D0085408

Stereotypes

Stereotypes

The Incidence and Impacts of Bias

Joel T. Nadler and Elora C. Voyles, Editors

 PRAEGER®

An Imprint of ABC-CLIO, LLC
Santa Barbara, California • Denver, Colorado

Library of Congress Cataloging-in-Publication Data

Names: Nadler, Joel T., editor. | Voyles, Elora C., editor.
Title: Stereotypes : the incidence and impacts of bias / Joel T. Nadler and
    Elora C. Voyles, editors.
Description: Santa Barbara, California : Praeger, an Imprint of ABC-CLIO,
    LLC, [2020] | Includes bibliographical references and index.
Identifiers: LCCN 2019030830 (print) | LCCN 2019030831 (ebook) | ISBN
    9781440868665 (print) | ISBN 9781440868672 (ebook)
Subjects: LCSH: Stereotypes (Social psychology)
Classification: LCC HM1096 .S743 2020 (print) | LCC HM1096 (ebook) | DDC
    303.3/85—dc23
LC record available at https://lccn.loc.gov/2019030830
LC ebook record available at https://lccn.loc.gov/2019030831

ISBN: 978-1-4408-6866-5 (print)
      978-1-4408-6867-2 (ebook)

24 23 22 21 20   1 2 3 4 5

This book is also available as an eBook.

Praeger
An Imprint of ABC-CLIO, LLC

ABC-CLIO, LLC
147 Castilian Drive
Santa Barbara, California 93117
www.abc-clio.com

This book is printed on acid-free paper ∞

Manufactured in the United States of America

*This work is dedicated to all who are in pursuit of
excellence and opportunity for all.*

Contents

Preface: The Purpose of Stereotypes

Elora C. Voyles and Joel T. Nadler

This book provides a cutting-edge examination of U.S. stereotypes and research. As discussed throughout this book, stereotypes have powerful influences on interpersonal interactions, reactions, and outcomes. We first provide a strong foundation on stereotypes research, including cognitive and social aspects and their impact. To further solidify the readers' foundation of knowledge, we also have included chapters on explicit and implicit stereotypes and bias. We also review the latest research on stereotype threat and the valence of stereotypes. These first four chapters provide a summary of broad stereotype concepts that permeate throughout many categories of stereotypes. The following eleven chapters examine group-specific stereotype content including age, race, citizenship, gender, sexual orientation, veteran status, weight, disability, and religion, and also examine the impacts. We also offer an in-depth review of research on each category, some of which are often neglected in other works. The conclusion discusses intersectionality and future directions for stereotypes researchers.

It should be noted that the stereotypes of social categories described in this book are bound to the culture in the United States. Stereotypes may differ in kind and degree in other countries and cultures, although many are shared across cultures. The social categories covered in this book are in no way exhaustive; the complete list of stereotyped groups in the United States alone would be extensive. We chose to dedicate chapters to social categories that are protected under employment law in the United States, and groups that have a substantial body of previous research. Members of these categories are often faced with discrimination based on these stereotypes.

In the final chapter of this book, we discuss the intersectional nature of stereotypes. Intersectionality refers to the unique interaction between identities. For example, picturing a Christian will bring a certain image to mind, but if instructed to think of a Black Christian, a different image may come to mind. This example illustrates the intersectional nature of stereotypes such that different combinations of identities bring about unique stereotypes that are qualitatively different from any of the stereotypes of the individual identities. Researchers' focus on the intersectionality of stereotypes is growing and knowledge of these intersecting identities and stereotypes is increasing.

Each peer-reviewed chapter in this book was written by experts in their respective areas of stereotype research. Their contributions have created a book that is a contemporary, educational, and enlightening guide for anyone interested in this harmful facet of human psychology and behavior, as well as those searching for potential solutions.

Acknowledgments

The editors wish to acknowledge the work of every person cited in the following book, as well as each contributor, and the undergraduate students, graduate students, coworkers, colleagues, and mentors whose help and support allowed the writing of this work.

CHAPTER ONE

The Cognitive and Motivational Aspects of Stereotypes and Their Impact in the United States

Jessica L. Cundiff

Across U.S. history, stereotypes have been used to justify social inequality and discrimination against certain groups (Allport, 1954; Lippmann, 1922). Slavery, for example, was justified by stereotypes of Blacks as savage, primitive, and intellectually inferior to Whites (Duckitt, 1992; Smedley & Smedley, 2005). Exclusion of women from the workplace and higher education in the nineteenth and early twentieth centuries was justified by stereotypes of women as emotionally irrational and unfit for intellectual pursuits (Shields, 1975, 2007). Restrictive immigration policies have been justified with stereotypes that depict immigrant groups as destitute, immoral "invaders" who threaten American society (O'Brien, 2003; Shinozuka, 2013). These stereotypes result from motivational processes that serve to promote and protect the self from threats, as well as from cognitive processes that serve to save mental energy by simplifying our social world. Today, motivationally and cognitively driven stereotypes continue to shape public opinion and policies on a broad range of topics, including welfare reform, immigration, affirmative action, sexual harassment, and law enforcement.

Understanding stereotypes is critical for understanding inequality. But what exactly are stereotypes? Where do they come from? And how do they affect us?

What Are Stereotypes?

A Brief History

Walter Lippmann (1922), a well-known journalist, is credited with coining the term "stereotype" as it is used by social scientists today. He described stereotypes as the "pictures we carry around in our head" of social groups that help us process and simplify our complex social world but also function to rationalize the social hierarchy. Lippmann's writings came at a time when historical and societal changes, including World War I, immigration patterns, and the Civil Rights Movement of the 1920s, prompted people to start viewing negative racial attitudes as a social problem rather than a natural response to supposed inherent group differences. As a result, early conceptualizations defined stereotypes as negative, inflexible, and inaccurate characterizations of groups based on faulty reasoning (Duckitt, 1992).

Early research (e.g., Katz & Braly, 1933, 1935) focused on measuring and identifying the content of stereotypes and later turned attention to understanding the source of the problem. In particular, the horrors of Nazi Germany in World War II spurred researchers to seek the root causes of stereotyping and prejudice. Theories, such as the one discussed in Adorno, Frenkel-Brunswik, Levinson, and Sanford's (1950) *The Authoritarian Personality*, focused on individual-level factors and posited that stereotyping and prejudice were pathological and driven by psychodynamic defense mechanisms and personality processes operating in the psyches of disturbed individuals.

Later theories (e.g., Allport, 1954) shifted focus away from individual differences and toward sociocultural processes as the source of stereotyping and prejudice. Attention turned toward social norms (Pettigrew, 1958), intergroup competition and conflict (Sherif & Sherif, 1953), and, later, mere categorization (Tajfel & Wilkes, 1963). With the cognitive revolution of the 1980s, stereotyping began to be viewed as an inevitable outcome of a natural and universal cognitive process that provided cognitive efficiency and simplified the complexity of the social world (Hamilton, 1981a). This view emphasized that stereotyping could result strictly from information processing even in the absence of motivated distortions or group conflict.

By the 1980s, it appeared that social norms had reduced self-reported stereotyping and prejudice in the United States, yet evidence of social inequality and discrimination remained (Gaertner & Dovidio, 1986). To explain this inconsistency between self-reported attitudes and continued disparities, researchers began theorizing that some processes may operate outside of conscious awareness. Dual-process theories emerged (e.g., Brewer & Feinstein, 1999; Devine, 1989; Fiske & Neuberg, 1990; see Chaiken & Trope, 1999, for review) that distinguished between automatic and controlled processes. This theoretical distinction shifted portrayals of perceivers as "cognitive misers," or lazy thinkers bent on conserving mental energy, to "motivated tacticians," or thoughtful thinkers who can overcome automatic stereotyping processes when motivated to do so. Technological advances in the 1990s and beyond led to the development of new, sophisticated methods for examining automatic and unconscious attitudes and beliefs, such as the Implicit Association Test (IAT; Greenwald, McGhee, & Schwartz, 1998), nonconscious priming procedures (e.g., Chen & Bargh, 1997), the process dissociation procedure (Jacoby, 1991; Payne, 2001), and the quadruple process model (Conrey, Sherman, Gawronski, Hugenberg, & Groom, 2005; for review, see Monteith, Woodcock, & Gulker, 2013).

Today research continues to examine the interplay between automatic and controlled processes. But rather than viewing stereotyping and prejudice as a purely cognitive phenomenon, researchers today integrate cognitive perspectives with motivational perspectives. In doing so, researchers today consider how stereotyping processes operate in individuals' minds and unfold in interpersonal and intergroup contexts (Dovidio, Hewstone, Glick, & Esses, 2010).

Current Conceptualizations

Today stereotypes are generally defined as overgeneralized beliefs about the characteristics of members of a particular group (Bodenhausen & Richeson, 2010; Schneider, 2004; Stangor, 2016). These beliefs contain information not only about group traits but also about other qualities such as social roles and within-group variability, that is, the degree to which members are perceived to share specific qualities.

Although stereotypes are often thought of as negative, they can also be positive and subjectively favorable beliefs about a group. For instance, women are stereotyped as nurturing and gentle (Eagly & Mladinic, 1989), Asian Americans are stereotyped as good at math (Ho & Jackson, 2001), and African Americans are stereotyped as naturally athletic (Stone, Lynch, Sjomeling, & Darley, 1999). Yet even positive stereotypes can have negative effects. Being the target of positive stereotypes can make individuals feel depersonalized and viewed in terms of their group membership rather than as individuals (Siy & Cheryan, 2013). Positive stereotypes can also put undue pressure on targeted group members to live up to the stereotype, which can interfere with performance (Cheryan & Bodenhausen, 2000). Additionally, positive stereotypes about stigmatized groups can suggest that negative stereotypes lurk close behind (Siy & Cheryan, 2016). For instance, stereotypes of Black athletes as having superior athletic ability subtly imply a corresponding deficiency in intellect (Walzer & Czopp, 2011). Even though positive stereotypes can seem affirming on the surface, they can ultimately patronize and restrict the stereotyped group, such as when women are directed into occupations and roles that best suit their assumed nurturing nature but are excluded from stereotypically masculine opportunities that would promote their careers (King et al., 2012). Positive stereotypes also serve to keep marginalized groups in subordinate positions through flattery and a seemingly just, fair distribution of benefits (Jackman, 1994; Kay et al., 2007).

Just as stereotypes do not have to be negative, they don't have to be completely false, either—beliefs about mean differences between groups may be accurate (Jussim et al., 2016). For example, Asian Americans as a group do outperform all other racial-ethnic groups on most standardized test measures, which corresponds with the "model minority" stereotype (Hsin & Xie, 2014). But even if mean differences between groups exist, the assertion that *all* Asian Americans are smarter than *all* members of other racial-ethnic groups is surely false. The problem with stereotyping is that people overgeneralize beliefs about a group to virtually all members of the group, regardless of actual variation among the members.

The overgeneralizing feature of stereotypes serves a purpose, but it comes at a cost. On one hand, stereotypes are functional. Stereotypes operate as cognitive schemas, or knowledge structures, that are used by social perceivers to process and fill in missing information about others (Hilton & von Hippel, 1996). Stereotypes help us organize and simplify the complex social knowledge we encounter every day, saving us mental energy and enhancing cognitive efficiency so we can make quick decisions easily and effortlessly. On the other hand, these benefits come at a cost: stereotypes are error prone, constraining, and can contribute to social inequality and discrimination.

Where Do Stereotypes Come From?

Multiple perspectives provide insight into where stereotypes come from (Sherman, Sherman, Percy, & Soderberg, 2013). This chapter focuses on two general perspectives: the cognitive perspective and the motivational perspective. These perspectives are not mutually exclusive or competing but rather are complementary perspectives that, together, provide a more complete analysis of stereotype formation.

The Cognitive Perspective

According to the cognitive perspective, stereotyping is an inevitable process that results from the natural way our brains are wired to process and organize information. At the heart of stereotyping is categorization. As stated by Allport (1954): "The human mind must think with the aid of categories . . . and once formed, categories are the basis for normal prejudgment. We cannot possibly avoid this process. Orderly living depends on it" (p. 20). We categorize nearly everything—types of furniture, animals, cars, even colors, and of course people. Categorizing helps us simplify and process the enormous amount of stimuli we confront.

We seem to have evolved a natural propensity to categorize people, but the specific features by which we choose to categorize people are likely shaped by environmental forces. According to developmental intergroup theory (Bigler & Liben, 2006, 2007), we divide people into groups based on the features that are psychologically salient. Features can become psychologically salient in many ways. First, some features draw attention because they are perceptually distinctive, such as race, gender, and age. Perceptual distinctiveness is not necessarily based on naturally occurring physical attributes, but it can be enhanced by cultural influences, such as when women and men adopt gender-distinctive clothing and hairstyles. Second, some features draw attention because they are rare. For instance, proportionally smaller groups are more distinctive than proportionally larger groups, making it more likely that members of the smaller group will be the target of stereotypes. Third, peers and role models can call attention to certain features by labeling those features in routine conversation (e.g., "Good morning, boys and girls") or by explicitly using those features to organize the environment (e.g., assigning teams based on gender). Finally, features can become psychologically salient when they are used to organize social environments implicitly without direction from authority figures, such as de facto segregation. People then perceive similarities among those who work, live, and socialize together, and assume that those similarities are important features by which to categorize people. In sum, those features that are psychologically salient—whether caused by explicit or implicit environmental forces—are the features that become psychologically meaningful and form the bases for social categorization.

Once categories are formed, people search for attributes that covary with category distinctions. Stereotypes arise from perceived correlations between attributes and social categories (Tajfel & Wilkes, 1963), suggesting that stereotypes are based on a *kernel of truth* about real group differences (Jussim et al., 2016). In fact, stereotypes are most likely to form for attributes that correlate most strongly with the categories, that is, attributes that maximize intergroup differences and minimize intragroup differences (Ford & Stangor, 1992). This is because traits that maximize differences between groups provide predictive power to the groupings, whereas traits that emphasize similarity within groups enhance inductive potential of the groupings. If all members of the group are similar, then attributes of one group member can be applied to all group members. Importantly, though, stereotype formation is susceptible to a cognitive bias known as "accentuation," in which differences between groups, as well as similarities within groups, are accentuated (Krueger & Rothbart, 1990). So even if a stereotype is based on a real (yet often small) group difference, accentuation processes can make it seem as though groups are more different from each other—and group members are more similar to each other—than they really are.

The effect of mere categorization on accentuation processes was first demonstrated in a classic study by Tajfel and Wilkes (1963). Their experiment involved having participants judge the length of eight lines. Each line differed from the previous line by a constant ratio of approximately 5 percent. In one condition, participants simply saw each line and made their judgment. In the other condition, Tajfel and Wilkes imposed category labels on the lines, such that the four shortest lines were each labeled as belonging to group "A" and the four longest lines were each labeled as belonging to group "B." In this way, there were real differences in average line lengths between groups A and B. What Tajfel and Wilkes wanted to know was whether the presence of category labels would lead people to exaggerate those differences. And that's exactly what they found—categorization distorted participants' perceptions in such a way that they perceived the lines from the two groups to be more different from each other, and the lines within each group to be more similar to each other, when the lines were categorized as belonging to a group versus not categorized. If people are susceptible to perceptual biases in a task as simple and easy as judging the length of lines, imagine how powerful such effects can be when judging people—a task that is neither easy nor simple.

We know that stereotypes can develop from observing real differences between groups, but can stereotypes develop even in the absence of a group difference? Research on the *illusory correlation* suggests yes (Hamilton & Gifford, 1976; see also Hamilton, 1981b). When two rare events co-occur, perceivers assume there is a connection between the two. For instance, minority members are rarer than majority members, and negative behaviors are rarer than positive behaviors. Rare events stick out in our minds such that we are more likely to remember when a minority member (as opposed to a majority member) engages in negative (as opposed to positive) behavior. The result is that we assume a correlation between being a minority member and negative behavior even when no correlation actually exists. Research on the illusory correlation is significant because it demonstrates that stereotypes can develop even in the absence of any real group difference and that stereotypes can develop from strictly cognitive processes that cannot be attributed to group conflict, social learning, ego justification, or some other motivational process. Even so, as we'll learn in the next section, motivational processes play an important role in stereotype formation.

The Motivational Perspective

The motivational perspective emphasizes the psychological needs and desires that lead to stereotyping. Two important motivations that help explain why humans develop stereotypes are the need for self-valuation and the need to justify and explain the social structure.

Self-Valuation Motives

Self-valuation motives involve the need to enhance favorable images of the self as well as protect against unfavorable images (Alicke & Sedikides, 2009). Stereotypes help fulfill self-valuation motives by protecting and promoting individuals' feelings of self-worth and well-being (Lippmann, 1922). Early approaches (e.g., Adorno et al., 1950) emphasized Freudian psychodynamic processes and defense mechanisms. Specifically, stereotypes were thought to aid in resolving threatening intrapsychic conflicts rooted in unconscious sexual and aggressive impulses derived from childhood experiences. Through the defense mechanism of displacement, these intolerable impulses and frustrations are redirected to targets other than the original source of the frustration; stereotypes form to justify the displacement of hostility toward the targeted group and defend the ego from threat. From this perspective, stereotypes were viewed as stemming primarily from troubled individuals who had unresolved psychological conflicts and problems (Adorno et al., 1950).

More recently, stereotypes have been viewed as stemming from a more general self-valuation motive among psychologically healthy people to promote a positive self-image and protect the self from ego threats. For instance, people show increased stereotyping of others after experiencing a blow to their self-esteem, such as after receiving negative feedback about their scores on an intelligence test (Fein & Spencer, 1997), a poor grade in a course (Sinclair & Kunda, 2000), or criticisms of their interpersonal skills (Sinclair & Kunda, 1999). Indeed, people who respond to negative feedback by derogating and stereotyping others experience a boost in self-esteem (Fein & Spencer, 1997). It seems that negatively stereotyping others serves to bolster and protect positive views of the self.

People are not only motivated to view themselves in a positive light, but they are also motivated to view the groups to which they belong in a positive light (Tajfel & Turner, 1979). Once people are assigned a group identity, they are motivated to view that identity favorably relative to group identities to which they do not belong. This occurs even when the groupings are arbitrary and meaningless. For instance, in the classic minimal group paradigm, merely being assigned to a meaningless group of either "underestimators" or "overestimators" led individuals to form more positive impressions and attribute more positive traits to their own group than the outgroup (Tajfel, Billig, Bundy, & Flament, 1971). The idea is that people can gain self-esteem by thinking highly of their own group and less highly of outgroups.

People are motivated to not only favor the ingroup but also protect it from group threats, such as competition with another group for scarce resources. Realistic group conflict theory (LeVine & Campbell, 1972; Sherif, 1966) posits that negative attitudes and stereotypes about outgroups develop as a natural response to the threat and frustration of real intergroup competition over desired resources. Realistic group conflict theory helps explain, for instance, why bias toward immigrant groups increases when economic times are tough and jobs are scarce (Butz & Yogeeswaran, 2011; Wilson, 2001).

More recent theories have focused on how competition, as well as relative group status, influences the specific content of stereotypes. The stereotype content model (Fiske, Cuddy, Glick, & Xu, 2002) predicts that groups that are perceived as competing with one's own group will be stereotyped as cold and dishonest, whereas cooperative groups will be stereotyped as warm and likable. Likewise, low-status groups will be stereotyped as incompetent, whereas high-status groups are stereotyped as competent. From this perspective, stereotypes form as a functional reaction to the threats posed by sociostructural relationships.

Justification Motives

In addition to promoting a positive self- and group-image and protecting the self from ego and group threats, stereotypes also fulfill a need to justify and explain why particular groups occupy particular social roles and statuses. According to social role theory (Eagly, 1987), stereotypes develop to explain the distribution of groups into roles. When people observe a correlation between group membership and a social role, they jump to the conclusion that the group must possess the traits necessary for that role. For example, people ascribe communal traits to novel groups that are assigned child-care roles and agentic traits to groups that are assigned city-worker roles as a way to justify the group assignments (Hoffman & Hurst, 1990). In this way, the content of stereotypes makes it seem as though the social roles are deserved and appropriate.

Stereotypes also develop to justify status differences among groups (Jost & Banaji, 1994). People have a tendency to misattribute observable group disparities (in income, academic achievement, incarceration, etc.) to unfounded inferences about the dispositional traits of the groups in question (Hetey & Eberhardt, 2018; Schaller & O'Brien, 1992). For instance, people rationalize status differences by stereotyping high-status groups as more intelligent and hardworking than low-status groups (Jost, 2001). The perception that high-status groups are intelligent and hardworking and, by implication, that low-status groups are incompetent and lazy helps to make sense of and justify existing social arrangements. However, such attributions can make it seem as though high-status groups unfairly "have it all," creating psychological discomfort and tension. To resolve this tension, people form complementary stereotypes that are flattering, yet status-irrelevant, for low-status groups (Kay et al., 2007). For instance, low-status groups may also be stereotyped as happy and honest, whereas high-status groups may be stereotyped as unhappy and greedy. These complementary stereotypes make it seem as though benefits and losses are evenly distributed across groups and, as a result, that the overarching social system is fair, legitimate, and justified (Jost, Kivetz, Rubini, Guermandi, & Mosso, 2005; Kay et al., 2007; Kay & Jost, 2003).

Stereotypes serve cognitive and motivational functions; they help us navigate our social worlds and make us feel better about ourselves and the world we live in. But they are not without consequence. The next section explores how stereotypes affect our perceptions and behaviors—sometimes in ways that we may not even notice or intend.

How Do Stereotypes Affect Us?

Impact on Perceivers

Stereotypes promote discrimination by systematically influencing perceptions, judgments, and behaviors. Stereotypes set up theories about what a person is like. But instead of testing our hypotheses systematically, humans have a general bias toward confirming our expectancies. We seek out, attend to, and remember information that is stereotype-consistent and ignore, disregard, and discount information that is stereotype-inconsistent. In this way, stereotypes produce a readiness to perceive ambiguous behavior in a stereotype-consistent manner and lead people to interpret the exact same behavior differently when it is performed by members of different social groups. For example, in one classic study (Darley & Gross, 1983), observers watched a video of a young girl taking an academic test. The observers formed strikingly different impressions of the girl's intellectual abilities depending on whether they had been led to believe the girl was from a high or low socioeconomic background. The socioeconomic information had biased the observers' expectations such that they latched on to evidence in the video that confirmed their expectations and ignored disconfirming evidence.

Stereotypes also affect the standards by which we evaluate others. Harsher standards are applied when judging the competence of negatively stereotyped groups (Foschi, 2000). When successful performance violates our stereotypic expectations, we do a double take; we scrutinize the performance and want to see additional evidence of competence. That is, we require extra proof from the stereotyped individuals to be convinced that they do not fit our stereotypic expectations. For example, in contexts where women are negatively stereotyped, women are judged as less competent than identically performing men (Moss-Racusin, Dovidio, Brescoll, Graham, & Handelsman, 2012), their successes are discounted and attributed to luck more often than men's successes are (Deaux & Emswiller, 1974), and they must provide more evidence of competence than men to be viewed as equally competent (Wennerås & Wold, 1997). When stereotyped individuals provide irrefutable evidence that counters our stereotypic expectations, such as when a woman provides extraordinary evidence of competence, we don't necessarily change our overall stereotype of the group. Instead, we subtype outliers as exceptions to the rule and place them in a new subcategory of their own so that we can maintain our existing stereotypes of the group in general (Richards & Hewstone, 2001).

Stereotypes influence not only our perceptions and judgments but also our behavior toward others in ways that can powerfully shape reality and contribute to inequalities between social groups (Klein & Snyder, 2003). In particular, stereotypic expectations can make us behave toward others in ways that elicit the expected behavior from them through a process known as the self-fulfilling prophecy. For example, imagine that you believe beautiful people are friendly (e.g., Snyder, Tanke, & Berscheid, 1977). This expectation may lead you to act more friendly toward an attractive stranger than an unattractive stranger. Your behavior is likely to elicit reciprocal responses, such that the attractive stranger will, in turn, respond in a warmer and friendlier manner than the unattractive stranger. As a result, you conclude that beautiful people really are friendly, unaware of your role in eliciting the stereotype-confirming behavior. The self-fulfilling prophecy effect has relevance for sustaining inequality across many contexts of societal importance, including educational settings (Rosenthal & Jacobson, 1968), interracial interactions (Word, Zanna, & Cooper, 1974), gendered interactions (Logel et al., 2009), and interactions between heterosexual and sexual minority individuals (Hebl, Foster, Mannix, & Dovidio, 2002).

Word et al. (1974) demonstrated the relevance of the self-fulfilling prophecy for maintaining racial inequality in a clever two-part experiment. In the first part of the experiment, the researchers found that White interviewers behaved in a less friendly manner toward Black job applicants than White job applicants. In the second part of the experiment, the researchers trained White interviewers to act in the same way that the original interviewers had acted toward either the Black applicants or the White applicants. This time, however, all the applicants were White. Applicants who were interviewed the way Black applicants had been interviewed in the first experiment responded in a more anxious and less effective manner than those who had been interviewed the way White applicants had been originally interviewed. These results suggest that our stereotypic expectations can unwittingly lead us to treat people in a way that elicits stereotype-confirming behavior and perpetuates social inequality.

The activation and application of stereotypes can happen automatically without our conscious awareness or intent (Monteith et al., 2013). Regardless of whether we believe stereotypes to be true or not, we all have knowledge about the stereotypes associated with particular groups because we are all exposed to similar cultural information. Stereotypic associations become ingrained and automatic such that once we categorize someone, stereotypes associated with the category often automatically come to mind and affect behavior, even if we don't consciously endorse the stereotype as true (Devine, 1989). Notably, automatic stereotypes influence behaviors that are difficult to control, such as nonverbal body language in interpersonal interactions; stereotypes we consciously endorse, by contrast, influence behavior that is more deliberate and controllable, such as verbal friendliness (Dovidio, Kawakami, & Gaertner, 2002).

Automatic stereotyping has relevance for many contexts, including racial injustice in police use of force. For example, African Americans are stereotypically associated with violence and crime (Eberhardt, Goff, Purdie, & Davies, 2004; Goff, Jackson, Di Leone, Culotta, & DiTomasso, 2014). If this stereotype is automatically activated upon seeing a Black person, then we would expect people to more often misidentify an object as a gun when it is held by a Black man than a White man and to more often mistakenly shoot an unarmed Black man than an unarmed White man. Indeed, experimental research has demonstrated the effects of target race on both weapon misidentification (Payne, 2001) and shooter bias (Correll, Park, Judd, & Wittenbrink, 2002). Notably, evidence suggests that these effects result more from knowledge of the cultural stereotype that Blacks are violent than from personal prejudice.

Automatic stereotyping is not inevitable, however, and can be moderated by a number of factors. Individual differences (Fazio, Jackson, Dunton, & Williams, 1995), availability of cognitive resources (Gilbert & Hixon, 1991), processing goals (Macrae, Bodenhausen, Milne, Thorn, & Castelli, 1997), motivations (Sinclair & Kunda, 1999), and the immediate context (Kahn & Davies, 2017) can all affect the extent to which stereotypes are automatically activated and applied. For example, the shooter bias described above is weaker when Black targets appear in nonthreatening contexts, such as a sunlit church, rather than a dark alley (Kahn & Davies, 2017). Automatic activation and application of stereotypes can also be controlled with practice. Consciously and consistently practicing nonprejudiced responses can result in automatic nonprejudiced responding over time through a process known as self-regulation (Monteith, 1993).

Impact on Targets

Thus far we have been looking at stereotyping from the perpetrator's perspective, but the target's perspective is just as important. Members of negatively stereotyped groups are typically aware of the stereotypes that others hold of them, and this awareness can have negative effects. One type of negative effect is attributional ambiguity (Major & Crocker, 1993). People want to know the causes of their treatment and outcomes in order to maintain a sense that their world is predictable and orderly. For members of negatively stereotyped groups, determining the causes of their experiences can be tricky; it can be unclear whether their experiences are due to the same causes as everyone else or whether they are due to stereotyping and prejudice. Did the police officer pull you over because of your race? Were you passed over for promotion because of your weight? Did you receive that scholarship because of your gender? The causes to which one attributes one's experiences can affect self-esteem, well-being, and personal growth. On one hand, attributing negative outcomes to prejudice rather than one's own failings can protect self-esteem and buffer well-being (Crocker, Voelkl, Testa, & Major, 1991; Hoyt, Aguilar, Kaiser, Blascovich, & Lee, 2007). On the other hand, such attributions can lead you to discount and ignore critical feedback that is necessary for growth and improvement (Cohen, Steele, & Ross, 1999). Likewise, attributing positive outcomes to prejudice can undermine the self-esteem boost that typically results from positive outcomes (Crocker et al., 1991; Hoyt et al., 2007) and can result in uncertainty about one's competence (Aronson & Inzlicht, 2004). Members of negatively stereotyped groups thus contend with attributional ambiguity and uncertainty, not knowing whether to take responsibility for their failures and successes or to blame prejudice and discrimination.

Awareness that one is the target of negative stereotypes can also result in stereotype threat. Stereotype threat is the fear of confirming a stereotype that exists about your group (Steele, Spencer, & Aronson, 2002). For example, a woman taking a difficult math exam may be concerned that performing poorly on the exam would confirm in others' eyes (and perhaps also her own eyes) the stereotype that women are worse at math than men. Ironically, this fear creates an extra psychological burden that can impair performance in a way that ends up confirming the stereotype (Spencer, Steele, & Quinn, 1999). Stereotype threat effects have been shown to undermine performance across a variety of contexts and social groups, including verbal test performance of African Americans (Steele & Aronson, 1995); driving performance of women (Yeung & von Hippel, 2008); memory performance of older adults (Chasteen, Bhattacharyya, Horhota, Tam, & Hasher, 2005); and emotional processing performance of men (Leyens, Désert, Croizet, & Darcis, 2000).

Stereotypes can thus pose a threat "in the air" that can hinder one's full potential in achievement settings, causing targets to doubt their own abilities and lose interest and motivation in domains where their group is negatively stereotyped (Steele, 1997).

Stereotypes also impact targets by steering people away from certain careers and opportunities. When people consider different career choices, they consider whether they will be successful, whether they will fit in with others, and whether the career will allow them to fulfill their goals and values (Eccles, 2011). Stereotypes, for better or worse, can inform all these considerations (for review, see Cundiff, 2018). For example, negative stereotypes about women's ability in science, technology, engineering, and math (STEM) can cause women to underestimate their own STEM competence and, as a result, express less interest in STEM careers (Correll, 2004). Additionally, stereotypes about the types of people and the types of work involved in STEM provide unrealistically narrow depictions that conflict with the way that many women view themselves. Such stereotypic depictions make STEM fields unattractive to many women and girls, as well as some men and boys, and lead many women to conclude that STEM fields are not for them (Cheryan, Master, & Meltzoff, 2015; Diekman, Steinberg, Brown, Belanger, & Clark, 2016).

Conclusion

Stereotypes are a double-edged sword. Stereotypes help us process enormous amounts of social information with relative ease and efficiency; they help us fill in gaps of information and provide a framework for how to understand and interact with others. However, stereotypes are also prone to error and are susceptible to cognitive and motivational biases. They are imperfect and sometimes inaccurate sources of information and can lead us to treat and judge others unfairly. In fact, stereotyping has been linked to a number of current social problems, including sexual harassment (Fiske & Glick, 1995), police brutality (Dukes & Kahn, 2017), and welfare reform (Hancock, 2004), among others.

Conceptualizations of stereotyping have evolved over the years, from viewing stereotyping as a problem primarily residing within troubled individuals to viewing it as a universal function of normal cognition. Research has advanced our understanding of the cognitive and motivational processes involved in stereotype formation, activation, and application, but there is still much work to be done. Stereotyping is a provocative, relevant field of study, and future research on stereotyping will continue to make important contributions to understanding and mitigating significant social problems.

References

Adorno, T. W., Frenkel-Brunswik, E., Levinson, D. J., & Sanford, R. N. (1950). *The authoritarian personality*. New York: Harper & Row.

Alicke, M., & Sedikides, C. (2009). Self-enhancement and self-protection: What they are and what they do. *European Review of Social Psychology, 20*, 1–48. doi:10.1080/10463280802613866

Allport, G. W. (1954). *The nature of prejudice*. Oxford, England: Addison-Wesley.

Aronson, J., & Inzlicht, M. (2004). The ups and downs of attributional ambiguity: Stereotype vulnerability and the academic self-knowledge of African American college students. *Psychological Science, 15*(12), 829–836. doi: 10.1111/j.0956-7976.2004.00763.x

Bigler, R. S., & Liben, L. S. (2006). A developmental intergroup theory of social stereotypes and prejudice. In R. V. Kail (Ed.), *Advances in child development and behavior* (pp. 39–89). San Diego, CA: Elsevier Academic Press.

Bigler, R. S., & Liben, L. S. (2007). Developmental intergroup theory: Explaining and reducing children's social stereotyping and prejudice. *Current Directions in Psychological Science, 16*(3), 162–166. doi:10.1111/j.1467-8721 .2007.00496.x

Bodenhausen, G. V., & Richeson, J. A. (2010). Prejudice, stereotyping, and discrimination. In R. F. Baumeister & E. J. Finkel (Eds.), *Advanced social psychology: The state of the science* (pp. 341–383). New York: Oxford University Press.

Brewer, M. B., & Feinstein, A. S. H. (1999). Dual processes in the cognitive representation of persons and social categories. In S. Chaiken & Y. Trope (Eds.), *Dual-process theories in social psychology* (pp. 255–270). New York: Guilford Press.

Butz, D. A., & Yogeeswaran, K. (2011). A new threat in the air: Macroeconomic threat increases prejudice against Asian Americans. *Journal of Experimental Social Psychology, 47*(1), 22–27. doi:10.1016/j.jesp.2010.07.01

Chaiken, S., & Trope, Y. (Eds.). (1999). *Dual-process theories in social psychology*. New York: Guilford Press.

Chasteen, A. L., Bhattacharyya, S., Horhota, M., Tam, R., & Hasher, L. (2005). How feelings of stereotype threat influence older adults' memory performance. *Experimental Aging Research, 31*(3), 235–260. doi:10.1080 /03610730590948177

Chen, M., & Bargh, J. A. (1997). Nonconscious behavioral confirmation processes: The self-fulfilling consequences of automatic stereotype activation. *Journal of Experimental Social Psychology, 33*(5), 541–560. doi:10.1006 /jesp.1997.1329

Cheryan, S., & Bodenhausen, G. V. (2000). When positive stereotypes threaten intellectual performance: The psychological hazards of "model minority" status. *Psychological Science, 11*, 399–402. doi:10.1111/1467-9280.00277

Cheryan, S., Master, A., & Meltzoff, A. N. (2015). Cultural stereotypes as gatekeepers: Increasing girls' interest in computer science and engineering by diversifying stereotypes. *Frontiers in Psychology, 6*(49), 1–8. doi:10.3389/fpsyg.2015.00049

Cohen, G. L., Steele, C. M., & Ross, L. D. (1999). The mentor's dilemma: Providing critical feedback across the racial divide. *Personality and Social Psychology Bulletin, 25*(10), 1302–1318. doi:10.1177/0146167299258011

Conrey, F. R., Sherman, J. W., Gawronski, B., Hugenberg, K., & Groom, C. J. (2005). Separating multiple processes in implicit social cognition: The quad model of implicit task performance. *Journal of Personality and Social Psychology, 89*(4), 469–487. doi:10.1037/0022-3514.89.4.469

Correll, J., Park, B., Judd, C. M., & Wittenbrink, B. (2002). The police officer's dilemma: Using ethnicity to disambiguate potentially threatening individuals. *Journal of Personality and Social Psychology, 83*(6), 1314–1329. doi:10.1037/0022-3514.83.6.1314

Correll, S. J. (2004). Constraints into preferences: Gender, status, and emerging career aspirations. *American Sociological Review, 69*(1), 93–113. doi:10.1177/000312240406900106

Crocker, J., Voelkl, K., Testa, M., & Major, B. (1991). Social stigma: The affective consequences of attributional ambiguity. *Journal of Personality and Social Psychology, 60*(2), 218–228. doi:10.1037/0022-3514.60.2.218

Cundiff, J. L. (2018). Subtle barriers and bias in STEM: How stereotypes constrain women's STEM participation and career progress. In J. T. Nadler & M. R. Lowery (Eds.), *War on women in the United States: Beliefs, tactics, and the best defenses* (pp. 97–116). Santa Barbara, CA: ABC-CLIO, LLC.

Darley, J. M., & Gross, P. H. (1983). A hypothesis-confirming bias in labeling effects. *Journal of Personality and Social Psychology, 44*(1), 20–33. doi:10.1037/0022-3514.44.1.20

Deaux, K., & Emswiller, T. (1974). Explanations of successful performance on sex-linked tasks: What is skill for the male is luck for the female. *Journal of Personality and Social Psychology, 29*(1), 80. doi:10.1037/h0035733

Devine, P. G. (1989). Stereotypes and prejudice: Their automatic and controlled components. *Journal of Personality and Social Psychology, 56*(1), 5–18. doi:10.1037/0022-3514.56.1.5

Diekman, A. B., Steinberg, M., Brown, E. R., Belanger, A. L., & Clark, E. K. (2016). A goal congruity model of role entry, engagement, and exit: Understanding communal goal processes in STEM gender gaps. *Personality and Social Psychology Review, 21*(2), 142–175. doi:10.1177/1088868316642141

Dovidio, J. F., Hewstone, M., Glick, P., & Esses, V. M. (2010). Prejudice, stereotyping and discrimination: Theoretical and empirical overview. In J. F. Dovidio, M. Hewstone, P. Glick, & V. M. Esses (Eds.), *The SAGE handbook of prejudice, stereotyping and discrimination* (pp. 3–29). Thousand Oaks, CA: SAGE Publications.

Dovidio, J. F., Kawakami, K., & Gaertner, S. L. (2002). Implicit and explicit prejudice and interracial interaction. *Journal of Personality and Social Psychology, 82*(1), 62–68. doi:10.1037//0022-3514.82.1.62

Duckitt, J. H. (1992). Psychology and prejudice: A historical analysis and integrative framework. *American Psychologist, 47*(10), 1182–1193. doi:10.1037/0003-066X.47.10.1182

Dukes, K. N., & Kahn, K. B. (2017). What social science research says about police violence against racial and ethnic minorities: Understanding the antecedents and consequences—An introduction. *Journal of Social Issues, 73*(4), 690–700. doi:10.1111/josi.12242

Eagly, A. H. (1987). *Sex differences in social behavior: A social-role interpretation.* Hillsdale, NJ: Lawrence Erlbaum.

Eagly, A. H., & Mladinic, A. (1989). Gender stereotypes and attitudes toward women and men. *Personality and Social Psychology Bulletin, 15*(4), 543–558. doi:10.1177/0146167289154008

Eberhardt, J. L., Goff, P. A., Purdie, V. J., & Davies, P. G. (2004). Seeing black: Race, crime, and visual processing. *Journal of Personality and Social Psychology, 87*(6), 876–893. doi:10.1037/0022-3514.87.6.876

Eccles, J. (2011). Gendered educational and occupational choices: Applying the Eccles et al. model of achievement-related choices. *International Journal of Behavioral Development, 35*(3), 195–201. doi:10.1177/0165025411398185

Fazio, R. H., Jackson, J. R., Dunton, B. C., & Williams, C. J. (1995). Variability in automatic activation as an unobtrusive measure of racial attitudes: A bona fide pipeline? *Journal of Personality and Social Psychology, 69*(6), 1013–1027. doi:10.1037/0022-3514.69.6.1013

Fein, S., & Spencer, S. J. (1997). Prejudice as self-image maintenance: Affirming the self through derogating others. *Journal of Personality and Social Psychology, 73*(1), 31–44. doi:10.1037/0022-3514.73.1.31

Fiske, S. T., Cuddy, A. J., Glick, P., & Xu, J. (2002). A model of (often mixed) stereotype content: Competence and warmth respectively follow from perceived status and competition. *Journal of Personality and Social Psychology, 82*(6), 878–902. doi:10.1037//0022-3514.82.6.878

Fiske, S. T., & Glick, P. (1995). Ambivalence and stereotypes cause sexual harassment: A theory with implications for organizational change. *Journal of Social Issues, 51*(1), 97–115. doi:10.1111/j.1540-4560.1995.tb01311.x

Fiske, S. T., & Neuberg, S. L. (1990). A continuum of impression formation, from category-based to individuating processes: Influences of information and motivation on attention and interpretation. *Advances in Experimental Social Psychology, 23*, 1–74.

Ford, T. E., & Stangor, C. (1992). The role of diagnosticity in stereotype formation: Perceiving group means and variances. *Journal of Personality and Social Psychology, 63*(3), 356–367. doi:10.1037/0022-3514.63.3.356

Foschi, M. (2000). Double standards for competence: Theory and research. *Annual Review of Sociology, 26*(1), 21–42. doi:10.1146/annurev.soc.26.1.21

Gaertner, S. L., & Dovidio, J. F. (1986). The aversive form of racism. In J. F. Dovidio & S. L. Gaertner (Eds.), *Prejudice, discrimination, and racism* (pp. 61–89). New York: Academic Press.

Gilbert, D. T., & Hixon, J. G. (1991). The trouble of thinking: Activation and application of stereotypic beliefs. *Journal of Personality and Social Psychology, 60*(4), 509–517. doi:10.1037/0022-3514.60.4.509

Goff, P. A., Jackson, M. C., Di Leone, B. L., Culotta, C. M., & DiTomasso, N. A. (2014). The essence of innocence: Consequences of dehumanizing Black children. *Journal of Personality and Social Psychology, 106*(4), 526–545. doi:10.1037/a0035663

Greenwald, A. G., McGhee, D. E., & Schwartz, J. K. (1998). Measuring individual differences in implicit cognition: The implicit association test. *Journal of Personality and Social Psychology, 74*(6), 1464–1480. doi:10.1037/0022-3514.74.6.1464

Hamilton, D. (Ed.). (1981a). *Cognitive processes in stereotyping and intergroup behavior.* Hillsdale, NJ: Erlbaum.

Hamilton, D. (1981b). Illusory correlation as a basis for stereotyping. In D. Hamilton (Ed.), *Cognitive processes in stereotyping and intergroup behavior* (pp. 115–144). Hillsdale, NJ: Erlbaum.

Hamilton, D. L., & Gifford, R. K. (1976). Illusory correlation in interpersonal perception: A cognitive basis of stereotypic judgments. *Journal of Experimental Social Psychology, 12*(4), 392–407. doi:10.1016/S0022-1031(76)80006-6

Hancock, A. M. (2004). *The politics of disgust: The public identity of the welfare queen.* New York: New York University Press.

Hebl, M. R., Foster, J. B., Mannix, L. M., & Dovidio, J. F. (2002). Formal and interpersonal discrimination: A field study of bias toward homosexual applicants. *Personality and Social Psychology Bulletin, 28*(6), 815–825. doi:10.1177/0146167202289010

Hetey, R. C., & Eberhardt, J. L. (2018). The numbers don't speak for themselves: Racial disparities and the persistence of inequality in the criminal justice system. *Current Directions in Psychological Science, 27*(3), 183–187. doi:10.1177/0963721418763931

Hilton, J. L., & von Hippel, W. (1996). Stereotypes. *Annual Review of Psychology, 47*(1), 237–271. doi:10.1146/annurev.psych.47.1.237

Ho, C., & Jackson, J. W. (2001). Attitudes toward Asian Americans: Theory and measurement. *Journal of Applied Social Psychology, 31*(8), 1553–1581. doi:10.1111/j.1559-1816.2001.tb02742.x

Hoffman, C., & Hurst, N. (1990). Gender stereotypes: Perception or rationalization? *Journal of Personality and Social Psychology, 58*(2), 197–208. doi:10.1037/0022-3514.58.2.197

Hoyt, C. L., Aguilar, L., Kaiser, C. R., Blascovich, J., & Lee, K. (2007). The self-protective and undermining effects of attributional ambiguity. *Journal of Experimental Social Psychology, 43*(6), 884–893. doi:10.1016/j.jesp.2006.10.013

Hsin, A., & Xie, Y. (2014). Explaining Asian Americans' academic advantage over Whites. *Proceedings of the National Academy of Sciences, 111*(23), 8416–8421. doi:10.1073/pnas.1406402111

Jackman, M. R. (1994). *The velvet glove: Paternalism and conflict in gender, class, and race relations*. Berkeley: University of California Press.

Jacoby, L. L. (1991). A process dissociation framework: Separating automatic from intentional uses of memory. *Journal of Memory and Language, 30*(5), 513–541. doi:10.1016/0749-596X(91)90025-F

Jost, J. (2001). Outgroup favoritism and the theory of system justification: A paradigm for investigating the effects of socioeconomic success on stereotype content. In G. B. Moskowitz (Ed.), *Cognitive social psychology: The Princeton symposium on the legacy and future of social cognition* (pp. 89–102). Mahwah, NJ: Lawrence Erlbaum Associates Publishers.

Jost, J. T., & Banaji, M. R. (1994). The role of stereotyping in system-justification and the production of false consciousness. *British Journal of Social Psychology, 33*(1), 1–27. doi:10.1111/j.2044-8309.1994.tb01008.x

Jost, J. T., Kivetz, Y., Rubini, M., Guermandi, G., & Mosso, C. (2005). System-justifying functions of complementary regional and ethnic stereotypes: Cross-national evidence. *Social Justice Research, 18*(3), 305–333. doi:10.1007/s11211-005-6827-z

Jussim, L., Crawford, J. T., Anglin, S. M., Chambers, J. R., Stevens, S. T., & Cohen, F. (2016). Stereotype accuracy: One of the largest and most replicable effects in all of social psychology. In T. D. Nelson (Ed.), *Handbook of prejudice, stereotyping, and discrimination* (pp. 31–63). New York: Psychology Press.

Kahn, K. B., & Davies, P. G. (2017). What influences shooter bias? The effects of suspect race, neighborhood, and clothing on decisions to shoot. *Journal of Social Issues, 73*(4), 723–743. doi:10.1111/josi.12245

Katz, D., & Braly, K. W. (1933). Racial stereotypes of one hundred college students. *The Journal of Abnormal and Social Psychology, 28*, 280–290.

Katz, D., & Braly, K. W. (1935). Racial prejudice and racial stereotypes. *The Journal of Abnormal and Social Psychology, 30*(2), 175.

Kay, A. C., & Jost, J. T. (2003). Complementary justice: Effects of "poor but happy" and "poor but honest" stereotype exemplars on system justification and implicit activation of the justice motive. *Journal of Personality and Social Psychology, 85*(5), 823–837. doi:10.1037/0022-3514.85.5.823

Kay, A. C., Jost, J. T., Mandisodza, A. N., Sherman, S. J., Petrocelli, J. V., & Johnson, A. L. (2007). Panglossian ideology in the service of system justification: How complementary stereotypes help us to rationalize inequality. *Advances in Experimental Social Psychology, 39*, 305–358. doi:10.1016/S0065-2601(06)39006-5

King, E. B., Botsford, W., Hebl, M. R., Kazama, S., Dawson, J. F., & Perkins, A. (2012). Benevolent sexism at work: Gender differences in the distribution of challenging developmental experiences. *Journal of Management, 38*(6), 1835–1866. doi:10.1177/0149206310365902

Klein, O., & Snyder, M. (2003). Stereotypes and behavioral confirmation: From interpersonal to intergroup perspectives. *Advances in Experimental Social*

Psychology, 35, 153–234. San Diego, CA: Academic Press. doi:10.1016/S0065-2601(03)01003-7

Krueger, J., & Rothbart, M. (1990). Contrast and accentuation effects in category learning. *Journal of Personality and Social Psychology, 59*(4), 651–663. doi:10.1037/0022-3514.59.4.651

LeVine, R. A., & Campbell, D. T. (1972). *Ethnocentrism: Theories of conflict, ethnic attitudes, and group behavior.* Oxford, England: John Wiley & Sons.

Leyens, J., Désert, M., Croizet, J., & Darcis, C. (2000). Stereotype threat: Are lower status and history of stigmatization preconditions of stereotype threat? *Personality and Social Psychology Bulletin, 26*(10), 1189–1199. doi:10.1177/0146167200262002

Lippmann, W. (1922). *Public opinion.* New York: Macmillan.

Logel, C., Walton, G. M., Spencer, S. J., Iserman, E. C., von Hippel, W., & Bell, A. E. (2009). Interacting with sexist men triggers social identity threat among female engineers. *Journal of Personality and Social Psychology, 96*(6), 1089–1103. doi:10.1037/a0015703

Macrae, C. N., Bodenhausen, G. V., Milne, A. B., Thorn, T. J., & Castelli, L. (1997). On the activation of social stereotypes: The moderating role of processing objectives. *Journal of Experimental Social Psychology, 33*(5), 471–489. doi:10.1006/jesp.1997.1328

Major, B., & Crocker, J. (1993). Social stigma: The consequences of attributional ambiguity. In D. M. Mackie & D. L. Hamilton (Eds.), *Affect, cognition, and stereotyping: Interactive processes in group perception* (pp. 345–370). San Diego, CA: Academic Press.

Monteith, M. J. (1993). Self-regulation of prejudiced responses: Implications for progress in prejudice-reduction efforts. *Journal of Personality and Social Psychology, 65*(3), 469–485. doi:10.1037/0022-3514.65.3.469

Monteith, M. J., Woodcock, A., & Gulker, J. E. (2013). Automaticity and control in stereotyping and prejudice: The revolutionary role of social cognition across three decades of research. In D. E. Carlston (Ed.), *The Oxford handbook of social cognition* (pp. 74–94). New York: Oxford University Press.

Moss-Racusin, C. A., Dovidio, J. F., Brescoll, V. L., Graham, M. J., & Handelsman, J. (2012). Science faculty's subtle gender biases favor male students. *Proceedings of the National Academy of Sciences, 109,* 16474–16479. doi:10.1073/pnas.1211286109

O'Brien, G. V. (2003). Indigestible food, conquering hordes, and waste materials: Metaphors of immigrants and the early immigration restriction debate in the United States. *Metaphor and Symbol, 18*(1), 33–47.

Payne, B. K. (2001). Prejudice and perception: The role of automatic and controlled processes in misperceiving a weapon. *Journal of Personality and Social Psychology, 81*(2), 181–192. doi:10.1037/0022-3514.81.2.181

Pettigrew, T. F. (1958). Personality and sociocultural factors in intergroup attitudes: A cross-national comparison. *Journal of Conflict Resolution, 2*(1), 29–42.

Richards, Z., & Hewstone, M. (2001). Subtyping and subgrouping: Processes for the prevention and promotion of stereotype change. *Personality and Social Psychology Review, 5*(1), 52–73. doi:10.1207/S15327957PSPR0501_4

Rosenthal, R., & Jacobson, L. (1968). *Pygmalion in the classroom: Teacher expectation and pupils' intellectual development.* New York: Holt, Rinehart & Winston.

Schaller, M., & O'Brien, M. (1992). "Intuitive analysis of covariance" and group stereotype formation. *Personality and Social Psychology Bulletin, 18*(6), 776–785. doi:10.1177/0146167292186014

Schneider, D. J. (2004). *The psychology of stereotyping.* New York: Guilford Press.

Sherif, M. (1966). *Group conflict and cooperation: Their social psychology.* London: Routledge & Kegan Paul.

Sherif, M., & Sherif, C. W. (1953). *Groups in harmony and tension: An integration of studies of intergroup relations.* Oxford, England: Harper & Brothers.

Sherman, S. J., Sherman, J. W., Percy, E. J., & Soderberg, C. K. (2013). Stereotype development and formation. In D. E. Carlston (Ed.), *The Oxford handbook of social cognition* (pp. 548–574). New York: Oxford University Press.

Shields, S. A. (1975). Functionalism, Darwinism, and the psychology of women. *American Psychologist, 30*(7), 739–754. doi:10.1037/h0076948

Shields, S. A. (2007). Passionate men, emotional women: Psychology constructs gender difference in the late 19th century. *History of Psychology, 10*(2), 92–110. doi:10.1037/1093-4510.10.2.92

Shinozuka, J. N. (2013). Deadly perils: Japanese beetles and the pestilential immigrant, 1920s–1930s. *American Quarterly, 65*(4), 831–852. doi:10.1353/aq.2013.0056

Sinclair, L., & Kunda, Z. (1999). Reactions to a Black professional: Motivated inhibition and activation of conflicting stereotypes. *Journal of Personality and Social Psychology, 77*(5), 885–904. doi:10.1037/0022-3514.77.5.885

Sinclair, L., & Kunda, Z. (2000). Motivated stereotyping of women: She's fine if she praised me but incompetent if she criticized me. *Personality and Social Psychology Bulletin, 26*(11), 1329–1342. doi:10.1177/0146167200263002

Siy, J. O., & Cheryan, S. (2013). When compliments fail to flatter: American individualism and responses to positive stereotypes. *Journal of Personality and Social Psychology, 104*(1), 87–102. doi:10.1037/a0030183

Siy, J. O., & Cheryan, S. (2016). Prejudice masquerading as praise: The negative echo of positive stereotypes. *Personality and Social Psychology Bulletin, 42*(7), 941–954. doi:10.1177/0146167216649605

Smedley, A., & Smedley, B. D. (2005). Race as biology is fiction, racism as a social problem is real: Anthropological and historical perspectives on the social construction of race. *American Psychologist, 60*(1), 16–26. doi:10.1037/0003-066X.60.1.16

Snyder, M., Tanke, E. D., & Berscheid, E. (1977). Social perception and interpersonal behavior: On the self-fulfilling nature of social stereotypes. *Journal of Personality and Social Psychology, 35*(9), 656–666. doi:10.1037/0022-3514.35.9.656

Spencer, S. J., Steele, C. M., & Quinn, D. M. (1999). Stereotype threat and women's math performance. *Journal of Experimental Social Psychology, 35*(1), 4–28. doi:10.1006/jesp.1998.1373

Stangor, C. (2016). The study of stereotyping, prejudice, and discrimination within social psychology: A quick history of theory and research. In T. D. Nelson (Ed.), *Handbook of prejudice, stereotyping, and discrimination* (pp. 3–27). New York: Psychology Press.

Steele, C. M. (1997). A threat in the air: How stereotypes shape intellectual identity and performance. *American Psychologist, 52*(6), 613–629. doi:10.1037/0003-066X.52.6.613

Steele, C. M., & Aronson, J. (1995). Stereotype threat and the intellectual test performance of African Americans. *Journal of Personality and Social Psychology, 69*(5), 797–811. doi:10.1037/0022-3514.69.5.797

Steele, C. M., Spencer, S. J., & Aronson, J. (2002). Contending with group image: The psychology of stereotype and social identity threat. *Advances in Experimental Social Psychology, 34,* 379–440. doi:10.1016/S0065-2601(02)80009-0

Stone, J., Lynch, C. I., Sjomeling, M., & Darley, J. M. (1999). Stereotype threat effects on Black and White athletic performance. *Journal of Personality and Social Psychology, 77*(6), 1213–1227. doi:10.1037/0022-3514.77.6.1213

Tajfel, H., Billig, M. G., Bundy, R. P., & Flament, C. (1971). Social categorization and intergroup behaviour. *European Journal of Social Psychology, 1*(2), 149–178. doi:10.1002/ejsp.2420010202

Tajfel, H., & Turner, J. (1979). An integrative theory of intergroup conflict. In W. G. Austin & S. Worchel (Eds.), *The social psychology of intergroup relations.* Monterey, CA: Brooks/Cole.

Tajfel, H., & Wilkes, A. L. (1963). Classification and quantitative judgement. *British Journal of Psychology, 54*(2), 101–114. doi:10.1111/j.2044-8295.1963.tb00865.x

Walzer, A. S., & Czopp, A. M. (2011). Able but unintelligent: Including positively stereotyped black subgroups in the stereotype content model. *The Journal of Social Psychology, 151*(5), 527–530. doi:10.1080/00224545.2010.503250

Wennerås, C., & Wold, A. (1997). Nepotism and sexism in peer review. *Nature, 387*(6631), 341–343.

Wilson, T. C. (2001). Americans' views on immigration policy: Testing the role of threatened group interest. *Sociological Perspectives, 44*(4), 485–501. doi:10.1525/sop.2001.44.4.485

Word, C. O., Zanna, M. P., & Cooper, J. (1974). The nonverbal mediation of self-fulfilling prophecies in interracial interaction. *Journal of Experimental Social Psychology, 10*(2), 109–120. doi:10.1016/0022-1031(74)90059-6

Yeung, N. J., & von Hippel, C. (2008). Stereotype threat increases the likelihood that female drivers in a simulator run over jaywalkers. *Accident Analysis and Prevention, 40*(2), 667–674. doi:10.1016/j.aap.2007.09.003

CHAPTER TWO

Explicit and Implicit Stereotypes: Current Models and Measurement of Attitudes

Amy L. Hillard

Psychologists face challenges in measuring concepts that exist inside the mind, such as stereotypes and prejudice. To examine these concepts from a scientific perspective, psychologists must identify and measure observable events or conditions that are indicative of prejudice and stereotyping; in other words, they develop operational definitions. However, prejudice and stereotypes are diverse; they exist for many social groups and can be expressed in differing ways. Still, our understanding of stereotyping and prejudice is dependent on how these concepts are operationally defined. As new measures developed, new questions and theories about stereotyping have been examined (Schneider, 2004). Stereotypes are cognitive structures, which are invisible. However, stereotypes can be made visible in differential emotions and behaviors that impact others. The challenge for psychologists is to measure stereotypes as they relate to behavioral outcomes; in other words, psychologists must make stereotypes visible.

To demonstrate the complexity of stereotypes and their relations to behavior, this chapter examines the ways stereotypes have been measured in empirical, psychological research. There are a variety of measures, each of which captures different facets of stereotyping and prejudice. This variety has implications for conceptualizations and theories of prejudice. I first examine the definitions and models of stereotypes, as well as changes over time therein. Next, specific operational definitions of explicit and implicit stereotypes are examined through widely used measures, along with the relationship between these measures and behavioral outcomes. The complexity in the measurement of stereotypes reflects the complexity of stereotypes and prejudice, as demonstrated across chapters in this book.

Definitions

Definitions of stereotypes vary, and researchers disagree on the essential qualities of stereotypes. As a result, empirical studies create operational definitions of stereotypes based on their research questions. Most definitions identify stereotypes as beliefs about traits associated with social groups. For example, Schneider (2004) defined stereotypes as "qualities perceived to be associated with particular groups or categories of people" (p. 24). Stereotypes are cognitive structures derived from culture and personal experience. The degree to which stereotypes are incorrect overgeneralizations (vs. generalizations containing a "kernel of truth") is an area of debate within the field. Early definitions included this component, but researchers now define stereotypes as perception, regardless of their relation to reality.

Stereotypes are functional because they provide a shortcut to understanding others based on previous experience (e.g., Hinton, 2017). In the absence of individuating information, stereotypes provide quick, easy information, which can facilitate predictions in interpersonal interactions. Although this "cognitive miser" perspective (Fiske & Taylor, 1991) explains why stereotypes are used habitually, there is extensive evidence about the ways stereotypes can be problematic. For example, stereotypes can rationalize or justify unequal treatment of others, thereby maintaining social hierarchies (Stangor, 2009). Although stereotypes are cognitions that exist in the mind and may seem harmless, they are related to feelings (i.e., prejudice) and behavior (i.e., discrimination) that influence others when expressed.

Models of Attitude Components

Through decades of research, attitudes are seen as having three interacting components: affect (i.e., feelings), behavior, and cognition (e.g., beliefs). Using this tripartite model of attitudes, prejudice can be understood as a general attitude toward a group or category of people. Research also defines prejudice as having an affective component (i.e., our feelings toward social groups); often prejudice is defined as negative affect toward groups, such as hostility or coldness. Prejudice reflects cognitions or stereotypic beliefs about groups. Behavior disadvantaging group members based on stereotypes or prejudice is then defined as discrimination. For example, sexism is a type of prejudice, which is supported by and related to negative feelings toward non-traditional women (i.e., affect), stereotypes about women's traits (e.g., cognitive beliefs that women are communal rather than agentic), and discriminatory behaviors against women (e.g., failing to consider women for stereotypically masculine jobs).

Consistent with the tripartite model of attitudes, stereotypes and prejudice are correlated, and affective and cognitive representations of groups are linked (Schneider, 2004). A meta-analysis showed that the affect is a strong predictor of racial discrimination, but stereotypes predict only self-reported discrimination (Talaska, Fiske, & Chaiken, 2008). On the other hand, information that challenges stereotypes can reduce racial bias (e.g., Cooley, Lei, Brown-Iannuzzi, & Boudrea, 2019). These relationships between attitude components may depend on type of prejudice and context. Another meta-analysis showed that racism and ageism, but not sexism, predicted workplace discrimination against job applicants as well as opposition to organizational diversity policies (Jones et al., 2017). Affective, behavioral, and cognitive components are related, with each explaining aspects of prejudice in a particular context.

The Stereotype Content Model (SCM; Fiske, Cuddy, Glick, & Xu, 2002) links stereotype content to affect toward stereotyped groups. According to SCM, group status and competition produce two dimensions, each ranging from low to high, that differentiate stereotypes: competence and warmth. Groups differ on the degree to which they are perceived as competent (e.g., high status and agentic) and warm (e.g., kind and sociable). These dimensions predict affect toward those groups, as shown in Figure 2.1. Groups stereotyped as low in competence and warmth (e.g., poor people) are subject to contempt. Groups stereotyped as low competence but high warmth (e.g., elderly and disabled people) are subject to pity and paternalistic stereotypes. Groups stereotyped as high competence but low warmth (e.g., Asian and Jewish people) are subject to envy and competition. Groups stereotyped as high in both competence and warmth are likely "ingroups" with which we identify, which are awarded admiration.

The SCM also explains complexity in and maintenance of stereotypes. Stereotypes can be ambivalent, considering the crossing of competence and warmth and tendencies to perceive these dimensions as inversely related (e.g., high warmth implies low competence and vice versa). Across cultures, greater stereotype ambivalence is associated with income inequality (Durante et al., 2012). Ambivalent stereotypes, then, can serve as beliefs that maintain social order. Inequality in the status quo can continue because stereotypes are ambivalent rather than uniformly negative. Further research has shown that stereotypes can be organized across dimensions of competence and warmth cross-culturally and that ambivalent stereotypes are common (Cuddy et al., 2009).

Stereotypes are associated with affect or emotion but also behavior toward social groups. Building on SCM, the Behaviors from Intergroup Affect and Stereotypes (BIAS) map (Cuddy, Fiske, & Glick, 2007) reflects affective, behavioral, and cognitive components of prejudice. As shown in Figure 2.1, the BIAS map includes two dimensions of behaviors: harm/facilitation and active/passive. Groups stereotyped as low in warmth are treated with harmful behavior, which can be active or passive, depending on perceived competence. Active harm (e.g., violence and harassment) is directed toward groups associated with both low competence and warmth, whereas passive harm (e.g., neglect or disregard) is directed toward groups with high competence and low warmth. Groups stereotyped as high in warmth are facilitated instead of harmed. Active facilitation (e.g., helping) is directed toward groups with high competence and warmth, whereas passive facilitation (e.g., cooperating) is directed toward groups with low competence and high warmth.

Consistent with the BIAS map, stereotypic warmth and competence predict behavior, both in the lab and the field (Jenkins, Karashchuk, Zhu, & Hsu, 2018). Perceived competence and warmth for twenty different social groups predicted behavior in economic games; over two-thirds of participants' resource allocation was explained by perceived competence and warmth. Further, the same model predicted discrimination against minority

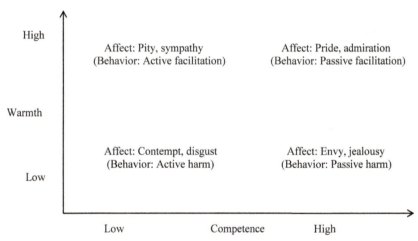

Figure 2.1 The SCM (Fiske et al., 2002) shows dimensions of stereotyping (e.g., warmth and competence) and the affect or emotion toward groups in that quadrant. Later, the BIAS map (Cuddy, Fiske, & Glick, 2007) integrated behavioral tendencies toward groups in each quadrant, which are indicated in parentheses.

and female applicants in labor and education. Discrimination documented in previous randomized field studies was predicted by other participants' ratings of perceived competence and warmth. Perceptions of competence and warmth account for the majority of overall evaluations of people, but warmth accounted for three times the effect of competence across behaviors in lab and field studies (Jenkins et al., 2018). Perceived competence and especially warmth may explain real-world disparities.

The Dual Nature of Attitudes

Another important distinction in the literature is between implicit and explicit attitudes. Explicit attitudes, which we are aware of and can self-report, are separate from implicit attitudes, which we are not aware of and cannot self-report. Implicit attitudes are sometimes called "the thumbprint of our culture" (Banaji & Greenwald, 2013; Vedantam, 2017) to reflect that they are learned through exposure to our environment and culture, even when explicit attitudes might contradict that exposure. Thus, explicit and implicit attitudes coexist but are independent, which allows for disagreement between explicit and implicit attitudes and for differing influences on behavior. For example, people may explicitly oppose a cultural stereotype, but knowledge of that cultural stereotype may still implicitly influence their behavior. Research shows that both cultural and personal stereotypes are related to prejudice, although personal stereotypes may be a stronger predictor (Schneider, 2004).

Stereotypes can function through controlled and automatic processes, consistent with dual process theories. The MODE model ("Motivation and Opportunity as DEterminants"; Fazio & Towles-Schwen, 1999) suggests that attitudes influence behaviors through two processes. One process is explicit and conscious, whereas the other is implicit and spontaneous, in which the attitude may not be directly considered before a behavioral response. The MODE model explains when deliberate or spontaneous processes are used based by motivation and opportunity. Although most of our interpersonal behavior is spontaneous (Schneider, 2004), a concern about accuracy can motivate more deliberate consideration of attitudes to determine behavior. Still, the opportunity must be present to spend the time necessary to undertake deliberate processing. Time pressure can increase stereotyping because the opportunity to engage in the deliberative processing is limited. Similarly, participants who have nonprejudiced explicit beliefs act in biased ways when they fail to recognize the propensity for bias (Devine, 1989). Lacking awareness of bias and thus motivation to overcome it, participants relied on automatic, cultural stereotypes rather than engaging the effort necessarily to use their personal (nonprejudiced) beliefs. Motivation to control prejudice also has been examined as an individual difference that can influence the extent to which stereotypes might be expressed and influence behavior (Schneider, 2004). Motivations to control prejudice can be internal (i.e., due to nonprejudiced personal beliefs) or external (i.e., due to social norms or pressure to avoid appearing prejudiced to others), with internal motivation more consistently reducing prejudiced responses.

In summary, prejudice is an attitude that is inter-related with affect (i.e., feelings toward social groups), behavior (i.e., differential treatment based on social group membership), and cognition (e.g., stereotypes of social groups). Research supporting the SCM and BIAS map suggests that cognitive beliefs about warmth and competence influence how we feel and act toward social groups. These dimensions explain ambivalence in cultural stereotypes and their effect on behavior. In addition, we can have implicit and explicit stereotypes, which potentially differ and separately influence behavior. Dual attitude models (e.g., MODE model) suggest that the automatic implicit stereotypes may influence behavior if the motivation and opportunity are not present for a nonprejudiced individual to override these automatic cultural associations. The dual nature of attitudes and stereotypes helps explain why people's behavior may be inconsistent with their beliefs. Given the complexity in prejudice and its components, it is not surprising that there is a diversity of conceptualizations about stereotyping and prejudice demonstrated in their theory, models, and measures, each of which have changed over time.

Changes Over Time and Measurement

When measured by support for interracial marriage and equal opportunity in education and employment, attitudes toward racial equality among White Americans shifted from opposition in the 1940s to widespread support in the 2000s (Krysan & Moberg, 2016). The gap in reported affect toward social groups on a "feeling thermometer" from 0 (*cold*) to 100 (*warm*) also reduced from 25 degrees cooler toward Black (vs. White) people in 1964 to seven degrees cooler in 2008 (Krysan & Moberg, 2016). Generally, psychologists have seen these trends as evidence of declining endorsement of prejudice, especially for race-based antipathy. From 1990 to 2004, White people were less likely to endorse negative stereotypes about Black people (e.g., less intelligent or hardworking); the percentage of White people reporting negative stereotypes was reduced by about half, with a minority rather than majority reporting negative stereotypes (Krysan & Moberg, 2016).

However, racial stereotype endorsement between 2004 and 2014 showed more stability than decline (Krysan & Moberg, 2016). Another study examined attitudes toward racial groups and other social groups from 2007 to 2016. Explicit and implicit attitudes became less negative (i.e., more neutral) toward minorities based on race, skin tone, and sexuality; however, stability was found for attitudes related to age and disability, and there were increasingly negative attitudes related to being overweight (Charlesworth & Banaji, 2019). Regardless of this decline in stereotyping and prejudiced attitudes related to race, a meta-analysis of field experiments found no change in hiring discrimination against Black job applicants over the last 25 years (Quillian, Pager, Hexel, & Midtbøen, 2017). Given evidence of continued racial discrimination, psychologists have examined explanations—other than less bias—for the decline in racial prejudice and stereotyping.

As reported prejudice has declined toward some groups, social norms encouraging tolerance and prohibiting explicit expressions of prejudice toward those groups may have also grown stronger. It is unclear what proportion of the decline in reported prejudice is attributable to less willingness to report (e.g., social desirability, social norms, self-presentation concerns), lack of awareness (e.g., implicit or unconscious attitudes/associations), or a shift in the conceptualization toward more subtle prejudice. In an attempt to disentangle a decline in internal prejudiced beliefs from a decline in external expressions of prejudice, psychologists have changed the ways in which they define and measure these concepts. Starting in the 1970s, theories and measures were developed to examine more subtle indicators of prejudice and stereotyping than blatant, old-fashioned prejudice (e.g., symbolic, modern, and aversive racism).

There are many measures of prejudice and stereotyping, making a full review of each beyond the scope of this chapter. Still, I offer several broad observations about these measures. First, as just mentioned, measures of prejudice have shifted from old-fashioned, traditional forms to more subtle forms. Second, most measures of prejudice focus on race and specifically Black-White attitudes (Olson & Zabel, 2016), which has influenced the creation of measures of other prejudices. Third, early work focused on the content of stereotypes, but the development of the field of social cognition led stereotyping to be examined, as a process, as well.

Before evaluating measures of stereotyping, some notes about psychometrics are necessary. There are two concerns relevant to the quality of a measure—reliability and validity—that determine whether a measure is "good." *Reliability* is the extent to which a measure is consistent and measures with minimal error (e.g., Price, Jhangiani, Chiang, Leighton, & Cuttler, 2017). All psychological measures contain some error, but reliability indicated by a correlation among the items and between the measure and a later administration of the same measure must be high. *Validity*, on the other hand, is the extent to which a measure accurately captures its intended concept (Price et al., 2017). To determine validity, the relationships between the measure and behavior or other existing measures are examined, again looking for high correlations with related behaviors and measures. To be a "good" measure, both reliability and validity are required, and researchers typically conduct multiple studies to provide evidence of both before new measures are used in other research. Most measures of stereotyping included in following review have high reliability, unless otherwise noted. Thus, the focus is on validity, or how well explicit and implicit measures predict behavior.

Explicit Measures

Stereotypes and prejudice can be assessed by measures that directly ask participants to report their attitudes toward groups of people. Measuring stereotyping using self-report is convenient and requires fewer resources than some implicit measures. However, self-report measures assume that participants are aware of and willing to report their attitudes. Participants often indicate the extent of agreement with statements that reflect stereotypes or prejudice. Scales can have many items, which can increase reliability, although even short scales can be reliable. Next, I describe measures organized by type, along with examples.

Stereotype Content

Research that examines the content of stereotypes has used a variety of methods. Free response measures are open-ended items in which the participants list traits associated with a group. Although free response can indicate strength of associations (i.e., earlier traits listed have a stronger association) and has the benefit of not "putting words in people's minds," the responses are qualitative, which comes with challenges of coding and quantifying the data (Schneider, 2004). Attribute checking avoids these issues by asking participants to report whether specific, provided attributes apply to members of a social group. However, this measure may reflect collective or cultural stereotypes rather than individual stereotyping (Schneider, 2004). The number of positive versus negative attributes checked also can be used as an evaluative measure, which may reflect affect associated with beliefs and thus better predict some behaviors.

Similarly, participants can be asked about the extent to which an attribute or trait describes a group using a scale rating (e.g., from "not at all" to "very much") or a semantic differential measure. For the latter, participants indicate where on a spectrum of opposing attributes (e.g., "competent" vs. "incompetent") members of social groups typically fall. These measures can be considered separately for social groups or relatively, by subtracting one group's rating from another.

Brigham's Individual Difference Measure examines the percentage of group members ascribed an attribute, which measures stereotyping by examining traits that are assigned high percentages (e.g., over 80%) and thus represent overgeneralized traits. Research shows that high perceived homogeneity within a group increases the likelihood that participants infer attributes about individual group members from group stereotypes (Schneider, 2004).

Racism

The majority of measures of prejudice focus on race/ethnicity and specifically on attitudes toward Black people. For example, the Prejudice Index (Bobo & Kluegel, 1993) and the Racial Stereotypes Measure (Peffley, Hurwitz, & Snidermann, 1997) examine White participants' endorsement of stereotypes of Black people, such as laziness and violence. The scales differ in that the Prejudice Index is a relative measure of attitudes toward Black versus White people (i.e., composite represents the difference between these groups), whereas the Racial Stereotypes Measure asks participants to rate the degree of accuracy of different attributes associated with Black people.

Similar to the measures just mentioned, scales for racism originally measured what is now called "old-fashioned prejudice," which is antipathy, hatred, and beliefs about inferiority that are associated with blatant acts of discrimination. For example, participants completing the Racial Attitudes Scale (Sidanius, Pratto, Martin, & Stallworth, 1991) respond to items concerning racial issues (e.g., support for interracial dating) toward a variety of racial/ethnic groups. Measures of this form of prejudice are easily recognizable as expressing racist attitudes and are counter to social norms favoring tolerance and prohibiting old-fashioned prejudice.

Recognizing greater sensitivity and/or reactivity toward items directly asking about race, modern measures of racism involve items that attempt to disguise the purpose of measuring stereotypes and prejudice. Disguised items address related issues, such as support for government programs (e.g., affirmative action) or belief in discrimination. Although the goal is to increase accuracy of responses by disguising the purpose, these changes introduce confounding concepts, such as political beliefs. For example, the Symbolic Racism 2000 Scale (Henry & Sears, 2002) blends racism and policy attitudes by asking participants whether they believe Black people are responsible for racial tension and are working hard enough to better their conditions. Similarly, participants completing the Modern Racism Scale (McConahay, Hardee, & Batts, 1981) answer items about violations of values. These disguised items measure stereotypic beliefs that are expressed in a more socially acceptable way and predict behaviors ranging from recommendations to hire job applicants to verdicts and sentencing. (For detailed reviews on measures of racism, see Biernat and Crandall [1999] and Olson and Zabel [2016].)

Sexism

Unlike many other social groups experiencing stereotyping and prejudice, gender represents a category wherein the groups are roughly equivalent in size. As a result, gender prejudice and stereotyping demonstrates ambivalence, which is necessary to gain support of both men and women. For example, the Ambivalent Sexism Inventory (Glick & Fiske, 1996) measures both hostile sexism (i.e., traditional, negative attitudes toward women) and benevolent sexism (i.e., a chivalrous attitude toward women, which seems more positive but is actually overprotective). These two forms of sexism function together to reinforce the status quo by punishing women acting outside their traditional gender roles with hostile sexism and rewarding women acting within their traditional role with benevolent sexism. These forms of sexism thus reflect beliefs about the traits "appropriate" for women and guides behavior toward women. For example, benevolent sexism reflects the belief that women are pure and wonderful but in need of protection, which results in paternalistic behaviors, whereas hostile sexism is related to aggression and other behaviors that reinforce male dominance (Connor, Glick, & Fiske, 2017).

Many researchers measure gender role attitudes, which are expectations about attributes and behaviors associated with men and women. Gender roles provide the basis for gender stereotypes, and both roles and stereotypes are cognitive components of sexism. Research suggests that endorsement of prescriptive gender roles and stereotypes is associated with discriminatory behavior. (For a review, see McHugh & Frieze, 1997.)

Other Types of Prejudice

Theories and measures of other types of prejudice are more recent compared to racism and sexism. New measures for different types of prejudice often start from the existing measures developed for racism and/or sexism. However, stereotypes related to race and/or gender may not capture stereotypes toward other groups. For example, reviews of measures of LGBT prejudice and discrimination (e.g., Morrison, Bishop, & Morrison, 2019; Morrison, Bishop, Morrison, & Parker-Taneo, 2016) indicate that assumptions of gender-related prejudice may have had undue influence on measures and that more work is needed. Another example is weight-related prejudice, which differs from other forms in that it is increasing over time (Charlesworth & Banaji, 2019). Measures of stereotypes of overweight or obese people, including beliefs about personality traits and willpower, have been assessed using explicit self-report measures. (See Lacroix, Alberga, Russell-Matthew, McLauren, and von Ranson [2017] for a psychometric review.)

Individual Differences Predicting Prejudice

Given that motivation and opportunity are related to tendencies to rely on stereotypes (e.g., MODE model), some measures examine an individual's motivation to express versus inhibit prejudice and stereotyping. Although these measures reflect the influence of implicit stereotypes, the measures themselves are explicit in that participants self-report their explicit attitudes. For example, Social Dominance Orientation (Pratto, Sidanius, Stallworth, & Malle, 1994) is a preference for social hierarchy, which is associated with prejudice and stereotyping toward groups stereotyped as "low status" (e.g., Christopher & Wojda, 2008). On the other hand, participants may be (successfully) motivated to avoid prejudice by either internal beliefs or external social pressure. The Motivation to Respond Without Prejudice Scale assesses both (Plant & Devine, 1998). Although originally developed for anti-Black prejudice, the scale has been adapted for various social groups (e.g., Klonis, Plant, & Devine, 2005). An internal motivation to avoid prejudice predicts lower discrimination regardless of whether the behavior is public, whereas external motivation to avoid prejudice predicts lower discrimination only when others are aware of responses (Klonis et al., 2005).

Summary

Measures of stereotype content, including those related to racism and sexism, are varied in order to address the facet of prejudice examined in empirical research. However, these measures come with concerns about reactivity, as self-presentation or social norms may distort participant responses. Also, some measures are domain specific; that is, they measure attitudes that may not apply to all groups or in all situations, which presents challenges for expanding the targets of stereotyping measured. While stereotype content is assessed using these measures, the strength of stereotypes is often not examined, unlike the implicit measures.

Implicit Measures

Implicit stereotypes are automatic associations with social groups. Given their unconscious nature, participants cannot directly report implicit stereotypes. However, measures and methods—often focusing on behaviors—have been developed to demonstrate implicit stereotypes participants may hold. Implicit measures can alternatively be called "indirect" measures because participants are not self-reporting stereotypes. Implicit associations influence behavior, especially more subtle or automatic behavior in intergroup interactions (e.g., Dovidio, Kawakami, & Gaetner, 2002). Implicit measures allow for assessing of the strength with which an attribute and social group are associated and for examining associations that participants may not be aware of. An additional advantage of implicit measures is that they are unobtrusive, and participants may not be able to adjust their responses out of social desirability concerns. Their disadvantage is that implicit measures often require more resources (e.g., technology) than explicit measures. Researchers also debate their reliability and validity, which is discussed next across variations in implicit measures.

Response Latency

Early research on implicit stereotypes examined the association between a social group and an attribute by measuring the latency of the response. In direct association measures, participants indicate the association, and the reaction time is measured. The faster participants answer, the more associated the social group and attributes are thought to be. Similar reasoning is used in a lexical decision task, in which participants determine whether pairs are words; faster responses are expected for stereotype consistent pairs. One study using the lexical decision task found that this measure was a predictor of White participants' nonverbal friendliness (as rated by confederates and observers) toward a Black partner, whereas explicit measures predicted verbal behavior (Dovido, Kawakami, & Gaertner, 2002).

Priming

Another method of assessing implicit stereotypes is through priming participants with a stereotype and examining the stereotype's effect on subsequent behavior. The logic is that participants' implicit stereotypes make associated concepts more easily and readily accessible. For example, memory measures can serve as measures of stereotypes, in which participants are asked to recall a list of words after being primed with a stereotype. Because of the increased accessibility of the concepts, stereotype-consistent words should be recalled at a higher rate. Sequential priming has been used to assess stereotype activation by measuring response times for pairs of words that are either stereotype congruent or incongruent. This paradigm has been used to examine a variety of stereotypes, including whether implicit racial stereotypes are generalized across target gender and age (Thiem, Neel, Simpson, & Todd, 2019). However, a recent meta-analysis indicates high variability in stereotype priming effects across methods (Kidder, White, Hinojos, Sandoval, & Crites, 2018). Affective priming has also been used as a stereotype measure, in which participants judge whether a target item is positive or negative. The target item is preceded by prime (e.g., words or images associated with a social group). If that social group is associated with negative stereotypes, the participants should respond more quickly to target items that are negative and more slowly to target items that are positive, because those concepts are more easily accessible as a result of the primed stereotype.

For example, the Affect Misattribution Procedure (AMP; Payne, Cheng, Govorun, & Stewart, 2005) has been used to measure implicit racial stereotypes. Participants are asked to judge whether a neutral image (e.g., a Chinese character) is pleasant or not pleasant by pressing keys. However, this target image is preceded by a prime, presented either subliminally or very briefly, associated with a social group (e.g., an image of either a Black or White face). Participants complete multiple trials, and implicit racial bias is indicated if the neutral targets are more likely to be judged as pleasant when proceeded by a White (vs. Black) face. In the absence of stereotyping, the target characters should be equally likely to be seen as pleasant or unpleasant. Primed with a social group, however, participants misattribute the associations with the prime to the neutral target, thus indicating their affective evaluation of the social group as pleasant or unpleasant.

Implicit Association Test

Since its introduction over twenty years ago (Greenwald, McGhee, & Schwartz, 1998), the Implicit Association Test (IAT) has been used extensively in research. It also has gained public visibility and awareness, and millions have completed online IATs through the Project Implicit website (https://implicit.harvard.edu). The IAT measures how quickly participants can associate social groups with positive versus negative words. After practice trials, participants complete trials in which they sort target items (e.g., names, photos) into paired categories by pressing corresponding keys. The categories include the social groups being assessed (e.g., Black and White) combined with evaluative words (e.g., Pleasant and Unpleasant). The paired categories are completely crossed across blocks of trials (e.g., stereotype inconsistent: Black + Pleasant vs. White + Unpleasant; stereotype consistent: Black + Unpleasant vs. White + Pleasant). Analyses compare response latencies for the stereotype consistent versus inconsistent trials. Faster responding to the stereotype consistent (vs. inconsistent) trials indicates stronger associations between the categories and thus more implicit stereotyping. Although the IAT is considered an implicit or indirect measure, participants report awareness of the purpose of the measure; that is, they notice while completing the IAT that the stereotype consistent trials are easier or faster than the stereotype inconsistent trials (Monteith, Voils, & Ashburn-Nardo, 2011).

The IAT has been used to measure a variety of stereotypes. The original Race IAT was just described, but the IAT can be adapted to measure implicit stereotypes between any social group and attribute. Although there is debate about what response times indicate and the extent of difference in responses times is indicative of a "preference," the researchers say that the results from the Race IAT indicate that 70 percent of participants have an implicit preference for White people over Black people (Nosek, Banaji, & Greenwald, 2002). Similarly, Age IATs, Weight IATs, and Sexuality IATs indicate implicit biases against older adults, obese individuals, and gay people, respectively (Nosek et al., 2002). The Gender-Science IAT and Gender-Career IAT show that most people more strongly associate men with science and careers but women with liberal arts and family (Nosek et al., 2002).

Variations of the IAT procedure rather than content have also developed over time. Participants completing a Go/No-go Association Test (GNAT; Nosek & Banaji, 2001) are asked to indicate the presence of a target (e.g., social group) paired with an evaluative attribute (e.g., good or bad) by pressing a key and to refrain from pressing the key when distractor pairings are presented. Thus, the GNAT assesses automatic associations to a single social category rather than contrasting social groups/categories as in the IAT, which makes the GNAT less relative. Both response latency and accuracy are calculated, and comparisons are made between the social category when paired with each extreme of the attribute, which indicates implicit associations. However, research has shown that the GNAT may have lower reliability than the IAT (Teige-Mocigemba, Kaluer, & Sherman, 2010). Other variations of the IAT include removing or adding categories, changes to the procedure (e.g., the block structure or response modality), and the length of the test (e.g., Brief IAT). For a review of variations, see Teige-Mocigemba et al. (2010) and/or Bar-Anan and Nosek (2013).

Although the IAT varies across content and procedure, controversy surrounds the measure's reliability and validity. The IAT's reliability is low in terms of being consistent over time. When the same IAT is given to the same people twice, the correlation between the test and retest is about $r = .4$ (Bar-Anan & Nosek, 2013; Gawronski, Morrison, Phills, & Gladi, 2017). Similar correlations are found for IATs over two weeks (Cunningham, Preacher, & Banaji, 2001) or two different versions of the IAT (i.e., images vs. names in the same session; Dasgupta, McGhee, & Greenwald, 2000). Even giving participants the same IAT one day later ($r = .65$; Lane, Banaji, Nosek, & Greenwald, 2007) does not meet conventions for reliability found among explicit measures. Implicit measures, including the IAT, are also less stable longitudinally than explicit measures (Gawronski et al., 2017).

Some researchers argue that the IAT also has low validity and is confounded with or contaminated by a range of factors, including cognitive ability, motivated processes, and cultural-level (rather than individual-level) associations. For example, IAT scores may reflect participants' knowledge of an existing cultural stereotype, regardless of their endorsement or acceptance of that cultural stereotype (see Olson, Fazio, and Han [2009] for a review). As a result, a "personalized" modification (i.e., replacing "Pleasant/Unpleasant" categories with "I like/I don't like") has been shown to predict behavior better than the standard IAT procedure (e.g., Olson & Fazio, 2004).

Even the researchers who developed the IAT have ceded that the IAT cannot predict individual behavior precisely enough to be used diagnostically; there are only weak correlations between individuals' IAT scores and their behavior. One meta-analysis showed the race IAT predicts 4–6 percent of discriminatory behavior in the lab (Greenwald, Poehlman, Uhlmann, & Banaji, 2009), although additional meta-analyses suggests that this estimate may be inflated, with the IAT's power to predict behavior at 2 percent or less (Carlsson & Agerström, 2016; Forscher et al., in press; Oswald, Mitchell, Blanton, Jaccard, & Tetlock, 2013). Correspondence between IAT type and behavior type has not been examined in meta-analyses but increases predictive validity. Specifically, a stereotype-based IAT predicted stereotypic expectations, whereas an evaluative IAT predicted physical distance in an interracial interaction (Amodio & Devin, 2006). Still, the evidence of the IAT's predictive validity is weaker than expected given its widespread use and notoriety.

Other Implicit Measures

Rather than categorizing words, another operational definition of implicit bias examines decisions in a meaningful context. The First Person Shooter Task (Correll, Park, Judd, & Wittenbrink, 2002) measures behavioral discrimination task by having participants decide whether to "shoot" by pressing a keyboard button. Participants are instructed to "shoot" armed targets but not unarmed targets. Participants are presented with images of Black and White men who are either armed or unarmed. The response rates and errors are tracked, and meta-analysis indicates that participants show racial bias in their decisions to shoot and reaction times (Mekawi & Breslin, 2015). Although the shooter task is a measure of discrimination, the decision to "shoot" is likely driven by stereotypic associations between Black men and dangerousness, criminality, and threat.

Although the implicit measures just reviewed require technology, pen and paper measures of implicit stereotypes have also been developed. (See Sekaquaptewa, Vargas, and von Hippel [2010] for a review.) For example, participants can be asked to complete word fragments or stems, which can either be completed in stereotype consistent or inconsistent ways. This implicit measure predicts guilt and discrimination in aversive racists (as cited in Sekaquaptewa et al., 2010).

Summary

Implicit measures have been criticized for low reliability (e.g., Olson & Zabel, 2016), but reliability ranges across situations (Payne & Lundberg, 2014). Also, the predictive validity of implicit measures for behavior continues to be debated. On one hand, implicit measures have been shown to predict subtle behaviors (Amodio & Devine, 2006; Dovidio et al., 2002), which are less monitored and controllable. On the other hand, priming tasks, AMP, and IAT have small associations with behavior (i.e., approximately $r = .3$; Cameron, Brown-Iannuzzi, & Payne, 2012; Greenwald et al., 1998, 2009). However, a recent meta-analysis found only small associations between implicit bias and behavior ($r = .11$; Forscher et al., in press). Further, interventions reduce implicit racial bias only temporarily (Lai et al., 2016), and changes in implicit bias did not predict changes in behavior (Forscher et al., in press). Implicit measures have clearly influenced psychological theories of prejudice. It is less clear, however, whether implicit bias is well measured and the extent to which these measures are meaningful predictors of behavior.

"Best" Measures?

There is likely no single best measure of prejudice and/or stereotyping. Instead, operational definitions reflect the type of stereotyping expected to have influence. Consistent with the dual process models, meta-analyses illustrate that implicit and explicit measures are related but separable. Implicit measures of bias generally have small to medium correlations with explicit measures (Cameron et al., 2012; Hofman, Gawronski, Gshwender, Le, & Schmitt, 2005; Greenwald et al., 2009), although a recent meta-analysis of 400+ studies found a smaller correlation between implicit and explicit measures ($r = .15$; Forscher et al., in press). Given this weak association, it is not surprising that implicit and explicit measures predict different behaviors (i.e., deliberate vs. spontaneous; Greenwald et al., 2009). Explicit but not implicit racial bias predicted controlled, deliberate decision-making in one recent study (Cooley, Lei, Brown-Iannuzzi, & Ellerkamp, 2019). Specifically, participants higher in explicit bias were more likely to find a White police officer who shot a Black man "not guilty" than participants lower in explicit bias, whereas implicit bias was not related to decisions about guilt or responsibility. However, meta-analyses indicate that implicit and explicit measures similarly predict behavior (Oswald et al., 2013) and even subtle discrimination (Jones et al., 2017). Until it is clear the conditions under which explicit and implicit measures predict differing behavioral outcomes, multiple measures are necessary to examine stereotyping and bias.

Concerns about social desirability led researchers to develop self-reported, explicit measures that disguised the purpose of measuring bias, often shifting language in items to be less direct. However, this approach may not have had the intended effect of better measuring bias (Axt, 2018). Coders rated over forty explicit measures commonly used to measure racial bias on directness (i.e., items were transparent rather than disguised in measured bias). The correlations between these explicit measures and implicit measures were examined, along with the gap between Black and White participants' feeling thermometer ratings toward racial groups. More direct explicit measures produced larger correlations with implicit attitudes than indirect explicit measures, even when controlling for social desirability. More direct explicit measures also better predicted gaps between Black and White participants' feelings toward racial groups than less direct measures; in other words, direct explicit measures detected bias against Black people (more often found in White than Black people) better than indirect measures. These findings suggest that, in an attempt to develop better measures of racial bias, researchers produced measures that are less likely to measure racial bias. The same likely applies to measures of other type of prejudice. In order to measure explicit prejudice and stereotypes, it may be best to directly ask about participants' attitudes, affect, and cognitions.

The complexity in conceptualizations, content, and theories related to prejudice and stereotyping suggest that there is no single best measure. Explicit and implicit measures highlight different facets of prejudice and stereotyping. Research suggests that the expression of stereotypes is influenced by a complex set of variables, which include the target group and situation (Lai et al., 2016). Explicit and implicit stereotypes are correlated but independent and thus have differing effects on behavior. Explicit measures may better predict controlled behavior, whereas implicit measures may predict spontaneous behavior. As such, when asking about the "best" measure, the answer depends on the context. Each measure captures a different aspect of the concepts of stereotyping and prejudice, although recent evidence suggests that direct self-report may better measure explicit bias (Axt, 2018). However, previous research indicates that stereotypes are not simply antipathy toward a group but instead may take the form of ambivalence toward groups. Thus, modern forms of stereotyping and prejudice may need multidimensional, complex measures.

This review raises issues for future research. First, there is an over-reliance on the IAT. Lack of diversity in measures of implicit bias is limiting to knowledge and theory development, because findings could be a result of that single operational definition of bias (Lai et al., 2016). The reliance on the IAT is especially problematic given evidence suggesting weak reliability and validity. Second, a focus on individual cognitive bias ignores powerful predictors of discrimination, such as affect (e.g., Talaska et al., 2008), culture (Hinton,

2017), and situations (Payne, Vuletich, & Lundberg, 2017). Shared stereotypes and biased expectations influence behaviors (e.g., Greenwald, Banaji, & Nosek, 2015; Hehman, Flake, & Calanchini, 2018) and likely produce social disparities (e.g., Jenkins et al., 2018). However, few studies take an aggregate approach, resulting in less knowledge about how prejudice and stereotypes are communicated, maintained, and/or disrupted at the level of culture. Cultural or social norms can be more powerful predictors of behaviors than personal beliefs, and communications influencing social norms can reduce (Paluck, 2009) or increase prejudice (Crandall, Miller, & White, 2018).

As noted at the start of this chapter, psychologists face challenges in measuring bias and making the invisible cognitions that drive bias visible. Stereotypes are not a single concept, which necessitates multiple measures to examine them. Measuring individual and cultural stereotyping predicts prejudice and discrimination, but no single measure is "best." Instead, measures reflect different aspects of stereotypes that are relevant to the research question or theory, which hopefully increases our understanding of stereotyping—and how to reduce it—in the real world.

References

Amodio, D. M., & Devine, P. G. (2006). Stereotyping and evaluation in implicit race bias: Evidence for independent constructs and unique effects on behavior. *Journal of Personality and Social Psychology, 91*, 652–661. doi:10.1037/0022-3514.91.4.652

Axt, J. R. (2018). The best way to measure explicit racial attitudes is to ask about them. *Social Psychological and Personality Science, 9*, 896–906. doi:10.1177/1948550617728995

Banaji, M. R., & Greenwald, A. G. (2013). *Blindspot: Hidden biases of good people.* New York: Delacorte Press.

Bar-Anan, Y., & Nosek, B. A. (2013). A comparative investigation of seven indirect attitude measures. *Behavior Research Methods, 46*, 668–688. doi:10.3758/s13428-013-0410-6

Biernat, M. B., & Crandall, C. S. (1999). Racial attitudes. In J. Robinson, P. Shaver, & L. Wrightsman (Eds.), *Measures of political attitudes* (2nd ed., pp. 297–411). New York: Academic Press.

Bobo, L., & Kluegel, J. (1993). Opposition to race-targeting: Self-interest, stratification ideology, or racial attitudes? *American Sociological Review, 58*, 443–464.

Cameron, C. D., Brown-Iannuzzi, J. L., & Payne, B. K. (2012). Sequential priming measures of implicit social cognition: A meta-analysis of associations with behavior and explicit attitudes. *Personality and Social Psychology Review, 16*, 330–350. doi:10.1177/1088868312440047

Carlsson, R., & Agerström, J. (2016). A closer look at the discrimination outcomes in the IAT literature. *Scandinavian Journal of Psychology, 57,* 278–287. doi:10.1111/sjop.12288

Charlesworth, T. E. S., & Banaji, M. R. (2019). Patterns of implicit and explicit attitudes: I. Long-term change and stability from 2007 to 2016. *Psychological Science, 30*(2), 174–192. doi:10.1177/0956797618813087

Christopher, A. N., & Wojda, M. R. (2008). Social dominance orientation, right-wing authoritarianism, sexism, and prejudice toward women in the workforce. *Psychology of Women Quarterly, 32,* 65–73.

Connor, R. A., Glick, P., & Fiske, S. (2017). Ambivalent sexism in the twenty-first century. In C. G. Sibley & F. K. Barlow (Eds.), *The Cambridge handbook of the psychology of prejudice* (pp. 295–320). Cambridge: Cambridge University Press.

Cooley, E., Lei, R., Brown-Iannuzzi, J., & Boudrea, C. (2019). Shifting stereotypes of welfare recipients can reverse racial biases in support for wealth redistribution. *Social Psychological and Personality Science.* Advance online publication. doi:10.1177/1948550619829062

Cooley, E., Lei, R., Brown-Iannuzzi, J., & Ellerkamp, T. (2019). Personal prejudice, other guilt: Explicit prejudice toward Black people predicts guilty verdicts for White officers who kill Black men. *Personality and Social Psychology Bulletin, 45*(5), 754–766. doi:10.1177/0146167218796787

Correll, J., Park, B., Judd, C. M., & Wittenbrink, B. (2002). The police officer's dilemma: Using ethnicity to disambiguate potentially threatening individuals. *Journal of Personality & Social Psychology, 83,* 1314–1329.

Crandall, C. S., Miller, J. M., & White, M. H. (2018). Changing norms following the 2016 U.S. presidential election: The Trump effect. *Social Psychological and Personality Science, 9,* 186–192. doi:10.1177/1948550617750735

Cuddy, A. J. C., Fiske, S. T., & Glick, P. (2007). The BIAS map: Behaviors from intergroup affect and stereotypes. *Journal of Personality and Social Psychology, 92,* 631–648. doi:10.1037/0022-3514.92.4.631

Cuddy, A. J. C., Fiske, S. T., Kwan, V. S. Y., Glick, P., Demoulin, S., Leyens, J., . . . Ziegler, R. (2009). Stereotype content model across cultures: Toward universal similarities and some differences. *British Journal of Social Psychology, 48,* 1–33. doi:10.1348/014466608x314935

Cunningham, W. A., Preacher, K. J., & Banaji, M. R. (2001). Implicit attitude measures: Consistency, stability, and convergent validity. *Psychological Science, 12,* 163–170.

Dasgupta, N., McGhee, D., & Greenwald, A. G. (2000). Automatic preference for White Americans: Ruling out the familiarity effect. *Journal of Experimental Social Psychology, 36,* 316–328.

Devine, P. G. (1989). Stereotypes and prejudice: Their automatic and controlled components. *Journal of Personality and Social Psychology, 56,* 5–18.

Dovido, J. F., Kawakami, K., & Gaertner, S. L. (2002). Implicit and explicit prejudice and interracial interaction. *Journal of Personality and Social Psychology, 82,* 62–68. doi:10.1037//0022-3514.82.1.62

Durante, F., Fiske, S. T., Kervyn, N., Cuddy, A. J. C., Akande, A., Adetoun, B. E., . . . Storori, C. C. (2012). Nation's income inequality predicts ambivalence in stereotype content: How societies mind the gap. *British Journal of Social Psychology, 52,* 726–746, doi:10.1111/bjso.12005

Fazio, R. H., & Towles-Schwen, T. (1999). The MODE model of attitude-behavior processes. In S. Chaiken & Y. Trope (Eds.), *Dual process theories in social psychology* (pp. 97–116). New York: Guilford Press.

Fiske, S. T., Cuddy, A. J., Glick, P., & Xu, J. (2002). A model of (often mixed) stereotype content: Competence and warmth respectively follow from perceived status and competition. *Journal of Personality and Social Psychology, 82,* 878–902.

Fiske, S. T., & Taylor, S. E. (1991). *Social cognition* (2nd ed.). New York: McGraw-Hill.

Forscher, P. S., Lai, C. K., Axt, J. R., Ebersole, R., Herman, M., Devine, P. G., & Nosek, B. A. (in press). *A meta-analysis of procedures to change implicit measures.* Retrieved from https://psyarxiv.com/dv8tu/

Gawronski, B., Morrison, M., Phills, C. E., & Galdi, S. (2017). Temporal stability of implicit and explicit measures: A longitudinal analysis. *Personality and Social Psychology Bulletin, 43,* 300–312. doi:10.1177/0146167216684131

Glick, P., & Fiske, S. T. (1996). The ambivalent sexism inventory: Differentiating hostile and benevolent sexism. *Journal of Personality and Social Psychology, 70,* 491–512.

Greenwald, A. G., Banaji, M. R., & Nosek, B. A. (2015). Statistically small effects of the Implicit Association Test can have societally large effects. *Journal of Personality and Social Psychology, 108,* 53–561. doi:10.1037/pspa0000016

Greenwald, A. G., McGhee, D. E., & Schwartz, J. L. K. (1998). Measuring individual differences in implicit cognition: The Implicit Association Test. *Journal of Personality and Social Psychology, 74,* 1464–1480. doi:10.1037/0022-3514.74.6.1464

Greenwald, A. G., Poehlman, T. A., Uhlmann, E. L., & Banaji, M. R. (2009). Understanding and using the Implicit Association Test: III. Meta-analysis of predictive validity. *Journal of Personality and Social Psychology, 97,* 17–41. doi:10.1037/a0015575

Hehman, E., Flake, J. K., & Calanchini, J. (2018). Disproportionate use of lethal force in policing is associated with regional racial biases of residents. *Social Psychological and Personality Science, 9,* 393–401. doi:10.1177/1948550617711229

Henry, P. J., & Sears, D. O. (2002). The symbolic racism 2000 scale. *Political Psychology, 23,* 253–283.

Hinton, P. (2017). Implicit stereotypes and the predictive brain: Cognition and culture in "biased" person perception. *Palgrave Communications, 3,* 17086. doi:10.1057/palcomms.2017.86

Hofman, W., Gawronski, B., Gshwender, T., Le, H., & Schmitt, M. (2005). A meta-analysis on the correlation between the Implicit Association Test and explicit self-report measures. *Personality and Social Psychology Bulletin, 31,* 1369–1385. doi:10.1177/0146167205275613

Jenkins, A. C., Karashchuk, P., Zhu, L., & Hsu, M. (2018). Predicting human behavior toward members of different social groups. *Proceedings of the National Academy of Sciences, 115,* 9696–9701. doi:10.1073/pnas .1719452115

Jones, K. P., Sabat, I. E., King, E. B., Ahmad, A., McCausland, T. C., & Chen, T. (2017). Isms and schisms: A meta-analysis of the prejudice-discrimination relationship across racism, sexism, and ageism. *Journal of Organizational Behavior, 38,* 1076–1110. doi:10.1002/job.2187

Kidder, C. K., White, K. R., Hinojos, M. R., Sandoval, M., & Crites, S. L., Jr. (2018). Sequential stereotype priming: A meta-analysis. *Personality and Social Psychology Review, 23,* 199–227. doi:10.1177/1088868317723532

Klonis, S. C., Plant, E. A., & Devine, P. G. (2005). Internal and external motivation to respond without sexism. *Personality and Social Psychology Bulletin, 31,* 1237–1249. doi:10.1177/0416167205275304

Krysan, M., & Moberg, S. (2016, August 25). Trends in racial attitudes. *University of Illinois Institute of Government and Public Affairs.* Retrieved from http:// igpa.uillinois.edu/programs/racial-attitudes

Lacroix, E., Alberga, A., Russell-Matthew, S., McLauren, L., & von Ranson, K. (2017). Weight bias: A systematic review of characteristics and psychometric properties of self-report questionnaires. *Obesity Facts, 10,* 223– 237. doi:10.1159/000346259

Lai, C. K., Skinner, A. L., Cooley, E., Murrar, S., Brauer, M., Devos, T., . . . Nosek, B. A. (2016). Reducing implicit racial preferences: II. Intervention effectiveness across time. *Journal of Experimental Psychology: General, 145,* 1001–1016.

Lane, K. A., Banaji, M. R., Nosek, B. A., & Greenwald, A. G. (2007). Understanding and using the Implicit Association Test: IV. What we know (so far). In B. Wittenbrink & N. S. Schwarz (Eds.), *Implicit measures of attitudes: Procedures and controversies* (pp. 59–102). New York: Guilford Press.

McConahay, J. B., Hardee, B. B., & Batts, V. (1981). Has racism declined in America? It depends on who is asking and what is asked. *Journal of Conflict Resolution, 25,* 563–579.

McHugh, M. C., & Frieze, I. H. (1997). The measurement of gender-role attitudes. *Psychology of Women Quarterly, 21,* 1–16.

Mekawi, Y., & Bresin, K. (2015). Is the evidence from racial bias shooting task studies a smoking gun? Results from a meta-analysis. *Journal of Experimental Social Psychology, 61,* 120–130. doi:10.1016/jesp.2015.08.002

Monteith, M. J., Voils, C. I., & Ashburn-Nardo, L. (2001). Taking a look underground: Detecting, interpreting, and reacting to implicit racial bias. *Social Cognition, 19,* 395–417.

Morrison, T. G., Bishop, C. J., & Morrison, M. A. (2019). A systematic review of the psychometric properties of composite LGBT prejudice and discrimination scales. *Journal of Homosexuality, 66*(4), 549–570. doi:10.1080/00918 369.2017.1422935

Morrison, T. G., Bishop, C. J., Morrison, M. A., & Parker-Taneo, K. (2016). A psychometric review of measures assessing discrimination against sexual minorities. *Journal of Homosexuality, 63,* 1086–1126. doi:10.1080/009183 69.2015.1117903

Nosek, B. A., & Banaji, M. R. (2001). The Go/No-Go Association Task. *Social Cognition, 19,* 625–666.

Nosek, B. A., Banaji, M. R., & Greenwald, A. G. (2002). Harvesting implicit group attitudes and beliefs from a demonstration website. *Group Dynamics, 6,* 101–115. doi:10.1037/1089-2699.6.1.101

Olson, M. A., & Fazio, R. H. (2004). Reducing the influence of extra-personal associations on the Implicit Association Test: Personalizing the IAT. *Journal of Personality and Social Psychology, 86,* 653–667.

Olson, M. A., Fazio, R. H., & Han, H. A. (2009). Conceptualizing personal and extrapersonal associations. *Social Psychology and Personality Compass, 3,* 152–170.

Olson, M. A., & Zabel, K. L. (2016). Measures of prejudice. In T. D. Nelson (Ed.), *Handbook of prejudice, stereotyping, and discrimination* (pp. 367–386). New York: Psychology Press.

Oswald, F. L., Mitchell, G., Blanton, H., Jaccard, J., & Tetlock, P. E. (2013). Predicting ethnic and racial discrimination: A meta-analysis of IAT criterion studies. *Journal of Personality and Social Psychology, 105,* 171–192. doi:10.1037/a0032734

Paluck, E. L. (2009). Reducing intergroup prejudice and conflict using the media: A field experiment in Rwanda. *Journal of Personality and Social Psychology, 96,* 574–587. doi:10.1037/a0011989

Payne, B. K., Cheng, C. M., Govorun, O., & Stewart, B. D. (2005). An inkblot for attitudes: Affective misattribution as implicit measurement. *Journal of Personality and Social Psychology, 89,* 277–293. doi:10.1037/0022-3514 .89.3.277

Payne, B. K., & Lundberg, K. (2014). The Affect Misattribution Procedure: Ten years of evidence on reliability, validity, and mechanism. *Social and Personality Psychology Compass, 8,* 672–686. doi:10.1111/spc3.12148

Payne, K., Vuletich, H. A., & Lundberg, K. B. (2017). The bias of crowds: How implicit bias bridges personal and systematic prejudice. *Psychological Inquiry, 28,* 233–248. doi:10.1080/104780X.1335568

Peffley, M., Hurwitz, J., & Snidermann, P. (1997). Racial stereotypes and whites' political views of blacks in the context of welfare and crime. *American Journal of Political Science, 41,* 30–60.

Plant, E. A., & Devine, P. G. (1998). Internal and external motivation to respond without prejudice. *Journal of Personality and Social Psychology, 75,* 811–832.

Pratto, F., Sidanius, J., Stallworth, L. M., & Malle, B. F. (1994). Social Dominance Orientation: A personality variable predicting social and political attitudes. *Journal of Personality and Social Psychology, 67,* 741–763.

Price, P. C., Jhangiani, R., Chiang, I. A., Leighton, D. C., & Cuttler, C. (2017). Psychological measurement. In *Research methods in psychology* (3rd ed.). Press Books. Retrieved from https://opentext.wsu.edu/carriecuttler/chapter/reliability-and-validity-of-measurement/

Quillian, L., Page, D., Hexel, O., & Midtbøen, A. H. (2017). Meta-analysis of field experiments shows no change in racial discrimination in hiring over time. *Proceedings of the National Academy of Sciences, 114*(41), 10870–10875. doi:10.1073/pnas.1706255114

Schneider, D. J. (2004). *The psychology of stereotyping.* New York: Guilford Press.

Sekaquaptewa, D., Vargas, P., & von Hippel, W. (2010). A practical guide to paper-and-pencil implicit measures of attitudes. In B. Gawronski & B. K. Payne (Eds.), *Handbook of implicit social cognition: Measurement, theory, and applications* (pp. 140–155). New York: Guilford Press.

Sidanius, J., Pratto, F., Martin, M., & Stallworth, L. M. (1991). Consensual racism and career track: Some implications of social dominance theory. *Political Psychology, 12,* 691–721.

Stangor, C. (2009). The study of stereotyping, prejudice, and discrimination within social psychology: A quick history of theory and research. In T. D. Nelson (Ed.), *Handbook of prejudice, stereotyping, and discrimination* (pp. 1–22). New York: Psychology Press.

Talaska, C. A., Fiske, S. T., & Chaiken, S. (2008). Legitimating racial discrimination: Emotions, not beliefs, best predict discrimination in a meta-analysis. *Social Justice Research, 21,* 263–296. doi:10.1007/s11211-008-0071-2

Teige-Mocigemba, S., Kaluer, K. C., & Sherman, J. W. (2010). A practical guide to Implicit Association Tests and related tasks. In B. Gawronski & B. K. Payne (Eds.), *Handbook of implicit social cognition: Measurement, theory, and applications* (pp. 117–139). New York: Guilford Press.

Thiem, K. C., Neel, R., Simpson, A. J., & Todd, A. R. (2019). Are Black women and girls associated with danger? Implicit racial bias at the intersection of target age and gender. *Personality and Social Psychology Bulletin.* Advance online publication. doi:10.1177/0146167219829182

Vedantam, S. (Host). (2017, June 5). The "Thumbprint of the Culture": Implicit Bias and Police Shootings. [Radio broadcast episode]. In M. Penman, J. Schmidt, R. Klahr, & R. Cohen (Producers), *Hidden brain.* National Public Radio. Retrieved from https://www.npr.org/2017/06/05/531578107/the-thumbprint-of-the-culture-implicit-bias-and-police-shootings

The Study of Microaggressive Behavior: Reflections on the Construct, Construct-Relevant Research, and Possible Future Research

Courtney Thomas and John J. Skowronski

A Tale We Shall Tell Thee: Introducing Microaggression

Imagine you connected online with someone named Chris. From your exchanges, you learn that Chris works in a management position at an IT company. You hit it off in your online conversations because Chris has likes and interests that resemble yours: Chris plays softball twice a week, watches sci-fi shows like Doctor Who, and loves to play fantasy football. You are both donors to the Republican Party and have both attended party conventions. You don't know what Chris looks like, or Chris's age or gender, because you both value privacy and have decided that you want to wait to meet each other before discovering this information.

Imagine that on your agreed meeting day, you are in a coffee shop, waiting for Chris to arrive. An athletic-looking older man wearing a suit walks in and orders a coffee. You think this must be him; a Republican manager in an IT firm would be a suit-wearing older man, right? The man sits alone at a table. As you head over to talk to him, a young, small, petite woman displaying a nose ring and several piercings walks up and asks if you're here for a meeting. Annoyed with the interruption of your action plan, with a sidelong glance and a brusque tone you inform the woman that you're here to meet Chris and you're in a hurry to go meet him. To your surprise (and perhaps to your chagrin, as well), this woman informs you that she is Chris!

Chris may have a negative reaction to both your nonverbal behavior (brusque tone, sidelong glance) and to the implied content (I am here to meet an important man) of your spoken message. If Chris experiences such reactions, then this scenario fits the definition of the term *microaggression* (for a comprehensive microaggression review, see Torino, Rivera, Capodilupo, Nadal, & Sue, 2018). As currently defined, a microaggression refers to a case in which (a) an actor manifests a subtle, sometimes nonconscious, and sometimes unintentional form of perceived discrimination toward a member of marginalized group (or to the group as a whole); (b) the discrimination may be perceived (by the recipient, and perhaps by an audience) to denigrate the minority group or its members via perceived negative messages conveyed by interpersonal communications or interpersonal behavior; and (c) the discrimination, or the perception of discrimination, then produces a negative reaction in the recipient (Sue, 2010).

One implication of this definition is that, as an observer in real-world contexts, one needs to be extremely cautious about definitively labeling a given scenario as an example of microaggression. To properly do so, one must have knowledge about all three of the definition's components. However, in many, if not most, real-world situations, it would be almost impossible for an observer to definitively know such things. For example, an observer might see an actor make a thoughtless comment that makes the person to whom that comment was directed angry, and thus conclude that the act was an example of a microaggression. However, if the act was not prompted by stereotyping or prejudice, the observer's inference would be wrong. Thus, one cannot gain precise knowledge about microaggressions from casual observation and inference. Instead, one must accumulate knowledge about microaggression via research that systematically explores the components that comprise such acts.

Our Purpose

Microaggression research has begun to pursue this task. However, this chapter is not intended to provide a comprehensive overview of the empirical literature on microaggression. There are many good and contemporary reviews available (e.g., Nadal, 2018; Torino et al., 2018). Instead, our purpose in this chapter is to provide informed commentary about, and clarification of, the microaggression construct and the existing research exploring that construct.

Why might conceptual clarification be in order? Our belief is that the construct of microaggression is often misunderstood. For example, some may not realize that while certain acts of microaggression might fit the generally accepted definition of aggressive behavior, other acts of microaggression may not do so: If both use the term "aggression," how can a "microaggression" *not* be an act of "aggression?" By clarifying the nature of microaggression, we hope to enlighten readers about such issues.

We also think that it is useful to clarify and update the scientific status of the microaggression construct. Scientists have not just perched on their couches and speculated about the existence of microaggressions: They have conducted research that explores the construct. How much can this research be trusted? The answer to this question might be especially important to a hypothetical human resources specialist at Humongous Corporation who thinks that the corporation should start training programs to combat microaggression. Does the state of the science justify such programs? Does the science inform how such programs should be constructed? We're not sure that the current science provides an affirmative answer to these questions. The reason is that, in our view, the research has been very good at documenting some elements of microaggression, but it has not done well at documenting other elements of microaggression. In this chapter, we will try to provide a bit of detail to justify this opinion.

However, that detail comes later. Our first task is to begin to describe the meaning of the term "microaggression." This task commences in the section that follows.

What Is a Microaggression?

The term "microaggression" was coined in 1970 by Chuck Pierce to highlight the social "gaslighting" that African Americans experienced in interactions with Whites (Pierce, 1970). Sue et al. (2007) later introduced a refined, expanded view. They defined microaggressions as "brief and commonplace daily verbal, behavioral, or environmental indignities, whether intentional or unintentional, that communicate hostile, derogatory, or negative racial slights and insults toward people of color" (p. 271). Those toward whom a microaggression has been directed are often described (e.g., Sue et al., 2007) as "targets"; those who engage in the acts are often described as "perpetrators" (but the term we prefer and use in this chapter is "actors"). Actor behaviors that can serve as microaggressions can range from verbal comments to enacted behaviors, and they can be exhibited on both personal (disregarding minority individuals) and cultural (recreating statues of only Whites) dimensions.

It should also be noted that microaggressive behaviors can be produced via at least two routes. Explicit microaggressions (see Brauer, Wasel, & Niedenthal, 2000) are exhibited with full perpetrator awareness (and perhaps even intent). In contrast, implicit microaggressions can be produced rapidly and unintentionally after encountering a triggering stimulus and may be accompanied by a lack of awareness about the behavior or its psychological source (e.g., Dasgupta, 2013). One implication of this hypothetical duality is that it is not only "bad people" (e.g., those who endorse stereotypes and prejudices) who can exhibit microaggressions: in theory, even people who do not endorse stereotypes and prejudices (but know of them), and who even may be vigilant against exhibiting discriminatory behavior, may be unintentionally prompted by their stereotypes and prejudices to exhibit microaggressions.

Additional insight into microaggressive acts comes from various taxonomies that have been created to precisely classify microaggressive behaviors. One widely used taxonomy includes the categories of microassaults, microinsults, and microinvalidations (see Sue et al., 2007, for a thorough review of these differentiations). Microassaults are described as intentional verbal or nonverbal racial belittlement. The intent of microassaults is to intentionally harm the target through the purposeful behaviors enacted. An example of a microassault would be to be influenced by patron color to intentionally serve a White person before a Person of Color in a restaurant. Microinsults are typically unconscious communications that are insulting and demeaning toward a person's racial identity. An example of a microinsult is when a White colleague, influenced by her stereotype, asks her colleague of color how she got her job, suggesting that the reason might be related to affirmative action. Finally, microinvalidations are actions that negate the thoughts, feelings, and experiences of targets, typically via subtle and nonconscious verbal or nonverbal communications. An example is when, influenced by stereotypes, a White American asks an Asian American where they were born, implying that they are foreigners in their own homeland.

Differentiating between Microaggression and Aggression

An understanding of the microaggression construct can be enhanced by considering the construct as it compares to related constructs, such as aggressive behavior. For example, when social psychologists describe aggressive behavior, they typically include only those behaviors that are enacted with the intent of harming another person who is motivated to avoid such harm (e.g., see Anderson & Bushman, 2002; Geen, 2001; Parrot & Giancola, 2007). Thus, microaggressive acts that are performed with explicit derogatory intent (e.g., President Donald Trump publicly calling Senator Elizabeth Warren "Pocahontas") can be considered to be examples of both aggression and microaggression. However, not all microaggressive acts are examples of aggression. To understand this distinction, one needs to know that, after a long debate, social psychologists reached a consensus: Behaviors that produce accidental harm or unintended harm are *not* typically judged to be instances of aggression. Thus, microaggressions that are enacted without intent to harm (e.g., someone thoughtlessly asking an Asian American to teach them words from their "native" language) are, by definition, not examples of aggression. Our opinion is that conceptual confusion may be present because of the semantic similarity between the terms "microaggression" and "aggression." To avoid confusion, we would prefer that another term, such as "subtle discrimination," be applied to the unintentional discrimination scenarios that are currently aggregated under the microaggression label.

However, given the history of the microaggression research area and the popular media usage rate of the term "microaggression" (the term now even has "official" status via its inclusion in English dictionaries), it is probably too late to induce researchers or research consumers to alter their use of this label. Thus, to avoid conceptual confusion, in our view, it is crucial that consumers of microaggression scholarship remain cognizant of the distinction between the meanings of the terms "aggression" and "microaggression." To reinforce this distinction, we repeat that, by definition, aggressive acts are always enacted with the intent of harming another. In contrast, microaggressive acts can, in theory, sometimes emerge without actor intent to harm. Indeed, of special interest to many microaggression researchers are the non-aggressive cases of microaggression in which a stereotype-knowledgeable perpetrator, either without intent to harm or even in the face of intent to avoid harm, engages in a stereotype-influenced action (e.g., insults) that makes the target uncomfortable and/or causes negative aftereffects in the target.

One other element that distinguishes between acts that are labeled as aggressive and acts that are labeled as microaggressive concerns the response of the target of the action. An aggressive act intends to harm another, regardless of whether it actually does so. For example, an actor can intentionally try to shoot and kill a target. That act is aggressive, even if the shot misses and the target is unaware that they were targeted. In contrast, given the way microaggression is currently defined, in our opinion, properly assigning the microaggression label to a stereotype-influenced act depends on a negative reaction from a target. For example, imagine that an actor says to an overweight dance partner, "Wow, I did not expect you to be so light on your feet." In our view, this scenario would only fit the current definition of microaggression if both the utterance was prompted by or linked to the actor's stereotype of, or prejudice against, overweight individuals and the overweight person took offense to the statement.

One implication of this line of thought is that, given the current definition of microaggression, it is theoretically possible for an actor to engage in behaviors that are stereotype-influenced or prejudice-influenced but that are not microaggressions (i.e., if they never produce a negative reaction in a recipient). Thus, if the overweight dance partner sees the "light on feet" comment as a compliment, the act is not a microaggression. However, how often might such total nonreactiveness be observed? Surely, there is at least one target out there who would view the comment through the lens of a stereotype or a prejudice and who would react negatively to the comment. Is only one negatively reacting person enough to define such acts as microaggressions? If not, one can ask, "Just how often must an act prompt a negative response in a recipient to be considered microaggressive?" To our knowledge, at this time, no one has established standards that can be used to make these determinations.

Given these considerations, in our view, the requirement that a negative reaction must occur for a scenario to be defined as a microaggression is overly restrictive. In our view, one key element is the emission of the stereotype-influenced or prejudice-influenced behavior. What is also important is that such behaviors have *some probability* of producing a negative reaction in a target, which is a step back from arguing that microaggressive events *must* include a negative target reaction. It is this probabilistic view of negative reaction production that we will have in mind when we use the term "microaggression" in the remainder of this chapter.

Microaggressions require a behavior that is prompted by actor stereotypes or prejudices. An understanding of the concept of microaggression is further complicated by the fact that a negative response to an act is not necessarily an infallible indicator of that act's origins in prejudices or stereotypes. That is, negativity in response to an act occur as the result of perceived prejudice or perceived stereotyping that did not actually prompt the act. This possibility is at the heart of some negative commentary that has appeared in the popular press regarding the microaggression concept (e.g., Ferguson, 2017) in which the study of microaggression is denigrated as "liberal hogwash" or "pseudoscience."

We similarly assert that the possibility that negative responses to an actor's behaviors may come from incorrect inferences about acts should not be discounted. For example, imagine that during a routine performance evaluation, a White supervisor says to a Person of Color, "I think that you are extremely articulate." Commenting on the person's communication skills may be a standard part of that company's job evaluation protocol, and the supervisor may have genuinely intended to convey praise. However, if the employee is unaware that such commentary is standard, the praise may be construed as derogatory by the message recipient because it is perceived to convey or link to the stereotypic expectation that People of Color are generally not articulate. From our point of view, this scenario would not reflect a microaggression because, despite the negative target reaction to the supervisor's statement, the supervisor's stereotypes or prejudices did not influence the supervisor commentary.

In our view, given the current conception of the microaggression concept, a scenario should only be labeled as an example of a microaggression only if one can show that the actor behavior is indeed linked to stereotypes or prejudices. In making this point, we do not intend to minimize the importance of negative interpretations of actor behavior by the behavior target, even when the actor behavior is not linked to stereotypes or prejudices. For example, in situations in which there is conflict among groups or in which prejudices and stereotypes are salient, it is easy to imagine how such misinterpretations can occur. Moreover, we believe (from considerable person perception research results in social psychology) that such misinterpretations frequently occur. For example, imagine that in our job evaluation scenario, there had been considerable racial strife at the company conducting the job evaluation. In the face of such strife, it might be especially likely that a minority group employee might misinterpret the standard communication fluency component of the evaluation to reflect stereotypes or prejudices. Moreover, there can clearly be severe consequences that can occur as a result of a target's misinterpretation of actor behavior as prejudice-motivated or as reflecting stereotypes. These can include employee job dissatisfaction, decreased job performance, high job turnover, and violent retaliatory behavior. These considerations suggest that these misinterpretations are clearly important topics of study. However, in our view, such misinterpretations do not fall under the umbrella of the term "microaggression," and their influence needs to be minimized in, or eliminated from, the study of the concept.

Indeed, in our view, inattention to the stereotype-based or prejudice-based sources of the actor's behavior is one major limitation of existing microaggression research. Why? Microaggression research (for reviews, see Lau & Williams, 2010; Nadal, 2013, 2018; Nadal, Whitman, Davis, Erazo, & Davidoff, 2016; Torino et al., 2018; Wong, Derthick, David, Saw, & Okazaki, 2014) has often relied on relatively general self-reports of perceived microaggression frequencies. One example comes from studies using the Racial Microaggressions Scale (Torres-Harding, Andrade, Jr., & Romero Diaz, 2012; for a similar scale, see Nadal, 2011). Items encountered on this scale include "I am treated like a second-class citizen because of my race" and "I am singled out by police or security people because of my race." Similar scales are typically employed when researchers attempt to explore the potential aftereffects of being a target of microaggressions. Results of such research typically assume that the more often one reports being a target of microaggression, the stronger the levels of negative feelings or symptoms (for a representative example, see Sohi & Singh, 2016; for a meta-analysis, see Lui & Quezada, 2019), including internalizing problems (e.g., depression), positive affectivity (e.g., self-esteem, well-being), and stress or negative affect. For example, in one study, rates of depressive symptoms and hospitalizations was higher for Native Americans who reported experiencing frequent microaggressions than for those who reported infrequent microaggression incidents (Walls, Gonzalez, Gladney, & Onello, 2015). In another example, Nadal, Wong, Griffin, Davidoff, and Sriken (2014) found that in a college student sample, the more microaggressions experienced, the lower the student self-esteem.

One concern is that this frequency self-report method may produce results that lump together microaggressive acts that were indeed influenced by stereotypes or prejudices with acts that were not. This would be the case if targets perceived microaggressions when none had been emitted (as when an actor's honest negative evaluation is perceived as motivated by prejudice). Hence, the self-report frequency method may lead researchers to overesti- mate the frequency with which microaggressive episodes occur. A second concern comes from the fact that the frequency judgments come from an observational methodology, not an experimental methodology. This observa- tional method does not pinpoint the direction of causality in a statistical relationship. This means that the direction of causality in observed microag- gression frequency-symptom relations may not flow from the perceptions of microaggressions to the symptoms, but may instead flow from the symptoms to the perceptions of microaggressions (e.g., those who are anxious may per- ceive a higher rate of microaggression). A third methodological criticism comes from scholars (e.g., Lui & Quezada, 2019) who suggest that research- ers have not done enough to tease out the effects of microaggressions on reported symptoms from the effects that other discrimination experiences may exert on those symptoms.

In our view, these criticisms are not to be taken lightly. However, it is also our view that it is unwise to fully discount all the results of the existing research because it has not yet done a good job of specifically linking actor stereotypes and prejudices to actor behaviors and, thence, to target responses and perceptions. Instead, our belief is that at least some of the existing target self report–based target frequency data will likely reflect actual instances of microaggression. One source of this belief lies in results provided by social psychology researchers that consistently reveal that people engage in dis- criminatory behaviors, and that sometimes they do so without realizing it. The studies describing such outcomes will be described later in this chapter. For now, we shall continue commenting on the construct of microaggression and the manner in which microaggression has been explored.

Microaggression: Additional Empirical and Conceptual Considerations

"Mushy" Microaggression? Concerns and Considerations. To many, our doubts about the extent to which the research documents microaggressions might be a surprise because the examples typically used to illustrate microaggressions

clearly imply that they are stereotype-driven or prejudice-driven (e.g., saying to a mixed-race person, "What are you, exactly?"). However, these examples may hide the fact that microaggressions are much more conceptually complex and elusive than such examples would suggest. Indeed, one of the major criticisms of microaggression is that in research, microaggression is often unreliably or improperly measured. Indeed, Lilienfeld (e.g., Lilienfeld, 2017a, 2017b) sees the lack of attention to the exact definition of microaggression and improper measurement of microaggression as significant deficiencies in the field. Some go even farther, claiming that the inability to exactly define, describe, or establish an a priori standard for microaggressions would seem to support the contention that many microaggressions are solely in the mind of the beholder, and as such, is "pseudoscientific nonsense" (e.g., Nagai, 2017).

While we agree that conceptual mushiness is a concern, our view is that such criticisms often ignore the fact that this "mushy" state of affairs is actually quite typical for many psychological concepts. Indeed, many psychological concepts are difficult to precisely define, but they can be understood largely via the specific examples that link to those concepts. Moreover, theories and data suggest that such fuzziness might be a "built in" feature of many constructs. Examples sometimes seem to be organized around concepts as fuzzy sets (for examples, see Dubois & Prade, 2016; Horowitz & Malle, 1993; Kochen, 1975; McCloskey & Glucksberg, 1978; Russell & Bullock, 1986). Mental representations of concepts that evince fuzzy set properties contain an idealized form (either a central tendency or an ideal type) and also contain examples that vary in their relation to this idealized form (see Kamp & Partee, 1995; Zadeh, 1965). For example, consider the concept of a bird. It is difficult to precisely and comprehensively define a bird. However, examples can be scaled in terms of their "birdiness." Robins tend to be seen as very "birdy," but penguins are not. Thus, the construct of "birdiness" can thus be understood by observing the judged "birdiness" of the various examples.

The psychological concept of a microaggression may exhibit similar characteristics. The concept may be difficult to precisely and comprehensively describe and define (e.g., in terms of necessary and/or sufficient features), but perceivers may nonetheless have a sense of those acts that are likely to be microaggressive and those that are not, and they ought to be able to report such perceptions. The advantage of using this type of approach is that it lets perceivers tell researchers about those acts that are microaggressive, rather than having researchers try to guess those acts (and their components) that may be microaggressive (for this kind of researcher-defined approach, see Sue, 2010). This is not to say that one should ignore the insights of the researchers as they explore the content of various behaviors—those insights may be a starting point for the selection of the behaviors to be explored. However, it makes sense to allow perceivers to be the final arbiters of those behaviors that are more or less likely to be perceived as microaggressions—after all, it is the targets of behaviors who are the ones affected by such behaviors, not the researchers.

Moreover, there is an additional advantage to such perceiver-driven scaling studies: The microaggression concept itself gains a measure of validity if perceivers are able to accomplish the judgment task, and if there are substantial variations among the behaviors in terms of their judged probability to act as microaggressors. For example, some race-based microaggression scales (see the RMAS developed by Torres-Harding et al., 2012) successfully assesses target *experiences* with microaggressions as they relate to constructs such as invisibility, criminality, cultural effects, sexualization, not belonging, and environmental invalidation. In a similar manner, Mekawi and Todd's (2018) Acceptability of Racial Microaggressions Scale (ARMS) successfully explores the *acceptability* of microaggressions in the multidimensional tool's evaluation of victim blaming, color evasion, power evasion, and exoticizing.

However, despite their success, one concern about such approaches is that they usually focus on post-hoc reports of experiences: Responses that occur after events have been encountered. Future research can benefit from an a priori approach. Part of this approach might involve attempts to scale via pretesting an act's microaggressive potential, then to observe actual responses to the act. For example, imagine that one wishes to conduct an experimental study that examines participant reactions to microaggressions. The context of the study might be a "practice" job interview conducted via Skype. The interviewer (a confederate of the research team) might be coached to insert different levels of microaggressive behaviors into the interview (for example, at levels of high, medium, low, and none). The levels would have been determined via pretesting. For example, it is reasonable to assume that pretest participants will view some acts as having a high potential to produce a negative reaction, others as moderately likely to produce a negative reaction, and others as only slightly likely to produce a negative reaction. The study could then look at the extent to which participants in the interview study had a negative response to an interview containing one of the acts. Given that one condition would be a control condition (no microaggressions), the study hypothesis would explore whether microaggressions did indeed prompt negative responses in the interview, and whether the magnitude of those responses was linked to the rated a priori likelihood (high, medium, low) of microaggressive behaviors producing a negative response. The conduct of such studies is eminently sensible and is aided immensely by predetermining perceived likelihood of a behavior as being perceived to act as a microaggressor by a set of potential behavior targets. Some studies have already explored microaggression using this approach (e.g., Hughey, Rees, Goss, Rosino, & Lesser, 2017; Tao, Owen, & Drinane, 2017).

Though such studies are desirable, we agree and acknowledge that measurement of microaggressive behaviors may present an unexpectedly high degree of difficulty. To understand why, we reiterate the manner in which we began this chapter. As currently defined, microaggressions evince three characteristics: (a) an actor manifests a subtle, sometimes nonconscious, and sometimes unintentional form of perceived discrimination toward a member of marginalized group (or to the group as a whole); (b) the discrimination is perceived (by the recipient, and perhaps by an audience) to denigrate the minority group or its members via perceived negative messages conveyed by interpersonal communications or interpersonal behavior; and (c) this perception then produces some form of negative reaction in the recipient. These characteristics imply to us that, given this definition (and note that we disagree with the negative response requirement), to properly label any given scenario as an example of microaggression, one needs to both assess whether an actor's behavior is linked to stereotypes or prejudices and to assess the reactions and interpretations of the target of the actor's behaviors. In the existing research, this is not often done. In our opinion, it needs to be done.

One other way that the area can respond to the "mushy concept" criticism is via methodological diversity. It is an axiom of research that all methods have potential flaws. These flaws can be potentially negated via the use of diverse research methodologies: The flaws in some methods studies serve to "cancel out" the flaws in other methods. Hence, even if the construct of issue in the research is a bit fuzzy, research that uses multiple methods, and that exhibits converging results, can compensate for this fuzziness.

Microaggression research is just beginning to exhibit this needed diversity. One major method is the cross-sectional survey design. In one study using this approach, Jones and Galliher (2015) evaluated the extent to which Native American identity related to microaggression experiences, specifically microinvalidations and microinsults. This study showed that Native Americans reported a strong connection to their Native culture and experienced mild microaggressions and found microinvalidations to be more upsetting than microinsults. Results from other methodologies provide evidence that converges with these findings. For example, using a qualitative approach, Ellis, Powell, Demetriou, Huerta-Bapat, and Panter (2019) coded the described microaggression experiences (e.g., microinsults, microassaults, microinvalidations) and microaffirmation experiences (e.g., microsupport, microvalidation, microcompliment) of first-generation college students. Among the themes were ideas that emerged related to academic merit assumptions, lack of preparation for college, and assumptions surrounding familial intelligence. This qualitative design provided highly detailed descriptions of experienced microaggressions and indicated that these types of behaviors influence the likelihood that targets feel connected to their college campuses.

However, because of the relative youth of the microaggression research area, our view is that there is not yet enough of this kind of diversity in the research methods exhibited by the area to be fully confident in the results reported. Hence, we encourage future microaggression researchers to "think outside the box" with regard to their studies of microaggression and to broaden the methodologies used to obtain an understanding of the construct.

Additional Criticisms of Microaggression Research. In this chapter, we have already touched on various ways in which the empirical case for microaggression can be strengthened. Such strengthening also needs to address a couple of additional concerns (see Lilienfeld, 2017a). One of these concerns involves lack of replication. Replication of existing results is an important task of science, and because the science of microaggression is relatively young, replications have not been attempted often enough (e.g., Williams, Oliver, Aumer, & Meyers, 2016). Recognizing this deficiency, there has been a call for more replication research in this area (e.g., Wong et al., 2014). We trust that this call will be heeded.

An additional concern pertains to the generality of the microaggression research findings. We believe that the scope of the descriptive findings is limited in that microaggression has not been sufficiently explored for many stigmatized groups, for many kinds of actors, and across cultures. Much of the research has been conducted in the context of western cultures and has focused on only some stereotypes and targets of prejudice (though research has explored microaggression in relation to People of Color (e.g., Sue et al., 2008), Asian Americans (e.g., Sue, Bucceri, Lin, Nadal, & Torino, 2009), Latinos (e.g., Nadal, Mazzula, Rivera, & Fujii-Doe, 2014), Muslim Americans (e.g., Nadal et al., 2012), LGBT individuals (e.g., Nadal et al., 2011), overweight individuals (e.g., Schafer, 2014), atheists (e.g., Cheng, Pagano, & Shariff, 2018), and women (e.g., Basford, Offermann, & Behrend, 2014). Furthermore, in our opinion, not enough research has explored the various potential consequences of experiencing microaggressions (for an example of research on aftereffects, see Sue, Capodilupo, & Holder, 2008). Finally, in our view, there is not enough research that documents the actual emission of stereotype-linked or prejudice-linked behaviors (as opposed to the perceived emission of such behaviors) and links those specific behaviors directly to the negative interpretations and reactions of a target.

A Brief Look at Social Psychological Research Potentially Relevant to Microaggression

As previously noted, one of the essential elements of science is convergence. This is the notion that one can gain increased confidence in a phenomenon by looking at it in various ways or from various perspectives. This principle of convergence can be used as a context in which to evaluate the microaggression concept. For example, one large thread in social psychological research is that the social world is a highly ambiguous place and that the behavior of others can often mean many things. Thus, people often use their existing knowledge to derive meaning from the behavior of others. This principle has been documented in many research areas, including research exploring perceiver trait judgments of actors and the perceiver causes of and explanations for actor behaviors (see Malle, 2011). Hence, from the view of social psychology, the assertion by microaggression critics that minority group targets may interpret innocuous actor behaviors in a negative light is highly plausible, and that should make one cautious about taking target reports of microaggression frequencies at face value.

However, the social psychology literature may surprise some in that it also lends support to the microaggression model. Social psychologists have extensively researched the notion that an actor's behaviors can be subtly influenced by their attitudes and beliefs, and the research has amply documented that such effects can occur. Moreover, the research has shown that an actor can, even sometimes unknowingly, evince stereotype-prompted or prejudice-prompted behaviors and perhaps will demonstrate them even when trying to avoid doing so. Because we see the emission of such behaviors as crucial to microaggression scenarios, and because this component is likely to provoke some controversy (because many people think that they never discriminate against others), we will provide a few examples of research showing that what actors believe and think and how they feel do indeed subtly influence how they act. These examples have been chosen because in our view it is especially plausible that they may apply to microaggression situations.

Learning from Research on Examining Subtle Cues

One such body of literature comes from the study of facial cues. It is well known that actors' faces vary in expression, and that these expressions provide cues to the actors' internal states (e.g., their emotions; see Miles & Johnston, 2007). While some of these cues are obvious, some are quite subtle. For example, it has been established that some elements of genuine facial expressions are relatively minor and difficult to control. For example, when people try to emit a fake smile, the pattern of cues in their face tends to be different than when they emit a real smile (see Ekman, Davidson, & Friesen, 1990). Perceivers can often detect these between-smile differences (e.g., Bernstein, Young, Brown, Sacco, & Claypool, 1998).

Another literature that fits with the idea that an actor's attitudes and beliefs can subtly influence their actions comes from the study of body language. Via gesture, posture, and movement, actors convey information to others (for an example, see Holler, Shovelton, & Beattie, 2009). Importantly, people often are unaware of their gestures, postures, and movements, so that they can convey information about their internal states without intending to do so (or even while trying to cover them up; Ekman & Friesen, 1969).

A set of studies showing that subtle behaviors can reflect an actor's internal cues explores nonverbal synchrony—the tendency of people, when interacting with others, to mimic the nonverbal behaviors emitted by an interaction partner. Actors have been shown to mimic, without awareness, a wide variety of cues exhibited by others, including postures, gestures, facial expressions, and speech patterns and accents (for a review, see Lakin & Chartrand, 2003). It is believed that such mimicry serves to "grease the skids" of interactions and works to produce liking among interaction partners. When interactions exhibit nonverbal synchrony, participants rate the interaction, and the interaction partner, especially positively.

So, what does any of this subtle behavior research have to do with microaggression derived from prejudices and stereotypes? Plenty. It provides important converging evidence for the first important element in microaggression: The assumption that people will emit (sometimes unintentionally) subtle cues that reveal their prejudices and stereotypes. However, better yet would be data showing that such behaviors can be specifically prompted by actor prejudices and stereotypes.

Learning from Research Examining Subtle Discrimination

Are there any empirical data suggesting that subtle discrimination specifically occurs in response to stereotypes and prejudices? The answer to this question is "yes"—and though scattered about, there is actually a large corpus of such data. For example, based on a review of pre-1980 studies exploring subtle White discrimination against Blacks, Crosby, Bromley, and Saxe (1980) offered three conclusions: (a) Whites tended to help Whites more often than they helped Blacks, especially when they did not have to face the person in need of help directly; (b) in competitive games or when administration of punishment was sanctioned and when consequences to the aggressor were low (aggressor anonymity, no possible retaliation, no censure from others); and (c) White nonverbal behavior displayed nonverbal hostility or discomfort as betrayed by cues such as tone of voice and enhanced seating distance.

Another example of the data describing subtle discrimination comes from the nonverbal mimicry research. Some researchers have sensibly investigated nonverbal mimicry in situation in which prejudice might exert a subtle influence on behavior. The results of such research suggest mimicry may be altered in mixed-race dyads and may be especially reduced in those who are highly prejudiced (Gutsell & Inzlicht, 2010; Yabar, Johnston, Miles, & Peace, 2006). Thus, simply because of alterations in patterns of nonverbal mimicry, people in mixed-race dyads may be less satisfied with the interaction and with their interaction partner, and this tendency may be exacerbated when one of the partners is highly prejudiced.

Learning from Measurement of Stereotypes and Prejudices in Social Psychology

The corpus of this kind of data has been considerably enhanced in recent years as psychologists have tried to measure prejudice and stereotypes without asking people directly. This has led to the development of a very large variety of tasks that allow actors' behaviors to reflect stereotypes and prejudices rather indirectly.

One set of such tasks has emerged in the form of various self-report scales. These include instruments such as the Modern Racism Scale (McConahay, 1986) and the Symbolic Racism Scale (Sears & Henry, 2005). The design of such scales (different versions of which target different groups) is such that they present self-report items that are influenced by actor stereotypes and/or prejudices, but do not directly ask respondents about those prejudices. Instead, responses to the items can be subtly influenced by stereotypes and prejudices, even if respondents believe that they are not prejudiced or that they do not endorse stereotypes.

However, some psychologists desire to obtain evidence about a person's stereotypes and prejudices without directly asking people to respond to self-report items. Many psychologists have pursued this desire by developing various laboratory techniques. These include the Affect Misattribution Procedure, the Sequential Priming Task, the Gun/Tool Priming Paradigm, the Implicit Association Test, and the Shooter Paradigm. While different in their design, these tasks are all bound together by the idea that people's responses to a stimulus can be subtly altered by their prejudices or stereotypes (for a recent exploration in the domain of prejudice, see Teige-Mocigemba, Becker, Sherman, Reichardt, & Christoph Klauer, 2017). Such techniques are often called *implicit measurement* techniques (or a review, see Gawronski & De Houwer, 2014). These measurement techniques are covered more in detail in Chapter two of this book.

We hasten to note that there is considerable controversy surrounding these kinds of tasks (see Gawronski & De Houwer, 2014). The interpretation of data that one obtains from such tasks is not always straightforward, and it is often a puzzle when results from these tasks do not always agree with each other (e.g., results from one task might indicate prejudice, and another might not). However, there are many studies that have used such tasks to explore stereotyping and prejudice, and the collective results from this large body of research are quite clear: An actor's prejudices and stereotypes can indeed subtly influence their behaviors, and moreover, they can do so without the actor's conscious knowledge of such influence.

Properly Viewing Microaggression in the Context of the Social Psychology Research

Some might wonder, given the support provided to the concept of microaggression by social psychology, what's the problem? Social psychology research says that actors, without their knowledge, can indeed emit subtle behaviors that reflect their stereotypes and prejudices without their knowledge (or even when trying to avoid doing so). Social psychology research says that people can interpret (or misinterpret) the meaning of the behavior of others. Social psychology research says that people can be sensitive to the subtle nonverbal cues emitted by others. These results all fit nicely with the propositions of microaggression theory. In the context of social psychology, microaggressions sure look plausible. So why do so many people (e.g., Lilienfeld, 2017a, 2017b; Nagai, 2017; Sue, 2017) seem to be so negative about it?

The reason is simple—plausibility is not fact. In our opinion, microaggression researchers have not yet conducted enough research to conclusively document either the various components of microaggression or the links among the components. Here, in our opinion, microaggression researchers would do well to adopt and mimic some of the approaches that social psychologists have used in the study of stereotyping, prejudice, and discrimination (our abbreviation will be SPD).

For example, some studies in the SPD area have focused on the actor who provides the behavior or communication component that is involved in microaggression. One element of such behavior is that it must be influenced by an actor's internalized knowledge (attitudes [prejudices] and beliefs [stereotypes]) about minority groups. However, social psychological research suggests that this internalized knowledge can come in various "flavors." For example, one actor might both know a stereotype about a minority group and believe it, while a second actor might know the stereotype but only because they have heard others using it—the actor may not personally believe the stereotype. One might suspect that only the actor who believes the stereotype might emit microaggressions, but some social psychological research suggests that this may not always be the case: Even the disbelieving actor might sometimes emit microaggressions (see Monteith, Parker, & Burns, 2015). This statement comes from social psychology's research indicating that peoples' behaviors can sometimes provide subtle cues about what they know or what they are thinking, even when they may be trying to hide their knowledge and thoughts.

Moreover, it is possible that these kinds of behavioral "leaks" can occur in response to knowledge that is possessed in the absence of conscious aware-ness of such knowledge. Psychologists call this kind of knowledge *implicit knowledge*. Social psychologists have extended this idea by suggesting that people can possess implicit stereotypes and implicit prejudices (see Devos, 2008; Greenwald & Banaji, 1995; Monteith, Voils, & Ashburn-Nardo, 2001). Indeed, a considerable amount of research has explored the distinction between implicit stereotypes/prejudices and explicit stereotypes/prejudices (as expressed earlier). One aspect of this research has looked at when implicit stereotypes/prejudices and explicit stereotypes/prejudices might differently predict behavior.

This body of research can be applied to the microaggression domain, for it leads to many interesting questions, such as: (a) "Are microaggressions more strongly related to implicit stereotypes/prejudices or explicit stereotypes/prejudices?"; (b) "Are some kinds of microaggressions more strongly pre-dicted by explicit knowledge and are some kinds of microaggressions more strongly predicted by implicit knowledge"; and (c) "How and when might the predictive links between implicit knowledge and microaggressions and explicit knowledge and microaggressions be affected by either the motivation to avoid discrimination or by the motivation to engage in discrimination?"

However, the actor is only one element in the microaggression scenario; the target of the action is the second important element. Indeed, as we have noted earlier, we believe that whether an action can be defined as a microag-gression or not depends on the response of the target. If an actor makes a stereotype-influenced untactful statement that unintentionally produces a negative reaction in a target, then the act fits the definition of a microaggres-sion. However, note that the untactful statement may not produce a negative reaction in all targets. For example, in the context of the hypothetical job review that we referred to earlier, person of Color A might view the statement about her articulateness as a slam against people of Color, while person of Color B might accept that statement as a personal compliment and not link the statement to stereotypes or to prejudice. Indeed, research suggests that there might be many individual differences that might explain such differen-tial reactions, including temporary state differences, differences in knowl-edge, and differences in personality (a recent example in the microaggression domain is Forrest-Bank & Cuellar, 2018).

The third element in the microaggression scenario is the context of the action (for examples of research exploring context effects, see Brauer, 2000; Tourangeau & Rasinski, 1988). Some acts might produce a negative reaction in targets only in some contexts. For example, imagine two different versions of the job evaluation scenario that we have used throughout this chapter. In one version, imagine that the evaluator who makes the statement praising the articulateness of the employee is White. In the second version, imagine that the same statement is made by an evaluator who is a Person of Color. One might guess that the statement might be perceived negatively in the first case, but not in the second. One reason may be related to an idea known as metacognition. This idea suggests that in interpersonal interactions people often make many assumptions about what is in the mind of the interaction partner. When the supervisor is White, the Person of Color employee may assume that the supervisor knows the stereotype that People of Color are not articulate and was thinking about that stereotype when reporting the evaluation. In contrast, when the evaluator is a fellow Person of Color, the employee may not have such thoughts, but may instead believe that the supervisor is making such a statement after the supervisor mentally reviews and summarizes the employee's objective performance.

These variables—actor, target, and context—have often been explored in the context of studies looking at how people act in situations and respond to situations, including situations that might be linked to stereotyping, prejudice, and discrimination. To our knowledge, very little of the existing research exploring microaggression has been explored in the context of this extensive body of knowledge. However, such research can, indeed should, be pursued.

Some Final Considerations

Conceptually, a microaggression is thought to occur when stereotypes or prejudices influence an actor to behave in a manner that induces a negative reaction in a target. However, it has been difficult for researchers to precisely define microaggressive acts, a state of affairs that has caused some to be skeptical about the concept. To be clear, we emphatically disagree with those who have used such criticisms to label the study of microaggression as a pseudoscience (e.g., Nagai, 2017). Such labeling fails to recognize that the problems that exist are not necessarily fatal problems with the science that has been done. Instead, the bigger concern is that the conclusions that people want to draw from the existing science may not be justified by the existing data. This is a solvable problem, and we look forward to seeing how microaggression research develops to solve this problem. We hope that the suggestions that we have offered in this chapter will be helpful to the pursuit of such research.

In this regard, we must point out that science generally proceeds much more slowly than people realize. In our view, this certainly applies to the study of microaggression.

Our opinion is that the empirical microaggression literature has made a good start, but it is also still in a preliminary phase: There is still much to be learned about microaggressions. That is, in our view we do not have as much empirical knowledge about microaggressions as we need to make a good scientific case for how, when, why, and for whom microaggressions work.

We fervently hope that this is one of the points that readers will "take away" and remember after reading this chapter.

What do we mean by "a good start"? Our reading of the empirical studies suggests that existing microaggression research strongly and reliably suggests that targets perceive that they often are the target of microaggressive acts. Our reading also suggests that there is reasonably good data linking the extent to which targets perceive themselves to be a target of microaggressive behaviors to many negative target outcomes (e.g., distress). These data ought not to be ignored.

However, in our view, there is much that microaggression researchers yet need to accomplish. In our view, it is crucial that future microaggression research can establish that negative effects occur in a target when microaggressions are actually emitted by an actor, as opposed to circumstances in which a target infers that actions are stereotype-influenced or prejudice-influenced, when in actuality such influence is not present. Related to this view is our opinion that microaggression researchers need to focus on situations in which they can document the influence of stereotypes and prejudices on subtle actions, and in which those specific actions can be linked to specific interpretations and/or negative outcomes in targets. Moreover, the validity of the microaggression concept can be enhanced by empirically documenting how microaggressions can vary by actor (e.g., more microaggressions emitted by prejudiced actors), target (e.g., those targets on whom a minority identity is central may be especially likely to have a negative reaction to a microaggression), and context (e.g., microaggressions might be both more likely to be emitted, and more likely to have negative effects, in a threatening intergroup context).

It is also important to note that optimism about the ultimate productivity of these attempts can be gleaned from a large corpus of social psychology research suggesting that the implications of research on microaggressions are quite plausible. Actors' behaviors are subtly influenced by their attitudes, beliefs, and emotions. These include the emotions and beliefs that are a part of, and are associated with, prejudices and stereotypes. However, it is important to also remember that plausibility is not fact. Despite the support offered by social psychological research, in our view, there is little empirical data from microaggression researchers that directly supports some of the major assertions that are contained in the microaggression concept.

We think that these kinds of cautions are especially important for those who want to improve the world. They may be especially interested in microaggression because they want to minimize or eliminate it. Indeed, some businesses and institutions already have training programs designed to minimize the emission of microaggressions. Such programs may include lists of statements that illustrate microaggressions, and attempt to induce employees to avoid such statements (see Barbash, 2015; Fisher, 2015; Gunn, 2016).

In our view, implementation of such programs is premature, and may even be a very risky proposition (see Haidt & Jussim, 2016). Not only is microaggression a relatively new area of knowledge, there is an even greater level of ignorance (e.g., not many clinical trials) about how to effectively ameliorate the problem (e.g., by reducing the emission of offensive behaviors or by minimizing negative reactions to such behaviors). This high level of ignorance suggests that the implementation of training programs designed to attack the microaggression problem (see Kang & Garran, 2018; Thurber & DiAngelo, 2018) may be of dubious effectiveness, or may even be counterproductive. Indeed, pulling from literature on diversity training programs aimed at reducing prejudice as a whole, it has been suggested that attempts to do so may actually backfire rather than lead to a reduction in behavior (Legault, Gutsell, & Inzlicht, 2011).

Thus, while we heartily applaud the intent underlying the effort to ameliorate microaggression, in our view, we simply do not know enough about microaggressions to know how to effectively combat their emergence and/or their impact. In our opinion, much more research is needed before effective microaggression-amelioration programs can be developed and implemented.

References

Anderson, C., & Bushman, B. (2002). Human aggression. *Annual Review of Psychology, 53*, 27–51. doi:10.1146/annurev.psych.53.100901.135231

Barbash, F. (2015, October 28). The war on "microaggressions": Has it created a "victimhood culture" on campuses? *Washington Post*. Retrieved from https://www.washingtonpost.com/news/morning-mix/wp/2015/10/28/the-war-over-words-literally-on-some-american-campuses-where-asking-where-are-you-from-is-a-microaggression/

Basford, T. E., Offermann, L. R., & Behrend, T. S. (2014). Please accept my sincerest apologies: Examining follower reactions to leader apology. *Journal of Business Ethics, 119*(1), 99–117. doi:10.1007/s10551-012-1613-y

Bernstein, M. J., Young, S. G., Brown, C. M., Sacco, D. F., & Claypool, H. M. (1998). Adaptive responses to social exclusion social rejection improves detection of real and fake smiles. *Psychological Science, 19*, 981–983. doi:10.1111/j.1467-9280.2008.02187.x

Brauer, M. (2000). Intergroup perception in the social context: The effects of social status and group membership on perceived out-group homogeneity and ethnocentrism. *Journal of Experimental Social Psychology, 37*, 15–31. doi:10.1006/jesp.2000.1432

Brauer, M., Wasel, W., & Niedenthal, P. (2000). Implicit and explicit components of prejudice. *Review of General Psychology, 4*, 79–101. doi:10.1037//1089-2680.4.1.79

Cheng, Z. H., Pagano, L. A., Jr., & Shariff, A. F. (2018). The development and validation of the Microaggressions Against Non-religious Individuals

Scale (MANRIS). *Psychology of Religion and Spirituality, 10*, 254. doi:10.1037/rel0000203

Crosby, F., Bromley, S., & Saxe, L. (1980). Recent unobtrusive studies of Black and White discrimination and prejudice: A literature review. *Psychological Bulletin, 87*, 546–563. doi:10.1037/0033-2909.87.3.546

Dasgupta, N. (2013). Implicit attitudes and beliefs adapt to situations: A decade of research on the malleability of implicit prejudice, stereotypes, and the self-concept. *Advances in Experimental Social Psychology, 47*, 233–279. doi:10.1016/B978-0-12-407236-7.00005-X

Devos, T. (2008). Implicit attitudes 101: Theoretical and empirical Insights. In W. D. Crano & R. Prislin (Eds.), *Attitudes and Attitude Change* (pp. 61–84). New York: Psychology Press.

Dubois, D., & Prade, H. (2016). Bridging gaps between several forms of granular computing. *Granular Computing, 1*(2), 115–126. doi:10.1007/s41066-015-0008-8

Ekman, P., Davidson, R. J., & Friesen, W. V. (1990). The Duchenne smile: Emotional expression and brain physiology II. *Journal of Personality and Social Psychology, 58*, 342–353. doi:10.1037/0022-3514.58.2.342

Ekman, P., & Friesen, W. V. (1969). Nonverbal leakage and clues to deception. *Journal for the Study of Interpersonal Processes, 32*, 88–106. doi:10.1080/00332747.1969.11023575

Ellis, J. M., Powell, C. S., Demetriou, C. P., Huerta-Bapat, C., & Panter, A. T. (2019). Examining first-generation college student lived experiences with microaggressions and microaffirmations at a predominately White public research university. *Cultural Diversity and Ethnic Minority Psychology, 25*(2), 266–279. doi:10.1037/cdp0000198

Ferguson, A. (2017, February 24). Microaggression and macrononsense. *The Weekly Standard*. Retrieved from https://www.weeklystandard.com/andrew-ferguson/microaggression-and-macrononsense

Fisher, A. (2015, November 15). How microaggressions can wreck your business. *Fortune*. Retrieved from http://fortune.com/2015/11/19/microaggressions-talent-business/

Forrest-Bank, S. S., & Cuellar, M. J. (2018). The mediating effects of ethnic identity on the relationships between racial microaggression and psychological well-being. *Social Work Research, 42*, 44–56. doi:10.1093/swr/svx023

Gawronski, B., & De Houwer, J. (2014). Implicit measures in social and personality psychology. In H. T. Reis & C. M. Judd (Eds.), *Handbook of research methods in social and personality psychology* (2nd ed., pp. 283–310). New York: Cambridge University Press.

Geen, R. G. (2001). *Human aggression* (2nd ed.). Philadelphia, PA: Open University Press.

Greenwald, A. G., & Banaji, M. R. (1995). Implicit social cognition: Attitudes, self-esteem, and stereotypes. *Psychological Review, 102*, 4–27. doi:10.1037/0033-295x.102.1.4

Gunn, S. (2016, June 14). University of Wisconsin students to undergo mandatory "cultural competency training." *EAGnews*. Retrieved from http://eagnews.org/university-of-wisconsin-students-to-undergo-mandatory-cultural-competency-training/

Gutsell, J. N., & Inzlicht, M. (2010). Empathy constrained: Prejudice predicts reduced mental simulation of actions during observation of outgroups. *Journal of Experimental Social Psychology, 46*, 841–845. doi:10.1016/j.jesp.2010.03.011

Haidt, J., & Jussim, L. (2016, May 6). Hard truths about race on campus. *Wall Street Journal*. Retrieved from http://www.wsj.com/articles/hard-truths-about-race-on-campus-1462544543GoogleScholar

Holler, J., Shovelton, H., & Beattie, G. (2009). Do iconic hand gestures really contribute to the communication of semantic information in a face-to-face context? *Journal of Nonverbal Behavior, 33*, 73–88. doi:10.1007/s10919-008-0063-9

Horowitz, L. M., & Malle, B. F. (1993). Fuzzy concepts in psychotherapy research. *Psychotherapy Research, 3*, 131–148. doi:10.1080/10503309312331333739

Hughey, M. W., Rees, J., Goss, D. R., Rosino, M. L., & Lesser, E. (2017). Making everyday microaggressions: An experimental vignette study on the presence and power of racial microaggressions. *Sociological Inquiry, 87*, 303–336. doi:10.1111/soin.12167

Jones, M. L., & Galliher, R. V. (2015). Daily racial microaggressions and ethnic identification among Native American young adults. *Cultural Diversity and Ethnic Minority Psychology, 21*, 1–9. doi:10.1037/a0037537

Kamp, H., & Partee, B. (1995). Prototype theory and compositionality. *Cognition, 57*(2), 129–191.

Kang, H., & Garran, A. M. (2018). Microaggressions in social work classrooms: Strategies for pedagogical intervention. *Journal of Ethnic & Cultural Diversity in Social Work: Innovation in Theory, Research & Practice, 27*, 4–16. doi:10.1080/15313204.2017.1413608

Kochen, M. (1975). Applications of fuzzy sets in psychology. In L. A. Zadeh, K. S. Fu, K. Tanaka, & M. Shimura (Eds.), *Fuzzy sets and their applications to cognitive and decision processes* (pp. 395–408). New York: Academic Press.

Lakin, J. L., & Chartrand, T. L. (2003). Using nonconscious behavioral mimicry to create affiliation and rapport. *Psychological Science, 14*, 334–339. doi:10.1111/14679280.14481

Lau, M. Y., & Williams, C. D. (2010). Microaggressions research: Methodological review and recommendations. In D. W. Sue (Ed.), *Microaggressions and marginality: Manifestation, dynamics and impact* (pp. 313–336). New York: John Wiley & Sons.

Legault, L., Gutsell, J. N., & Inzlicht, M. (2011). Ironic effects of antiprejudice messages: How motivational interventions can reduce (but also increase) prejudice. *Psychological Science, 22*(12), 1472–1477. doi:10.1177/0956797611427918

Lilienfeld, S. O. (2017a). Microaggressions: Strong claims, inadequate evidence. *Perspectives on Psychological Science, 12,* 138–169. doi:10.1177/174569 1616659391

Lilienfeld, S. O. (2017b). Through a glass, darkly: Microaggressions and psychological science. *Perspectives on Psychological Science, 12,* 178–180. doi:10.1177/1745691616669098

Lui, P. P., & Quezada, L. (2019). Associations between microaggression and adjustment outcomes: A meta-analytic and narrative review. *Psychological Bulletin, 145*(1), 45–78. doi:10.1037/bul0000172

Malle, B. F. (2011). Attribution theories: How people make sense of behavior. In D. Chadee (Ed.), *Theories in social psychology* (pp. 72–95). Malden, MA: Wiley-Blackwell.

McCloskey, M. E., & Glucksberg, S. (1978). Natural categories: Well defined or fuzzy sets? *Memory & Cognition, 6,* 462–472. doi:10.3758/BF03197480

McConahay, J. B. (1986). Modern racism, ambivalence, and the Modern Racism Scale. In J. F. Dovido & S. L. Gaertner (Eds.), *Prejudice, discrimination and racism* (pp. 91–126). Orlando, FL: Academic Press.

Mekawi, Y., & Todd, N. R. (2018). Okay to say?: Initial validation of the acceptability of racial microaggressions scale. *Cultural Diversity and Ethnic Minority Psychology, 24,* 346–362. doi:10.1037/cdp0000201

Miles, L., & Johnston, L. (2007). Detecting happiness: Perceiver sensitivity to enjoyment and non-enjoyment smiles. *Journal of Nonverbal Behavior, 31,* 259–275. doi:10.1007/s10919-007-0036-4

Monteith, M. J., Parker, L. R., & Burns, M. D. (2015). The self-regulation of prejudice. In T. D. Nelson (Ed.), *Handbook of stereotyping, prejudice, and discrimination* (2nd ed., pp. 409–432). New York: Psychology Press.

Monteith, M. J., Voils., C. I., & Ashburn-Nardo, L. (2001). Taking a look underground: Detecting, interpreting and reacting to implicit racial biases. *Social Cognition, 19,* 395–417. doi:10.1521/soco.19.4.395.20759

Nadal, K. L. (2011). The Racial and Ethnic Microaggressions Scale (REMS): Construction, reliability, and validity. *Journal of Counseling Psychology, 58,* 470–480. doi:10.1037/a0025193

Nadal, K. L. (2013). *That's so gay! Microaggressions and the lesbian, gay, bisexual, and transgender community.* Washington, D.C.: American Psychological Association.

Nadal, K. L. (2018). *Microaggressions and traumatic stress: Theory, research, and clinical treatment.* Washington, D.C.: American Psychological Association.

Nadal, K. L., Griffin, K. E., Hamit, S., Leon, J., Tobio, M., & Rivera, D. P. (2012). Subtle and overt forms of Islamophobia: Microaggressions toward Muslim Americans. *Journal of Muslim Mental Health, 6*(2), 15–37. doi:10.3998 /jmmh.10381607.0006.203

Nadal, K. L., Mazzula, S. L., Rivera, D. P., & Fujii-Doe, W. (2014). Microaggressions and Latina/o Americans: An analysis of nativity, gender, and ethnicity. *Journal of Latina/o Psychology, 2*(2), 67. doi:10.1037 /lat0000013

Nadal, K. L., Whitman, C. N., Davis, L. S., Erazo, T., & Davidoff, K. C. (2016). Microaggressions toward lesbian, gay, bisexual, transgender, queer, and genderqueer people: A review of the literature. *Journal of Sex Research, 53,* 488–508. doi:10.1080/00224499.2016.1142495

Nadal, K. L., Wong, Y., Griffin, K. E., Davidoff, K., & Sriken, J. (2014). The adverse impact of racial microaggressions on college students' self-esteem. *Journal of college student development, 55*(5), 461–474. doi:10.1353/csd.2014.0051

Nadal, K. L., Wong, Y., Issa, M. A., Meterko, V., Leon, J., & Wideman, M. (2011). Sexual orientation microaggressions: Processes and coping mechanisms for lesbian, gay, and bisexual individuals. *Journal of LGBT Issues in Counseling, 5*(1), 21–46. doi:10.1080/15538605.2011.554606

Nagai, A. (2017, March 29). The pseudo-science of microaggressions. *National Association of Scholars.* Retrieved from https://www.nas.org/articles/the_pseudo_science_of_microaggressions

Parrot, D. J., & Giancola, P. R. (2007). Addressing "the criterion problem" in the assessment of aggressive behavior: Development of a new taxonomic system. *Aggression and Violent Behavior, 12,* 280–299. doi:10.1016/j.avb.2006.08.002

Pierce, C. M. (1970). Black psychiatry one year after Miami. *Journal of the National Medical Association, 62,* 471–473. Retrieved from https://www.ncbi.nlm.nih.gov/pmc/articles/PMC2611929/

Russell, J. A., & Bullock, M. (1986). Fuzzy concepts and the perception of emotion in facial expressions. *Social-Cognition, 4,* 309–341. doi:10.1521/soco.1986.4.3.309

Schafer, K. J. (2014). *Weight-based microaggressions experienced by obese women in psychotherapy* (Unpublished Doctoral dissertation). University of Nevada, Las Vegas, NV.

Sears, D. O., & Henry, P. J. (2005). Over thirty years later: A contemporary look at symbolic racism and its critics. *Advances in Experimental Social Psychology, 37,* 95–150. doi:10.1016/S0065-2601(05)37002-X

Sohi, K. K., & Singh, P. (2016). Experiencing microaggression: Invisibility, distress, and self stereotyping among northeasterners in India. *Frontiers in Psychology, 7,* 1–7. doi:10.3389/fpsyg.2016.01995

Sue, D. W. (2010). *Microaggressions in everyday life: Race, gender, and sexual orientation.* Hoboken, NJ: John Wiley & Sons, Inc.

Sue, D. W. (2017). Microaggressions and "Evidence": Empirical or experiential reality? *Perspectives on Psychological Science, 12,* 170–172. doi:10.1177/1745691616664437

Sue, D. W., Bucceri, J., Lin, A. I., Nadal, K. L., & Torino, G. C. (2009). Racial microaggressions and the Asian American experience. *Asian American Journal of Psychology, S*(1), 88–101. doi:10.1037/1948-1985.S.1.88

Sue, D. W., Capodilupo, C. M., & Holder A. M. (2008). Racial microaggressions in the life experience of black Americans. *Professional Psychology: Research and Practice, 39,* 329–336. doi:10.1037/0735-7028.39.3.329

Sue, D. W., Capodilupo, C. M., Torino, G. C., Bucceri, J. M., Holder, A. M. B., Nadal, K. L., & Esquilin, M. (2007). Racial microaggressions in everyday life: Implications for clinical practice. *American Psychologist, 62*, 271–286. doi:10.1037/0003-066X.62.4.271

Sue, D. W., Nadal, K. L., Capodilupo, C. M., Lin, A. I., Torino, G. C., & Rivera, D. P. (2008). Racial microaggressions against Black Americans: Implications for counseling. *Journal of Counseling & Development, 86*(3), 330–338. doi:10.1002/j.1556-6678.2008.tb00517.x

Tao, K. W., Owen, J., & Drinane. J. M. (2017). Was that racist? An experimental study of microaggression ambiguity and emotional reactions for racial-ethnic minority and white individuals. *Race and Social Problems, 9*, 262–271. doi:10.1007/s12552-017-9210-4

Teige-Mocigemba, S., Becker, M., Sherman, J. W., Reichardt, R., & Christoph Klauer, K. (2017). The affect misattribution procedure: In search of prejudice effects. *Experimental Psychology, 64*, 215–230. doi:10.1027/1618-3169/a000364

Thurber, A., & DiAngelo, R. (2018). Microaggressions: Intervening in three acts. *Journal of Ethnic & Cultural Diversity in Social Work: Innovation in Theory, Research & Practice, 27*, 17–27. doi:10.1080/15313204.2017.1417941

Torino, G. C., Rivera, D. P., Capodilupo, C. M., Nadal, K. L., & Sue, D. W. (Eds.). (2018). *Microaggression theory: Influence and implications.* Hoboken, NJ: John Wiley & Sons, Inc.

Torres-Harding, S. R., Andrade, A. L., Jr., & Romero Diaz, C. E. (2012). The Racial Microaggressions Scale (RMAS): A new scale to measure experiences of racial microaggressions in people of color. *Cultural Diversity and Ethnic Minority Psychology, 18*, 153–164. doi:10.1037/a0027658

Tourangeau, R., & Rasinski, K. A. (1988). Cognitive processes underlying context effects in attitude measurement. *Psychological Bulletin, 103*, 299–314. doi:10.1037/00332909.103.3.299

Walls, M. L., Gonzalez, J., Gladney, T., & Onello, E. (2015). Unconscious biases: Racial microaggressions in American Indian health care. *The Journal of the American Board of Family Medicine, 28*(2), 231–239. doi:10.3122/jabfm.2015.02.140194

Williams, A., Oliver, C., Aumer, K., & Meyers, C. (2016). Racial microaggressions and perceptions of Internet memes. *Computers in Human Behavior, 63*, 424–432. doi:10.1016/j.chb.2016.05.067

Wong, G., Derthick, A. O., David, E. J. R., Saw, A., & Okazaki, S. (2014). The what, the why, and the how: A review of racial microaggressions research in psychology. *Race and Social Problems, 6*, 181–200. doi:10.1007/s12552-013-9107-9

Yabar, Y., Johnston, L., Miles, L., & Peace, V. (2006). Implicit behavioral mimicry: Investigating the impact of group membership. *Journal of Nonverbal Behavior, 30*, 97–113. doi:10.1007/s10919-006-0010-6

Zadeh, L. A. (1965). Fuzzy sets. *Information and control, 8*(3), 338–353. doi:10.1016/S0019-9958(65)90241-X

Performance Stereotypes in Action: Stereotype Threat Consequences, Mechanisms, and Potential Interventions

Jade S. Jenkins

For the past few decades, institutions and organizations have increasingly pursued contributions from members of diverse social groups (Roberson & Kulik, 2007). During this time, increased participation in fields where group members have been historically underrepresented has also been observed. Indeed, educational trends for adults twenty-five years old and older reveal that the gender gap in the attainment of bachelor's degrees is no longer statistically significant and that the rates of bachelor's degree attainment for racial minority groups have all increased over the past few decades (Ryan & Bauman, 2016). Furthermore, women's participation in science and engineering professions increased 6 percent between 1993 and 2010, while participation from members of racial minority groups in these professions increased 14 percent during this same period (National Science Foundation, 2014).

However, despite the progress that has been made in these areas (and others), research indicates that stereotypes in evaluative performance contexts continue to serve as barriers to achieving equitable representation of social groups in valued domains (Schmader & Hall, 2014). These effects are robust and extend beyond laboratory experiments to predict many "real world" outcomes (Spencer, Logel, & Davies, 2016). Therefore, eradicating social group discrepancies across all levels of society will be difficult without addressing the adverse effects of pervasive performance stereotypes. To do so, one must understand: (1) the content and power of positive and negative performance stereotypes; (2) the nature of stereotype threat; (3) the consequences and mechanisms of stereotype threat; and (4) possible interventions that may prevent and reduce the costs of stereotype threat.

The Content and Power of Positive and Negative Performance Stereotypes

Members of social groups are often viewed through the lens of multiple performance stereotypes. Performance contexts help determine which performance stereotypes are relevant to perceivers' judgments and which ones are not. In some contexts, performance stereotypes associated with members of a specific social group can be positive—making that group *stereotypically favored* in those contexts because those group members would be expected to perform well. However, sometimes performance stereotypes associated with members of a social group can be negative—causing that same group to be viewed as *stereotypically disadvantaged* in other performance contexts because those group members would not be expected to perform well. Thus, social groups are often ascribed both positive and negative traits simultaneously, with performance expectations that correspond with the stereotypes.

For example, stereotypes of Black individuals suggest that they are physically strong, rhythmic, and athletic (Schneider, 2004; Stone, Lynch, Sjomeling, & Darley, 1999). As a result, they may be expected to perform well in performance situations in which success requires these attributes. However, Black individuals may also be expected to have poor general intellect, to have poor health, and to be unambitious (Jones et al., 2013; Schneider, 2004; Steele & Aronson, 1995). Thus, they would be stereotypically disadvantaged in situations where success rests upon their ability to exercise attributes that they are stereotypically perceived to lack. Stereotypes of members of other social groups often suggest a similar interplay of positive and negative performance expectations. Indeed, stereotypes of women suggest that they have high verbal ability and are gifted in the arts and humanities (Schneider, 2004; Shih, Pittinsky, & Ambady, 1999). However, stereotypes also suggest that women may have poor quantitative and spatial abilities, are physically weak, are not strong negotiators, and are bad drivers (Fogliati & Bussey, 2013; Kray, Thompson, & Galinski, 2001; Schneider, 2004; Shih et al., 1999). Relative to stereotypes of younger adults, stereotypes of older adults suggest that they are wise, dependable, and trustworthy. At the same time, they are also stereotyped to have poor memory abilities, to be less skilled with technology, and to be less motivated (and able) to learn (Barber & Mather, 2013; Postuma & Campion, 2008). Asian Americans may be perceived as intelligent—especially in regard to STEM-related capabilities—but may also be expected to be physically short, to have poor verbal skills, and to not have leadership potential (Mukkamala & Suyemoto, 2018; Schneider, 2004; Shih et al., 1999). Stereotypes of gay men suggest that they are rhythmic, have high emotional intelligence and verbal skills, and have stylish aesthetic tastes (Morrison & Bearden, 2007). However, gay men may also be presumed to have poor sexual health (Custer, Murcia, Robinson, McFarland, & Raymond, 2018; Schneider, 2004; Tilcsik, 2011). Hispanic Americans (particularly those perceived to be of Mexican origin) may be seen as hardworking, but they may also be seen as uneducated with high potential for criminality (Romero, Gonzalez, & Smith, 2015; Schneider, 2004). People who have mental illnesses may be stereotypically perceived as creative, but they may also be perceived as having poor social skills and as being less committed to their health (Corrigan & Blink, 2016; Schneider, 2004). Many more social groups are associated with positive and negative performance stereotypes, and the performance stereotypes mentioned here do not reflect a comprehensive list for the previously mentioned social groups.

Importantly, performance stereotypes have wielded a powerful influence over a host of outcomes in settings ranging from education (Mukkamala & Suyemoto, 2018; Romero et al., 2015; Schneider, 2004) and health care (Custer et al., 2018; Quinn, Williams, & Weisz, 2015) to the workplace (e.g., Bertrand & Mullainathan, 2004; Carli, Alawa, Lee, Zhao, & Kim, 2016; Mukkamala & Suyemoto, 2018; Postuma & Campion, 2008; Tilcsik, 2011). Regarding evaluative performance contexts in particular, consider the example that women are stereotypically perceived to have strong verbal skills but are not perceived to have strong negotiation skills (relative to men). Research suggests that in relevant performance contexts, women would be more likely to achieve positive performance outcomes when reminded of the positive ingroup performance stereotype ("women have strong verbal skills"; Shih et al., 1999) or the negative outgroup performance stereotype ("men do not have strong verbal skills"; Walton & Cohen, 2003). However, although research suggests that women might sometimes achieve favorable performance outcomes when reminded of the negative ingroup performance stereotype ("women are not gifted negotiators"; Kray et al., 2001), research has overwhelmingly focused on how negative ingroup performance stereotypes lead to poor performance outcomes due to stereotype threat (Steele & Aronson, 1995).

The Nature of Stereotype Threat

Stereotype threat occurs when people enter an evaluative performance context, encounter a negative performance stereotype that is relevant to one of their social group memberships within that performance context, and become concerned that performing poorly will be taken as evidence by others that the performance stereotype is true. Furthermore, they may fear that perceived confirmation of the stereotype may result in negative judgments from others, interpersonal mistreatment, and other potential consequences. Personal endorsement of the stereotype is not a necessary precursor to stereotype threat; one need only believe that others are aware of the stereotype and may even endorse it themselves (Schmader, Johns, & Barquissau, 2004; Steele & Aronson, 1995).

Although stereotype threat may share characteristics with other sources of performance-related discomfort, it is distinct from these other sources in important ways (Schmader, Hall, & Croft, 2015). For example, stereotype threat has sometimes been compared to test anxiety or to having a fear of being evaluated critically by others. However, stereotype threat tends to emerge in stereotype-relevant performance contexts, whereas mere test anxiety and fear of critical social evaluations may occur across many performance contexts regardless of whether performance stereotypes are relevant to any given context (Zeidner & Matthews, 2005). Stereotype threat has also been compared to belongingness threat—the feeling that one does not belong within a performance domain (see Walton & Cohen, 2007). Although chronic stereotype threat could lead someone to conclude that they do not belong in a stereotype-relevant setting, that same person could question whether they belong for reasons that have nothing to do with performance stereotypes (such as workload, pay, and other factors). Finally, stereotype threat has also been compared to the phenomenon of choking under pressure, in which the pressure to perform well leads to performance outcomes that are worse than expected (DeCaro, Thomas, Albert, & Beilock, 2011). Although stereotype threat and choking under pressure often lead to similar performance outcomes, causes other than stereotype reminders are often responsible for eliciting choking effects (e.g., manipulating performance pressure; see Gray, 2004).

Given that people may struggle to anticipate which situations might put them at risk for stereotype threat (Steele, Spencer, & Aronson, 2002), research has extensively tried to identify situational moderators of stereotype threat effects. This research has shown that being asked to complete a task that is difficult, diagnostic of one's ability, and relevant to a negative ingroup performance stereotype may trigger stereotype threat (Roberson & Kulik, 2007; Steele & Aronson, 1995). Furthermore, the performance context must also be capable of reinforcing negative ingroup performance stereotypes—and this effect can be achieved in several ways. For example, perceiving that one of our ingroups is underrepresented within a performance domain (e.g., a White man realizing that he is the only White player on a men's athletic team) may create a favorable condition for stereotype threat (Purdie-Vaughns, Steele, Davies, Ditlmann, & Crosby, 2008; Roberson & Kulik, 2007). Having unpleasant interactions with members of a stereotypically favored group or suspecting that they may endorse negative performance stereotypes about your ingroup may also increase one's chances of experiencing stereotype threat (Spencer et al., 2016). Furthermore, stereotype threat may also occur when one believes that other people will witness or find out about their potentially poor performance outcome (Shapiro & Neuberg, 2007).

Characteristics of situations may also determine the type(s) of stereotype threat that negatively stereotyped group members may experience in relevant performance domains. According to the multithreat framework (Shapiro & Neuberg, 2007), stereotype threats may be distinguished from each other depending on (1) the target of the threat, including whether the threat impacts (a) one's self-perceptions; or (b) how they view their social group; and (2) the source of the threat, including whether the threat originates from (a) within the self; (b) from outgroup members; or (c) from ingroup members. Thus, threatened people at any given time may be experiencing one (or more) of six possible types of stereotype threat.

Consider the example of an employee named Dan, an older adult who is aware of the stereotype that older adults struggle with memory. When Dan experiences stereotype threat, it could be characterized by (1) *self-concept threat* (fear that poor performance would indicate that Dan, as an older adult, may indeed struggle with memory); (2) *group concept threat* (fear that poor performance would mean that older adults really do struggle with memory); (3) *outgroup threat to own reputation* (fear that poor performance could cause young employees to perceive that Dan is the type of older adult who struggles with memory); (4) *outgroup threat to group reputation* (fear that poor performance would cause Dan's young coworkers to infer that all older adults struggle with memory); (5) *ingroup threat to own reputation* (fear that other older adults will take Dan's memory failures as evidence that the negative stereotype applies to Dan); and (6) *ingroup threat to group reputation* (fear that Dan's memory failures could cause other older adults to conclude that the stereotype is true for ingroup members).

It is important to note that these different types of stereotype threat may manifest in response to different situational triggers (Shapiro & Neuberg, 2017). Consider the previously mentioned situational trigger of having other people know about one's poor performance. If Dan believes at the time that he is expected to demonstrate his memory skills that his results won't ever be shared with at least one other person, then self-concept threat and group-concept threat will be the only forms of stereotype threat that could possibly emerge. If no one else learns about the performance outcome, then one cannot feel threatened by other people's negative judgments and possible mistreatment resulting from poor performance. However, if Dan's performance is public or he believes that details will be shared with at least one other person at some point later in time, any type of stereotype threat could possibly emerge.

To complicate matters even further, personal characteristics—including one's knowledge base, level of skill, beliefs, feelings, traits, and other personal characteristics—may help determine how severely one experiences any type of threat. For example, stereotype threat may have limited effects on a person who doesn't realize that he or she belongs to the negatively stereotyped group or who doesn't strongly identify with a known group membership (Schmader et al., 2015). A Hispanic American woman with undiagnosed dyslexia, for instance, might be aware of the fact that she is Hispanic American but be unaware of her dyslexia. Given this, she would be susceptible to stereotype threat in response to performance stereotypes about Hispanic Americans. However, because she is unaware of her dyslexia diagnosis, reminders of negative dyslexia performance stereotypes may not elicit stereotype threat (Shapiro & Neuberg, 2007). Exposure to negative performance stereotypes also matter. Someone who has infrequently encountered negative performance stereotypes about their group may feel less threatened than someone who has frequently encountered them. Indeed, this reasoning may help explain why first-generation Black immigrants to the United States demonstrate less evidence of experiencing stereotype threat relative to second-generation Black immigrants (Deaux et al., 2007). Stereotype threat may also be especially likely to occur when someone highly values and identifies with the performance domain (Schmader et al., 2015), suspects that the stereotype might be true or that others may believe that it is true (Shapiro & Neuberg, 2007), or often feels that they will be stereotyped by others (i.e., stigma consciousness; Brown & Pinel, 2003).

Consequences and Mechanisms of Stereotype Threat

Unfortunately, research has revealed that stereotype threat is associated with a host of short-term and long-term consequences. These consequences extend to the following domains: (1) learning outcomes; (2) performance on stereotype-relevant tasks; (3) career planning and work outcomes; (4) health and well-being outcomes; and (5) the self and self-improvement.

Learning

Research has shown that preschool-aged children exhibit awareness of social group stereotypes (Schneider, 2004) and that children's and teenagers' formative educational years can be negatively impacted by stereotype threat (Ambady, Shih, Kim, & Pittinsky, 2001). If individuals do not successfully obtain a baseline set of knowledge or learned skills, it will be difficult for them to keep up with others who are moving on to develop more complex knowledge and skills. To prevent group members from falling behind in domains in which they are negatively stereotyped, we must understand how stereotype threat may negatively affect learning.

Research suggests that stereotype threat may impair learning because the target of a negative performance stereotype may adopt maladaptive learning strategies. For example, Rydell, Shiffrin, Boucher, Van Loo, and Rydell (2010) asked women to complete a series of visual search training tasks. These tasks could be completed in an easy manner (characterized by a search method that demanded relatively little attention) or in a relatively difficult manner (characterized by an effortful search method that demanded attention). Attention attraction was used as a metric for learning. Relative to nonthreatened women who demonstrated more attention attraction (learning) over time, women under stereotype threat failed to demonstrate attention attraction. The group of threatened women may have underperformed because they chose the effortful, attention-demanding search strategy—perhaps because they expended extra effort in an attempt to prove that negative performance stereotypes about women are incorrect.

Stereotype threat may also impair the process of storing and retrieving information. Rydell, Rydell, and Boucher (2010) demonstrated that women experiencing stereotype threat demonstrated deficits in information encoding (the storage of new information into memory) but not in information retrieval (recalling information that had been stored in memory). These findings may represent failures of motivation (i.e., disengaging from the performance domain), working memory issues (i.e., reduced mental resources as a result of monitoring the environment for stereotype information), or both (Rydell & Boucher, 2017). Of course, in research focused on members of other social groups, poor recall can occur in response to stereotype threat (e.g., in older adults threatened by the stereotype of poor memory performance; Barber & Mather, 2013). Differences in consequences and processes across social groups is consistent with the notion that different groups may experience stereotype threat in different ways (Shapiro & Neuberg, 2007).

Performance

In the first published stereotype threat paper, Steele and Aronson (1995) demonstrated that threatened Black test-takers underperformed on diagnostic tests of intellectual ability (relative to White test-takers and nonthreatened Black test-takers). Additional research has shown that stereotype threat impairs achievement for members of other social groups in a variety of other performance domains as well, such as athletic performance (i.e., Stone et al., 1999), managerial decision-making (i.e., Bergeron, Block, & Echtenkamp, 2006), negotiation performance (i.e., Kray et al., 2001), and leadership (i.e., Ho, Shih, & Walters, 2012), among many other domains.

Of course, people belong to multiple social groups, and task demands can often be interpreted from more than one perspective. Empirical consideration of these notions has revealed that performance on stereotype-relevant tasks can be malleable. For example, stereotypes of women maintain that they will perform poorly on math tasks, whereas stereotypes of Asian Americans maintain that they will excel on math tasks. Shih et al. (1999) demonstrated that Asian American women who had been reminded of their gender underperformed on quantitative tasks relative to a control group (who did not receive reminders of any group membership). However, Asian American women outperformed the control group when they had been reminded of their racial identity. Thus, performance can change as a result of manipulating the stereotypical relevance of tasks. In a similar vein, reframing the nature of performance tasks can also matter. Indeed, men may underperform (relative to women) when asked to complete a task framed as an "arts and crafts" project or as a test of "perspective-taking," but they may outperform women if the same task is described as a "building task" or as a test of "spatial ability" (Ho et al., 2012; Wraga, Helt, Jacobs, & Sullivan, 2007).

What psychological mechanisms can help explain why stereotype threat impairs performance? Stereotype threat is theorized to tax working memory capacity, which reduces the amount of mental resources that are available to help someone successfully perform a difficult task (Beilock & Carr, 2005). Stereotype threat may also elicit performance motivation that causes someone to override a dominant response expected to have a higher likelihood of success on a difficult task (Spencer et al., 2016). Additionally, stereotype threat can have negative effects by motivating the selection of performance tactics that will allow someone to preserve their positive self-views, at the expense of performance (Schmader, Johns, & Forbes, 2008). Stereotype threat also causes stress, as indicated by physiological measures (i.e., Townsend, Major, Gangi, & Mendes, 2011) and can trigger negative thoughts and emotions, which the performer must then try to suppress (Schmader & Hall, 2014). Finally, stereotype threat can cause someone to become preoccupied with monitoring their performance and perusing the environment for potentially threatening cues (i.e., see Schmader et al., 2015).

Career Planning and Work

Despite incremental progress in recruiting members of underrepresented groups to lucrative, prestigious, and/or in-demand industries, discrepancies across social groups remain. These discrepancies are often consistent with performance stereotypes. In 2010, the science and engineering workforce consisted of 28 percent women and ranged from 5 percent to 19 percent across Asian American workers, Hispanic American workers, and Black workers (National Science Foundation, 2014). Members of these social groups also remain significantly underrepresented in workplace leadership positions (Hekman, Johnson, Foo, & Yang, 2017), report similar discrepancies in compensation (National Science Foundation, 2014), and are more hesitant than their male and/or White counterparts to pursue entrepreneurial projects (Casad & Bryant, 2016). Of course, consistent with stereotypes, men remain underrepresented in other high-demand fields (such as nursing; Hodges et al., 2017) and White individuals may be underrepresented as athletes in revenue-generating sports (though they are well represented in sport leadership positions; Cunningham & Singer, 2010).

One way that stereotype threat may contribute to these social group discrepancies is by shaping career interests. For example, chronic experiences with stereotype undermine racial minority science students' identification with the science domain, along with their intentions to pursue STEM careers (Woodcock, Hernandez, Estrada, & Schultz, 2012). Furthermore, women may develop a distaste for careers with highly competitive cultures because those environments are likely to trigger stereotype threat (Casad & Bryant, 2016). Threatened group members who work in fields where their group is underrepresented may be less likely to recommend those fields to other ingroup members (von Hippel, Sekaquaptewa, & McFarlane, 2015). These patterns undermine organizational efforts to spark underrepresented group members' interest in various industries and to recruit them to their organization.

Members of negatively stereotyped groups who do overcome obstacles to healthy career interest development may nonetheless struggle to overcome additional challenges in the workplace. Many of the same stereotype threat mechanisms that impact performance undermine employees' ability to thrive in the workplace as well, causing applicants under stereotype threat to underperform on selection tests used to make hiring decisions (Kirnan, Alfieri, Bragger, & Harris, 2009) and in interviews (i.e., Latu, Mast, & Stewart, 2015). In organizations, stereotype threat may lead employees to demonstrate high absenteeism (Walton, Murphy, & Ryan, 2015), report low work engagement and motivation (Roberson & Kulik, 2007), and experience impaired well-being (von Hippel et al., 2015). Threatened employees from negatively stereotyped groups may also be seen as poor performers who aren't competitive for promotions, which could inform stereotypically disadvantaged group members' greater turnover intentions relative to members of stereotypically favored groups (Hom, Roberson, & Ellis, 2008; Walton et al., 2015).

Stereotype threat may also weaken organizational return on investment in some programs designed to foster a culture of inclusivity and respect. For example, stereotype threat may cause female employees to perceive that participating in family-friendly programs at work would be associated with negative career consequences (von Hippel, Kalokerinos, & Zacher, 2017). When training opportunities and management styles are explicitly designed to assist specific groups that are vulnerable to stereotype threat (i.e., when age-awareness Human Resource Management (HRM) practices are used to help older workers), they may have the unintended effect of worsening stereotype threat rather than buffering it (Oliveira & Cabral-Cardoso, 2018). Furthermore, the discomfort and concern that these programs elicit may generalize beyond the specific social groups that they were designed to help (Cundiff, Ryuk, & Cech, 2018).

Health and Well-Being

Assessments of health and well-being include both examinations of temporary fluctuations in health and observations of long-term health patterns and outcomes. Unfortunately, research has revealed that health disparities exist across many social groups in society and that stereotype threat may contribute to these disparities (e.g., Fingerhut & Abdou, 2017). Rather than eliciting a broad effect, research suggests that stereotype threat undermines health and well-being in multiple specific ways.

First, stereotype threat directly affects the body—such as by triggering physiological stress responses. For example, research has shown that Black research participants who were induced to experience stereotype threat demonstrated an increase in blood pressure (Blascovich, Spencer, Quinn, & Steele, 2001). Given that Black individuals may frequently encounter situations in which stereotype threat is present, these findings could help explain the relatively high incidence of hypertension among Black individuals in the United States. Stereotype threat is associated with other physiological indicators of stress as well, including increased sympathetic nervous system activity (Murphy, Steele, & Gross, 2007) and heightened levels of cortisol (Townsend et al., 2011). Furthermore, stereotype threat triggers inflammation, an essential component of many disease development processes (John-Henderson, Rheinschmidt, Mendoza-Denton, & Francis, 2014). Much more research is needed to clarify the relationship between stereotype threat, physiological reactions to threat, and health outcomes. Nonetheless, available evidence suggests that chronic stereotype threat could make it more difficult to prevent stress-related illnesses and disease.

Stereotype threat may also strain the relationship between patients who are members of negatively stereotyped groups and providers who may (erroneously or accurately) be perceived as harboring bias toward members of those groups (Aronson, Burgess, Phelan, & Juarez, 2013). For example, patients who experience stereotype threat may choose to avoid providers whom they suspect of bias and delay scheduling preventative tests and exams (Jones et al., 2013). Threatened patients may also be less likely to disclose accurate medical information (out of fear of judgment) and tend to report that interactions with providers were shorter and less patient-focused than desired (i.e., Aronson et al., 2013; Street, Makoul, Arora, & Epstein, 2009). These findings are problematic, given that research has shown that the quality of interactions between providers and their patients is paramount and sometimes may even be a more important predictor of patient outcomes than the provider's medical training or expertise (Street et al., 2009).

Finally, stereotype threat may make it more difficult for patients to adhere to treatment plans. Patients who experience stereotype threat may struggle with their treatment plans because they may discount treatment information, struggle to understand the details of their treatment plans, or struggle to recall vital information (Aronson et al., 2013). Stereotype threat could make it more difficult for patients to engage in health-conscious behaviors that are consistent with their treatment plans. For example, managing chronic stereotype threat could tax the mental resources patients need to willfully avoid unhealthy behaviors (i.e., overeating; see Inzlicht & Kang, 2010). Furthermore, patients may avoid engaging in health-conscious behaviors as a means of coping with stereotype threat (e.g., by avoiding the gym when one is overweight) or may turn to unhealthy behaviors as a means of trying to eliminate the stigma (e.g., by turning to disordered eating in order to lose weight; see Hunger, Major, Blodorn, & Miller, 2015).

Self-Perceptions and Self-Improvement

Stereotype threat produces internal conflict by pitting negative stereotypes about one's group against one's desire to (usually) see themselves positively (Schmader et al., 2008). In response to this conflict, people may become motivated to engage in psychological and/or behavioral strategies aimed at reducing or eliminating the discrepancy. One strategy may be to alter one's self-perceptions and stereotype-relevant behaviors. Indeed, research has shown that women who strongly identify with mathematics may respond to stereotype threat by distancing themselves from feminine characteristics that are strongly associated with stereotypes of women (Pronin, Steele, & Ross, 2004). Furthermore, women may adopt a masculine communication style when reminders of leadership ability stereotypes trigger stereotype threat (von Hippel, Wiryakusuma, Bowden, & Shochet, 2011). By shifting to less feminine self-views and behaviors, the applicability of the negative stereotype is reduced (which, in turn, may help buffer the self against stereotype threat).

Ironically, people may also choose to respond to situations capable of eliciting stereotype threat by endorsing a negative ingroup stereotype. For example, embracing a negative stereotype after failing on a stereotypical task helps preserve how people feel about themselves as individuals—especially if they have high self-esteem (Burkley & Blanton, 2008). In other words: To cope with stereotype threat, an otherwise confident Asian American person could reference the stereotype that Asian Americans have poor verbal skills to explain their recent poor performance on a verbal task. People with high self-esteem may also deploy a self-handicapping strategy, in which they embrace a negative stereotype prior to performance on a stereotypical task if failure seems likely (Kim, Lee, & Hong, 2012). These results suggest that high self-esteem individuals may be invoking negative stereotypes strategically. Doing so may allow people to shift the blame from the self to the group—and by excusing themselves for poor performance in this way, people may preserve how they see themselves as individuals (Burkley & Blanton, 2009). As one might expect, the benefits of preserving one's self-views may be offset by negative perceiver evaluations when such excuses lead others to suspect that poor performance will continue in the future (Jenkins & Skowronski, 2016).

Stereotype threat may also impact whether (and how) people choose to pursue important feedback. For example, stereotype threat may undermine one's ability to accurately assess one's own learning because threatened individuals may avoid sources of potentially helpful learning feedback or may discount positive feedback (see Rydell & Boucher, 2017). Threatened employees may also discount positive feedback and are more likely to engage in indirect feedback-seeking strategies (i.e., observing and thinking about how one is performing in relation to others) instead of direct feedback-seeking strategies (i.e., asking one's supervisor for feedback; Roberson, Deitch, Brief, & Block, 2003). Furthermore, stereotype threat may simply decrease one's desire to improve (Fogliati & Bussey, 2013).

Possible Interventions for Stereotype Threat

Many interventions could be successful in combating stereotype threat. Tailoring interventions to the specific type(s) of stereotype threat that may be elicited in various situations is paramount for success (Shapiro, Williams, & Hambarchyan, 2013). Ideally, potential targets of stereotype threat could use this information to predict which situations may elicit stereotype threat and to better understand their personal experiences with stereotype threat. Furthermore, institutions and organizations could use this information to better manage environments and people so that many types of stereotype threat are less likely to occur. Research is continuing to emerge and shed a light on which threats could occur in which situations (see Shapiro et al., 2013, for a starting point). Nonetheless, stereotype threat research has produced many data-informed ideas of what a stereotype threat intervention toolbox could consist of. The following discussion focuses on potential interventions that (1) potential targets of stereotype threat could choose to pursue to protect themselves against stereotype threat; and (2) institutions, organizations, and other entities could pursue to address the costs of stereotype threat.

Targets

Research suggests that when people are trained to shift their perspective in situations capable of eliciting stereotype threat, negative outcomes can be minimized or prevented. For example, negatively stereotyped individuals could be encouraged to prioritize learning and personal development goals (growth mindset) rather than performance goals (Rydell & Boucher, 2017). Stereotype threat may also be reduced when people reflect upon their core beliefs and values, which helps protect their sense of self-integrity from threat (Cohen, Garcia, Apfel, & Master, 2006; but see Voisin, Brick, Vallee, & Pascual, 2019, for words of caution). By preserving self-integrity, members of negatively stereotyped groups may respond less defensively to the threat and choose effective strategies to help them successfully navigate the threat (Rydell & Boucher, 2017). Interventions focused on fostering a sense of social belongingness can also be helpful (Spencer et al., 2016; Walton & Cohen, 2007). Indeed, by training members of negatively stereotyped groups to view challenges as a common feature of new experiences, they may be less likely to view challenges as indicators that they don't belong in the threatening context (Walton et al., 2015). Potential targets of stereotype threat can also be trained to view their stereotypical traits as assets that are essential for success rather than as liabilities that hinder success (Wang, Whitson, Anicich, Kray, & Galinsky, 2017).

Coping resources and training can also be beneficial. Although stereotype threat research has often focused on threats to singular group identities, people tend to belong to multiple groups. Therefore, teaching people to embrace a context-relevant identity that reflects positive characteristics of the stigmatized group or personal characteristics of the individual may help (Schmader et al., 2015). Furthermore, people may successfully combat stereotype threat by practicing situational disengagement. By temporarily disengaging one's self-worth from a task, one may respond to the threat with less defensiveness (Spencer et al., 2016). Although adopters of this strategy should try their best to avoid succumbing to long-term disengagement, research suggests that temporary disengagement may help people persist longer in domains where they are negatively stereotyped (Morgan & Mehta, 2004). People can also be trained to perceive anxiety and stress as a source of motivation rather than as a sign that one may not perform well (Schmader & Hall, 2014). By wielding preperformance stress in a productive way, members of negatively stereotyped groups may be able to prevent or buffer the adverse effects of stereotype threat. Finally, people could be trained to monitor their stereotype threat coping responses so that spillover effects of the threat into non-threatening domains can be buffered or even prevented (Inzlicht & Kang, 2010). By increasing awareness of the scope of stereotype threat's consequences, it may be possible to limit the negative impact of stereotype threat.

It has been suggested that targets of negative stereotypes could also simply avoid threatening situations by carefully conducting research on where to go to school, where to accept a job offer, and where to receive medical treatment. To this end, organizational webpages, websites like LinkedIn and Glassdoor, review websites, and one's own extended network can all be great resources of information. Although these steps may be helpful, people may struggle to identify situations where stereotype threat could become a risk (Steele et al., 2002). Furthermore, even with careful planning, situational triggers of stereotype threat cannot always be avoided and may tend to remain outside of negatively stereotyped group members' control. For example, a prospective female college student pursuing a STEM-related career may carefully research and choose an academic program that promotes a culture of inclusion. However, other cues she encounters in that environment could still trigger stereotype threat. Should group members desire opportunities to learn how to protect themselves from the negative effects of stereotype threat, they will find that many possible options are available to them. However, the burden of combating stereotype threat should not be placed solely on the shoulders of people who belong to negatively stereotyped groups.

Institutions and Organizations

Stereotype threat-eliciting cues must be identified and minimized across various contexts. Given the importance of perceived underrepresentation to the activation of negative ingroup performance stereotypes (Purdie-Vaughns et al., 2008), one approach might be to focus on increasing recruitment of members from negatively stereotyped groups to "critical mass" (see Roberson & Kulik, 2007). There are many ways to improve representation through recruitment, ranging from favoring predictive selection indicators that are less susceptible to stereotype threat to discouraging organizational referral programs that may be reinforcing current organizational demographics (Walton et al., 2015). Affirmative action plans (AAPs) may also increase participation from underrepresented group members to critical mass over time. However, these policies remain poorly understood and may be met with resistance and hostility in the short term (Schmader et al., 2015). Using nonpreferential AAPs, clearly communicating (and publicizing) their use, and making the business case for them by linking them to context and business strategy may all help improve the practice and acceptance of AAPs (Kravitz, 2008).

Until critical mass is achieved, institutions and organizations can still take steps to reduce the salience of negative ingroup performance stereotypes. For example, stereotype threat may be prevented if demographic questions are moved to the end of standardized exams and tests used for personnel selection purposes (Walton et al., 2015). The salience of role models from negatively stereotyped groups can also be boosted to help improve perceptions of belongingness (Aronson et al., 2013). Finally, institutions and organizations can promote identity-safe environments by not adopting a "colorblind" philosophy (Schmader & Hall, 2014). A colorblind approach may foster distrust among members of negatively stereotyped groups, especially when representation of those groups has not yet reached critical mass (Purdie-Vaughns et al., 2008). Instead, institutions and organizations may consider all-inclusive multiculturalism (AIM; Plaut, Garnett, Buffardi, & Sanchez-Burks, 2011). Relative to other philosophies (i.e., colorblind vs. multicultural), all-inclusive multiculturalism may be received particularly well. This is because stereotypically favored groups do not feel that inclusion efforts targeting stereotypically disadvantaged groups are overlooking, devaluing, or excluding their contributions (see Walton et al., 2015, for a review).

The ways people are socialized into new environments can also have implications for stereotype threat. Educators, health practitioners, and employers can be encouraged to describe tasks in terms of the characteristics that are shared by members of all groups (Roberson & Kulik, 2007). For example, negotiation success can be framed as requiring characteristics that both men and women have in common rather than prescribing gendered characteristics (i.e., being "rational and assertive" rather than "emotional and passive") as necessary for success (Kray et al., 2001). In doing this, the stereotype relevance of tasks may be reduced, which should help reduce the risk of stereotype threat. Organizations should also favor training programs that are broad and all-inclusive. Although usually implemented with good intentions, programs tailored to address members of a negatively stereotyped group on tasks relevant to the negative stereotype may (1) trigger backlash; (2) cause group members to perceive that the institution or organization is endorsing the stereotype; and (3) increase stereotype threat rather than reduce it (Cundiff et al., 2018; Oliveira & Cabral-Cardoso, 2018). In conjunction with inclusive training, educators, health practitioners, and employers should also acknowledge and talk openly about the harmful effects of stereotype threat. Doing so may help students, patients, and employees persist in spite of stereotype threat because these conversations may help them realize that their struggles may be due to stereotype threat rather than due the validity of negative stereotypes (Roberson & Kulik, 2007).

Cultural changes can also help prevent stereotype threat. For example, educational and professional environments that promote a "sink-or-swim" culture of identifying performance "stars" while weeding out everyone else may heighten stereotype threat (Walton et al., 2015). While these cultures tend to be broad in their focus rather than group-specific, they could trigger stereotype threat by increasing the salience and importance of performance goals and fixed mindsets of ability (Rydell & Boucher, 2017). Members of negatively stereotyped groups may not thrive within this type of culture, given that they may already feel that they have to protect perceptions of their ability (Walton et al., 2015). Institutions and organizations should also expand the ways in which they train educators, health providers, and managers. Just as it is important for them to take responsibility for their own beliefs and attitudes toward members of negatively stereotyped groups, so, too, is it important for them to take responsibility for enforcing a positive cultural environment (Roberson & Kulik, 2007).

Institutions and organizations can also improve the ways in which they develop and foster positive personal growth in members from negatively stereotyped groups. For example, educators, health practitioners, and employers may avoid giving critical feedback to members of negatively stereotyped groups because they don't want to demotivate members of those groups and may also fear being accused of bias. However, by utilizing *wise feedback*—in which the feedback giver conveys both their high standards for performance and their belief in the feedback recipient's ability to meet that standard—consequences such as these may be avoided (Cohen, Steele, & Ross, 1999; Walton et al., 2015). During such feedback sessions, managers may also consider setting performance goals, providing stretch assignments, and providing strategies that members from negatively stereotyped groups may utilize to combat stereotype threat (Roberson & Kulik, 2007). And finally, because evaluative feedback situations themselves may induce stereotype threat (Rydell & Boucher, 2017), the effectiveness of feedback can be enhanced by providing feedback recipients with clearly written information, instructions, and explanations from the feedback session (Aronson et al., 2013).

Conclusion

Reminders of negative ingroup performance stereotypes can exert detrimental short-term and long-term effects on learning, task performance, workplace outcomes, health, and self-views (Aronson et al., 2013; Fogliati & Bussey, 2013; Pronin et al., 2004; Rydell & Boucher, 2017; Steele & Aronson, 1995; Walton et al., 2015). These effects contribute to social group discrepancies observed throughout society. Given the reach and complexity of the psychological mechanisms that predict stereotype threat-related outcomes, successful interventions will rest upon having multiple parties (members of negatively stereotyped groups, institutions, and organizations) tackle the problem in partnership. Although negatively stereotyped groups should not shoulder the burden of addressing stereotype threat on their own, providing them with institutional and organizational resources can help raise awareness of stereotype threat processes. These resources could help members of various social groups cope with stereotype threat and persist longer in domains where stereotype threat may occur. However, successful management of educational, professional, and healthcare settings is also critical.

References

Ambady, N., Shih, M., Kim, A., & Pittinsky, T. L. (2001). Stereotype susceptibility in children: Effects of identity activation on quantitative performance. *Psychological Science, 12*, 385–390.

Aronson, J., Burgess, D., Phelan, S. M., & Juarez, L. (2013). Unhealthy interactions: The role of stereotype threat in health disparities. *American Journal of Public Health, 103*, 50–56.

Barber, S. J., & Mather, M. (2013). Stereotype threat can both enhance and impair older adults' memory. *Psychological Science, 24*, 2522–2529.

Beilock, S. L., & Carr, T. H. (2005). When high-powered people fail: Working memory and "choking under pressure" in math. *Psychological Science, 16*, 101–105.

Bergeron, D. M., Block, C. J., & Echtenkamp, A. (2006). Disabling the able: Stereotype threat and women's work performance. *Human Performance, 19*, 133–158.

Blascovich, J., Spencer, S. J., Quinn, D., & Steele, C. (2001). African Americans and high blood pressure: The role of stereotype threat. *Psychological Science, 12*, 225–229.

Brown, R. P., & Pinel, E. C. (2003). Stigma on my mind: Individual differences in the experience of stereotype threat. *Journal of Experimental Social Psychology, 39*, 626–633.

Burkley, M., & Blanton, H. (2008). Endorsing a negative in-group stereotype as a self-protective strategy: Sacrificing the group to save the self. *Journal of Experimental Social Psychology, 44*, 37–49.

Burkley, M., & Blanton, H. (2009). The positive (and negative) consequences of endorsing negative self-stereotypes. *Self and Identity, 8*, 286–299.

Carli, L. L., Alawa, L., Lee, Y., Zhao, B., & Kim, E. (2016). Stereotypes about gender and science: Women ≠ scientists. *Psychology of Women Quarterly, 40*, 244–260.

Casad, B. J., & Bryant, W. J. (2016). Addressing stereotype threat is critical to diversity and inclusion in organizational psychology. *Frontiers in Psychology, 7*, 8.

Cohen, G. L., Garcia, J., Apfel, N., & Master, A. (2006). Reducing the racial achievement gap: A social-psychological intervention. *Science, 313*, 1307–1310.

Cohen, G. L., Steele, C. M., & Ross, L. D. (1999). The mentor's dilemma: Providing critical feedback across the racial divide. *Personality and Social Psychology Bulletin, 25*, 1302–1318.

Corrigan, P. W., & Blink, A. B. (2016). The stigma of mental illness. *Encyclopedia of Mental Health, 4*, 230–234.

Cundiff, J. L., Ryuk, S., & Cech, K. (2018). Identity safe or threatening? Perceptions of women-targeted professional programs. *Group Processes and Intergroup Relations, 21*(5), 745–766.

Cunningham, G. B., & Singer, J. N. (2010). "You'll face discrimination wherever you go": Athletes intentions to enter the coaching profession. *Journal of Applied Social Psychology, 40*, 1708–1727.

Custer, B., Murcia, K., Robinson, W. T., McFarland, W., & Raymond, H. F. (2018). Blood donation history and eligibility assessment in a community-based sample of men who have sex with men. *Transfusion, 58*, 969–973.

Deaux, K., Bikmen, N., Gilkes, A., Ventuneac, A., Joseph, Y., Payne, Y. A., & Steele, C. M. (2007). Becoming American: Stereotype threat effects in Afro-Caribbean immigrant groups. *Social Psychology Quarterly, 70*, 384–404.

DeCaro, M. S., Thomas, R. D., Albert, N. B., & Beilock, S. L. (2011). Choking under pressure: Multiple routes to skill failure. *Journal of Experimental Psychology: General, 140*, 390–406.

Fingerhut, A. W., & Abdou, C. M. (2017). The role of healthcare stereotype threat and social identity threat in LGB health disparities. *Journal of Social Issues, 73*, 493–507.

Fogliati, V. J., & Bussey, K. (2013). Stereotype threat reduces motivation to improve: Effects of stereotype threat and feedback on women's intentions to improve mathematical ability. *Psychology of Women Quarterly, 37*, 310–324.

Gray, R. (2004). Attending to the execution of a complex sensorimotor skill: Expertise differences, choking, and slumps. *Journal of Experimental Psychology: Applied, 10*, 42–54.

Hekman, D. R., Johnson, S. K., Foo, M., & Yang, W. (2017). Does diversity-valuing behavior result in diminished performance ratings for non-White female leaders? *Academy of Management Journal, 60*, 771–797.

Ho, G. C., Shih, M., & Walters, D. J. (2012). Labels and leaders: The influence of framing on leadership emergence. *The Leadership Quarterly, 23*, 943–952.

Hodges, E. A., Rowsey, P. J., Gray, T. F., Kneipp, S. M., Giscombe, C. W., Foster, B. B., . . . Kowlowitz, V. (2017). Bridging the gender divide: Facilitating the educational path for men in nursing. *Journal of Nursing Education, 56*, 295–299.

Hom, P. W., Roberson, L., & Ellis, A. D. (2008). Challenging conventional wisdom about who quits: Revelations from corporate America. *Journal of Applied Psychology, 93*, 1–34.

Hunger, J. M., Major, B., Blodorn, A., & Miller, C. T. (2015). Weighed down by stigma: How weight-based social identity threat contributes to weight gain and poor health. *Social and Personality Psychology Compass, 9*, 255–262.

Inzlicht, M., & Kang, S. K. (2010). Stereotype threat spillover: How coping with threats to social identity affects aggression, eating, decision making, and attention. *Journal of Personality and Social Psychology, 99*, 467–481.

Jenkins, J. S., & Skowronski, J. J. (2016). The effects of invoking stereotype excuses on perceivers' character trait inferences and performance attributions. *Social Psychology, 47,* 4–14.

John-Henderson, N. A., Rheinschmidt, M. L., Mendoza-Denton, R., & Francis, D. D. (2014). Performance and inflammation outcomes are predicted by different facets of SES under stereotype threat. *Social Psychological and Personality Science, 5,* 301–309.

Jones, P. R., Taylor, D. M., Dampeer-Moore, J., Van Allen, K. L., Saunders, D. R., Snowden, C. B., & Johnson, M. B. (2013). Health-related stereotype threat predicts health services delays among Blacks. *Race and Social Problems, 5,* 121–136.

Kim, H., Lee, K., & Hong, Y. (2012). Claiming the validity of negative in-group stereotypes when foreseeing a challenge: A self-handicapping account. *Self and Identity, 11,* 285–303.

Kirnan, J. P., Alfieri, J. A., Bragger, J. D., & Harris, R. S. (2009). An investigation of stereotype threat in employment tests. *Journal of Applied Social Psychology, 39,* 359–388.

Kravitz, D. A. (2008). The diversity-validity dilemma: Beyond selection—The role of affirmative action. *Personnel Psychology, 61,* 173–193.

Kray, L. J., Thompson, L., & Galinsky, A. (2001). Battle of the sexes: Gender stereotype confirmation and reactance in negotiations. *Journal of Personality and Social Psychology, 80,* 942–958.

Latu, I. M., Mast, M. S., & Stewart, T. L. (2015). Gender bias in (inter) action: The role of interviewers' and applicants' implicit and explicit stereotypes in predicting women's job interview outcomes. *Psychology of Women Quarterly, 39,* 539–552.

Morgan, S. L., & Mehta, J. D. (2004). Beyond the laboratory: Evaluating the survey evidence for the disidentification explanation of black-white differences in achievement. *Sociology of Education, 77,* 82–101.

Morrison, T. G., & Bearden, A. G. (2007). The construction and validation of the homopositivity scale: An instrument measuring endorsement of positive stereotypes about gay men. *Journal of Homosexuality, 52,* 63–89.

Mukkamala, S., & Suyemoto, K. L. (2018). Racialized sexism/sexualized racism: A multimethod study of intersectional experiences of discrimination for Asian American women. *Asian American Journal of Psychology, 9,* 32–46.

Murphy, M. C., Steele, C. M., & Gross, J. J. (2007). Signaling threat: How situational cues affect women in math, science, and engineering settings. *Psychological Science, 18,* 879–885.

National Science Foundation. (2014). *Women and Minorities in the S&E Workforce.* Retrieved from https://www.nsf.gov/statistics/seind14/index.cfm/chapter-3/c3s5.htm#s1-1

Oliveira, E. A. D. S., & Cabral-Cardoso, C. J. (2018). Buffers or boosters? The role of HRM practices in older workers' experience of stereotype threat. *The Journal of Psychology, 152,* 36–59.

Plaut, V. C., Garnett, F. G., Buffardi, L., & Sanchez-Burks, J. (2011). What about me? Perceptions of exclusion and Whites' reactions to multiculturalism. *Journal of Personality and Social Psychology, 10,* 337–353.

Postuma, R. A., & Campion, M. A. (2008). Age stereotypes in the workplace: Common stereotypes, moderators, and future research directions. *Journal of Management, 35,* 158–188.

Pronin, E., Steele, C. M., & Ross, L. (2004). Identity bifurcation in response to stereotype threat: Women and mathematics. *Journal of Experimental Social Psychology, 40,* 152–168.

Purdie-Vaughns, V., Steele, C. M., Davies, P. G., Ditlmann, R., & Cosby, J. R. (2008). Social identity contingencies: How diversity cues signal threat or safety for African Americans in mainstream institutions. *Journal of Personality and Social Psychology, 94,* 615–630.

Quinn, D. M., Williams, M. K., & Weisz, B. M. (2015). From discrimination to internalized mental illness stigma: The mediating roles of anticipated discrimination and anticipated stigma. *Psychiatric Rehabilitation Journal, 38,* 103–108.

Roberson, L., Deitch, E. A., Brief, A. P., & Block, C. J. (2003). Stereotype threat and feedback seeking in the workplace. *Journal of Vocational Behavior, 62,* 176–188.

Roberson, L., & Kulik, C. T. (2007). Stereotype threat at work. *Academy of Management Perspectives, 21,* 24–40.

Romero, A. J., Gonzalez, H., & Smith, B. A. (2015). Qualitative exploration of adolescent discrimination: Experiences and responses of Mexican-American parents and teens. *Journal of Child and Family Studies, 24,* 1531–1543.

Ryan, C. L., & Bauman, K. (2016). *Education attainment in the United States: 2015.* Washington, D.C.: U.S. Census Bureau.

Rydell, R. J., & Boucher, K. L. (2017). Stereotype threat and learning. *Advances in Experimental Social Psychology, 56,* 81–129.

Rydell, R. J., Rydell, M. T., & Boucher, K. L. (2010). The effects of negative performance stereotypes on learning. *Journal of Personality and Social Psychology, 99,* 883–896.

Rydell, R. J., Shiffrin, R., Boucher, K. L., Van Loo, K., & Rydell, M. T. (2010). Stereotype threat prevents perceptual learning. *Proceedings of the National Academy of Sciences of the United States of America, 107,* 14042–14047.

Schmader, T., & Hall, W. (2014). Stereotype threat in school and at work: Putting science into practice. *Policy Insights from the Behavioral and Brain Sciences, 1,* 30–37.

Schmader, T., Hall, W., & Croft, A. (2015). Stereotype threat in intergroup relations. In M. Mikulincer & P. R. Shaver (Eds.), *APA handbook of personality and social psychology: Vol. 2* (pp. 447–471). Washington, D.C.: American Psychological Association.

Schmader, T., Johns, M., & Barquissau, M. (2004). The cost of accepting gender differences: The role of stereotype endorsement in women's experience in the math domain. *Sex Roles, 50,* 835–850.

Schmader, T., Johns, M., & Forbes, C. (2008). An integrated process model of stereotype threat on performance. *Psychological Review, 115,* 336–356.

Schneider, D. J. (2004). *The psychology of stereotyping.* New York: Guilford Press.

Shapiro, J. R., & Neuberg, S. L. (2007). From stereotype threat to stereotype threats: Implications of a multi-threat framework for causes, moderators, mediators, consequences, and interventions. *Personality and Social Psychology Review, 11,* 107–130.

Shapiro, J. R., Williams, A. M., & Hambarchyan, M. (2013). Are all interventions created equal? A multi-threat approach to tailoring stereotype threat interventions. *Journal of Personality and Social Psychology, 104,* 277–288.

Shih, M., Pittinsky, T. L., & Ambady, N. (1999). Stereotype susceptibility: Identity salience and shifts in quantitative performance. *Psychological Science, 10,* 80–83.

Spencer, S. J., Logel, C., & Davies, P. G. (2016). Stereotype threat. *Annual Review of Psychology, 67,* 415–437.

Steele, C. M., & Aronson, J. (1995). Stereotype threat and the intellectual performance of African Americans. *Journal of Personality and Social Psychology, 69,* 797–811.

Steele, C. M., Spencer, S. J., & Aronson, J. (2002). Contending with group image: The psychology of stereotype and social identity threat. *Advances in Experimental Social Psychology, 34,* 379–440.

Stone, J., Lynch, C. I., Sjomeling, M., & Darley, J. M. (1999). Stereotype threat effects on Black and White athletic performance. *Journal of Personality and Social Psychology, 77,* 1213–1227.

Street, R. L., Makoul, G., Arora, N. K., & Epstein, R. M. (2009). How does communication heal? Pathways linking clinician-patient communication to health outcomes. *Patient Education and Counseling, 74,* 295–301.

Tilcsik, A. (2011). Pride and prejudice: Employment discrimination against openly gay men in the United States. *American Journal of Sociology, 117,* 586–626.

Townsend, S. S. M., Major, B., Gangi, C. E., & Mendes, W. B. (2011). From "in the air" to "under the skin": Cortisol responses to social identity threat. *Personality and Social Psychology Bulletin, 37,* 151–164.

Voisin, D., Brick, C., Vallee, B., & Pascual, A. (2019). When stereotype threat does not impair performance, self-affirmation can be harmful. *Self and Identity, 18*(3), 331–348.

von Hippel, C., Kalokerinos, E. K., & Zacher, H. (2017). Stereotype threat and perceptions of family-friendly policies among female employees. *Frontiers in Psychology, 7,* 2043.

von Hippel, C., Sekaquaptewa, D., & McFarlane, M. (2015). Stereotype threat among women in finance: Negative effects on identity, workplace well-being, and recruiting. *Psychology of Women Quarterly, 39,* 405–414.

von Hippel, C., Wiryakusuma, C., Bowden, S., & Shochet, M. (2011). Stereotype threat and female communication styles. *Personality and Social Psychology Bulletin, 37,* 1312–1324.

Walton, G. M., & Cohen, G. L. (2003). Stereotype lift. *Journal of Experimental Social Psychology, 39*, 456–467.

Walton, G. M., & Cohen, G. L. (2007). A question of belonging: Race, social fit, and achievement. *Journal of Personality and Social Psychology, 92*, 82–96.

Walton, G. M., Murphy, M. C., & Ryan, A. M. (2015). Stereotype threat in organizations: Implications for equity and performance. *Annual Review of Organizational Psychology and Organizational Behavior, 2*, 523–550.

Wang, C. S., Whitson, J. A., Anicich, E. M., Kray, L. J., & Galinsky, A. D. (2017). Challenge your stigma: How to reframe and revalue negative stereotypes and slurs. *Current Directions in Psychological Science, 26*, 75–80.

Woodcock, A., Hernandez, P. R., Estrada, M., & Schultz, P. W. (2012). The consequences of chronic stereotype threat: Domain disidentification and abandonment. *Journal of Personality and Social Psychology, 103*, 635–646.

Wraga, M., Helt, M., Jacobs, E., & Sullivan, K. (2007). Neural basis of stereotype-induced shifts in women's mental rotation performance. *Social Cognitive and Affective Neuroscience, 2*, 12–19.

Zeidner, M., & Matthews, G. (2005). Evaluation anxiety: Current theory and research. In A. J. Elliot & C. S. Dweck (Eds.), *Handbook of competence and motivation* (pp. 141–163). New York: Guildford Publications.

CHAPTER FIVE

Stereotyping Never Gets Old: Exploring the Persistence, Popularity, and Perniciousness of Age Stereotypes

Cody Cox and Friederike Young

The World Health Organization estimates that individuals over sixty years old will make up more than 20 percent of the world's population by 2025 (World Health Organization, 2014). In the United States specifically, these changes in demographics will result in substantial changes in the working population as older workers become the fastest growing demographic in the workforce (Bureau Labor of Statistics, 2019). People are living longer and staying healthier further into older age and, consequently, experiencing the need to stay active in their communities and the workforce longer than in previous generations (Truxillo, Cadiz, & Hammer, 2015). Unfortunately, the perceptions people have of both older and younger individuals—as well as the perceptions people have of themselves as older and younger individuals—are often shaped by stereotypes. In research, younger individuals are viewed as more materialistic, less reliable, more narcissistic, and less loyal to organizations (Twenge & Campbell, 2008; Van Dalen, Henkens, & Schippers, 2010). Older individuals are often perceived to be resistant to change, intolerant, unable to use technology and incapable of learning (Patel, Tinker, & Corna, 2018; Posthuma & Campion, 2009; Rosen & Jerdee, 1976; Wrenn & Maurer, 2004). Paradoxically, even though older individuals are living longer, healthier lives, attitudes toward older individuals and aging remains largely negative (Levy, 2017). Thus, as communities and workplaces are becoming more age diverse, stereotypes about older and younger people are becoming both more common and more negative (Costanza & Finkelstein, 2015; Ng, Allore, Trentalange, Monin, & Levy, 2015).

The prevalence of these stereotypes has several implications for both older and younger individuals in all aspects of society. Managers increasingly need to ensure that age stereotypes do not impact workplace decisions in hiring, promoting, and deciding which employees should receive opportunities to develop. Medical practitioners need to work to ensure that age-related stereotypes do not impact their diagnoses and prognoses of their patients. Individuals also need to be resilient against the detrimental and even harmful effects of age-related stereotypes on their own motivation, cognitive performance and health. The purpose of this chapter is to review the recent research surrounding age-related stereotypes. First, we explore some of the history and prevalence of age stereotypes today. Then we will explore the effects of the prevalence of these stereotypes. Finally, we will review the research on how to mitigate and manage age stereotypes effectively.

History and prevalence of age stereotypes

Research on age stereotypes can be considered an extension of research into ageism. Ageism was originally defined by Butler (1969) as prejudice between individuals of different age groups. In the years since then, researchers have explored many examples of ageism, such as denying resources to older individuals (Palmore, 2001), treating employees differently depending on their ages (e.g., Terrell, 2018), manifesting implicit attitudes toward older individuals (Perdue & Gurtman, 1990) and providing different medical treatment as a function of patients' ages (Kane & Kane, 2005). Researchers have argued that bias against older individuals is a relatively recent phenomenon, reflecting the perceived need for the skills associated with younger workers in an increasingly industrialized workforce (Nelson, 2005). This may explain why a lot of the literature around stereotypes toward older and younger people focuses on age-related prejudice in organizations. For example, researchers exploring exposure to stereotypes in the workforce have found that both older and younger individuals experience more exposure to stereotypes in the workplace than middle-aged individuals (von Hippel et al., 2018). Researchers have also found that while both older workers and younger workers are perceived to have strengths (e.g., reliability for older workers and trainability for younger workers), the perceived strengths of younger workers are more valued by employers (Abrams, Swift, & Drury, 2016; Van Dalen et al., 2010).

Generational Stereotypes and Ageism

Researchers who examine age-related stereotypes have often noted that whereas stereotypes about older individuals are both positive and negative, stereotypes about younger individuals tend to be uniformly positive. One important exception, however, is in the research around generational differences. Millennials, often described as the generation of individuals born after 1980 and before 1996, are frequently described in more negative terms than older generations are, leading many Millennials to distance themselves from the label (Pew Research Center, 2015). Researchers have noted that Millennials, compared to older generations, are more neurotic and narcissistic (e.g., Twenge & Campbell, 2008), less focused on work (Twenge, 2010) and less interested in altruistic work (Twenge, Campbell, Hoffman, & Lance, 2010). Thus, there are negative stereotypes about younger individuals as well, particularly when younger individuals are described as Millennials. Relatedly, it is important to note that generational labels such as Millennial or Baby Boomer are not related to individuals' current age; instead, the label is based on birth year. Indeed, there is already some exploration of the characteristics of the next generation (e.g., Twenge, 2017). Thus, the labels "Millennial" and "younger" will not always be aligned, and as Generation Z moves into the workforce, it will be interesting to see where the stereotypes about Generation Z overlap with stereotypes about younger employees generally (e.g., in terms of technological sophistication) and where they differ.

While discussion about generational differences is common, other researchers have recently argued that some generalizations about generational differences are drawn from research with methodological limitations (Parry & Urwin, 2011; Costanza & Finkelstein, 2015). These concerns have led researchers to explore whether generational differences might be considerably smaller than previously believed; one large meta-analysis, for example, failed to find substantial evidence of generational differences in work-related values (Costanza, Badger, Fraser, Severt, & Gade, 2012; see also Carmichael, 2016). Thus there is some concern that many broad generalizations that are drawn about differences between generations may not always be based on scientific evidence.

In discussing the lack of evidence for generational differences, Costanza and Finkelstein (2015) noted that generational labels could lead to more prejudice against older and younger workers. They note, for example, that while older workers are protected by law, there is no law protecting members of different generations, and previous research has indicated that attitudes toward older workers are more positive when people believe older workers are protected by law. Further, there is some evidence that generational labels lead to differential treatment for both older and younger individuals. One study, for example, found that job candidates who were identified as Baby Boomers and Millennials received higher ratings in terms of motivation and adaptability than candidates described as sixty years old or twenty-nine years old, respectively (Perry et al., 2017). Conversely, another study found that participants were more likely to hire, more likely to train, and more likely to advocate for employees described as "older workers" than employees described as "Baby Boomers" (Cox, Young, Guardia, & Bohmann, 2018). Overall, negative stereotypes about Millennials are common, but there is some debate about whether generational stereotypes generally are valid and whether generational stereotypes may be harmful for older or younger individuals.

The Origin of Age Stereotypes

The prevalence of age stereotypes has led to some examination of where age stereotypes originate. Negative age-related stereotypes are introduced early in the lifespan and reinforced throughout one's life. Levy (2009) noted that children quickly learn to categorize people based on age, noting that stories for children frequently describe characters based on age-related characteristics. It is important to note that people encounter stereotypes about older individuals at young ages in which these stereotypes do not apply to themselves. That is, although members of stereotyped groups (e.g., African Americans, women) initially encounter those stereotypes at younger ages during identity formation and develop methods for dismissing or distancing themselves from these stereotypes, individuals develop attitudes toward older individuals while still young and while those stereotypes do not apply to them (Levy, Slade, Kunkel, & Kasl, 2002). Thus, as these stereotypes do not apply to younger individuals, younger people are less motivated to dismiss them and are more susceptible to adopting stereotyped beliefs about older individuals (Levy & Banaji, 2002). These negative age stereotypes are frequently conveyed and reinforced through media such as television programs; one study found that hours spent watching television predicted negative attitudes toward older adults (Donlon, Ashman, & Levy, 2005; Levy, 2003). Researchers have noted that television shows such as *The Simpsons* often portray older characters as being incompetent, ill-tempered, and inconsequential (Blakeborough, 2008). Haboush, Warren, and Benuto (2012) found that the extent to which Western ideas of beauty—which, the authors argued, are promulgated by Western media—was internalized by participants predicted the participants' negative attitudes toward aging. Thus age stereotypes are conveyed through many mediums, and people are exposed to these stereotypes at young ages.

Age stereotypes are universal; negative attitudes and discrimination against older adults is a phenomenon that is observed around the world (Ayalon, 2013). Broadly speaking, Cuddy, Norton, and Fiske (2005) found that older individuals are viewed as warmer, but less competent across six different countries. The Stereotype Content Model (SCM) supports these divisive stereotypes for a group by finding that status predicted competence but competition predicted low warmth. Mixed stereotypes often involve two separate dimensions but are not considered psychologically inconsistent as sometimes elderly are perceived as nice but incapable of learning new things or another group may be considered efficient but not warm (Fiske, Cuddy, Glick, & Xu, 2002). Though these findings may seem contradictory, many stereotypes for groups have been found to have multiple dimensions according to the model mentioned above. In a large survey of participants in twenty-six countries, researchers found that younger individuals are universally believed to be more impulsive and more friendly than older individuals. Moreover, these stereotypes corresponded to self-report measures of personality in these countries as well, leading the researchers to conclude that age-stereotypes—in regard to personality, at least—may be somewhat accurate (Chan et al., 2012). Other researchers explored cultural differences in perceptions of older individuals. Though researchers anticipated that Eastern cultures might possess more positive views of aging, meta-analytic evidence demonstrates, surprisingly, that older individuals are viewed more negatively in Eastern cultures than they are in Western cultures (North & Fiske, 2015). Chiu, Chan, Shape, and Redman (2001) also found that respondents from a Western sample (i.e., UK respondents) viewed older workers as more productive but less adaptable than respondents from an Eastern sample (i.e., Hong Kong residents). Overall, there is considerable evidence that positive and negative stereotypes about older and younger individuals are pervasive worldwide.

Stereotypes are not only pervasive, they are also changing. Specifically, there is some evidence that stereotypes about older individuals in particular are becoming increasingly negative. Ng et al. (2015) demonstrated an increase in negativity of age stereotypes across 200 years of evidence from a database of 400 million words. By creating an exhaustive list of synonyms for the word *elderly*, the researchers also identified one hundred words that co-occurred most frequently with these synonyms. With this system, they identified that age stereotypes have become more negative over the last two centuries in the United States. Similarly, Mason, Kuntz, and McGill (2015) found that older individuals have been described more negatively in books over the course of the twentieth century. This increasingly negative view of older workers is consistent with the notion that negative stereotypes about older workers reflect the increased need among industries for the skills stereotypically associated with younger individuals (Nelson, 2005), though this has not been explored empirically.

The prevalence of age-related stereotypes has led some researchers to explore whether age-related stereotypes serve some sociological or psychological function in society. North and Fiske (2013), for example, suggest that stereotypes about older individuals serve a *prescriptive* purpose; that is, these stereotypes do not simply reflect how older individuals do act but rather how they should act. Specifically, they argue that prescriptive negative stereotypes are maintained because they encourage older individuals to be generous with resources and to refrain from adopting youthful behavior. They conducted six studies exploring how younger individuals react to older and middle-aged individuals violating these prescriptive stereotypes (e.g., refusing to provide money to a relative in need or demonstrating a preference for the Black Eyed Peas over Frank Sinatra). They found that younger people reacted more negatively to older individuals behaving this way than younger or middle-aged individuals and concluded that the prescriptive stereotypes are enforced by younger individuals to ensure access to resources and maintenance of their identities. Thus, the prevalence of age stereotypes may reflect the persistence of these prescriptive norms.

Overall, there is considerable evidence that age stereotypes are pervasive, cross-cultural, evolving, and potentially prescriptive. Additionally, it is important to note that most recent studies find little evidence to support the negative views of older adults. In a series of meta-analyses, Ng and Feldman (2008, 2009, 2012) found that older individuals are just as engaged with their work, successful in their work, creative, willing to change, trusting, and healthy as younger workers and—further—were more likely to stay in their jobs, promote workplace safety, and go above and beyond at work, though they were less successful and less willing to participate in training. These meta-analyses indicate that age stereotypes, in addition to being common, persistent, and universal, are also frequently inaccurate.

Impact of Age Stereotypes

The impact of age stereotypes on individuals has been explored closely through research on stereotype threat. Stereotype threat is a phenomenon in which individuals who are exposed to a negative stereotype feel themselves at risk of demonstrating and conforming to the stereotype about their social group. Additionally, they show worse performance than similar individuals not exposed to the same stereotype (Steele, 1997). Thomas Hess and colleagues have demonstrated across several studies that presenting older adults with negative stereotypes about older adults—inducing stereotype threat—can reduce the performance of older adults on memory tasks (e.g., Hess,

Auman, Colcombe, & Rahhal, 2003). Stereotypes threat can be caused by explicitly mentioning specific age-related stereotypes that are either supported by empirical evidence—such as memory declines (e.g., O'Brien & Hummert, 2006)—or using unfounded stereotypes (Abrams, Eller, and Bryant, 2006; Lamont, Swift, & Abrams, 2015). Stereotype threat can also be explicitly discussed or implied by informing older participants that their performance will be compared to younger participants (e.g., Swift, Lamont, & Abrams, 2012). These stereotypes can be presented subliminally and still affect older adults' performance (Levy, 1996). Interestingly, the stereotypes do not need to be believed in order to produce an effect; merely being exposed to the stereotypes impacts older adults (Lamont et al., 2015).

Beyond deficits in memory performance, there is considerable evidence that age-based stereotypes impact motivation among older adults. Age-related stereotypes, for example, have the effect of reducing older individuals' confidence; one study found that exposing older adults to negative age-related stereotypes reduced their confidence in their driving but, importantly, did not impact their actual driving performance (Chapman, Sargent-Cox, Horswill, & Anstey, 2016). Age stereotypes appear to impact the performance of younger adults as well. Hehman and Bugental (2013) found that exposing older adults to age-related stereotypes (i.e., that age was negatively associated with performance on a task) impaired their performance on the task, much as other researchers have found. However, they also found that younger individuals actually demonstrated greater performance when told their age would be a disadvantage, but this is only if they experienced an external sense of control. The authors argued that younger individuals see stereotypes as challenges to be overcome and thus actually demonstrate better performance under threat.

Age stereotypes have the ability to impact not only individual performance and motivation, but they can also impact the contact between individuals of different ages. For many years, researchers have long explored how age stereotypes are expressed in communication between individuals of different ages. These researchers have noted that younger individuals often adopt shorter sentences and simpler vocabulary when speaking with older individuals (Giles, Fox, Harwood, & Williams, 1994; Hummert, Shaner, Garstka, & Henry, 1998). This form of speech has been called "secondary baby talk" (Ryan, Bourhis, & Knops, 1991, p. 442). In research, participants are more likely to utilize this communication with despondent older adults than with positive older adults, but older speakers were less likely to incorporate this type of language overall (Hummert et al., 1998). Though these accommodations are made due to older adults' perceived declining cognitive function, researchers have noted that even experienced caregivers tend to adopt simplified language for all older adults regardless of perceived cognitive function (Kempler & Zelinski, 1994). While this communication may be well-intentioned, researchers have noted that this language can reinforce stereotypes and reduce the self-esteem of older adults (O'Connor & Rigby, 1996).

Age Stereotypes around Us

Age stereotypes have some of their largest effects in the workplace. One recent meta-analysis, for example, found that older workers are rated lower in their potential for advancement, lower in the likelihood of being hired, lower in job performance, and lower in interpersonal skills than younger employees (Bal, Reiss, Rudolph, & Baltes, 2011). One recent study found that older individuals were less likely to be hired due to the perception that they did not possess the traits the position required (Abrams et al., 2016). von Hippel et al. (2018) found that exposure to stereotypes led to increase rumination for older employees, which led to less job satisfaction, less well-being, and increased intention to quit. They also found that the extent to which stereotype threat was perceived as a challenge to be overcome lessened the impact on organizational outcomes, leading the researchers to suggest that framing organizational obstacles as challenges to be overcome may reduce the impact of stereotype threat on organizational performance.

There is also a growing literature exploring the effects of age stereotypes on individual's health. Age stereotypes, for example, may also affect the practice of medicine. One study found that older women in particular were likely to believe that ageism affected their doctor's diagnosis of their chronic health problems (Chrisler, Barney, & Palatino, 2016). Further, attributing health outcomes to age also has negative effects for older individuals. Negative beliefs about aging have been associated with decreased life expectancy, increased risk for cardiovascular problems, and decreased likeliness to pursue health-promoting behavior (Levy & Myers, 2004; Levy et al., 2002; Levy, Zonderman, Slade, & Ferrucci, 2009). Indeed, researchers have found that attributing negative health outcomes to age is associated with worse health outcomes for older adults, even when controlling for actual symptom severity (Stewart, Chipperfield, Perry, & Weiner, 2012). In addition to predicting more negative health outcomes generally, negative views on aging may impair older adults' ability to recover from negative health events. Wurm, Warner, Zielgelmann, Wolff, and Schuz (2013) found that negative health events predicted the adoption of more positive health behaviors for older adults, but this relationship was moderated by attitudes toward getting older such that individuals who experience a health event would be less likely to adopt healthier practices if they held a negative view about aging. Thus, age stereotypes may affect both older individuals' experiences with medical treatment and their ability to manage their own health.

More recently, researchers exploring the effects of stereotypes have started to focus on the impact and effects of age *metastereotypes*. A metastereotype is defined by Vorauer, Main, and O'Connell (1998) as "a person's beliefs regarding the stereotype that outgroup members hold about his/her own group" (p. 917). Researchers have consistently found that individuals are concerned about the viewpoints of others who see them through the lens of specific stereotypes (Vorauer, Hunter, Main, & Roy, 2000). Finkelstein and colleagues specifically explored the accuracy and content of age metastereotypes of three groups: younger workers (aged eighteen to thirty), middle-aged workers (thirty-one to fifty) and older workers (over fifty-one). A total of 247 individuals completed a survey about stereotypes held of the age groups other than their own. Afterward, the participants completed the survey by identifying stereotypes they believed others had of their own group. The survey results identified twelve sets of descriptors from each age group and the stereotypes held of each group. In ten out of twelve cases, the authors found that people have lower opinions of their own age group than do those who are not a part of their group (Finkelstein, King, & Voyles, 2015). Further, Ryan, King, and Finkelstein (2015) found that younger workers were more dissatisfied with their older coworkers when they believed their older coworkers viewed them negatively. Future research may explore these impacts of metastereotypes on intergroup relations, employee engagement, and intergenerational communication and perhaps even begin to explore methods of reducing the impact of these perceptions.

Combating Age-Related Stereotypes

There is a large body of research demonstrating the impact of age-related stereotypes. Remedying the effects of these stereotypes has received less attention. One common method for improving intergroup relations is by increasing intergroup contact; the *contact hypothesis* argues that, under particular conditions, intergroup contact often improves relations between groups (Hewstone & Brown, 1986). However, the evidence for the effectiveness of the contact hypothesis for dispelling age-related stereotypes appears to be mixed. One study, for example, found that self-reported contact with older adults did reduce the likelihood that individuals would engage in condescending language when speaking with older adults (Hehman, Corpuz, & Bugental, 2012). On the other hand, another study of physicians found that the amount of time interacting with elderly patients that the physicians reported was actually associated with more negative attitudes toward the health of elderly patients (Revenson, 1989). Similarly, Reyna, Goodwin, and Ferrari (2007) surveyed a sample of care providers at residential homes for the elderly and found that contact with elderly patients did not reduce stereotypes about the elderly, but increased education did. Iweins, Desmette,

Yzerbyt, and Stinglhamber (2013), however, found that intergenerational contact does promote more positive stereotypes, but this effect was dependent on the extent to which individuals identified both as members of their generation and members of their organization (a dual identity; see Gómez, Dovidio, Huici, Gaertner, & Cuadrado, 2008). Thus, there is mixed evidence that contact with older individuals improves attitudes toward older individuals.

Interestingly, even though contact may not improve attitudes toward older individuals, contact (even imagined contact) with younger individuals may reduce the impact of age-related stereotype threat on older adults' performance. Abrams et al. (2008) found that older individuals completing a math test under conditions of stereotype threat performed better when they had either recently visited their grandchildren or imagined visiting their grandchildren. Likewise, Abrams et al. (2006) found that the more positive the contact with younger individuals, the more resilient older adults were to the effect of stereotype threat on performance. Taken together, these studies suggest that the evidence that contact with older individuals improves attitudes toward older individuals is somewhat mixed; however, contact with younger individuals (even imagined contact) does seem to improve older individuals' resilience to the effects of stereotypes.

Outside of the contact hypothesis, other researchers have explored alternative methods for alleviating the effects of negative age-related stereotypes. Researchers have found that when one's age and one's organizational identity are integrated, this relationship can reduce the impact of stereotype threat on work-related outcomes for older adults (Manzi, Paderi, Benet-Martínez, & Coen, 2018). Donlon et al. (2005) also found that simply asking older participants to note the older characters on television increased their awareness of negative age stereotypes on television (and, consequently, reduced their desire to watch television in the future). Thus, making individuals aware of positive age–role models or age-stereotypes may reduce the impact of age-related stereotypes.

Researchers have also found that implicit attitudes toward older individuals can be improved by priming participants with examples of positive older individuals. Dasgupta and Greenwald (2001) primed older and younger individuals with examples of admired older individuals (e.g., Willie Nelson and Barbara Walters) and disliked older individuals (e.g., Jim Bakker and Ted Kaczinsky) before asking participants to complete an age-focused IAT. They found that exposure to admired older individuals and disliked younger individuals (e.g., Erik and Lyle Menendez) reduced—but did not eliminate—bias toward younger targets.

Other research suggests that how stereotypes are perceived might determine their effect. Von Hippel et al. (2018) found that individuals who view the perception that their job is inappropriate for someone their age as a challenge to overcome are less likely to experience reduced job performance when exposed to age stereotypes. This suggests that encouraging older adults to view their age as a challenge to be overcome rather than a hindrance to their performance may reduce the negative impacts of age-related stereotypes. Additional research suggests that the effects of stereotyping can be fully mediated by describing the task appropriately. Rahhal, Hasher, and Colcombe (2001) found that describing a recall task as a "learning" task rather than a "memory" task fully mediated the differences in recall between older and younger participants. Together, these findings suggest describing the task or framing a task in such a way as to avoid threat may help older participants overcome the negative effects of stereotypes. Coaching older workers to view age-related issues as challenges to be overcome and framing these challenges in terms that avoid negative stereotypes may improve the workplace experiences of older workers.

Conclusions

The negative impact of intergenerational stereotypes has led some writers to call for avoiding media perpetuating stereotypes and companies that promote stereotypes (Schofield, 2017). Age-related stereotypes affect intergenerational communication and interactions. Moreover, there is a consistent and growing literature examining the effects of negative stereotypes on the cognitive performance and motivation of older adults. Researchers exploring metastereotypes and generational stereotypes are also discovering additional effects of age-related stereotypes. Fortunately, there is also an emerging body of literature suggesting that these effects can be remedied by intergenerational contact, framing activities as challenges rather than hurdles, and encouraging an intergenerational identity. As age diversity continues to increase and older adults remain in the workforce longer, communities, businesses, and health care providers will all have an interest in discovering new methods for eliminating and remedying the impact of these stereotypes.

References

Abrams, D., Crisp, R. J., Marques, S., Fagg, E., Bedford, L., & Provias, D. (2008). Threat inoculation: Experienced and imagined intergenerational contact prevents stereotype threat effects on older people's math performance. *Psychology and Aging, 23*(4), 934–939.

Abrams, D., Eller, A., & Bryant, J. (2006). An age apart: The effects of intergenerational contact and stereotype threat on performance and intergroup bias. *Psychology and Aging, 21*(4), 691–702.

Abrams, D., Swift, H. J., & Drury, L. (2016). Old and unemployable? How age-based stereotypes affect willingness to hire job candidates. *Journal of Social Issues, 72*(1), 105–121.

Ayalon, L. (2013). Feelings towards older vs. younger adults: Results from the European Social Survey. *Educational Gerontology, 39*(12), 888–901.

Bal, A. C., Reiss, A. E., Rudolph, C. W., & Baltes, B. B. (2011). Examining positive and negative perceptions of older workers: A meta-analysis. *Journals of Gerontology Series B: Psychological Sciences and Social Sciences, 66*(6), 687–698.

Blakeborough, D. (2008). "Old people are useless": Representations of aging on The Simpsons. *Canadian Journal on Aging/La Revue Canadienne du Vieillissement, 27*(1), 57–67.

Bureau Labor of Statistics. (2019). Projected job growth in occupations with large shares of older workers. Retrieved from https://www.bls.gov/careeroutlook/2019/data-on-display/older-workers-and-occupational-employment-growth.htm

Butler, R. N. (1969). Age-ism: Another form of bigotry. *The Gerontologist, 9*(4_Part_1), 243–246.

Carmichael, S. G. (2016). Millennials are actually workaholics, according to research. *Harvard Business Review.* Retrieved from https://hbr.org/2016/08/millennials-are-actually-workaholics-according-to-research

Chan, W., McCrae, R. R., De Fruyt, F., Jussim, L., Löckenhoff, C. E., De Bolle, M., . . . Nakazato, K. (2012). Stereotypes of age differences in personality traits: Universal and accurate? *Journal of Personality and Social Psychology, 103*(6), 1050–1066.

Chapman, L., Sargent-Cox, K., Horswill, M. S., & Anstey, K. J. (2016). The impact of age stereotypes on older adults' hazard perception performance and driving confidence. *Journal of Applied Gerontology, 35*(6), 642–652.

Chiu, W. C. K., Chan, A. W., Snape, E., & Redman, T. (2001). Age stereotypes and discriminatory attitudes towards older workers: An East-West comparison. *Human Relations, 54*(5), 629–661.

Chrisler, J. C., Barney, A., & Palatino, B. (2016). Ageism can be hazardous to women's health: Ageism, sexism, and stereotypes of older women in the healthcare system. *Journal of Social Issues, 72*(1), 86–104. doi:10.1111/josi.12157

Costanza, D. P., Badger, J. M., Fraser, R. L., Severt, J. B., & Gade, P. A. (2012). Generational differences in work-related attitudes: A meta-analysis. *Journal of Business and Psychology, 27*(4), 375–394.

Costanza, D. P., & Finkelstein, L. M. (2015). Generationally based differences in the workplace: Is there a there there? *Industrial and Organizational Psychology, 8*(3), 308–323.

Cox, C. B., Young, F. K., Guardia, A. B., & Bohmann, A. K. (2018). The Baby Boomer bias: The negative impact of generational labels on older workers. *Journal of Applied Social Psychology, 48*(2), 71–79.

Cuddy, A. J., Norton, M. I., & Fiske, S. T. (2005). This old stereotype: The pervasiveness and persistence of the elderly stereotype. *Journal of Social Issues, 61*(2), 267–285.

Dasgupta, N., & Greenwald, A. G. (2001). On the malleability of automatic attitudes: Combating automatic prejudice with images of admired and disliked individuals. *Journal of Personality and Social Psychology, 81*(5), 800.

Donlon, M. M., Ashman, O., & Levy, B. R. (2005). Re-vision of older television characters: A stereotype-awareness intervention. *Journal of Social Issues, 61*(2), 307–319. doi:10.1111/j.1540-4560.2005.00407.x

Finkelstein, L. M., King, E. B., & Voyles, E. C. (2015). Age metastereotyping and cross-age workplace interactions: A meta view of age stereotypes at work. *Work, Aging and Retirement, 1*(1), 26–40.

Fiske, S. T., Cuddy, A. J., Glick, P., & Xu, J. (2002). A model of (often mixed) stereotype content: Competence and warmth respectively follow from perceived status and competition. *Journal of Personality and Social Psychology, 82*(6), 878.

Giles, H., Fox, S., Harwood, J., & Williams, A. (1994). Talking age and aging talk: Communicating through the life span. In M. L. Hummert, J. M. Wiemann, & J. F. Nussbaum (Eds.), *Sage focus editions, Vol. 173. Interpersonal communication in older adulthood: Interdisciplinary theory and research* (pp. 130–161). Thousand Oaks, CA: SAGE Publications.

Gómez, Á., Dovidio, J. F., Huici, C., Gaertner, S. L., & Cuadrado, I. (2008). The other side of we: When outgroup members express common identity. *Personality and Social Psychology Bulletin, 34*(12), 1613–1626.

Haboush, A., Warren, C. S., & Benuto, L. (2012). Beauty, ethnicity, and age: Does internalization of mainstream media ideals influence attitudes towards older adults? *Sex Roles, 66*(9–10), 668–676.

Hehman, J. A., & Bugental, D. B. (2013). "Life stage-specific" variations in performance in response to age stereotypes. *Developmental Psychology, 49*(7), 1396–1406.

Hehman, J. A., Corpuz, R., & Bugental, D. (2012). Patronizing speech to older adults. *Journal of Nonverbal Behavior, 36*(4), 249–261.

Hess, T. M., Auman, C., Colcombe, S. J., & Rahhal, T. A. (2003). The impact of stereotype threat on age differences in memory performance. *The Journals of Gerontology Series B: Psychological Sciences and Social Sciences, 58*(1), P3–P11.

Hewstone, M. E., & Brown, R. E. (1986). *Contact and conflict in intergroup encounters.* Oxford, England: Basil Blackwell.

Hummert, M. L., Shaner, J. L., Garstka, T. A., & Henry, C. (1998). Communication with older adults: The influence of age stereotypes, context, and communicator age. *Human Communication Research, 25*(1), 124–151.

Iweins, C., Desmette, D., Yzerbyt, V., & Stinglhamber, F. (2013). Ageism at work: The impact of intergenerational contact and organizational multi-age perspective. *European Journal of Work and Organizational Psychology, 22*(3), 331–346.

Kane, R., & Kane, R. (2005). Ageism in healthcare and long-term care. *Generations, 29*(3), 49–54.

Kempler, D., & Zelinski, E. M. (1994). Language function in dementia and normal aging. In F. A. Huppert, C. Brayne, & D. O'Connor (Eds.), *Dementia and normal aging* (pp. 331–365). Cambridge: Cambridge University Press.

Lamont, R. A., Swift, H. J., & Abrams, D. (2015). A review and meta-analysis of age-based stereotype threat: Negative stereotypes, not facts, do the damage. *Psychology and Aging, 30*(1), 180.

Levy, B. R. (2003). Mind matters: Cognitive and physical effects of aging self-stereotypes. *The Journals of Gerontology Series B: Psychological Sciences and Social Sciences, 58*(4), P203–P211.

Levy, B. R. (2009). Stereotype embodiment: A psychosocial approach to aging. *Current Directions in Psychological Science, 18*(6), 332–336.

Levy, B. R. (2017). Age-stereotype paradox: Opportunity for social change. *The Gerontologist, 57*, S118–S126. doi:10.1093/geront/gnx059

Levy, B. R., & Banaji, M. R. (2002). Implicit ageism. In T. Nelson (Ed.), *Ageism: Stereotyping and prejudice against older persons*. Cambridge, MA: MIT Press.

Levy, B. R., & Myers, L. M. (2004). Preventive health behaviors influenced by self-perceptions of aging. *Preventive Medicine, 39*(3), 625–629.

Levy, B. R., Slade, M. D., Kunkel, S. R., & Kasl, S. V. (2002). Longevity increased by positive self-perceptions of aging. *Journal of Personality and Social Psychology, 83*(2), 261.

Levy, B. R., Zonderman, A. B., Slade, M. D., & Ferrucci, L. (2009). Age stereotypes held earlier in life predict cardiovascular events in later life. *Psychological Science, 20*(3), 296–298.

Manzi, C., Paderi, F., Benet-Martínez, V., & Coen, S. (2018). Age-based stereotype threat and negative outcomes in the workplace: Exploring the role of identity integration. *European Journal of Social Psychology, 49*(4), 705–716.

Mason, S. E., Kuntz, C. V., & McGill, C. M. (2015). Oldsters and Ngrams: Age stereotypes across time. *Psychological Reports, 116*(1), 324–329.

Nelson, T. D. (2005). Ageism: Prejudice against our feared future self. *Journal of Social Issues, 61*(2), 207–221.

Ng, R., Allore, H. G., Trentalange, M., Monin, J. K., & Levy, B. R. (2015). Increasing negativity of age stereotypes across 200 years: Evidence from a database of 400 million words. *PLoS One, 10*(2), e0117086.

Ng, T. W., & Feldman, D. C. (2008). The relationship of age to ten dimensions of job performance. *Journal of Applied Psychology, 93*(2), 392–423.

Ng, T. W., & Feldman, D. C. (2009). Re-examining the relationship between age and voluntary turnover. *Journal of Vocational Behavior, 74*(3), 283–294.

Ng, T. W., & Feldman, D. C. (2012). Evaluating six common stereotypes about older workers with meta-analytical data. *Personnel Psychology, 65*(4), 821–858.

North, M. S., & Fiske, S. T. (2013). Act your (old) age: Prescriptive, ageist biases over succession, consumption, and identity. *Personality and Social Psychology Bulletin, 39*(6), 720–734.

North, M. S., & Fiske, S. T. (2015). Modern attitudes toward older adults in the aging world: A cross-cultural meta-analysis. *Psychological Bulletin, 141*(5), 993–1021.

O'Brien, L. T., & Hummert, M. L. (2006). Memory performance of late middle-aged adults: Contrasting self-stereotyping and stereotype threat accounts of assimilation to age stereotypes. *Social Cognition, 24*(3), 338–358.

O'Connor, P., & Rigby, H. (1996). Perceptions of baby talk, frequency of receiving baby talk and self-esteem among community and nursing home residents. *Psychology and Aging, 11*, 147–154.

Palmore, E. (2001). The ageism survey: First findings. *The Gerontologist, 41*(5), 572–575.

Parry, E., & Urwin, P. (2011). Generational differences in work values: A review of theory and evidence. *International Journal of Management Reviews, 13*(1), 79–96.

Patel, J., Tinker, A., & Corna, L. (2018). Younger workers' attitudes and perceptions towards older colleagues. *Working with Older People, 22*(3), 129–138.

Perdue, C. W., & Gurtman, M. B. (1990). Evidence for the automaticity of ageism. *Journal of Experimental Social Psychology, 26*(3), 199–216.

Perry, E. L., Golom, F. D., Catenacci, L., Ingraham, M. E., Covais, E. M., & Molina, J. J. (2017). Talkin' 'bout your generation: The impact of applicant age and generation on hiring-related perceptions and outcomes. *Work, Aging and Retirement, 3*(2), 186–199.

Pew Research Center. (2015, September 3). *Most Millennials resist the Millennial label.* Retrieved from http://www.people-press.org/2015/09/03/most -millennials-resist-the-millennial-label/

Posthuma, R. A., & Campion, M. A. (2009). Age stereotypes in the workplace: Common stereotypes, moderators, and future research directions. *Journal of Management, 35*(1), 158–188.

Rahhal, T. A., Hasher, L., & Colcombe, S. J. (2001). Instructional manipulations and age differences in memory: Now you see them, now you don't. *Psychology and Aging, 16*(4), 697–706.

Revenson, T. A. (1989). Compassionate stereotyping of elderly patients by physicians: Revising the social contact hypothesis. *Psychology and Aging, 4*(2), 230–234.

Reyna, C., Goodwin, E. J., & Ferrari, J. R. (2007). Older adult stereotypes among care providers in residential care facilities: Examining the relationship between contact, education, and ageism. *Journal of Gerontological Nursing, 33*(2), 50–55.

Rosen, B., & Jerdee, T. H. (1976). The nature of job-related age stereotypes. *Journal of Applied Psychology, 61*(2), 180.

Ryan, E. B., Bourhis, R. Y., & Knops, U. (1991). Evaluative perceptions of patronizing speech addressed to elders. *Psychology and Aging, 6*(3), 442.

Ryan, K. M., King, E. B., & Finkelstein, L. M. (2015). Younger workers' metastereotypes, workplace mood, attitudes, and behaviors. *Journal of Managerial Psychology, 30*(1), 54–70.

Schofield, G. H. (2017, November). 7 ways to eliminate stereotypes about aging. *Forbes*. Retrieved from https://www.forbes.com/sites/nextavenue/2017/11/19/7-ways-to-eliminate-stereotypes-about-aging/#10c9b3171d6a

Stewart, T. L., Chipperfield, J. G., Perry, R. P., & Weiner, B. (2012). Attributing illness to "old age": Consequences of a self-directed stereotype for health and mortality. *Psychology & Health, 27*(8), 881–897.

Swift, H. J., Lamont, R. A., & Abrams, D. (2012). Are they half as strong as they used to be? An experiment testing whether age-related social comparisons impair older people's hand grip strength and persistence. *BMJ Open, 2*(3), e001064.

Terrell, K. (2018, August). Age discrimination common in the workplace, survey says. *AARP.* Retrieved from https://www.aarp.org/work/working-at-50-plus/info-2018/age-discrimination-common-at-work.html

Truxillo, D. M., Cadiz, D. M., & Hammer, L. B. (2015). Supporting the aging workforce: A review and recommendations for workplace intervention research. *Annual Review of Organizational Psychology and Organizational Behavior, 2*(1), 351–381.

Twenge, J. M. (2010). A review of the empirical evidence on generational differences in work attitudes. *Journal of Business and Psychology, 25*(2), 201–210.

Twenge, J. M. (2017). *iGen: Why today's super-connected kids are growing up less rebellious, more tolerant, less happy—And completely unprepared for adulthood*. New York, NY: Atria Books.

Twenge, J. M., & Campbell, S. M. (2008). Generational differences in psychological traits and their impact on the workplace. *Journal of Managerial Psychology, 23*(8), 862–887.

Twenge, J. M., Campbell, S. M., Hoffman, B. R., & Lance, C. E. (2010). Generational differences in work values: Leisure and extrinsic values increasing, social and intrinsic values decreasing. *Journal of Management, 36*(5), 1117–1142.

Van Dalen, H. P., Henkens, K., & Schippers, J. (2010). Productivity of older workers: Perceptions of employers and employees. *Population and Development Review, 36*(2), 309–330.

von Hippel, C., Kalokerinos, E. K., Haanterä, K., & Zacher, H. (2018). Age-based stereotype threat and work outcomes: Stress appraisals and rumination as mediators. *Psychology and Aging*. Retrieved from https://doi-org.blume.stmarytx.edu/10.1037/pag0000308.supp

Vorauer, J. D., Hunter, A. J., Main, K. J., & Roy, S. A. (2000). Meta-stereotype activation: Evidence from indirect measures for specific evaluative concerns experienced by members of dominant groups in intergroup interaction. *Journal of Personality and Social Psychology, 78*(4), 690–707.

Vorauer, J. D., Main, K. J., & O'Connell, G. B. (1998). How do individuals expect to be viewed by members of lower status groups? Content and implications of meta-stereotypes. *Journal of Personality and Social Psychology, 75*(4), 917.

World Health Organization. (2014). *Ageing and the life course: Facts about ageing.* Retrieved November 19, 2018, from http://www.who.int/ageing/about/facts/en

Wrenn, K. A., & Maurer, T. J. (2004). Beliefs about older workers' learning and development behavior in relation to beliefs about malleability of skills, age-related decline, and control 1. *Journal of Applied Social Psychology, 34*(2), 223–242.

Wurm, S., Warner, L. M., Ziegelmann, J. P., Wolff, J. K., & Schüz, B. (2013). How do negative self-perceptions of aging become a self-fulfilling prophecy? *Psychology and Aging, 28*(4), 1088–1097.

CHAPTER SIX

Stereotypes of African Americans

*Sheretta T. Butler-Barnes, Phylicia C. Allen,
Maya A. Williams, and Ashley N. Jackson*

Recently, mainstream media attention has focused on racial encounters involving incidents wherein individuals who identify as African American were treated unjustly while engaging in normal day-to-day activities. These activities include barbequing, grocery shopping, vending, or entering their own homes from a day out. For instance, "BBQ Becky" called 911 on two African American men barbequing in a designated grilling zone; "Permit Patty" called the police on an eight-year-old African American girl for selling water on a sidewalk; and "Pool Patrol Paula" used racial slurs while telling a fifteen-year-old African American boy that he didn't belong at a pool (*Washington Post*, 2018). Moreover, "Coupon Carl" called the police on an African American woman who used a coupon at CVS that the customer service representative did not recognize (*Washington Post*, 2018). "ID Adam" demanded identification from an African American woman in a community pool (*Washington Post*, 2018). "Jogger Joe" destroyed a homeless African American man's belongings (CNN, 2018) while jogging in the neighborhood. These incidents have become commonplace in the United States.

Additional reports gaining national attention include the following incidents: Starbucks, where a report was made to police about two African American men (NPR, 2018); Smith College, where an employee called the police on an African American student for eating lunch there (American

Civil Liberties Union, 2018); and Yale University, where police were called on a student napping in the common area (BBC, 2018). Unfortunately, these racial encounters have become a norm for African Americans in society. The two common denominators in these encounters is that African Americans were the victims and they were innocent. Media reports also show that in all incidents, the aggressor was a White American. Stereotypes drive these racial incidents where African Americans are perceived as breaking the law and are seen as suspicious and/or as not belonging—occupying what is perceived as White space. Identity contingencies (the encounters individuals experience based on their social identity) ultimately influence individual reactions to these experiences (Steele, 2010). Literature shows that these stereotypes are imposed on African Americans and have become socially acceptable (Moskowitz & Carter, 2018).

The media's coverage of these racial encounters has highlighted the unfair actions of others; however, these experiences are not new to African Americans. For example, stereotypes are a result of the attitudes and values one has, influencing the way individuals are perceived and treated, and are likely rooted in the racial profiling of African Americans (Harris, 2006). Historical cases (e.g., slavery, Jim Crow laws, discriminatory housing policies) rooted in systemic oppression give evidence to the views individuals have about minorities and African Americans in particular. This chapter sheds light on cases that have been reported in the United States; however, there are a plethora that remain unreported. Following the inception of the Civil Rights Act, covert forms of racism began to manifest. Hence, racial profiling occurs, whereby an individual is approached and treated differently based on their racial/ethnic background (Harris, 2006). According to the American Civil Liberties Union (2018), racial profiling is defined as the discriminatory practice by law enforcement of targeting individuals suspicious of a crime based on their racial/ethnic group membership, religion, and/or national origin. Although these actions are covert, acts of racial profiling and imposing stereotypes are also enforced by everyday citizens, making it imperative that we acknowledge the different experiences that African Americans face.

Recent data on racial profiling illuminate the disparities in these experiences based on one's racial/ethnic background. For instance, Davis, Whyde, and Langton (2018) found that African Americans were significantly more likely to be stopped by police compared to White Americans and Hispanics. There are also similar findings in terms of street stops while in a public place or a parked car, where African Americans were approached more often. Also, when participants were asked about their most recent contact with the police, African Americans were more likely to experience police-initiated contact compared to Whites. In terms of use of force, during the most recent police-initiated contact, African Americans were twice as likely to experience nonfatal threats or use of force by the police compared to Whites. Types of force included being threatened, handcuffed, pushed/grabbed/hit/kicked, pepper sprayed, shocked, or held at gunpoint.

Antonovics and Knight (2009) examined racial profiling among Boston Police Department law enforcement officers. In this study, they examined the distinction between preference-based discrimination, wherein "police have discriminatory preferences against members of a particular group and act as if there is some nonmonetary benefit associated with arresting or detaining members of that group" (Antonovics & Knight, 2009, p. 2), and statistical discrimination, wherein "law enforcement officials are uncertain about whether a suspect has committed a particular crime" (Antonovics & Knight, 2009, p. 2). They found that when there was a racial mismatch, officers were more likely to search someone if the race of the officer and race of the driver differed. Roh and Robinson (2009) examined traffic stop data on micro and macro levels and found racial disparities in traffic stops and police treatment, particularly in communities where higher numbers of African Americans lived, confirming the hypothesis made around minority threat in which the dominant race (e.g., White Americans) imposes forms of social control on minorities. Prior findings also show that although Whites are arrested for engaging in criminal behavior at higher rates, there is a disproportionately high number of African Americans who are incarcerated (Department of Justice, 2016a, 2016b; Prison Policy Initiative, 2016). Additionally, an analysis of racial stereotyping of criminals from the civil rights movement to the present highlights the rise of the notion of the "criminal predator" used to label African American male youth. These general associations of violence with African Americans as opposed to Whites are due in large part to the War on Drugs during the 1980s (Brooms & Perry, 2016; Welch, 2007).

Thus, based on the catalyst of some of the racialized experiences of African Americans in often unprovoked encounters, targeted racist attacks (e.g., Charleston church shooting), and racial profiling (e.g., Henry Louis Gates Jr.), it's important to understand how stereotypes, beliefs, and endorsements are detrimental to the psychological well-being of African Americans and how they elucidate most of the social problems impacting African Americans today (Steele, 2010). Additionally, based on the role of social identities (race/ethnicity, gender, and class) we center the experiences of African American men and African American women to understand how stereotypes over time have shaped current societal beliefs and attitudes about African Americans.

Guiding Framework

In the current review, we use the Integrative Model for the Study of Stress in Black American Families (Murry, Butler-Barnes, Mayo-Gamble, & Inniss-Thompson, 2018). The model highlights the historical vestiges of slavery and Jim Crow laws (i.e., path A), in particular, how racist practices and policies associated with economic, social, and political structures was the origin of stereotypes for African Americans. These encounters shape African Americans' racialized and gendered experiences as they pertain to racism, prejudice, discrimination, oppression, and marginalization (i.e., path B) while centering their social position—race/ethnicity, social class, and gender (i.e., path C). We emphasize the racialized experiences of African Americans by discussing the genesis of stereotypes and the impact on various developmental competencies. We focus on African American men and African American women by underscoring their racial, gendered, and class experiences. Due to the sociohistorical realities of the experiences of African Americans within the United States, a study of how stereotypes have impacted African American women and African American men is warranted. This review is not to compare or contrast African American women or African American men, but to note the way in which stereotypes have uniquely shaped their experiences. Collectively, paths A to C are associated with the types of stressors (i.e., path D) that African American women and African American men experience and the lasting impact on their development, adjustment, and adaption (i.e., path G). Finally, we suggest specific cultural strength-based coping assets (i.e., path F) that may reduce the negative impact of stereotypes on African Americans' psychological well-being (see Figure 6.1).

Ain't I Woman? African American Women and Stereotypes

The stereotypes of African American women are rooted in in slavery (Collins, 2000). Sarah Baartman's experiences epitomize the negative attitudes and beliefs regarding women of African descent. Baartman was an enslaved African woman who was objectified and put on public display because of her large buttocks and exploited under the name "Hottentot Venus"; this was the impetus for the "Jezebel" stereotype for African American women (Gordon-Chipembere, 2011). Jezebel is a woman who is viewed as promiscuous, loose, and overtly sexual (Davis & Tucker-Brown, 2013; Mitchell & Herring, 1998). Within the biblical text, Jezebel is synonymous with a wicked woman (Revelation 2:20)—sexually immoral. In the present day, this stereotype has persisted through social media (e.g., freaks/sexually promiscuous, gold diggers, and baby mamas) (Medina, 2011; Stephens & Phillips, 2003). These images within the media have a deleterious impact on the development of African American women. Davis and Tucker-Brown (2013) conducted focus groups and interviews with African American younger adult women and found general themes around the negative stereotypes promoted through media. More specifically, they found that endorsement of negative stereotypes was associated with engaging in risky sexual behavior. Townsend, Neilands, Thomas, and Jackson (2010) reported that endorsing more Jezebel stereotypic messages (e.g., sexually promiscuous) was associated with rejection of African

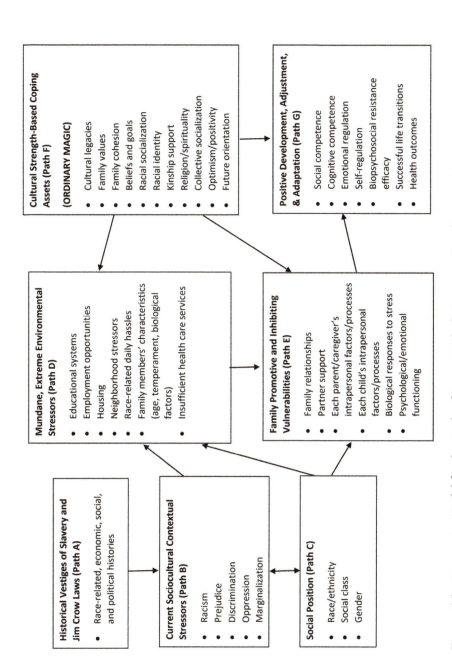

Figure 6.1 Integrative Model for the Study of Stress in Black American Families.

Cultural Strength-Based Coping Assets (Path F)

(ORDINARY MAGIC)

- Cultural legacies
- Family values
- Family cohesion
- Beliefs and goals
- Racial socialization
- Racial identity
- Kinship support
- Religion/spirituality
- Collective socialization
- Optimism/positivity
- Future orientation

Positive Development, Adjustment, & Adaptation (Path G)

- Social competence
- Cognitive competence
- Emotional regulation
- Self-regulation
- Biopsychosocial resistance efficacy
- Successful life transitions
- Health outcomes

Mundane, Extreme Environmental Stressors (Path D)

- Educational systems
- Employment opportunities
- Housing
- Neighborhood stressors
- Race-related daily hassles
- Family members' characteristics (age, temperament, biological factors)
- Insufficient health care services

Family Promotive and Inhibiting Vulnerabilities (Path E)

- Family relationships
- Partner support
- Each parent/caregiver's intrapersonal factors/processes
- Each child's intrapersonal factors/processes
- Biological responses to stress
- Psychological/emotional functioning

Historical Vestiges of Slavery and Jim Crow Laws (Path A)

- Race-related, economic, social, and political histories

Current Sociocultural Contextual Stressors (Path B)

- Racism
- Prejudice
- Discrimination
- Oppression
- Marginalization

Social Position (Path C)

- Race/ethnicity
- Social class
- Gender

American beauty standards, colorism, and engaging in risky behavior for early adolescent African American girls. With regard to the impact of stereotypes on specific developmental periods, younger African American women were more likely to endorse the Jezebel stereotypes (Brown, White-Johnson, & Griffin-Fennell, 2013). Barrie et al. (2016) also noted that the deleterious impact of African American adolescent girls internalizing negative stereotypes was associated with perceived stress.

In addition to being stereotyped as the Jezebel, African American women have also been stereotyped as the "mammy"—the faithful servant (Collins, 2000). The mammy stereotype is the African American woman who is obese and dark-complexioned with African features. She is also subservient, and her primary role is one of domestic service, where she is employed for long hours (see West, 1995). Brown Givens and Monahan (2005) primed participants with either stereotypical images of African American women, such as the mammy or Jezebel, or a nonstereotypic image by watching a video of these exaggerated stereotypes. Findings indicate that during the mock interviews, in comparison to the control group, the experimental group of participants were more likely to associate African American women with these negative stereotypes. In a study conducted by Thomas, Witherspoon, and Speight (2004), results revealed that for African American women, the role of consistently serving others and being nurturing (i.e., mammy stereotype) was a predictor of low self-esteem. Wingfield (2007) interviewed professional African American women about their experiences in their workplace and found that a majority of African American women reported encountering the image of the modern-day mammy.

Another stereotype that African American women are labeled with is the "Sapphire" stereotype. Sapphire is viewed as being aggressive, masculine, hostile, and nagging (e.g., complaining) (West, 2004). This woman is seen as stubborn and bitchy as well (Ladson-Billings, 2009, p. 89). The stereotype also has its roots in the infamous "Amos & Andy" show, which has led to the current casting of African American women as aggressive and nagging (West, 2004). Endorsing this image was associated with poor coping mechanisms for African American women (Walley-Jean, 2009). Additionally, Morris (2007) conducted interviews with school officials and found that many of them labeled Black girls as loud. Interestingly enough, because of these stereotypes—often loaded with stereotypes as being "manly"—this is frequently associated with the sociopolitical plights of the Black family (see Walley-Jean, 2009). More specifically, this negative stereotype of African American women penalizes single African American women and has been suggested as the cause for the deterioration of the Black family (e.g., Moynihan, 1967). In contrast, when not viewed as the Sapphire, African American women are also viewed as the "crack mother" or the "welfare mother" (Carpenter, 2012; Masters, Lindhorst, & Meyers, 2014). For instance, Masters et al. (2014) interviewed caseworkers and found that they often associated African American women as welfare recipients—mirroring some of the negative stereotypes put forth about African American mothers in the Moynihan Report (1967), which continue to be perpetuated (Kennelly, 1999).

Furthermore, several studies have documented the negative stereotypes of African American women as promiscuous, loud, and, most recently, angry (Jones & Shorter-Gooden, 2003; Koonce, 2012; Morris, 2007; Thomas, Hacker, & Hoxha, 2011; Thomas & King, 2007). Most importantly, the views of the "Angry Black Woman" continue to prevail despite the evidence that African American women are less angry than other demographic groups in situations where they receive criticism and perceived disrespect (Walley-Jean, 2009). However, African American women continue to be portrayed as the "Angry Black Woman"—argumentative, aggressive, and confrontational (Smith, 2013; Tyree, 2011). Additionally, due to ideologies enforced through mainstream media, Black women are often viewed based on presumed gendered stereotypes (Anyiwo, Ward, Day Fletcher, & Rowley, 2018). For example, Jerald, Ward, Moss, Thomas, and Fletcher (2017) examined the impact of media on shaping the stereotypes about African American women and found a significant positive association between media exposure (hours of television watched) and perceived realism (content reflective of day-to-day interactions).

Another stereotype associated with African American women is being a "Strong Black Woman," which portrays African American women as resilient, strong, and self-sacrificing (Beauboeuf-Lafontant, 2009; Harrington, Crowther, & Shipherd, 2010; Harris-Lacewell, 2001; Romero, 2000). These images of African American women are situated within previous stereotypes (e.g., mammy) as the strong Black woman who takes care of everybody (Collins, 2004; Mullings, 2002). Conversely, often to her own detriment, this stereotype has negative consequences on health. To demonstrate, the strong Black woman stereotype has a negative impact on mental health, leading to stressful outcomes (Donovan & West, 2015). More importantly, endorsement of the strong Black woman stereotype was also associated with more perceived stress (Woods-Giscombé, 2010) and depression (Beauboeuf-Lafontant, 2009; Collier, Taylor, & Peterson, 2017; Speight, Isom, & Thomas, 2013; Watson & Hunter, 2015; West, Donovan, & Daniel, 2016; Wyatt, 2008).

Overall, the stereotypes associated with African American women have a negative impact on their well-being (Littlefield, 2008). In addition to their racial and gendered experiences, these stereotypes also cut across class. For instance, Hayes (2012) draws parallels between the images and perceptions of African American women in the White House and in academia, referencing the strong Black woman in both cases. In particular, the stereotypes that were often mentioned about Michelle Obama were similar to ways that African American women in higher education are labeled. Despite being an accomplished lawyer and a Princeton and Harvard graduate, she was often viewed in terms of her phenotypic features and as being an angry Black woman. Additionally, Sacks (2018) found that in an effort to avoid being stereotyped, middle-class African American women utilized various strategies to be treated respectfully (e.g., dressing the part), having a role in the healing process with regard to their health, and being educated about their health issues (e.g., cultural health capital). In the instance of health issues, African American women took additional steps to essentially prove that they were educated in what was going on with their bodies and that they could also be helpful in their own healing in hopes of reducing the negative stereotypes associated with African American women.

It is also important to note that metastereotypes (e.g., being aware that others hold negative beliefs and attitudes about your group membership) is detrimental (Vorauer, Main, & O'Connell, 1998). For instance, among African American women, understanding that others hold negative views or stereotypes is associated with higher levels of depression, anxiety, and anger (Jerald, Cole, Ward, & Avery, 2017). With regard to educational outcomes, Chavous, Harris, Rivas, Helaire, and Green (2004), found that stereotypic expectations (perceptions of biased treatment) was associated with a lower sense of belonging, lower academic competence, and lower grade point average.

Currently, an overwhelming amount of research indicates the severe consequences stereotypes have on African American women. Some of the consequences have negative impacts on their families and health outcomes. The aforementioned research reports that negative stereotyping leads to several detrimental outcomes on Black women, including depression, increased stress, and low self-esteem (e.g., Jerald et al., 2017; Woods-Giscombé, 2010). Therefore, additional research on the experiences of African American girls and women is crucial to appropriately understand the effects of these stereotypes in other aspects of their lives. Previous literature could be expanded to discuss their experiences within the health care system, education, employment, and the criminal justice system. Conclusively, it is imperative to listen, respect, and address the concerns of African American girls and women. These conversations could help reduce barriers and increase access to societal resources essential for their future success.

I Can't Breathe! African American Males and Stereotypes

Recently, a woman now publicly recognized as "Cornerstore Carolina" accused a nine-year-old African American boy of sexual assault, only to discover that his bookbag bumped against her (Martinez, 2018). Emmett Till was accused of offending a White woman in a grocery store in 1955; however, recent reports show that the woman lied (see Tyson, 2017). The stereotypes that are often associated with African American men are that they are criminals, lazy, dangerous, and hypersexual (Collins, 2004; hooks, 2004). Similarly, to African American women, stereotypes originated during slavery, beginning with "Sambo." Sambo has its genesis in slavery, as Black men were viewed as dumb, lazy, and often childlike (Boskin, 1988). Black men were also viewed as "savages," who must be tamed like wild animals, and perceived to have low intellectual capacity (Green, 1999). These stereotypes of African American men permeate throughout our society as African American men are racially profiled and continue to be labeled with negative stereotypes (Smith, Allen, & Danley, 2007).

The finding from a case study on aggressive interactions with police officers shows that these encounters can affect the psychosocial functioning of African American men (Brooms & Perry, 2016). These experiences can also extend to the educational setting as stereotypes are often reinforced through racist policies and practices. Due to the historic legacy of African American men and boys being viewed as inferior and loaded with stereotypes— dangerous Black man—these labels exacerbate the school-to-prison pipeline (Carter, Skiba, Arrendondo, & Pollack, 2017). The school-to-prison pipeline stemmed from police presence in schools, over-reliance on punitive discipline, and the increased usage of "zero tolerance" policies, which criminalize trivial transgressions (Heitzeg, 2009). Moreover, the school-to-prison pipeline excludes minority students from quality education time and funnels them into the criminal justice system (Skiba, Arredondo, & Williams, 2014). This occurs through increased detentions, suspensions, expulsions, and referrals to police and juvenile detention centers (Jones, 2013). The school-to-prison pipeline is also reflected in the racial disparities in school suspensions. According to the Department of Education suspension data, African American boys are three times as likely to be suspended as White boys (Crenshaw, Ocen, & Nanda, 2015).

In addition, African American males who engage in adverse behaviors face disapproving stereotypes whereby they are perceived as troublesome and threatening, leading them to receive more frequent and harsh punishment (Monroe, 2005). Instead of focusing on restorative practices, African American males are criminalized by both practitioners who enforce punitive actions and researchers who illuminate this narrative (Monroe, 2005). This disproportionate minority contact is reflected through the system of mass incarceration. Although African Americans only accounted for 13 percent of the total U.S. population, they represented 40 percent of the prison population in 2012 (Fasching-Varner, Mitchell, Martin, & Bennett-Haron, 2014). Therefore, stereotypes that a dominant group may uphold continue to fuel the disproportionately high levels of African American men who make up the U.S. criminal justice system.

Additionally, African American male victims continue to be viewed as the aggressors and blamed for their own deaths in discriminatory racial encounters. Smiley and Fakunle (2016) argue that the role of the media is to fixate on a victim's past or current behavior, phenotypic features (e.g., stature), residential history (e.g., residing in a poor community), and lifestyle. These authors centered their analyses on the killings of six unarmed African American males (i.e., Eric Garner, Michael Brown, Akai Gurley, Tamir Rice, Tony Robinson, and Freddie Gray). Dukes and Gaither (2017) also found that when negative stereotypes about African American men were given, Black men were viewed to be at fault for their own killing. Further, when race was held constant, the shooter was viewed as less at fault when presented with stereotypic information (Dukes & Gaither, 2017). Studies have found that stereotyped phenotypic features of African American men (e.g., skin tone, facial features, and stature) were associated with eyewitness misidentification (Kleider-Offutt, Knuycky, Clevinger, & Capodanno, 2017). This indicates that individuals can be wrongly accused in the criminal justice system, based on a description of African American features. Dixon and Linz (2000), found that African American men were more likely to be portrayed as lawbreakers. With regard to interpersonal violence (e.g., aggressive provocation or escalation), Harrison and Esqueda (1998) found that White Americans were more likely to call the police in interpersonal violent or aggressive situations than an African American male. More specifically, even in aggressive or violent encounters where African American men were innocent, phone calls by others reporting the incident were still more likely to be made than similar instances involving other ethnic groups.

Several studies illuminate the impact of negative stereotypes on African American males' educational outcomes. Robertson and Chaney (2015), found that there were stereotypes associated with the academic ability of African American males that significantly impacted their academic success. Todd, Simpson, Thiem, and Neel (2016) found that stereotyping and awareness of others' perceptions is also associated with a stress response to racism known as racial battle fatigue (e.g., shock, anger, disappointment, anxiety, and fear) for African American men on predominately White campuses. Another study showed that African American male college students have experienced being stereotyped on and off campus through increased surveillance by the police, which has led to psychological stress and feelings of racial battle fatigue (Smith et al., 2007). Similarly, Smith, Mustaffa, Jones, Curry, and Allen (2016) examined African American males' experiences on an elite, predominately White university and found that African American males reported being stereotyped, marginalized, and surveilled, which cause psychological distress.

As a result, because African American men are stereotyped as criminal, thugs, violent, and sexually aggressive (Smiley & Fakunle, 2016; Wendt, 2007), they are more likely to be racially profiled (see Hall, Hall, & Perry, 2016). Research indicates that between the years of 2010 and 2012, Black males were twenty-one times more likely to be killed by a police officer in comparison to White males (Gabnelson, Jones, & Sagara, 2014). Thus, due to the racialized and gendered experiences of African American males, various health consequences contribute to poor health outcomes (Gilbert et al., 2015; Haritatos, Mahalingam, & James, 2007).

Although African American males are also more likely to be associated with negative (e.g., criminal) stereotypes, studies also shed light on stereotypes that are positive (e.g., athletic) can be potentially harmful, too (see Czopp, Monteith, & Mark, 2006). Consequently, the role of being an athlete (e.g., positive), but also being Black (e.g., negative) cannot be separated from one another, indicating that the negative stereotypes of being Black overshadows positive stereotypes (Moskowitz & Carter, 2018). For instance, it was found that White individuals perceive a lack of work ethic from African American men with athletic ability (Moskowitz & Carter, 2018).

Overall, African American men encounter both overt and covert racialized experiences that impact their immediate and long-term outcomes. However, these experiences can alter the ways African American boys and men navigate various spaces, focusing on their strengths and capabilities to overcome these obstacles (Gaylord-Harden, Barbarin, Tolan, & Murry, 2018; Smith et al., 2007). Therefore, continued research could shed light on the experiences of African American boys and men in different contexts. These studies could increase the understanding of their experiences in the United States and aid in the creation of specific interventions.

Conclusion and Future Research

The Integrative Model for the Study of Stress in Black American Families (Murry et al., 2018) places the experiences of African American men and African American women at the center, demonstrating the inception of stereotypes while documenting the detrimental impact it has on the development of Black Americans. However, protective mechanisms (path F), such as racial identity and racial socialization, can buffer against these negative experiences as a result of harmful stereotypes. To demonstrate, Davis, Aronson, and Salimas (2006) found that African American college students who internalized racial identity beliefs had higher GRE scores. In comparison, African American college students who did not endorse a healthy racial identity had lower GRE scores. Adams-Bass, Stevenson, and Kotzin (2014) found that private regard (e.g., "I am proud of the significant accomplishments of Blacks") was associated with viewing more positive Black images in the media as well. Race-related messages provided to adolescents who are coping with racial discrimination experiences may also buffer against internalizing negative stereotypes. Because awareness about one's racial group develops during adolescence, cultivating a healthy, strong racial identity is especially important for African American youth (Swanson, Cunningham, & Spencer, 2003).

The aims of this review were to emphasize the role and effect of stereotypes in the lives of African Americans. Overall, this research highlights the impact stereotypes have on the psychological, educational, and social outcomes of African Americans. As reported in the literature, African American men (Welch, 2007) and African American women experience stereotypes (Davis & Tucker-Brown, 2013); the stereotypical images of African American men and African American women, portrayed through media, influence how this population is viewed in society (Dukes & Gaither, 2017). From a global perspective, understanding the overarching depictions of African Americans and the effects they have on Black individuals, families, and communities is crucial. The primary work of scholars and human service professionals can challenge this narrative by opposing current policies that intentionally depict African Americans as an inferior group, by creating inclusive policies; and by pushing forward positive views of African American women and men.

Results from previous literature and media outlets suggest that the initiation, impact, and outcomes of stereotypes contribute to the way in which African Americans self-identify (Swanson et al., 2003; Davis & Tucker-Brown, 2013; Dukes & Gaither, 2017). Consequently, scholars are encouraged to increase their self-awareness on issues affecting the well-being of African Americans through stereotypes that are repeated and endorsed. This review recommends that future research integrate interventions and practices, which are culturally responsive and address the negative impact stereotypes have had on African Americans. Furthermore, additional literature should expound on qualitative methods that will highlight the voices of African Americans while providing key inside perspective. Ultimately, non-Black individuals can play a crucial role in unpacking, dispelling, and eliminating stereotypes that have harmed African Americans by understanding the cause of stereotype initiation, the perpetuation of these stereotypes, and challenging their existence to create a society that celebrates the positive contributions and aspects of African American communities.

References

Adams-Bass, V. N., Stevenson, H. C., & Kotzin, D. S. (2014). Measuring the meaning of Black media stereotypes and their relationship to the racial identity, Black history knowledge, and racial socialization of African American youth. *Journal of Black Studies, 45*(5), 367–395.

American Civil Liberties Union. (2018). *A Smith College employee called the police on me for eating lunch while Black*. Retrieved from https://www.aclu.org/blog/racial-justice/race-and-criminal-justice/smith-college-employee-called-police-me-eating-lunch

Antonovics, K., & Knight, B. G. (2009). A new look at racial profiling: Evidence from the Boston police department. *The Review of Economics and Statistics, 91*, 163–177.

Anyiwo, N., Ward, L. M., Day Fletcher, K., & Rowley, S. (2018). Black adolescents' television usage and endorsement of mainstream gender roles and the strong Black woman schema. *Journal of Black Psychology, 44*(4), 0095798418771818.

Barrie, R. E., Langrehr, K., Jerémie-Brink, G., Alder, N., Hewitt, A., & Thomas, A. (2016). Stereotypical beliefs and psychological well-being of African American adolescent girls: Collective self-esteem as a moderator. *Counselling Psychology Quarterly, 29*(4), 423–442.

BBC. (2018). *Police called after black Yale student fell asleep in common room.* Retrieved from https://www.bbc.com/news/world-us-canada-44068305

Beauboeuf-Lafontant, T. (2009). *Behind the mask of the strong Black woman: Voice and the embodiment of a costly performance.* Philadelphia, PA: Temple University Press.

Boskin, J. (1988). *Sambo: The rise and demise of an American jester.* New York: Oxford University Press.

Brooms, D. R., & Perry, A. R. (2016). "It's simply because we're Black men": Black men's experiences and responses to the killing of Black men. *The Journal of Men's Studies, 24*(2), 166–184.

Brown, D. L., White-Johnson, R. L., & Griffin-Fennell, F. D. (2013). Breaking the chains: Examining the endorsement of modern Jezebel images and racial-ethnic esteem among African American women. *Culture, Health & Sexuality, 15*(5), 525–539.

Brown Givens, S. M., & Monahan, J. L. (2005). Priming mammies, jezebels, and other controlling images: An examination of the influence of mediated stereotypes on perceptions of an African American woman. *Media Psychology, 7*(1), 87–106.

Carpenter, T. R. (2012). Construction of the crack mother icon. *Western Journal of Black Studies, 36*(4), 264.

Carter, P. L., Skiba, R., Arredondo, M. I., & Pollock, M. (2017). You can't fix what you don't look at: Acknowledging race in addressing racial discipline disparities. *Urban Education, 52*(2), 207–235.

Chavous, T. M., Harris, A., Rivas, D., Helaire, L., & Green, L. (2004). Racial stereotypes and gender in context: African Americans at predominantly Black and predominantly White colleges. *Sex Roles, 51*(1–2), 1–16.

CNN. (2018). *This jogger was caught throwing a homeless man's belongings into a lake. The community wasn't having it.* Retrieved from https://www.cnn.com/2018/06/14/us/jogger -joe-homeless-thrown-in-lake-trnd/index.html

Collier, J. M., Taylor, M. J., & Peterson, Z. D. (2017). Reexamining the "Jezebel" stereotype: The role of implicit and psychosexual attitudes. *Western Journal of Black Studies, 41*, 92–104.

Collins, P. H. (2000). Mammies, matriarchs, and other controlling images. In P. H. Collins (Ed.), *Black feminist thought: Knowledge, consciousness, and the politics of empowerment* (Rev. 10th anniversary ed.). New York: Routledge.

Collins, P. H. (2004). *Black sexual politics: African Americans, gender and the new racism.* New York: Routledge.

Crenshaw, K., Ocen, P., & Nanda, J. (2015). *Black girls matter: Pushed out, overpoliced, and underprotected.* New York: Center for Intersectionality and Social Policy Studies, Columbia University.

Czopp, A. M., Monteith, M. J., & Mark, A. Y. (2006). Standing up for a change: Reducing bias through interpersonal confrontation. *Journal of Personality and Social Psychology, 90*(5), 784.

Davis, C., III, Aronson, J., & Salinas, M. (2006). Shades of threat: Racial identity as a moderator of stereotype threat. *Journal of Black Psychology, 32*(4), 399–417.

Davis, E., Whyde, A., & Langton, L. (2018). *Contacts between police and the public, 2015* (NCJ251145). Washington, D.C.: U.S. Department of Justice, Office of Justice Programs, Bureau of Justice Statistics.

Davis, S., & Tucker-Brown, A. (2013). Effects of black sexual stereotypes on sexual decision making among African American women. *Journal of Pan African Studies, 5*(9), 111–128.

Dixon, T. L., & Linz, D. (2000). Race and the misrepresentation of victimization on local television news. *Communication Research, 27*(5), 547–573.

Donovan, R. A., & West, L. M. (2015). Stress and mental health: Moderating role of the strong black woman stereotype. *Journal of Black Psychology, 41*(4), 384–396.

Dukes, K. N., & Gaither, S. E. (2017). Black racial stereotypes and victim blaming: Implications for media coverage and criminal proceedings in cases of police violence against racial and ethnic minorities. *Journal of Social Issues, 73*(4), 789–807.

Fasching-Varner, K. J., Mitchell, R. W., Martin, L. L., & Bennett-Haron, K. P. (2014). Beyond school-to-prison pipeline and toward an educational and penal realism. *Equity & Excellence in Education, 47*(4), 410–429.

Gabnelson, R., Jones, R. G., & Sagara, E. (2014, October 10). *Deadly force, in Black and White.* Retrieved from http://www.propublica.org/article/deadly-force-in-black-andwhite#update-note

Gaylord-Harden, N. K., Barbarin, O., Tolan, P. H., & Murry, V. M. (2018). Understanding development of African American boys and young men: Moving from risks to positive youth development. *American Psychologist, 73*(6), 753.

Gilbert, K. L., Elder, K., Lyons, S., Kaphingst, K., Blanchard, M., & Goodman, M. (2015). Racial composition over the life course: Examining separate and unequal environments and the risk for heart disease for African American men. *Ethnicity & Disease, 25*(3), 295.

Gordon-Chipembere, N. (Ed.). (2011). *Representation and black womanhood: The legacy of Sarah Baartman.* New York: Springer Publishing Company.

Green, L. (1999). Stereotypes: Negative racial stereotypes and their effect on attitudes toward African-Americans. *Perspectives on Multiculturalism and*

Cultural Diversity, 9(1). Retrieved from http://www.ferris.edu/jimcrow /links/VCU.htm

Hall, A. V., Hall, E. V., & Perry, J. L. (2016). Black and blue: Exploring racial bias and law enforcement in the killings of unarmed black male civilians. *American Psychologist, 71*(3), 175.

Haritatos, J., Mahalingam, R., & James, S. A. (2007). John Henryism, self-reported physical health indicators, and the mediating role of perceived stress among high socio-economic status Asian immigrants. *Social Science & Medicine, 64*(6), 1192–1203.

Harrington, E. F., Crowther, J. H., & Shipherd, J. C. (2010). Trauma, binge eating, and the "strong Black woman." *Journal of Consulting and Clinical Psychology, 78*, 469–479. doi:10.1037/a0019174

Harris, D. A. (2006). US experiences with racial and ethnic profiling: History, current issues, and the future. *Critical Criminology, 14*(3), 213–239.

Harris-Lacewell, M. (2001). No place to rest: African American political attitudes and the myth of Black women's strength. *Women & Politics, 23*(3), 1–33.

Harrison, L. A., & Esqueda, C. W. (1998). Race stereotypes and perceptions about black males involved in interpersonal violence. *Journal of African American Men*, American Psychology-Law Society Biennial Conference, Redondo Beach, CA, March 5–7.

Hayes, D. (2012). The Black woman's burden. *Diverse: Issues in Higher Education, 29*(2), 18–19.

Heitzeg, N. A. (2009). Education or incarceration: Zero tolerance policies and the school to prison pipeline. *Forum on Public Policy, 2009*(2), 21. (ERIC Document Reproduction Service No. EJ870076).

hooks, b. (2004). *We real cool: Black men and masculinity*. New York: Routledge.

Jerald, M. C., Cole, E. R., Ward, L. M., & Avery, L. R. (2017). Controlling images: How awareness of group stereotypes affects Black women's well-being. *Journal of Counseling Psychology, 64*(5), 487.

Jerald, M. C., Ward, L. M., Moss, L., Thomas, K., & Fletcher, K. D. (2017). Subordinates, sex objects, or sapphires? Investigating contributions of media use to Black students' femininity ideologies and stereotypes about Black women. *Journal of Black Psychology, 43*(6), 608–635.

Jones, C., & Shorter-Gooden, K. (2003). *Shifting: The double lives of African American Women in America*. New York: Harper Collins.

Jones, H. T. (2013). *Restorative justice in school communities: Successes, obstacles, and areas for improvement*. Austin, TX: The University of Texas at Austin.

Kennelly, I. (1999). "THAT SINGLE-MOTHER ELEMENT": How white employers typify Black women. *Gender & Society, 13*(2), 168–192.

Kleider-Offutt, H. M., Knuycky, L. R., Clevinger, A. M., & Capodanno, M. M. (2017). Wrongful convictions and prototypical black features: Can a face-type facilitate misidentifications? *Legal and Criminological Psychology, 22*(2), 350–358.

Koonce, J. B. (2012). "Oh, those loud Black girls!": A phenomenological study of Black girls talking with an attitude. *Journal of Language and Literacy Education, 8*(2), 26–46.

Ladson-Billings, G. (2009). "Who you callin' nappy-headed?" A critical race theory look at the construction of Black women. *Race Ethnicity and Education, 12*(1), 87–99.

Littlefield, M. B. (2008). The media as a system of racialization: Exploring images of African American women and the new racism. *American Behavioral Scientist, 51*(5), 675–685.

Martinez, G. (2018). *Woman dubbed "Cornerstore Caroline" faces backlash after falsely accusing a 9-year-old boy of sexual assault.* Retrieved from https://time.com/5426067/cornerstore-caroline-backlash-sexual-assault-boy

Masters, N. T., Lindhorst, T. P., & Meyers, M. K. (2014). Jezebel at the welfare office: How racialized stereotypes of poor women's reproductive decisions and relationships shape policy implementation. *Journal of Poverty, 18*(2), 109–129.

Medina, C. (2011). An alternative strategy: Sex scripts, and women of color. *Social Work and Public Health, 26,* 260–277.

Mitchell, A., & Herring, K. (1998). *What the blues is: Black women overcoming stress and depression.* New York: Perigee.

Monroe, C. R. (2005). Why are "bad boys" always black?: Causes of disproportionality in school discipline and recommendations for change. *The Clearing House: A Journal of Educational Strategies, Issues and Ideas, 79*(1), 45–50.

Morris, E. W. (2007). "Ladies" or "loudies"? Perceptions and experiences of black girls in classrooms. *Youth & Society, 38*(4), 490–515.

Moskowitz, G. B., & Carter, D. (2018). Confirmation bias and the stereotype of the black athlete. *Psychology of Sport and Exercise, 36,* 139–146.

Moynihan, D. P. (1967). *The Negro family: The case for national study action.* In L. Rainwater & W. L. Yancey, *The Moynihan report and the politics of controversy* (pp. 39–124). Cambridge, MA: MIT Press.

Mullings, L. (2002). The sojourner syndrome: Race, class, and gender in health and illness. *Voices, 6*(1), 32–36.

Murry, V. M., Butler-Barnes, S. T., Mayo-Gamble, T. L., & Inniss-Thompson, M. N. (2018). Excavating new constructs for family stress theories in the context of everyday life experiences of Black American families. *Journal of Family Theory & Review, 10*(2), 384–405.

National Public Radio. (2018). *Men arrested at Philadelphia Starbucks speak out; police commissioner apologizes.* Retrieved from https://www.npr.org/sections/thetwo-way/2018/04/19/603917872/they-can-t-be-here-for-us-men-arrested-at-philadelphia-starbucks-speak-out

Prison Policy Initiative. (2016). *Mass incarceration: The whole pie 2016.* Retrieved from https://www.prisonpolicy.org/reports/pie2016.html

Robertson, R. V., & Cassandra, C. (2015). The influence of stereotype threat on the responses of black males at a predominantly White college in the South. *The Journal of Pan African Studies, 7*(8), 20–42.

Roh, S., & Robinson, M. (2009). A geographic approach to racial profiling. *Police Quarterly, 12*, 137–169.

Romero, R. E. (2000). The icon of the strong Black woman: The paradox of strength. In L. C. Jackson & B. Greene (Eds.), *Psychotherapy with African American women: Innovations in psychodynamic perspectives* (pp. 225–238). New York: Guilford Press.

Sacks, T. K. (2018). Performing Black womanhood: A qualitative study of stereotypes and the healthcare encounter. *Critical Public Health, 28*(1), 59–69.

Skiba, R. J., Arredondo, M. I., & Williams, N. T. (2014). More than a metaphor: The contribution of exclusionary discipline to a school-to-prison-pipeline. *Equity and Excellence in Education, 47*(4), 546–564.

Smiley, C., & Fakunle, D. (2016). From "brute" to "thug": The demonization and criminalization of unarmed Black male victims in America. *Journal of Human Behavior in the Social Environment, 26*(3–4), 350–366.

Smith, S. (2013). And still more drama! A comparison of the portrayals of African American women and African American men on BET's College Hill. *Western Journal of Black Studies, 37*, 39–47

Smith, W. A., Allen, W. R., & Danley, L. L. (2007). "Assume the position . . . you fit the description" psychosocial experiences and racial battle fatigue among African American male college students. *American Behavioral Scientist, 51*(4), 551–578.

Smith, W. A., Mustaffa, J. B., Jones, C. M., Curry, T. J., & Allen, W. R. (2016). "You make me wanna holler and throw up both my hands!": Campus culture, Black misandric microaggressions, and racial battle fatigue. *International Journal of Qualitative Studies in Education, 29*(9), 1189–1209.

Speight, S. L., Isom, D. A., & Thomas, A. J. (2013). From Hottentot to superwoman. In E. N. Williams (Ed.), *The handbook of feminist multicultural counseling psychology* (pp. 115–130). Oxford, England: Oxford University Press.

Steele, C. M. (2010). *Whistling Vivaldi: And other clues to how stereotypes affect us (issues of our time)*. New York: W. W. Norton & Company.

Stephens, D. P., & Phillips, L. D. (2003). Freaks, gold diggers, divas, and dykes: The sociohistorical development of adolescent African American women's sexual scripts. *Sexuality & Culture, 7*, 3–47.

Swanson, D. P., Cunningham, M., & Spencer, M. B. (2003). Black males' structural conditions, achievement patterns, normative needs, and "opportunities." *Urban Education, 38*(5), 608–633.

Thomas, A. J., Hacker, J. D., & Hoxha, D. (2011). Gendered racial identity of Black young women. *Sex Roles, 64*(7–8), 530–542.

Thomas, A. J., & King, C. T. (2007). Gendered racial socialization of African American mothers and daughters. *The Family Journal: Counseling and Therapy for Couples and Families, 15*, 137–142.

Thomas, A. J., Witherspoon, K. M., & Speight, S. L. (2004). Toward the development of the stereotypic roles for Black women scale. *Journal of Black Psychology, 30*(3), 426–442.

Todd, A. R., Simpson, A. J., Thiem, K. C., & Neel, R. (2016). The generalization of implicit racial bias to young Black boys: Automatic stereotyping or automatic prejudice? *Social cognition, 34*(4), 306–323.

Townsend, T., Neilands, T., Thomas, A., & Jackson, T. (2010). I'm no Jezebel; I am young, gifted, and Black: Identity, sexuality, and Black girls. *Psychology of Women Quarterly, 34*, 273–285.

Tyree, T. (2011). African American stereotypes in reality television. *Howard Journal of Communications, 22*, 394–413.

Tyson, T. B. (2017). *The blood of Emmett Till.* New York: Simon and Schuster.

U.S. Department of Justice. (2016a). *Crime in the United States, 2016.* Retrieved March 26, 2019, from https://ucr.fbi.gov/crime-in-the-u.s/2016/crime-in -the-u.s.- 2016/topic-pages/tables/table-21

U.S. Department of Justice. (2016b). *Prisoners in 2016.* Retrieved March 26, 2019, from https://www.bjs.gov/content/pub/pdf/p16.pdf

Vorauer, J. D., Main, K. J., & O'Connell, G. B. (1998). How do individuals expect to be viewed by members of lower status groups? Content and implications of meta-stereotypes. *Journal of Personality and Social Psychology, 75*(4), 917.

Walley-Jean, J. C. (2009). Debunking the myth of the "angry Black woman": An exploration of anger in young African American women. *Black Women, Gender & Families, 3*(2), 68–86.

Washington Post. (2018). BBQ Becky, Permit Patty and Cornerstore Caroline: Too "cutesy" for those white women calling police on black people? Retrieved from https://www.washingtonpost.com/news/morning-mix/wp /2018/10/19/bbq-becky-permit-patty-and-cornerstore-caroline -too-cutesy-for-those-white-women-calling-cops-on-blacks

Watson, N. N., & Hunter, C. D. (2015). Anxiety and depression among African American women: The costs of strength and negative attitudes toward psychological help-seeking. *Cultural Diversity and Ethnic Minority Psychology, 21*(4), 604.

Welch, K. (2007). Black criminal stereotypes and racial profiling. *Journal of Contemporary Criminal Justice, 23*(3), 276–288.

Wendt, S. (2007). "They finally found out that we really are men": Violence, nonviolence and Black manhood in the civil rights era. *Gender & History, 19*(3), 543–564.

West, C. M. (1995). Mammy, Sapphire, and Jezebel: Historical images of Black women and their implications for psychotherapy. *Psychotherapy: Theory, Research, Practice, Training, 32*(3), 458.

West, C. M. (2004). Mammy, Jezebel, and Sapphire: Developing an "oppositional gaze" toward the images of black women. In J. C. Chrisler, C. Golden, & P. D. Rozee (Eds.), *Lectures on the psychology of women* (3rd ed., pp. 237–252). Boston: McGraw-Hill.

West, L. M., Donovan, R. A., & Daniel, A. R. (2016). The price of strength: Black college women's perspectives on the strong Black woman stereotype. *Women & Therapy, 39*(3–4), 390–412.

Wingfield, A. H. (2007). The modern mammy and the angry Black man: African American professionals' experiences with gendered racism in the workplace. *Race, Gender & Class, 14,* 196–212.

Woods-Giscombé, C. L. (2010). Superwoman schema: African American women's views on stress, strength, and health. *Qualitative Health Research, 20*(5), 668–683.

Wyatt, J. (2008). Patricia Hill Collins's Black sexual politics and the genealogy of the Strong Black Woman. *Studies in Gender and Sexuality, 9*(1), 52–67.

CHAPTER SEVEN

Latinx Stereotypes: Myths and Realities in the Twenty-First Century

Kara Harris, Angel D. Armenta,
Christine Reyna, and Michael A. Zárate

The history of Latinx populations in the United States is complex and reflects the United States' ambivalent relationship with Latin America broadly (Keller, 2016). On the one hand, Latin American countries are our close neighbors, and Mexico in particular has been a political and economic ally for generations. On the other hand, the United States has engaged in various armed conflicts throughout Latin America, either overtly (e.g., the Mexican-American War), or covertly (e.g., military interventions in El Salvador, Nicaragua, and the "war" on drugs). To this day, the hostilities and mistrust run deep. The United States also has a long history of economic collaboration and immigration with Latin America, which has forged enduring, if often uncomfortable, bonds.

The United States' complex relationship with Latin America often mirrors ambivalent perceptions of people of Latin American descent (called Latinxs). Prevailing stereotypes paint Latinxs as either scourges in our society or as symbols of the promise of the American dream. On one hand, Latinxs are viewed as hardworking (Fox, 2004), but on the other, they are viewed as prone to criminal behavior (Madriz, 1997). They are viewed as incompetent and simultaneously as warm (Fiske, Xu, & Cuddy, 1999). They are viewed as aggressive as well as family-oriented and happy (Kay & Jost, 2003; Kay et al., 2007). More recently, Latinxs have been blamed for economic instability, crime, and unwanted demographic changes in America that paint Latinxs as perpetual threats (Keller, 2016). In this chapter, we will review stereotypes of Latinxs in America and how these beliefs lead to intrapersonal stress, as well as intergroup discord. We will examine the media's role in progressing and maintaining certain stereotypes and their consequences both historically and in modern times.

Stereotypes of Latinxs in America

The Latinx population is the largest ethnic minority population in the country (U.S. Census Bureau, 2017). Yet, the empirical research on stereotypes and prejudice toward Latinx groups is surprisingly small given the size and influence of this group and their salience in media and political discourse. Multiple studies investigate how Latinx *immigrants* (particularly from Mexico) are viewed (see "Latinx as Foreign" below), but relatively few studies investigate how Americans of Latin American descent, or any other specific Latinx groups, are viewed. One reason for the lack of research, may be that researchers (like the rest of the population) are vulnerable to the outgroup homogeneity effect (Ostrom & Sedikides, 1992), wherein Latinx groups might appear to be one monolithic group with a common heritage and experience (Menéndez Alarcón, 2014). For instance, the stereotype that "Latinxs are immigrants" or are otherwise foreign may diminish the need to explore these stereotypes beyond anti-immigrant stereotypes.

As a result, there are few actual studies that have focused on the content of Latinx stereotypes and how those stereotypes influence day to day treatment of Latinx individuals. In the following sections, we hope to broaden the understanding of Latinx stereotypes. We will review the three prevailing stereotypes about Latinxs in America (i.e., Latinxs as foreign, criminals, and low-skill laborers), examine the gendered nature of Latinx stereotypes, and address some of the consequences of these stereotypes.

Latinxs as Foreign

According to the Pew Research Center, there are 56.5 million Latinxs living in the U.S., but only about a third are foreign-born (Flores, 2017). Despite this fact, the tendency to conflate "Latinx" with immigrant, and unauthorized immigrant in particular, drives much of the stereotyping regarding the Latinx population. In an investigation of ethnic/racial minority stereotypes, "illegal immigrant" and "speaks with an accent" were the two most prevalent stereotypes of Latinxs (Zou & Cheryan, 2017, Study 3). Although Latinx Americans and Black Americans share stereotypes associated with lower status (e.g., less intelligent, less competent, and more prone to crime; Zou & Cheryan, 2017), Latinxs (but not Blacks) are associated with stereotypes related to foreignness.

In the United States, one might label ethnic/racial groups along two dimensions: their "intellectual, economic or occupational prestige" (inferiority-superiority) and a group's perceived distance between the prototypes of dominant/majority group and foreign (foreign-American). To test this racial positioning model, Zou and Cheryan (2017) examined a variety of racial/ethnic groups in America, including Latinx, Black, Asian, and White. They report that Latinx populations, even U.S.-born citizens, are perceived as both inferior and foreign compared to White Americans. Blacks were also seen as inferior, but they were seen as relatively more American.

A group's position along the foreignness dimension has consequences. Latinxs are often treated like unwanted and unassimilable strangers (Molina, 2014; Ngai, 2014; Takaki, 1998). When participants were asked to indicate positive attributes of European and Latinx individuals, participants reported over forty positive items for Europeans (who are seen as more similar to Americans; Devos & Banaji, 2005) but only sixteen for Latinxs (Tomkiewicz & Adeyemi-Bello, 1997). The more Latinxs are perceived as foreign, the fewer opportunities are granted to them and the lower their sense of belonging in their own country (Dovidio, Gluszek, John, Ditlmann, & Lagunes, 2010). Thus, Latinx U.S. citizens are much more likely to experience pressures to "go back to where [they] came from" than are groups low in foreignness.

The representation of Latinxs in the media perpetuates stereotypes of Latinxs as "illegal aliens," "foreign," or "illegal immigrants" who are threatening U.S. domestic populations and the cultural values of America (Chávez, 2013; Mastro, Tukachinsky, Behm-Morawitz, & Blecha, 2014; Steinberg, 2004; Zárate, Garcia, Garza, & Hitlan, 2004). Recently, prejudice toward Latinx groups has been amplified by the rise in nationalist, protectionist, and anti-immigrant rhetoric and policies in the United States. For example, in 2015, then-presidential candidate Donald Trump galvanized potential voters around foreboding anti-Latinx stereotypes. He famously stated: "When Mexico sends its people, they're not sending their best. They're not sending you. . . . They're sending people that have lots of problems, and they're bringing those problems with us. They're bringing drugs. They're bringing crime. They're rapists. And some, I assume, are good people" (*Washington Post*, 2015, June 16).

Although Mr. Trump was referring to Mexican immigrants, these stereotypes affected Latinx people across America, regardless of their citizenship status (due in part to the broad bush used to paint Latinxs as foreign). Hostile or discriminatory rhetoric by national leaders can change norms and make it more acceptable to express prejudice against stereotyped groups. After President Trump was elected, individuals reported greater willingness to express prejudice toward groups directly targeted by President Trump (like Latinxs) but did not express more prejudice toward groups not targeted by Trump (Crandall, Miller, & White, 2018). There has also been an increase in anti-Latinx hate crimes. According to FBI statistics, hate crimes doubled after the 2016 election, with the most dramatic increase in hate crimes against Latinx, which increased by 176 percent (Levin, Nolan, & Reitzel, 2017).

In addition to hate crimes, day-to-day harassment of Latinx people also appears more prevalent. Social media is replete with examples of individuals harassing others simply for speaking Spanish, be it in a supermarket, restaurant, park, or just walking down the street. In all these instances, all the bystanders knew about the victims was that they spoke Spanish. English-only speakers express more anger and prejudice when they feel alienated by Spanish speakers (Hitlan, Zarate, Kelly, & DeSoto, 2016). Speaking a language other than English can serve as a cue signaling foreignness, insularity, and incompatible cultures and worldviews.

Stereotypes of Latinxs as foreigners in America can trigger both realistic and symbolic threats. Realistic threats consist of barriers to the political, economic, or educational welfare of the ingroup (Esses, Jackson, & Armstrong, 1998). Symbolic threats come from the perception of differences in morals, traditions, values, or norms between the ingroup and outgroup (Stephan, Ybarra, & Morrison, 2008). When cultural norms are threatened (e.g., English as the common language in America), fear of change may rise in non-Latinx Americans. This fear can manifest as pressure from the ingroup to suppress the outgroup's culture and force them to assimilate into the ingroup (Esses et al., 1998; Zárate et al., 2004). In social media, we see this assimilation motive in people berating Latinx to "speak English since this is America," which highlights both symbolic threat and the common stereotype that "all Latinxs are immigrants."

Symbolic threats are also associated with the desire to be rid of the worldview-threatening outgroup; they can manifest as anything from social distancing to isolationist policies to genocide (Esses et al., 1998; Stephan et al., 2008). Thus, stereotypes of foreignness can have life-altering consequences for Latinx Americans. One recent example concerns immigration laws. Arizona law SB 1070, for instance, required Arizona law enforcement to detain and possibly arrest individuals that police have a "reasonable suspicion" of being an immigrant. As a result, police targeted and sometimes arrested and deported U.S. citizens of Latinx descent for not carrying identification at all times. The policy inspired similar laws to be passed around the country (Archibold, 2010). A recent report found that 59 percent of second-generation Latinx citizens reported being asked for proof of citizenship by law enforcement (Morales, Delgado, & Curry, 2018). These laws were in violation of basic human rights for all Latinxs, especially those of lower-income status, just because they "looked illegal" (Archibold, 2010). (For more on stereotypes of immigrants, see the "Stereotypes of Immigrants" chapter in this volume.)

Latinxs as Criminals

The stereotypes of Latinxs as foreign is associated with another stereotype—that Latinxs are criminals. As implied in the quote from Donald Trump above, a prevailing narrative is that Latinxs (who "come to this country") are drug dealers, gang members, and lawbreakers. "Criminal" is among the top ten most common stereotypes of Latinxs (Zou & Cheryan, 2017), and one of the most common stereotypes of a criminal is being Black or Latinx (or recent immigrant; Madriz, 1997). The stereotypical Latinx criminal is perceived to have short hair, dark skin, tattoos, and baggy clothing (MacLin & Herrera, 2006). However, some of these attributes (e.g., ill-fitting clothing) can also be signs of poverty rather than criminality.

The association between Latinxs and crime has been a persistent stereotype throughout U.S. history. In times of economic stress, cultural flux, or shifts in the dominant groups' social and/or political status, the Latinx community has been a scapegoat. Vivid stereotypes of criminal and opportunistic "foreigners" fuel those accusations. Whether Latinxs were portrayed as wild "banditos" in the nineteenth century or as abusive alcoholics, gang-banging "Cholos," or murderous members of drug cartels in more modern times (Brown, 2016), Latinx people have been stereotyped as dangerous and prone to crime (Reyna, Dobria, & Wetherell, 2013; see Holmes, Smith, Freng, & Muñoz, 2008).

The media plays a role in cultivating these stereotypes. Latinxs are more likely than Whites to be portrayed in the media as perpetrators of crime, whereas Whites are more likely to be portrayed as defenders of the law (Dixon & Linz, 2000). These patterns can have important consequences for how Latinxs are perceived by the broader society. The majority of non-Latinx Americans have few meaningful encounters with the Latinx culture and its people (Martinez, 2014). This lack of social contact can lead to an overreliance on the media to shape beliefs about Latinx people, whether positively or negatively (Martinez, 2014). If Latinx people are predominantly portrayed in the media as threatening or violent, these stereotypes can have dire consequences.

One consequence is how Latinxs are treated in the criminal justice system. These stereotypes can influence every stage of the criminal justice process. Police officers are exposed to the same media and stereotypes as the general public, and the prevalence of negative stereotypes about Latinxs related to criminality, illegal immigration, and social/economic instability likely influences police-citizen relations (Epstein & Goff, 2011; Timberlake, Howell, Grau, & Williams, 2015). Police brutality is positively correlated with percentage of Latinxs in a population and the ratio of Latinx citizens to Latinx police officers (Smith & Holmes, 2003). Among minority groups in the United States, Latinxs are second to Blacks in number of police stops, use-of-force incidents, and fatal police shootings (Downs, 2016; Goldstein, 2013; Hyland, Langton, & Davis, 2015).

Trust in police has suffered because of the Latinx crime stereotype. Traditionally, Latinxs have trusted their community police officers and reported being confident that the police in the community will enforce the law in a fair manner (Lopez & Livingston, 2009). Since the Trump administration entered the White house and promoted extreme anti-immigrant policies against Latinx immigrants, cities with high Latinx populations (e.g., Los Angeles and Houston) have reported a significant drop in Latinxs who report crime—perhaps an indication of growing mistrust toward police officers and other authority figures (Arthur, 2017).

The impact of the "Latinxs-are-criminals" stereotype is also reflected in how Latinxs are treated in the courts. Latinxs, especially those of low socio-economic status, are more likely to receive harsher punishments compared to Whites for the same offense (Willis-Esqueda, Espinoza, & Culhane, 2008). This can lead to overrepresentation of Latinxs in our prisons. For example, Latinxs account for 17.8 percent of those residing within the United States (U.S. Census Bureau, 2017) but make up approximately 40 percent of all sentenced federal offenders (Pew Research Center, 2009). The number of Latinx federal offenders has nearly doubled since in the 1990s.

Another factor is how prevailing stereotypes intersect with prominent issues of the day. In 1991, during the height of the "war on drugs," 60 percent of crimes involving Latinxs were drug related, and only 20 percent were immigration related. At a time when drug crime was largely associated with Latinxs, federal court data from the 1990s suggest that Latinxs received harsher punishment for drug offenses than other groups (Steffensmeier & Demuth, 2000), which partially accounted for their higher incarceration rates. Due to shifts in political priorities and the perception of the ways Latinxs break the law, the reasons for incarceration have shifted. In 2007, 48 percent of Latinx offenders were sentenced to federal courts for immigration related offenses and only 37 percent for drug offenses (Pew Research Center, 2009). Thus, incarceration rates are at least partially influenced by policy priorities and how Latinx stereotypes relate to these issues.

Political attitudes and voting behaviors may also be influenced by Latinx crime-related stereotypes. An analysis of GOP debates in the last few election cycles revealed that Latinx populations (especially Latinx immigrants) were regularly framed in terms of crime, suggesting that conservative politicians view this frame as effective in mobilizing their voting base (Brown, 2016).

This strategy is not new. Support for California's Proposition 187—legislation in 1994 designed to prevent unauthorized immigrants from getting government assistance and education—was associated (at least partly) with negative attitudes and perceived realistic threat from Mexicans and "commitment to legal obedience" (Lee, Ottati, & Hussain, 2001).

The stereotype that Latinxs (especially immigrants), are associated with crime is misguided. Often referred to as the "immigrant paradox," crime rates are lower across the country in places with high immigrant populations, which in the United States, tend to be Latinx immigrants (Martinez, Stowell, & Lee, 2010). For example, neighborhoods with large Latinx immigrant communities actually have lower rates of violent crime compared to communities with lower numbers of immigrants (Martinez et al., 2010), a trend due to a variety of factors beyond underreporting crime (see Martinez & Lee, 2000). Thus, the criminal stereotype is partially driven by the increased incarceration of Latinxs at disproportional rates. Latinxs are more likely to be stopped by police, arrested, and sentenced longer for the same offenses than are Whites. However, the Latinx paradox and crime rates along the border suggest that the Latinx-criminal stereotype, like most stereotypes, is misleading.

Latinxs as (Uneducated, Low-Skill) Laborers

When Americans think of Latinxs, a particular type of person often comes to mind: poor, uneducated, low-skilled people doing manual or service labor. Content analyses of television shows find that Latinxs are commonly portrayed as having nonprofessional occupations and low authority in the workplace (Mastro & Behm-Morawitz, 2005). This stereotype results in a paradox: Latinxs are often seen as low-skilled but hardworking laborers (Brammer, 2016), who are simultaneously seen as lazy (Fox, 2004). This contradiction stems in part from the pervasive stereotype that Latinxs are mostly immigrants. First-generation Latinxs, in particular, tend to have lower wages and educational attainment (Kochhar, 2005), but this association decreases dramatically with subsequent generations. It is also true that, historically, Latinxs occupy a large percentage of nonprofessional and service-related jobs such as janitorial work and food preparation (Kochhar, 2005).

Despite the fact that these jobs contribute to economic stability in the United States, these jobs do not have prestige and have very little job security during nationwide economic downturns. During the great recession (2007–2009), for instance, lack of job security led to many Latinxs losing their jobs. The Latinx unemployment rate reached a peak of 12.7 percent in 2009 compared to 5.9 percent at the start of the recession (Kochhar, 2014), further contributing to the "Latinx as lazy" stereotype. In reality, Latinxs come from a wide array of socioeconomic statuses and occupations; however, the overrepresentation of Latinxs in low-waged jobs has led to an overrepresentation of Latinxs in poverty—22 percent of Latinxs live in poverty compared to the national average of 14.2 percent (Flores, Lopez, & Radford, 2017).

Since the economic recovery, however, job growth has brought many Latinxs back to work, especially in industries such as manufacturing and service (Kochhar, 2014). However, this trend can activate another common stereotype—that Latinxs steal jobs from hardworking, White Americans (Citrin, Green, Muste, & Wong, 1997). The perception of Latinxs as sources of realistic threat is triggered when rhetoric associating Latinxs to job loss and wage suppression are in the news. The narrative of jobs being stolen is one threat that is consistently associated with Latinxs in America (Esses et al., 1998) and can lead to discrimination in labor, housing, and other opportunities for all members of the Latinx community, including citizens (Esses et al., 1998; Zárate et al., 2004).

Whites' jobs loss to Latinxs, especially Latinx immigrants, is often misunderstood. Although a higher number of jobs after the recession went to Latinxs and other minority groups compared to Whites, it is partly due to the fact that fewer Whites were unemployed during the recession compared to people of color, and thus a higher number of people of color, especially Latinxs, re-entered the workforce (Jan, 2016). Furthermore, many of these jobs are jobs that are not desirable to many White Americans because they are dangerous or involve long hours of manual labor (Felbab-Brown, 2017). This argument is reflected on both sides of the political spectrum supporting Latinx labor. It is argued that if Latinxs were denied the opportunity to work in the United States, then no one would do the "jobs Americans don't want to do" (Brammer, 2016).

Contact with members of the Latinx community can influence which contradictory stereotype (hard working vs. lazy) a person believes. The extent to which people believe these stereotypes is related to Latinx population size (Fox, 2004). Overall, as the Latinx population increases in a given region, the more positive perceptions Whites have regarding Latinxs' work ethic. When the proportion of Latinxs to Whites is small, Latinxs are seen as lazier (Fox, 2004).

Despite disparaging stereotypes portraying Latinxs as low-skilled and/or lazy, Latinxs in America are largely a success story. Latinxs are more likely than White Americans to believe in the American dream and that one can get ahead if one is willing to work hard (Taylor, Lopez, Martinez, & Velasco, 2012). Belief in this American ethos largely reflects the progress made by Latinxs regarding new business and entrepreneurship. According to the Stanford Latino Entrepreneurship Initiative (Orozco, Oyer, & Porras, 2018), between 2007 and 2012, the growth rate of Latinx firms outpaced the growth rate of firms by all other racial/ethnic groups. Finally, and contradicting stereotypes of Latinas in particular (see below), nearly half of new Latinx businesses are Latina owned firms (compared to a third of White firms owned by women). Using new business startups as the key indicator, the economic outlook for Latinxs in America is tremendous; with most growth models demonstrating greater economic growth for Latinx businesses than non-Latinx businesses.

Gendered Stereotypes of Latinxs

To fully understand Latinx stereotypes in America, it is important to recognize that Latinx stereotypes are largely gender-specific. Only 3.9 percent of prime-time television shows include Latinxs (Mastro & Behm-Morawitz, 2005), and many of these media portrayals regularly reinforce gender-specific stereotypes. Latinos are often portrayed as either simple laborers, threatening criminals, or charismatic Latin Lovers—but always traditionally masculine. Latinas in the media are also portrayed with diametric imagery. Latinas are either portrayed as the "fiery Latina" (i.e., verbally aggressive, lazy, and unintelligent; Mastro & Behm-Morawitz, 2005), the "sexual temptress" who uses her sex appeal to manipulate others, or as "the virgin" (i.e., obedient, Catholic, and family-oriented; Rodríguez, 2008).

A popular framework reflecting the gendered stereotypes of Latinxs is "machismo and marianismo" (Stevens, 1973). Machismo (attributed to Latinos) is perceived to be exaggerated toughness and male chauvinism, whereas marianismo (attributed to Latinas) is an exaggerated sense of submission (to men), efforts to fit traditional domestic roles, and a desire to have a lot of children. However, data contradict these stereotypes. When Latinxs are asked if husbands should have a final say in family matters, only 24 percent of Latinas agree, while half of Latinos agree. These beliefs do not differ by generation status in the United States—61 percent of first-, second-, and third-generation Latinxs report that husbands should not have a final say in family matters (Pew Research Center, 2009).

Another manifestation of the machismo stereotype is that Latinos are more likely to abuse their female partners. Again, research on relationship violence dispels this stereotype. The literature shows that intimate partner violence is as frequent in Latinx relationships as it is in non-Latinx relationships (Klevens, 2007). Furthermore, current research demonstrates that intimate partner violence committed by Latinos is unrelated to their degree of acculturation to U.S. culture (Alvarez, Oviedo Ramirez, Frietze, Field, & Zarate, 2018). Thus, male dominance as a function of Latinx culture is not supported by the empirical evidence.

Just as negative stereotypes can carry consequences for Latinos, so too can the stereotypes of Latinas. Latinas are highly sexualized in the media. The belief that Latinas are overly sexual "baby-making machines" feeds into narratives about Latinxs exploiting welfare and the social safety net and increases concerns about the changing demographic and cultural makeup of America. At the most extreme, President Donald Trump has proposed ending birthright citizenship (i.e., the law that anyone born in the United States is automatically a citizen) in order to discourage pregnant immigrants from Latin America coming to the United States (Davis, 2018).

These "baby-making machine" stereotypes contradict the life priorities of Latinxs. Latinxs report that being successful in a career is more important to them than having children, being married, living a religious life, or being wealthy (Pew Research Center, 2009). For Latinxs between the ages of sixteen and twenty-five, more report being successful in a career as an important life priority compared to the general population. Moreover, those in the general population are more likely than Latinxs to report that having children is an important life priority (Pew Research Center, 2009).

The Impact of Stereotypes on Latinxs' Psychological Well-Being

Benevolent and hostile stereotypes displayed in the media can influence how Latinxs in America see themselves, their cultural identity, and their place in their community. Because of the disparaging implications of many Latinx stereotypes, those in the Latinx community may feel the need to alter their behavior for fear of confirming negative stereotypes associated with their ethnic group—called stereotype threat (Steele & Aronson, 1995). Stereotype threat can have negative psychological and performance consequences that result from the stress of trying to disprove stereotypes, and can arise in different settings such as professional, academic, athletic or interpersonal settings where a stereotype might be applied (Steele, 2011). For Latinxs, negative stereotypes of their ethnic group cause psychological distress that interferes with achievement-based performance and interactions in day-to-day encounters (Ojeda, Navarro, Meza, & Arbona, 2012).

In academic settings, Latinx students face stereotypes portraying them as unproductive, illiterate, and unintelligent by non-Latinx teachers and classmates (Ojeda et al., 2012; Reyna, 2000). A meta-analysis found that teachers hold lower expectations for Latinx students than for White students (Tenenbaum & Ruck, 2007). Presenting Latinx students with easier materials or not giving enough attention causes both stereotype threat and self-fulfilling prophecies (Guyll, Madon, Prieto, & Scherr, 2010), both of which reduce student performance. Such educational biases against Latinx students begin in preschool and grade school and can be perpetuated by the family (through lower parent involvement) and/or educational system (through prolonged neglect and reduced opportunities for Latinx students, especially English-language learners) (Verdugo, 2006). Reduced expectations can reduce motivation, reinforce the belief that they and/or their group are inadequate (Guyll et al., 2010; Reyna, 2000; Tenenbaum & Ruck, 2007), and can eventually lead to disengagement from domains wherein they are stereotyped, like academic settings (Reyna & Zimmerman, 2017; Woodcock, Hernandez, Estrada, & Schultz, 2012). For example, a lifetime of resisting negative stereotypes and discrimination can undermine dreams to go to college (Llagas & Snyder, 2003; Verdugo, 2006). Constant vigilance to disprove stereotypes also carries over into social interactions wherein Latinxs are hypervigilant in interactions with non-Latinx people, which can lead to lower self-esteem over time (Ojeda et al., 2012; Shorey, Cowan, & Sullivan, 2002).

Ethnic identity plays a major role in the awareness of discrimination and the fear of confirming a stereotype (Erba, 2017). Latinxs with strong ethnic identity are more prone to stereotype threat compared to those with low ethnic identity (Armenta, 2010; Erba, 2017). Furthermore, those who identify strongly with their Latinx heritage experience more cognitive overload from chronic efforts to distance themselves from the negative stereotypes about their group, compared to Latinxs who are less ethnically identified (Contrada et al., 2001). As a result, some Latinxs may start to disassociate from their ethnic group if they struggle with separating negative stereotypes from their ethnic identity (Contrada et al., 2001). This disassociation, called ethnic group conformity (Contrada et al., 2000), happens when individuals trying to disassociate from stereotypes purposefully disassociate from their culture. This can have consequences within the Latinx community as well. For example, in academic settings, Latinx students' pressure to achieve in a White world can lead to accusations of them being "a coconut" (i.e., brown on the outside, White on the inside), "acting White," and being "disloyal to the Latinx culture" (Lopez, 2005). Regardless, stereotype threat coupled with ethnic identity in Latinxs causes high levels of stress and a decrease in self-esteem due to pressures from either the ingroup or the outgroup, or both (Contrada et al., 2000).

Despite this, ethnic identity can also be a protective factor. Having a positive ethnic identity can improve psychological well-being, social interactions, and coping mechanisms when faced with prejudice and discrimination (Umaña-Taylor, Diversi, & Fine, 2002; see also Reyna & Zimmerman, 2017). Strong ethnic identity predicts greater educational attainment, fewer unplanned pregnancies, and less alcohol abuse (Rivas-Drake et al., 2014).

Conclusion

Latinxs in America face unique discrimination due to the stereotypes associated with them. Stereotypes paint an unflattering and often inaccurate portrayal of their citizenship status, moral integrity, occupations, gender roles, intelligence, and the overall threat that they pose to Americans and American values. Disparaging stereotypes, perpetuated through media, politicians, and

U.S. culture, create challenges for the Latinx community both externally (e.g., discrimination) and internally (e.g., stereotype threat). There are, however, multiple driving factors that predict the widespread prejudice Latinx communities face. In a classic example of the outgroup homogeneity effect, policies that are intended to police a subset of the Latinx population have repercussions to the whole community. For example, Latinxs in general are seen as foreign, and laws designed to target undocumented immigrants threaten all Latinxs in America, including Latinx citizens. Stereotypes also influence the daily discrimination Latinxs face (e.g., narrow job choices with few opportunities for advancement), which in turn perpetuates other stereotypes pertaining to work ethic and Latinx culture (e.g., laziness or lower skill).

Moreover, the recent political rhetoric has increased the discrimination Latinxs face. Consistent with the influence of norms and leadership on group-level prejudice (e.g., Crandall et al., 2018), as the negative rhetoric regarding Latinx communities increases, so have the instances of daily discrimination and hate crimes. It is no accident that the increase in hate crimes is particularly high for Latinx (and Muslim) populations—the groups targeted in recent political rhetoric (e.g., Müller & Schwarz, 2018). Thus, leadership and norms matter. As the Latinx population continues to grow, so does the perception of threat and prejudice among Americans toward Latinxs (Craig & Richeson, 2014; see Zárate, Reyna, & Alvarez, 2019 for review). Simply reminding Whites that they will no longer be the majority group triggers anti-immigrant and antiminority attitudes and prejudice (Outten, Schmitt, Miller, & Garcia, 2012). The increasing prejudice Latinx communities face is in direct contrast to the limited empirical research that has examined the content and veracity of these stereotypes. Contrary to the perceptions of threat and negative stereotypes, Latinxs have enriched our economy, culture, policies, and progress as a nation (New American Economy, 2017).

References

Alvarez, M., Ramirez, S. O., Frietze, G., Field, C., & Zarate, M. A. (2018). A meta-analysis of Latinx acculturation and intimate partner violence. *Trauma, Violence, & Abuse*, 1524838018801327. doi:10.1177/1524838018 801327

Archibold, R. C. (2010, April 23). Arizona enacts stringent law on immigration. *The New York Times*. Retrieved from https://www.nytimes.com/2010/04 /24/us/politics/24immig.html

Armenta, B. E. (2010). Stereotype boost and stereotype threat effects: The moderating role of ethnic identification. *Cultural Diversity and Ethnic Minority Psychology, 16*(1), 94–98.

Arthur, R. (2017, May 18). Latinos in three cities are reporting fewer crimes since Trump took office. *Five Thirty Eight*. Retrieved from https://fivethirtyeight

.com/features/latinos-report-fewer-crimes-in-three-cities-amid
-fears-of-deportation/

Brammer, J. P. (2016, September 24). Latinos are more than "The jobs Americans don't want to do." *Huffington Post.* Retrieved from https://www .huffingtonpost.com/john-paul-brammer/latinos-are-more-than-the b8189724.html

Brown, J. A. (2016). Running on fear: Immigration, race and crime framings in contemporary GOP presidential debate discourse. *Critical Criminology, 24*(3), 315–331.

Chávez, L. R. (2013). *The Latino threat: Constructing immigrants, citizens, and the nation.* Stanford, CA: Stanford University Press.

Citrin, J., Green, D. P., Muste, C., & Wong, C. (1997). Public opinion toward immigration reform: The role of economic motivations. *The Journal of Politics, 59*(3), 858–881.

Contrada, R. J., Ashmore, R. D., Gary, M. L., Coups, E., Egeth, J. D., Sewell, A., . . . Chasse, V. (2000). Ethnicity-related sources of stress and their effects on well-being. *Current Directions in Psychological Science, 9,* 136–139.

Contrada, R. J., Ashmore, R. D., Gary, M. L., Coups, E., Egeth, J. D., Sewell, A., . . . Goyal, T. M. (2001). Measures of ethnicity-related stress: Psychometric properties, ethnic group differences, and associations with well-being. *Journal of Applied Social Psychology, 31,* 1775–1820.

Craig, M. A., & Richeson, J. A. (2014). More diverse yet less tolerant? How the increasingly diverse racial landscape affects white Americans' racial attitudes. *Personality and Social Psychology Bulletin, 40*(6), 750–761.

Crandall, C., Miller, J. M., & White, M. H. (2018). Changing norms following the 2016 U.S. presidential election: The Trump effect on prejudice. *Social Psychological and Personality Science, 9,* 186–192. doi:10.1177/1948550617 750735

Davis, J. H. (2018, October 30). President wants to use executive order to end birthright citizenship. *The New York Times.* Retrieved from https://www .nytimes.com/2018/10/30/us/politics/trump-birthright-citizenship.html

Devos, T., & Banaji, M. R. (2005). American = white? *Journal of Personality and Social Psychology, 88*(3), 447–466.

Dixon, T. L., & Linz, D. (2000). Overrepresentation and underrepresentation of African Americans and Latinos as lawbreakers on television news. *Journal of Communication, 50*(2), 131–154.

Dovidio, J. F., Gluszek, A., John, M. S., Ditlmann, R., & Lagunes, P. (2010). Understanding bias toward Latinos: Discrimination, dimensions of difference, and experience of exclusion. *Journal of Social Issues, 66*(1), 59–78.

Downs, K. (2016). Why aren't more people talking about Latinos killed by police? *PBS Newshour.* Retrieved from https://www.pbs.org/newshour /nation/black-men-werent-unarmed-people-killed-police-last-week

Epstein, L. M., & Goff, P. A. (2011). Safety or liberty?: The bogus trade-off of cross-deputization policy. *Analyses of Social Issues and Public Policy, 11*(1), 314–324.

Erba, J. (2017). Media representations of Latina/os and Latino students stereotype threat Behavior. *Howard Journal of Communications, 29*(1), 83–102. doi:10.1080/10646175.2017.1327377

Esses, V. M., Jackson, L. M., & Armstrong, T. L. (1998). Intergroup competition and attitudes toward immigrants and immigration: An instrumental model of group conflict. *Journal of Social Issues, 54*(4), 699–724.

Felbab-Brown, V. (2017, August). The wall: The real costs of a barrier between the United States and Mexico. *Brookings.* Retrieved from https://www .brookings.edu/essay/the-wall-the-real-costs-of-a-barrier-between-the -united-states-and-mexico/

Fiske, S. T., Xu, J., & Cuddy, A. C. (1993). (Dis)respecting versus (Dis)liking: Status and interdependence predict ambivalent stereotypes of competence and warmth. *Journal of Social Issues, 55*(3), 473–489.

Flores, A. 2017. *Facts on U.S. Latinos, 2015.* Retrieved from https://www .pewresearch.org/hispanic/2017/09/18/facts-on-u-s-latinos

Flores, A., Lopez, G., & Radford, J. (2017, September 18). Facts on U.S. Latinos, 2015. *Pew Research Center.* Retrieved from https://www.pewhispanic.org /2017/09/18/facts-on-u-s-latinos-trend-data/

Fox, C. (2004). The changing color of welfare? How Whites' attitudes toward Latinos influence support for welfare. *American Journal of Sociology, 110*(3), 580–625.

Goldstein, J. (2013, April 12). Judge rejects New York's stop-and-frisk policy. *The New York Times.* Retrieved from https://www.nytimes.com/2013/08/13 /nyregion/stop-and-frisk-practice-violated-rights-judge-rules.html (last viewed: 3/29/19).

Guyll, M., Madon, S., Prieto, L., & Scherr, K. C. (2010). The potential roles of self-fulfilling prophecies, stigma consciousness, and stereotype threat in linking Latino/a ethnicity and educational outcomes. *Journal of Social Issues, 66*(1), 113–130. doi:10.1111/j.1540-4560.2009.01636.x

Hitlan, R. T., Zarate, M. A., Kelly, K., & DeSoto, M. C. (2016). Linguistic ostracism causes prejudice: Support for a serial mediation effect. *Journal of Social Psychology, 156*(4), 422–436. doi:10.1080/00224545.2015.1119668

Holmes, M. D., Smith, B. W., Freng, A. B., & Muñoz, E. A. (2008). Minority threat, crime control, and police resource allocation in the Southwestern United States. *Crime & Delinquency, 54*(1), 128–152.

Hyland, S., Langton, L., & Davis, E. (2015). *Police use of nonfatal force, 2002–11.* Washington, D.C.: US Department of Justice, Office of Justice Programs, Bureau of Justice Statistics.

Jan, T. (2016, December 17). No, minority workers are not taking jobs away from white people. *The Washington Post.* Retrieved from https://www .washingtonpost.com/news/wonk/wp/2016/12/17/no-minority-workers -are-not-taking-jobs-away-from-whitepeople/

Kay, A. C., & Jost, J. T. (2003). Complementary justice: Effects of "poor but happy" and "poor but honest" stereotype exemplars on system justification and implicit activation of the justice motive. *Journal of Personality and Social Psychology, 85,* 823–837. doi:10.1037/0022- 3514.85.5.823

Kay, A. C., Jost, J. T., Mandisodza, A. N., Sherman, S. J., Petrocelli, J. V., & Johnson, A. L. (2007). Panglossian ideology in the service of system justification: How complementary stereotypes help us to rationalize inequality. In M. P. Zanna (Ed.), *Advances in Experimental Social Psychology* (pp. 305–358). San Diego, CA: Elsevier Academic.

Keller, R. (2016, March 03). U.S.-Mexican relations from Independence to the present. *Oxford Research Encyclopedia of American History*. Retrieved March 29, 2019, from http://oxfordre.com/americanhistory/view/10.1093/acrefore/9780199329175.001.0001/acrefore-9780199329175-e-269

Klevens, J. (2007). Overview of intimate partner violence among Latinos. *Violence Against Women, 13*(2), 111–122.

Kochhar, R. (2005, December 15). *The occupational status and mobility of Hispanics*. Pew Research Center. Retrieved from http://www.pewhispanic.org/2005/12/15/the-occupational-status-and-mobility-of-hispanics/

Kochhar, R. (2014, June 19). Latino jobs growth driven by U.S. Born. *Pew Research Center*. Retrieved from http://www.pewhispanic.org/2014/06/19/latino-jobs-growth-driven-by-u-s-born/

Lee, Y. T., Ottati, V., & Hussain, I. (2001). Attitudes toward "illegal" immigration into the United States: California proposition 187. *Hispanic Journal of Behavioral Sciences, 23*(4), 430–443.

Levin, B., Nolan, J. J., & Reitzel, J. D. (2017, June 26). New data shows U.S. hate crimes continued to rise in 2017. *The Conversation*. Retrieved from http://theconversation.com/new-data-shows-us-hate-crimes-continued-to-rise-in-2017-97989

Llagas, C., & Snyder, T. (2003, April 15). Status and trends in the education of Hispanics. *National Center for Educational Statistics*. Retrieved from https://nces.ed.gov/pubs2017/2017051.pdf

Lopez, J. D. (2005). Race-related stress and sociocultural orientation among Latino students during their transition into a predominately White, highly selective institution. *Journal of Hispanic Higher Education, 4*, 354–365.

Lopez, M. H., & Livingston, G. (2009, April 7). *Hispanics and the criminal justice system*. Pew Research Center. Retrieved from http://www.pewhispanic.org/2009/04/07/hispanics-and-the-criminal-justice-system/

Maclin, K. M., & Herrera, V. (2006). The criminal stereotype. *North American Journal of Psychology, 8*(2), 197–208.

Madriz, E. (1997). Images of criminal and victims: A study on women's fear and social control. *Gender & Society, 11*(3), 342–356.

Martinez, M. S. (2014). *Stranger in a strange land: A study of the effect of foreignness on perceptions of Latinos* (Unpublished doctoral dissertation). The University of Texas at Austin, Austin, Texas.

Martinez, R., Jr., & Lee, M. T. (2000). On immigration and crime. *Criminal justice, 1*(1), 486–524.

Martinez, R., Jr., Stowell, J. I., & Lee, M. L (2010). Immigration and crime in an era of transformation: A longitudinal analysis of homicides in San Diego neighborhoods, 1980–2000. *Criminology, 48*(3), 797–829.

Mastro, D., Tukachinsky, R., Behm-Morawitz, E., & Blecha, E. (2014). News Coverage of Immigration: The Influence of Exposure to Linguistic Bias in the News on Consumers Racial/Ethnic Cognitions. *Communication Quarterly, 62*(2), 135–154. doi:10.1080/01463373.2014.890115

Mastro, D. E., & Behm-Morawitz, E. (2005). Latino representation on primetime television. *Journalism & Mass Communication Quarterly, 82*(1), 110–130.

Menéndez Alarcón, A. V. (2014). Latin American culture: A deconstruction of stereotypes. *Studies in Latin American Popular Culture, 32*, 72–96.

Molina, N. (2014). How race is made in America: Immigration, citizenship, and the historical power of racial scripts. *Western Historical Quarterly, 46*(2), 241–242. doi:10.2307/westhistquar.46.2.0241

Morales, M. C., Delgado, D., & Curry. T. (2018). Variations in citizenship profiling by generational status: Individual and neighborhood characteristics of Latina/os questioned by law enforcement about their legal status. *Race and Social Problems, 10*(4), 293–305. doi:10.1007/s12552-018-9235-3

Müller, K., & Schwarz, C. (2018). Making America hate again? Twitter and hate crime under Trump. *SSRN*. Retrieved from https://papers.ssrn.com/sol3/papers.cfm?abstract_id=3149103

New American Economy. (2017). How Hispanics contribute to the U.S. economy. *New American Economy*. Retrieved from http://research.newamericaneconomy.org/wp-content/uploads/sites/2/2017/12/Hispanic_V5.pdf

Ngai, M. M. (2014). *Impossible subjects: Illegal aliens and the making of modern America*. Princeton, NJ: Princeton University Press.

Ojeda, L., Navarro, R. L., Meza, R. R., & Arbona, C. (2012). Too Latino and not Latino enough. *Journal of Hispanic Higher Education, 11*(1), 14–28. doi:10.1177/1538192711435553

Orozco, M., Oyer, P., & Porras, J. I. (2018, February). 2017 State of Latino entrepreneurship. Stanford Latino Entrepreneurship Initiative. *Stanford Business School*. Retrieved from https://www.gsb.stanford.edu/faculty-research/publications/state-latino-entrepreneurship-2017

Ostrom, T. M., & Sedikides, C. (1992). Out-group homogeneity effects in natural and minimal groups. *Psychological Bulletin, 112*(3), 536–552.

Outten, H. R., Schmitt, M. T., Miller, D. A., & Garcia, A. L. (2012). Feeling threatened about the future: Whites' emotional reactions to anticipated ethnic demographic changes. *Personality and Social Psychology Bulletin, 38*(1), 14–25.

Pew Research Center. (2009, December 11). *Life satisfaction, priorities and values*. Pew Research Center. Retrieved from http://www.pewhispanic.org/2009/12/11/vii-life-satisfaction-priorities-and-values/

Reyna, C. (2000). Lazy, dumb, or industrious: When stereotypes convey attribution information in the classroom. *Educational Psychology Review, 12*(1), 85–110.

Reyna, C., Dobria, O., & Wetherell, G. (2013). The complexity and ambivalence of immigration attitudes: Ambivalent stereotypes predict conflicting attitudes toward immigration policies. *Cultural Diversity and Ethnic Minority Psychology, 19*(3), 342–356.

Reyna, C., & Zimmerman, J. L. (2017). Issues of status and power in interracial problems and solutions. In Blume, A. W. (Ed.), *Social issues in living color: Challenges and solutions from the perspective of ethnic minority psychology.* Santa Barbara, CA: Praeger.

Rivas-Drake, D., Seaton, E. K., Markstrom, C., Quintana, S., Syed, M., Lee, R. M., . . . Ethnic and Racial Identity in the 21st Century Study Group. (2014). Ethnic and racial identity in adolescence: Implications for psychosocial, academic, and health outcomes. *Child Development, 85*(1), 40–57.

Rodríguez, C. E. (2008). *Heroes, lovers, and others: The story of Latinos in Hollywood.* Oxford, England: Oxford University Press.

Shorey, H. S., Cowan, G., & Sullivan, M. P. (2002). Predicting perceptions of discrimination among Hispanics and Anglos. *Hispanic Journal of Behavioral Sciences, 24*(1), 3–22.

Smith, B. W., & Holmes, M. D. (2003). Community accountability, minority threat, and police brutality: An examination of civil rights criminal complaints. *Criminology, 41*(4), 1035–1064.

Steele, C. M. (2011). *Whistling Vivaldi: And other clues to how stereotypes affect us (issues of our time).* New York: W. W. Norton & Company.

Steele, C. M., & Aronson, J. (1995). Stereotype threat and the intellectual test performance of African Americans. *Journal of Personality and Social Psychology, 69*(5), 797–811. doi:10.1037//0022-3514.69.5.797

Steffensmeier, D., & Demuth, S. (2000). Ethnicity and sentencing outcomes in U.S. federal courts: Who is punished more harshly? *American Sociological Review, 65*(5), 705–729.

Steinberg, S. L. (2004). Undocumented immigrants or illegal aliens? Southwestern media portrayals of Latino immigrants. *Humboldt Journal of Social Relations, 28*(1), 109–133.

Stephan, W. G., Ybarra, O., & Morrison, K. R. (2008). Intergroup threat theory. In T. D. Nelson (Ed.), *Handbook of prejudice, stereotyping, and discrimination.* Mahwah, NJ: Lawrence Erlbaum Associates.

Stevens, E. P. (1973). Machismo and marianismo. *Society, 10*(6), 57–63.

Takaki, R. T. (1998). *Strangers from a different shore a history of Asian Americans.* Boston: Little, Brown.

Taylor, P., Lopez, M. H., Martinez, J., & Velasco, G. (2012, April 4). When labels don't fit: Hispanics and their views of identity. *Pew Research Center.* Retrieved from http://www.pewhispanic.org/2012/04/04/iii-the-american-experience/

Tenenbaum, H. R., & Ruck, M. D. (2007). Are teachers' expectations different for racial minority than for European American students? A meta-analysis. *Journal of Educational Psychology, 99*(2), 253–273. doi:10.1037/0022-0663.99.2.253

Timberlake, J. M., Howell, J., Grau, A. B., & Williams, R. H. (2015). Who "they" are matters: Immigrant stereotypes and assessments of the impact of immigration. *The Sociological Quarterly, 56*(2), 267–299.

Tomkiewicz, J., & Adeyemi-Bello, A. (1997). Perceptual differences in racial descriptions of Euro-American and Hispanic persons. *Psychological Reports, 80*(3), 1339–1343.

Umaña-Taylor, A. J., Diversi, M., & Fine, M. A. (2002). Ethnic identity and self-esteem of Latino adolescents. *Journal of Adolescent Research, 17*(3), 303–327. doi:10.1177/0743558402173005

US Census Bureau. (2017, August 31). *Newsroom*. Retrieved from https://www.census.gov/newsroom/facts-for-features/2017/hispanic-heritage.html

Verdugo, R. (2006). Report on the status of Hispanics in education: Overcoming a history of neglect. *National Education Association*. Retrieved from https://files.eric.ed.gov/fulltext/ED569183.pdf

Washington Post Staff. (2015, June 16). Full Text: Donald Trump announces presidential bid. *The Washington Post*. Retrieved from https://www.washingtonpost.com/news/post-politics/wp/2015/06/16/full-text-donald-trump-announces-a-presidential-bid/

Willis-Esqueda, C., Espinoza, R. K. E., & Culhane, S. E. (2008). The effects of ethnicity, SES, and crime status on juror decision making: A cross-cultural examination of European American and Mexican American mock jurors. *Hispanic Journal of Behavioral Sciences, 30*, 181–199.

Woodcock, A., Hernandez, P. R., Estrada, M., & Schultz, P. (2012). The consequences of chronic stereotype threat: Domain disidentification and abandonment. *Journal of Personality and Social Psychology, 103*(4), 635–646.

Zárate, M. A., Garcia, B., Garza, A. A., & Hitlan, R. (2004). Cultural threat and perceived realistic group conflict as predictors of attitudes towards Mexican immigrants. *Journal of Experimental Social Psychology, 40*, 99–105.

Zárate, M. A., Reyna, C., & Alvarez, M. (2019). Cultural inertia, identity and intergroup dynamics in a changing context. In J. Oleson (Ed.), *Advances in Experimental Social Psychology* (pp. 176–234). San Diego, CA: Elsevier Academic.

Zou, L. X., & Cheryan, S. (2017). Two axes of subordination: A new model of racial position. *Journal of Personality and Social Psychology, 112*(5), 696–717. doi:10.1037/pspa0000080

CHAPTER EIGHT

Stereotypes of Immigrants and Immigration in the United States

*Andrea Bellovary, Angel D. Armenta,
and Christine Reyna*

"Give me your tired, your poor/your huddled masses yearning to breathe free."

In the United States, demographics are changing dramatically. By 2055, Whites will no longer be the dominant racial group in America. This change is driven to a large degree by immigration (Cohn & Caumont, 2016). As a result, who is coming into the United States, where they are from, and what they do while they are here continues to be hotly debated. However, despite the outward appearance of polarization, many Americans experience ambivalent feelings and hold contradictory beliefs toward immigrant groups.

The clash over immigration policies centers on whether or not immigrants are viewed as helping or hurting the nation they are entering. Opponents argue that immigrants exhaust societal resources, steal jobs, and erode national culture, while supporters argue that immigrants bring a wealth of knowledge and experience, improve the economy, and enrich national culture. To understand the current debate around immigration, we must first understand that attitudes toward immigration are often associated with stereotypes about the immigrant groups and what these stereotypes imply about an immigrant's potential for contribution or threat. Stereotypes about immigrants can come from many sources, such as family, friends, community, political rhetoric, and the media. The complex and often contradictory stereotypes around immigrants in the United States can help explain the ambivalent attitudes Americans hold about immigration itself and associated policies.

In this chapter, we explore the current literature on immigrant stereotypes in the United States and how immigration and immigrants are depicted in our culture, the media, and our nation's laws and policies. We argue that immigrants serve as a perpetual scapegoat for economic, security, and symbolic threats. We will review stereotypes of immigrants in general and highlight the ways these stereotypes manifest across specific groups, paying special attention to three groups that have dramatically shaped immigration attitudes and policies in the last few decades—Asian, Arab/Muslim,[1] and Hispanic immigrants. We will contextualize these stereotypes within changing cultural and economic circumstances in America, discuss the ambivalence that ensues when stereotypes contradict each other, and discuss real world immigration outcomes.

Immigration in America: Who, from Where, and Why

Immigrants in the United States represent a wide array of races, ethnicities, cultures, religions, and language preferences. They come from East Asia (27%), Mexico (27%), Central and South America (15%), Europe/Canada (13%), the Caribbean (10%), the Middle East (4%) and sub-Saharan Africa (4%) (Lopez, Bialik & Radford, 2018). Historically, Latin-American groups have been the most likely to migrate into the United States; however, recent trends suggest that this pattern is shifting (Radford & Budiman, 2018). In terms of new arrivals, Asian immigrants are outnumbering Hispanics, and are expected to be the largest immigrant group in America by 2055 (Lopez et al., 2018). Americans' attitudes toward immigrants depend in part on where the group comes from. Overall, nearly half of Americans hold more favorable attitudes toward Asian (47%) and European (44%) immigrants, whereas only about a fifth of U.S.-born Americans view immigrants from Latin America (26%), the Middle East (20%), and Africa (26%) positively (Pew Research Center, 2015).

Stereotypes about immigrants are often associated with the reasons and methods by which immigrants migrate. Although illegal immigration is often at the forefront of public discourse, immigration is multifaceted and includes

---

[1]Arabs and Muslims are only partially overlapping identities. Not all Arabs are Muslim, and not all Muslims are of Arab ancestry. However, stereotypes in America conflate these two identities and thus shape literature on stereotypes about these groups.

many different reasons for immigration—such as economics, family reunification, and asylum. For many, the process of migrating often takes years, or even decades. For others, fleeing their country is an urgent matter of life or death (American Immigration Council, 2016).

One of the most prevalent stereotypes of immigrants is that the majority of (especially Latin American) immigrants are in the country illegally. "Undocumented" and "illegal" are common words used to describe immigrants (Pew Research Center, 2015). However, this is a misconception. The vast majority of immigrants are in the United States legally (76%) (Lopez et al., 2018). Despite this, stereotypes of the "illegal immigrant" dominate narratives about immigration in America. In 2016, president-elect Donald Trump ran a campaign centered on stoking fear about the security and economic threats caused by illegal immigrants. He promised to build a wall stretching across the U.S.-Mexico border to stop the "tidal wave of drugs and crime" (Trump, 2018, October 6) that he claimed will accompany Latin Americans crossing the border illegally (Pramuk, 2018). These disparaging stereotypes have psychological consequences. People have more negative attitudes, experience more intergroup anxiety, and perceive more realistic threat toward unauthorized immigrants compared to authorized immigrants (Murray & Marx, 2013). Trends in the American National Election Studies between 2012 and 2016 suggest that, although attitudes toward Hispanics have improved over time, attitudes toward "illegal immigrants" have worsened (Reyna & Motyl, 2017).

Even among authorized (i.e., legal) immigrants, the reasons for immigration matter in terms of how immigrants are perceived and treated. Economic immigrants have purposely traveled to a new country for better economic opportunities. American citizens prefer highly skilled or educated immigrants who plan to work in high-status jobs (e.g., health care, technology), compared to low-skilled, poorly educated immigrants (Hainmueller & Hiscox, 2010; Hainmueller & Hopkins, 2014). Refugees are immigrants who are forced to leave their homes and have little say about when or where they are relocated for asylum. They have little time to prepare for the transition to America and therefore tend to have poor English skills and few resources (Capps et al., 2015). Asylum seekers are often stereotyped as threatening the host country both economically and culturally (Canetti, Snider, Pedersen, & Hall, 2016). Americans generally disapprove of the United States accepting large numbers of refugees from war-torn countries, with 54 percent of Americans believing that it is not the United States' responsibility to accept refugees (Krogstad & Radford, 2017). These negative attitudes toward refugees likely stem from the stereotypes directed toward immigrants in general, and they may be amplified by factors such as lack of resources or poor English-speaking and writing skills. The disadvantaged position that refugees are in when they arrive in a new country fuels the presumption that they are low-class citizens and marks them as an unproductive strain on society.

Stereotypes of Immigrants as Sources of Realistic and Symbolic Threats

Throughout American history, immigrants have been depicted with a common set of stereotypes regardless of their country of origin or the period of time. Whether they were Germans, Irish, Italians, Eastern Europeans, Jews, or Chinese in the nineteenth and early twentieth centuries, or Africans, Arabs, and Latin Americans today, immigrants are consistently stereotyped as uncivilized, uneducated, poor, dirty, immoral, prone to crime, and un-American (Wilson, 2002). These stereotypes persevere through the generations and transfer to newer, less established immigrant groups. To understand these common stereotypes and prejudices against immigrants, it is important to understand that anti-immigrant beliefs stem to a large degree from perceptions that immigrants are sources of threat (Esses, Dovidio, Jackson, & Armstrong, 2002).

Once a group is established, like that of Anglo-Saxon Americans, members of the group engage in a variety of behaviors and develop elaborate worldviews to protect and promote their group (the ingroup). People react, sometimes violently, against threats to the ingroup posed by outside groups (called outgroups; e.g., Kinder & Sears, 1981). This can manifest as *realistic threats* (e.g., taking away jobs, lowering wages or depleting the social safety net) or threats to safety (e.g., beliefs that immigrants are sources of crime or terrorism), or it can manifest as *symbolic threats* (e.g., that immigrants dilute or undermine American values and culture).

Stereotypes of Immigrants as Sources of Realistic Threats

Realistic threats are defined as perceived threats to tangible resources, such as jobs, wages, power, or security (LeVine & Campbell, 1972; Sherif, 1966). Because a primary reason for immigration is access to better resources and opportunities, immigration is associated with various forms of realistic threat.

Economic Threats

Citizens are often concerned that immigrants are going to affect them or their ingroup by taking away or diminishing valuable resources. When an outgroup like immigrants competes, or is perceived to be competing, for these resources, prejudice toward the competitive group increases (Langford & Ponting, 1992; Sherif & Sherif, 1969; Zárate, Garcia, Garza, & Hitlan, 2004). Even when not directly affected by the perceived competition, people will react negatively to the competitor on behalf of their ingroup (Bobo, 1983). According to the instrumental model of group conflict (Esses, Jackson & Armstrong, 1998), when resources are stressed and competitive outgroups are salient, people are more likely to perceive zero-sum competition with these groups and attempt to remove or otherwise disempower the group. Gallup surveys since 1993 show that people are more likely to stereotype immigrants as hurting the economy following economic downturns (Swift, 2017). In statewide surveys, citizens had higher negative attitudes toward unauthorized immigrants every year as the unemployment rate increased and the gross domestic product decreased (Diaz, Saenz, & Kwan, 2011), suggesting that unauthorized immigrants are perceived more negatively in times of stress and are used as scapegoats for economic concomitants.

As with European and Chinese immigrants in the mid-1800s and early 1900s (Choy, Dong, & Hom, 1995; Massey, 1995), Hispanic immigrants today are blamed for "stealing" jobs from citizens and depressing wages to the point that citizens can no longer support their families. However, these stereotypes are inaccurate (Hoban, 2017). According to a report by the Brookings Institute (Felbab-Brown, 2017), most low-skilled immigrants work in dangerous or difficult jobs that require long hours of manual labor in undesirable conditions (e.g., farm work) that few Americans seek. In reality, immigrants bring in new skills and do important jobs that Americans will not or cannot do (Hoban, 2017). Likewise, immigrants do not necessarily depress wages. Many industries invest money to recruit talent from overseas and often pay higher wages to immigrants (Ruiz & Krogstad, 2017) in order to retain them in hard-to-fill jobs.

Another common stereotype is that immigrants pose an economic burden through tax evasion, poverty, and a poor work ethic. Contrary to stereotypes, both unauthorized and authorized immigrants contribute billions of dollars a year to the U.S. economy in terms of purchasing power and taxes, with foreign-born Hispanics paying a total of $96.9 billion in taxes (Gee, Gardner, & Wiehe, 2016; Joint Economic Committee, 2016; New American Economy, 2017). Hispanic immigrants also make up a large portion of entrepreneurs in the United States. In 2012, 1.4 million Hispanic immigrants were self-employed (New American Economy, 2017). In 2015, Hispanic immigrants contributed a total of $27.2 billion in business income (New American Economy, 2017). Furthermore, as our country's population ages, government programs such as Medicare and social security are increasingly reliant on immigrant support. Immigrants tend to be younger and therefore stay longer in the workforce, paying taxes. As a result, immigrants pay billions of dollars into social security and Medicare—including illegal immigrants, who pay into these systems but cannot reap any benefits—keeping these systems solvent for a longer period of time (New American Economy, 2017).

Immigrants from Asia are also stereotyped about economic threats, but quite differently from Hispanics. Before and shortly after World War II Asians were dehumanized as animalistic and violent (Yam, 2017). However, stereotypes of Asians have since shifted to the "model minority"—smart, hardworking and successful (Lin, Kwan, Cheung, & Fiske, 2005; Sue & Kitano, 1973). These stereotypes have remained relatively stable over the past several decades (Brand, 1987; Chou & Feagin, 2008; Taylor & Stern, 1997). Asians are consistently portrayed in the media as studious, industrious, and diligently working in business, technology, or other successful careers (Deo, Lee, Chin, Milman, & Wang Yuen, 2008; Taylor & Stern, 1997). These media representations translate into stereotypes; Asians are more likely than other racial groups to be stereotyped as high academic achievers and as "nerds" (Zhang, 2010). The model minority stereotype, on its face, appears to be positive. However, it can reinforce beliefs that Asians pose realistic threats.

Asians have been seen as economic threats to Whites since the mid-1800s. These sentiments resulted in extreme anti-Asian immigration laws such as the Chinese Exclusion Act of 1882, which barred all Chinese laborers from entering the country (Calavita, 2000; Choy, Dong, & Hom, 1995; Deo et al., 2008). Now, as immigration from Asian countries has increased dramatically, Asians are once again seen as a source of realistic, competitive threats in the eyes of the White majority (Chou & Feagin, 2008; Kawai, 2005; Maddux, Galinsky, Cuddy, & Polifroni, 2008). Asian immigrants are perceived as being "unfair competition," hindering others' upward mobility (Lee, 1996). From 1988–1990 Asians accounted for nearly half of all professionals immigrating to the United States (Kanjanapan, 1995). Two-thirds of the foreign-born engineering workforce in Silicon Valley are Asian immigrants, and Asian immigrants make up a quarter of senior executives in these tech companies (Saxenian, 2002). As lower-skilled jobs become more automated, competition for higher-skilled jobs will become fiercer, making Asian immigrants more vulnerable to threat stereotypes.

Security Threats

Up until recently, the issue of immigration per se has not intersected with issues of national security; immigration in America has always been predominantly about economics. After the attacks of September 11, 2001, national security agencies and immigration laws were formally intertwined to an unprecedented degree (American Bar Association, 2012). Although most Americans did not blame immigrants in general for the attacks, they did scapegoat Arab and Muslim immigrants.

The media's portrayal of Arabs and Muslims shifted dramatically near the end of the twentieth century and in particular post-9/11. Since then, portrayals of Arabs in the media changed from the "comic villains" (exotic but uncivilized) to the more modern "foreign devils," thereby intensifying the stereotype of Arab and foreign-born Muslims as dangerous (Arti, 2007). After 9/11 national leaders and pundits espoused rhetoric depicting Arabs as evil, bloodthirsty, and animalistic (Merskin, 2004). Beliefs about security threats became the primary determinant of negative attitudes toward Muslims (Wike & Grim, 2010).

These stereotypes have real-world consequences. Across political orientations, Americans endorsed more aggressive, restrictive, and authoritarian policies when they perceived a threat of terrorism (Hetherington & Suhay, 2011; Norris, 2017). Americans were also more willing to support torturing a detainee when that person had an Arabic name and was an alleged terrorist (Conrad, Croco, Gomez, & Moore, 2017). Some chose to act directly on these stereotypes. After 9/11 hate crimes against Arabs, Muslims, and others of Middle Eastern descent rose dramatically (Akram & Johnson, 2001; Goodstein & Tamar, 2001).

Threat-based stereotypes became a justification for policies that undermined civil liberties across America (Ciuk, 2015). Immigration law became a tool for meeting national security objectives and spawned the creation of new immigration agencies with unprecedented powers (American Bar Association, 2012). The nation became engulfed in fear of another attack and became more accepting of aggressive measures racially targeting Arab and Muslim minorities (Gross & Livingston, 2002; Saleem, Prot, Anderson, & Lemieux, 2017). The government passed dozens of policies and initiatives within the year following 9/11, fifteen of which targeted Arabs and potential immigrants from Arab nations (Cainkar, 2004). The Department of Homeland Security deported approximately 6,000 men from various Middle Eastern countries (Cainkar, 2004) and detained hundreds of Arab and Muslim men without due process (American Bar Association, 2012). Over a decade after the 9/11 attacks, Muslim immigrants are still singled out for discrimination. According to a *New York Times* report, the 2018 travel ban aimed to bar anyone from several predominantly-Muslim countries from entering the United States on the grounds that they posed a national security threat (Gladstone & Sugiyama, 2018).

Efforts to demonize immigrants as criminals have had mixed success. When asked directly about crime rates caused by immigrants, especially unauthorized immigrants, U.S.-born Americans are torn. Sixty-five percent of Americans do not believe that unauthorized immigrants are more likely to commit serious crimes than U.S.-born citizens (Pew Research Center, 2018). When these statistics are stratified by political affiliation, the results diverge. Eighty percent of Democrats report that unauthorized immigrants are no more likely than U.S.-born citizens to commit serious crimes, whereas only 46 percent of Republicans report similar attitudes (Pew Research Center, 2018). However, there has been concerted effort to frame immigration, especially unauthorized immigration, in terms of security threat, despite the fact that unauthorized immigrants commit fewer crimes per capita than U.S.-born citizens (Light & Miller, 2018). These stereotypes can stoke fears that make draconian immigration policies seem justifiable and can galvanize an otherwise moderate constituency to consider more extreme policies and candidates if they promise greater security. Therefore, stereotyping immigrants in terms of security threat can be a powerful political tool in times of instability.

Stereotypes of Immigrants as Sources of Symbolic Threat

Unlike realistic threats that pertain to tangible resources and outcomes, symbolic threats undermine more abstract but deeply important things like personal or national identity, cherished values, worldviews, and culture (Henry & Reyna, 2007; Sears, 1988; Stephan & Stephan, 1996). Often, symbolic threats from immigrants are stronger predictors of intergroup prejudice than realistic threats (Danbold & Huo, 2015; Hainmueller & Hopkins, 2014; Sniderman, Hagendoorn, & Prior, 2004; Zárate, Garcia, Garza, & Hitlan, 2004).

What does it mean to be American? In order to understand how immigration is associated with perceptions of symbolic threat and associated stereotypes, it is important to understand how Americans perceive their culture and what it means to be American. Only 32 percent of people surveyed nationally believed it was important to be born in the United States to be American, whereas 70 seventy of those surveyed believed that speaking English was important to be American (Stokes, 2017a, 2017b). For many, however, being American means being White (Danbold & Huo, 2015). A study by Devos and Banaji (2005) found that Americans were faster at associating American symbols with Whites than with any other racial/ethnic group. This trend was so robust that participants were more likely to associate being American with well-known, *foreign*, White celebrities over well-known American-born, Asian celebrities (Study 4; Devos & Banaji, 2005).

The tendency to equate "American" with Whiteness is even prevalent among people of color. Racial/ethnic minorities are less likely than Whites to see themselves as being a typical American (Rodriguez, Schwartz, & Whitbourne, 2010; Schwartz et al., 2012; Weisskirch, 2005). Immigrants themselves associate being American with being White, affluent, and privileged (Bloemraad, 2013). Even after naturalization, immigrants still felt as though they were outsiders and perceived as foreign (Bloemraad, 2013; Rodriguez et al., 2010).

Symbolic Threats to American Values

Negative attitudes toward immigrants are related to how much immigrants are stereotyped as threatening cultural values (e.g., Esses, Haddock, & Zanna, 1993; Esses, Hodson, & Dovidio, 2003; Huddy & Sears, 1995; McLaren, 2003). Those with a strong American identity may feel especially threatened by groups that do not appear to conform to American ideals. For example, national identity is a critical predictor of anti-immigrant attitudes, above and beyond that of economic considerations (Sniderman et al., 2004). The degree to which Americans perceive immigrants as supporting or weakening American culture appears to be partially ideological. For example, according to a 2018 Pew Research Center survey, 79 percent of Democrats say that current immigrants are more willing or as willing to adapt to American culture as immigrants from the 1900s, whereas only 38 percent of Republicans report similar attitudes (Lopez et al., 2018).

Those who do not conform to the ingroup's culture can be perceived as threatening the very foundation of society. In periods of societal instability, immigrants become the perfect scapegoat for American fears that their way of life is in flux. According to cultural inertia theory, people are motivated to avoid cultural change and to maintain their cultural status quo (Zárate & Shaw, 2010). The threat of change, in and of itself, leads to perceived threat to one's morals, values, money, politics, security, and so on (see Zárate, Reyna, & Alvarez, 2019, for review). People expressed greater perceived threat, greater cultural angst, and greater endorsement of anti-immigrant legislation when biased to believe that mainstream American culture was changing due to the influx of unauthorized Latino immigrants (Quezada, Shenberger-Trujillo, & Zárate, 2011).

Immigrant groups differ in how "Western" or "American" they seem. Immigrants who speak other languages, practice different religions or customs, or wear different attire (such as face or hair coverings) are more vulnerable to stereotypes suggesting symbolic threat. When differences are visible, it is much easier for those of the majority to label the newly arrived immigrants as an outgroup. For example, Asians (whose ancestors come from a different continent and culture) are stereotyped as the "perpetual foreigner," even if they have lived in the United States for many generations (Armenta et al., 2013). Asians also suffer from stereotypes that they are "clannish" and do not assimilate to American culture and values (Armenta et al., 2013; Zou & Cheryan, 2017).

Historically, Arabs and Muslims have been portrayed as "backward" in Western media (Arti, 2007). An analysis of over 900 Hollywood films showed that 95 percent of Arab portrayals showed them as brutal, uncivilized, religious fanatics (Shaheen, 2003). Historical and media representations of Arabs and Muslims have stereotyped them as either exotic (e.g., with images of harems and veiled women; Alsultany, 2012) or depraved (e.g., as terrorists, anti-West, antiwoman, and anti-human-rights; Hamada, 2001). Altogether, the media paints a stark image of Arabs as against all things "American." These media portrayals affect stereotypes. Arab immigrants are perceived as more fanatical, aggressive, quick-tempered, and vengeful than almost all other immigrant groups measured (Reyna, Dobria, & Wetherell, 2013).

One challenge that Arabs and Muslims face is that religion is often conflated with culture (a common stereotype is that most Arabs are Muslim and most Muslims are Arab). As a result, Arabs and/or Muslims are a unique group because they are both a religious minority and have cultural practices different from mainstream America. In essence, these differences create a double "otherness" for Arab and Muslim immigrants. Groups defined by their cultural differences are especially likely to trigger feelings of symbolic threat. When context was framed around cultural threats to the United States, people expressed more negative affect toward Muslims (Hellwig & Sinno, 2017), indicating that the public associates Muslims specifically with being culturally different.

As perceived differences between the ingroup and outgroup increase, negative attitudes toward the outgroup also increase (Dunbar, Saiz, Stela, & Saez, 2000; Sawires & Peacock, 2000). Customs, religions, or ways of dress that are uncommon in the United States can distinguish an immigrant as different or less "American." These differences (as well as other stereotypes about the group) can cause some Americans to fear that their way of life is being threatened and therefore cause them to react negatively to the new group. The more the media reinforces narratives of immigrants undermining or eroding American ideals and values, the more Americans will see immigrants in general as symbolic threats.

Ambivalent and Contradictory Stereotypes of Immigrants

Another hallmark of immigrant stereotypes is that they are often contradictory and reflect ambivalent beliefs and attitudes. These conflicting beliefs can result in seemingly diametric, if not outright polarized, policy positions that ultimately make immigration an intractable challenge.

Lee and Fiske (2006) used the stereotype content model (SCM) to assess how immigrant subgroups are perceived as a function of nationality, ethnicity, documentation status, and social class. According to SCM, people evaluate groups along two dimensions ranging from a) warm to cold, which indicates ally status, and b) competent to incompetent, which indicates their capacity for threat (Fiske, Cuddy, & Glick, 2007). Their findings revealed that most immigrant groups are perceived as having ambivalent traits. People appear to form impressions of immigrants first based on perceptions of generic immigrants (low competence and low warmth), but as additional information (e.g., ethnicity, socio-economic status, etc.) is available, perceptions change and become more like stereotypical warmth and competence levels of those specific groups. For example, documented, third-generation, European, and Indian immigrants are viewed as having warmth and competence levels similar to those of college students (moderately high warmth, moderate competence). Undocumented, Mexican, Latinx, South American, and African immigrants are viewed as having similar warmth and competence levels of poor people (moderate warmth, low competence). Asian, Chinese, Korean, and Japanese immigrants receive similar warmth and competence levels as professionals and rich people (low warmth, high competence).

Where immigrant groups fall along these two dimensions has consequences. For example, although seen as successful, Asians struggle against stereotypes that they are quiet, passive, and socially awkward (Reyna et al., 2013)—a low warmth, high-competence pattern. This "shy" stereotype may keep Asians out of certain industries that value sociability, such as entertainment, or assertiveness like the military. A lawsuit was filed against Harvard and other top universities for limiting their number of Asian admissions due to stereotyping Asians as smart but not outgoing or creative (Zimmerman, 2018).

Ambivalence goes beyond warmth and competence beliefs. Stereotypes of immigrants are contingent on how other facets of their identities, behaviors, and circumstances are perceived, often reflecting a complex and sometimes contradictory array of traits and attributes (Reyna et al., 2013). Much of these contradictions are rooted in the complexities associated with immigration in America. For example, when you examine the contradictory media and political rhetoric surrounding Hispanic immigrants, it is as though Hispanic immigrants are two diametric groups. The media has portrayed Hispanic immigrants as a boon to the U.S. economy (McGirt, 2016), and the scapegoat for the slow economic recovery (Gomez, 2017). They are depicted both as brave, loving families trying to protect vulnerable children from atrocities, and criminal "invaders" coming to our country to sell drugs, murder, and rape our citizenry (Mathema, 2018). Immigrants from Latin American countries are often stereotyped as untrustworthy, poor, prone to criminal behavior, and taking jobs away from Americans (Casas & Cabrera, 2011; Cowan, Martinez, & Mendiola, 1997; Hitlan, Carrillo, Zárate, & Aikman, 2007; Reyna et al., 2013). However, they were also more likely to be perceived as friendly, family oriented, helpful, and devout (Reyna et al., 2013).

These group-specific stereotypes predict support for specific immigration policies that reflect these attitudes (Reyna et al., 2013). For example, Mexican immigrants' *lower-status* stereotype negatively predicts attitudes and, simultaneously, positively predicts endorsement of punitive policies (e.g., automatic deportation); however, the belief that Mexican immigrants are *persecuted* predicts positive attitudes and, simultaneously, negatively predicts endorsement of isolation and punitive policies. This pattern extends to other immigrant groups. The *aggressive/vengeful* stereotype of Arab immigrants positively predicts endorsement of isolation policies (e.g., placing higher restrictions on visitors from certain countries), while their *smart* stereotype predicts positive immigrant group attitudes and support for pro-immigration policies (e.g., promoting work visa and guest worker programs).

These findings suggest that people can simultaneously hold positive and negative stereotypes of immigrants. More importantly, they suggest that ambivalent beliefs can lead to inconsistencies concerning how and when society supports or disapproves of immigration and the social structures from which it is regulated. Stereotypes of Mexican immigrants being *dangerous* as well as *family-oriented*, for example, may lead to endorsement of deportation practices while simultaneously stoking national ire when immigrant families are separated by law enforcement (Matthews, 2018). The stereotype that Arab immigrants are *vengeful* and *smart* may lead to issuing more student visas to these individuals, while simultaneously ramping up security when these individuals arrive in our country. Sadly, these contradictory stereotypes and policy attitudes likely contribute to an overly complex and convoluted immigration code, and political gridlock when it comes to immigration reform.

Conclusion

Immigration is one of the most important and divisive issues in America in the twenty-first century. Stereotypes that portray immigrants as threatening American jobs, wages, safety, and way of life have been used as political tools to galvanize disaffected voters and further divide partisans from both sides of the political aisle. This tactic is not new. Although America is a country founded by immigrants, stoking prejudice and fear toward immigrants has been a hallmark of our history. The groups targeted for derision have changed over generations—from Western and Eastern Europeans, to Asians and Arabs, Africans and Latin Americans—but the basic narrative remains the same: immigrants are the "perpetual outgroup" that a populace struggling in rapidly changing cultural and economic times can blame for their insecurity or misfortune. Immigrants have been portrayed as less deserving of our moral considerations through outright dehumanization (by associating them with animals or vermin) or through stereotypes that portray them as threatening in one manner or another. In spite of these stereotypes and their consequences, immigrants continue to do for this country what they have always done: enrich our culture, innovate novel ideas, technologies, and industries, generate work and wealth, and enable our country to progress forward.

References

Akram, S. M., & Johnson, K. R. (2001). Race, civil rights, and immigration law after September 11, 2001: The targeting of Arabs and Muslims. *New York University Annual Survey of American Law, 58*(3), 295–356.

Alsultany, E. (2012). *Arabs and Muslims in the Media: Race and Representation after 9/11*. New York: New York University Press.

American Bar Association. (2012). 9/11 and the transformation of U.S. immigration law and policy. *Human Rights Magazine, 38.* Retrieved from https://www.americanbar.org/groups/crsj/publications/human_rights_magazine_home/human_rights_vol38_2011/human_rights_winter2011/9-11_transformation_of_us_immigration_law_policy

American Immigration Council. (2016). How the United States immigration system works. *American Immigration Council.* Retrieved from https://americanimmigrationcouncil.org/research/how-united-states-immigration-system-works

Armenta, B. E., Lee, R. M., Pituc, S. T., Jung, K. R., Park, I. J., Soto, J. A., . . . Schwartz, S. J. (2013). Where are you from? A validation of the Foreigner Objectification Scale and the psychological correlates of foreigner objectification among Asian Americans and Latinos. *Cultural Diversity and Ethnic Minority Psychology, 19*(2), 131.

Arti, S. (2007). The evolution of Hollywood's representation of Arabs before 9/11: The relationship between political events and the notion of "otherness." *Journal of the MeCCSA Postgraduate Network, 1*(2), 1–20.

Bloemraad, I. (2013). Being American/becoming American: Birthright citizenship and immigrants' membership in the United States. *Law, Politics, and Society, 60,* 55–84.

Bobo, L. (1983). Whites' opposition to busing: Symbolic racism or realistic group conflict? *Journal of Personality and Social Psychology, 45*(6), 1196.

Brand, D. (1987). The new whiz kids: Why Asian Americans are doing so well and what it costs them. *Time, 130,* 42–46.

Cainkar, L. (2004). Post 9/11 domestic policies affecting U.S. Arabs and Muslims: A brief review. *Comparative Studies of South Asia, Africa, and the Middle East, 24*(1), 245–248.

Calavita, K. (2000). The paradoxes of race, class, identity, and "passing": Enforcing the Chinese Exclusion Acts, 1882–1910. *Law & Social Inquiry, 25*(1), 1–40.

Canetti, D., Snider, K. L., Pedersen, A., & Hall, B. J. (2016). Threatened or threatening? How ideology shapes asylum seekers' immigration policy attitudes in Israel and Australia. *Journal of Refugee Studies, 29*(4), 583–606.

Capps, R., Newland, K., Fratzke, S., Groves, S., Auclair, G., Fix, M., & McHugh, M. (2015). *The integration outcomes of U.S. refugees: Successes and challenges.* Washington, D.C.: Migration Policy Institute.

Casas, J., & Cabrera, A. P. (2011). Latino/a immigration: Actions and outcomes based on perceptions and emotions or facts? *Hispanic Journal of Behavioral Sciences, 33,* 283–303.

Chou, R., & Feagin, J. R. (2008). *The myth of the model minority: Asian Americans facing racism.* Boulder, CA: Paradigm Publishers.

Choy, P., Dong, L., & Hom, M. (1995). *The coming main: 19th century American Perceptions of the Chinese.* Seattle, WA: University of Washington Press.

Ciuk, D. J. (2015). Americans' value preferences pre- and post-9/11. *Social Science Quarterly, 97*(2), 407–417.

Cohn, D., & Caumont, A. (2016). 10 demographic trends that are shaping the U.S. and the world. *Pew Research Center.* Retrieved from http://www .pewresearch.org/fact-tank/2016/03/31/10-demographic-trends-that-are -shaping-the-u-s-and-the-world/

Conrad, C. R., Croco, S. E., Gomez, B. T., & Moore, W. H. (2017). Threat perception and American support for torture. *Political Behavior,* 1–21.

Cowan, G., Martinez, L., & Mendiola, S. (1997). Predictors of attitudes toward illegal Latino immigrants. *Hispanic Journal of Behavioral Sciences, 19,* 403–415.

Danbold, F., & Huo, Y. J. (2015). No longer "All-American"? Whites' defensive reactions to their numerical decline. *Social Psychological and Personality Science, 6*(2), 210–218.

Deo, M. E., Lee, J. J., Chin, C. B., Milman, N., & Wang Yuen, N. (2008). Missing in action: "Framing" race on prime-time television. *Social Justice, 35*(2), 145–162.

Devos, T., & Banaji, M. R. (2005). American = white? *Journal of Personality and Social Psychology, 88*(3), 447.

Diaz, P., Saenz, D. S., & Kwan, V. S. (2011). Economic dynamics and changes in attitudes toward undocumented Mexican immigrants in Arizona. *Analyses of Social Issues and Public Policy, 11*(1), 300–313.

Dunbar, E., Saiz, J. L., Stela, K., & Saez, R. (2000). Personality and social group value determinants of out-group bias: A cross-national comparison of Gough's Pr/To scale. *Journal of Cross-Cultural Psychology, 31,* 267–275.

Esses, V. M., Dovidio, J. F., Jackson, L. M., & Armstrong, T. L. (2002). The immigration dilemma: The role of perceived group competition, ethnic prejudice, and national identity. *Journal of Social Issues, 57*(3), 389–412.

Esses, V. M., Haddock, G., & Zanna, M. P. (1993). Values, stereotypes, and emotions as determinants of intergroup attitudes. In D. M. Mackie & D. L. Hamilton (Eds.), *Affect, cognition, and stereotyping: Interactive processes in group perception.* New York: Academic Press.

Esses, V. M., Hodson, G., & Dovidio, J. F. (2003). Public attitudes toward immigrants and immigration. In C. M. Beach, A. G. Green, & J. F. Reitz (Eds.), *Canadian immigration policy for the 21st century.* Montreal, Canada: McGill-Queen's Press.

Esses, V. M., Jackson, L. M., & Armstrong, T. L. (1998). Intergroup competition and attitudes toward immigrants and immigration: An instrumental model of group conflict. *Journal of Social Issues, 54*(4), 699–724.

Felbab-Brown, V. (2017). The wall: The real costs of a barrier between the United States and Mexico. *The Brookings.* Retrieved from https://www.brookings .edu/essay/the-wall-the-real-costs-of-a-barrier-between-the-united -states-and-mexico/

Fiske, S. T., Cuddy, A. J., & Glick, P. (2007). Universal dimensions of social cognition: Warmth and competence. *Trends in Cognitive Sciences, 11*(2), 77–83.

Gee, L. C., Gardner, M., & Wiehe, M. (2016). Undocumented immigrants' state & local tax contributions. *Institute on Taxation & Economic Policy,* 1–22. Retrieved from https://itep.org/wp-content/uploads/immigration2016.pdf

Gladstone, R., & Sugiyama, S. (2018). Trump's travel ban: How it works and who is affected. *The New York Times.* Retrieved from https://www.nytimes.com/2018/07/01/world/americas/travel-ban-trump-how-it-works.html

Gomez, A. (2017). Jobs report disputes Trump claim that immigration hurts U.S. workers and lowers wages. *USA Today.* Retrieved from https://www.usatoday.com/story/news/2017/08/04/jobs-report-disputes-trump-claim-immigration-hurts-u-s-workers-and-lowers-wages/540206001/

Goodstein, L., & Tamar, L. (2001). Victims of mistaken identity, Sikhs pay a price for turbans. *New York Times.* Retrieved from https://www.nytimes.com/2001/09/19/us/nation-challenged-violence-harassment-victims-mistaken-identity-sikhs-pay-price.html

Gross, S. R., & Livingston, D. (2002). Racial profiling under attack. *Columbia Law Review, 102*(5), 1413–1438.

Hainmueller, J., & Hiscox, M. (2010). Attitudes toward highly skilled and low-skilled immigration: Evidence from a survey experiment. *American Political Science Review, 104*(1), 61–84.

Hainmueller, J., & Hopkins, D. J. (2014). Public attitudes toward immigration. *Annual Review of Political Science, 17,* 225–249.

Hamada, B. I. (2001). The Arab image in the minds of western image-markers. *Journal of International Communication, 7*(1), 7–35.

Hellwig, T., & Sinno, A. (2017). Different groups, different threats: Public attitudes towards immigrants. *Journal of Ethnic and Migration Studies, 43*(3), 339–358.

Henry, P. J., & Reyna, C. (2007). Value judgments: The impact of perceived value violations on American political attitudes. *Political Psychology, 28*(3), 273–298.

Hetherington, M. J., & Suhay, E. (2011). Authoritarianism, threat, and Americans' support for the war on terror. *American Journal of Political Science, 55*(3), 546–560.

Hitlan, R. T., Carrillo, K., Zárate, M. A., & Aikman, S. N. (2007). Attitudes toward immigrant groups and the September 11 terrorist attacks. *Peace and Conflict, 13,* 135–152.

Hoban, B. (2017). Do immigrants "steal" jobs from American workers? *Brookings.* Retrieved from https://www.brookings.edu/blog/brookings-now/2017/08/24/do-immigrants-steal-jobs-from-american-workers/

Huddy, L., & Sears, D. O. (1995). Opposition to bilingual education: Prejudice or the defense of realistic interests? *Social Psychology Quarterly, 58,* 133–143.

Joint Economic Committee. (2016). *The 2016 joint economic report.* Washington, D.C.: U.S. Government printing office.

Kanjanapan, W. (1995). The immigration of Asian professionals to the United States: 1988-1990. *The International Migration Review, 29*(1), 7–32.

Kawai, Y. (2005). Stereotyping Asian Americans: The dialectic of the model minority and the yellow peril. *Howard Journal of Communication, 16,* 109–130.

Kinder, D. R., & Sears, D. O. (1981). Prejudice and politics: Symbolic racism versus racial threats to the good life. *Journal of Personality and Social Psychology, 40*(3), 414.

Krogstad, J. M., & Radford, J. (2017). *Key facts about refugees to the U.S.* Pew Research Center. Retrieved from http://www.pewresearch.org/fact-tank /2017/01/30/key-facts-about-refugees-to-the-u-s/

Langford, T., & Ponting, J. R. (1992). Canadians' responses to aboriginal issues: The roles of prejudice, perceived group conflict and economic conservatism. *Canadian Review of Sociology/Revue Canadienne de Sociologie, 29*(2), 140–166.

Lee, S. J. (1996). *Unraveling the "model minority" stereotype: Listening to Asian American youth.* New York: Teachers College Press.

Lee, T. L., & Fiske, S. T. (2006). Not an outgroup, not yet an ingroup: Immigrants in the stereotype content model. *International Journal of Intercultural Relations, 30,* 751–768.

LeVine, R. A., & Campbell, D. T. (1972). *Ethnocentrism: Theories of conflict, ethnic attitudes, and group behavior.* Oxford, England: John Wiley & Sons.

Light, M. T., & Miller, T. (2018). Does undocumented immigration increase violent crime? *Criminology, 56*(2), 370–401.

Lin, M. H., Kwan, V. S., Cheung, A., & Fiske, S. T. (2005). Stereotype content model explains prejudice for an envied outgroup: Scale of anti-Asian American stereotypes. *Personality and Social Psychology Bulletin, 31*(1), 34–47.

Lopez, G., Bialik, K., & Radford, J. (2018). Key findings about U.S. immigrants. *Pew Research Center.* Retrieved from http://www.pewresearch.org /fact-tank/2018/09/14/key-findings-about-u-s-immigrants/

Maddux, W. W., Galinsky, A. D., Cuddy, A. J. C., & Polifroni, M. (2008). When being a model minority is good . . . and bad: Realistic threat explains negativity toward Asian Americans. *Personality and Social Psychology Bulletin, 34*(1), 74–89.

Massey, D. S. (1995). The new immigration and ethnicity in the United States. *Population and Development Review, 21*(3), 631–652.

Mathema, S. (2018). They are (still) refugees: People continue to flee violence in Latin American countries. *Center for American Progress.* Retrieved from https://www.americanprogress.org/issues/immigration/reports/2018 /06/01/451474/still-refugees-people-continue-flee-violence-latin-ameri can-countries/

Matthews, D. (2018). Polls: Trump's family separation policy is very unpopular—except among Republicans. *The Vox.* Retrieved from https:// www.vox.com/policy-and-politics/2018/6/18/17475740/family-separation -poll-polling-border-trump-children-immigrant-families-parents

McGirt, E. (2016). Latinos power the U.S. economy. *Fortune.* Retrieved from http://fortune.com/2016/12/07/latinos-power-the-u-s-economy/

McLaren, L. M. (2003). Anti-immigrant prejudice in Europe: Contact, threat perception, and preferences for the expulsion of migrants. *Social Forces, 81,* 909–936.

Merskin, D. (2004). The construction of Arabs as enemies: Post-September 11 discourse of George W. Bush. *Mass Communication & Society, 7*(2), 157–175.

Murray, K. E., & Marx, D. M. (2013). Attitudes toward unauthorized immigrants, authorized immigrants, and refugees. *Cultural Diversity and Ethnic Minority Psychology, 19*(3), 332–341.

New American Economy. (2017). How Hispanics contribute to the U.S. economy. *New American Economy.* Retrieved from http://research.newameri caneconomy.org/wp-content/uploads/sites/2/2017/12/Hispanic_V5.pdf

Norris, G. (2017). Authoritarianism and privacy: The moderating role of terrorist threat. *Surveillance & Society, 15*, 573–581.

Pew Research Center. (2015). U.S. public has mixed views of immigrants and immigration. *Pew Research Center.* Retrieved from http://www .pewhispanic.org/2015/09/28/chapter-4-u-s-public-has-mixed-views-of -immigrants-and-immigration/

Pew Research Center. (2018). Shifting public views on legal immigration into the US. *Pew Research Center.* Retrieved from http://www.people-press.org /2018/06/28/shifting-public-views-on-legal-immigration-into-the-u-s/

Pramuk, J. (2018, April). *President Trump wants Congress to "act now" on immigration, but that's unlikely to happen. CNBC: Politics.* Retrieved from https:// www.cnbc.com/2018/04/02/trump-wants-congress-to-pass-daca -border-wall-bill.html (last viewed: 11/23/18).

Quezada, S. A., Shenberger-Trujillo, J., & Zárate, M. A. (2011). [Latino immigration in the United States]. Unpublished raw data.

Radford, J., & Budiman, A. (2018). Facts on U.S. immigrants, 2016: Statistical portrait of the foreign-born population in the United States. *Pew Research Center.* Retrieved from http://www.pewhispanic.org/2018/09/14/facts-on -u-s-immigrants/

Reyna, C., Dobria, O., & Wetherell, G. (2013). The complexity and ambivalence of immigration attitudes: Ambivalent stereotypes predict conflicting attitudes toward immigration policies. *Cultural Diversity and Ethnic Minority Psychology, 19*(3), 342.

Reyna, C., & Motyl, M. (2017). *2016 U.S. Election Town Hall.* Presentation given at the Society for the Psychological Study of Social Issues, Summer 2017 Conference.

Rodriguez, L., Schwartz, S. J., & Whitbourne, S. K. (2010). American identity revisited: The relation between national, ethnic, and personal identity in a multiethnic sample of emerging adults. *Journal of Adolescent Research, 25*(2), 324–349.

Ruiz, N. G., & Krogstand, J. M. (2017). Salaries have risen for higher-skilled foreign workers in U.S. on H-1B visas. *Pew Research Center.* Retrieved from http://www.pewresearch.org/fact-tank/2017/08/16/salaries-have-risen -for-high-skilled-foreign-workers-in-u-s-on-h-1b-visas/

Saleem, M., Prot, S., Anderson, C. A., & Lemieux, A. F. (2017). Exposure to Muslims in media and support for public policies harming Muslims. *Communication Research, 44*(6), 841–869.

Sawires, J. N., & Peacock, M. J. (2000). Symbolic racism and voting behavior on Proposition 209. *Journal of Applied Social Psychology, 30*(10), 2092–2099.

Saxenian, A. (2002). Silicon valley's new immigrant high-growth entrepreneurs. *Economic Development Quarterly, 16*(1), 20–31.

Schwartz, S. J., Park, I. J. K., Hurnh, Q., Zamboanga, B. L., Umana-Taylor, A. J., Lee, R. M., . . . Agocha., V. B. (2012). The American identity measure: Development and validation across ethnic group and immigrant generation. *Identity: An International Journal of Theory and Research, 12*, 93–128.

Sears, D. O. (1988). Symbolic racism. In *Eliminating racism* (pp. 53–84). Boston: Springer.

Shaheen, J. G. (2003). Reel bad Arabs: How Hollywood vilifies a people. *The Annals of the American Academy of Political and Social Science, 588*(1), 171–193.

Sherif, M. (1966). *Group conflict and cooperation.* London: Routledge and Kegan Paul.

Sherif, M., & Sherif, C. W. (1969). Ingroup and intergroup relations: Experimental analysis. *Social Psychology* (pp. 221–266). New York: Harper & Row.

Sniderman, P. M., Hagendoorn, L., & Prior, M. (2004). Predisposing factors and situational triggers: Exclusionary reactions to immigrant minorities. *American Political Science Review, 98*(1), 35–49.

Stephan, W. G., & Stephan, C. W. (1996). Predicting prejudice. *International Journal of Intercultural Relations, 20*(3–4), 409–426.

Stokes, B. (2017a). Refugees in the mind of the west. *Real Clear World.* Retrieved from https://www.realclearworld.com/articles/2017/02/08/refugees_in_the_mind_of_the_west_112209.html

Stokes, B. (2017b). What it takes to truly be "one of us." *Pew Research Center.* Retrieved from http://www.pewglobal.org/2017/02/01/language-the-cornerstone-of-national-identity/

Sue, S., & Kitano, H. H. (1973). Stereotypes as a measure of success. *Journal of Social Issues, 29*(2), 83–98.

Swift, A. (2017). More Americans say immigrants help rather than hurt economy. *Gallup.* Retrieved from https://news.gallup.com/poll/213152/americans-say-immigrants-help-rather-hurt-economy.aspx

Taylor, C. R., & Stern, B. B. (1997). Asian-Americans: Television advertising and the "model minority" stereotype. *Journal of Advertising, 26*(2), 47–61.

Trump, D. (2018, October 6). *President Trump rally in Topeka, Kansas.* Retrieved from https://www.c-span.org/video/?452582-1/president-trump-rally-topeka-kansas

Weisskirch, R. S. (2005). Ethnicity and perceptions of being a "typical American" in relationship to ethnic identity development. *International Journal of Intercultural Relations, 29*(3), 355–366.

Wike, R., & Grim, B. J. (2010). Western views toward Muslims: Evidence from a 2006 cross-national survey. *International Journal of Public Opinion Research, 22*(1), 4–25.

Wilson, J. (2002). *Coming to America: A history of immigration and ethnicity in American life* (2nd ed.). Salem Press Pasadena, CA: Magill Book Reviews.

Yam, K. (2017). These anti-Japanese signs from World War II are a warning against bigotry today. *Huffington Post.* Retrieved from https://www

.huffingtonpost.com/entry/pearl-harbor-japanese-americans_us
_5a283fb8e4b02d3bfc37b9f6

Zárate, M. A., Garcia, B., Garza, A. A., & Hitlan, R. T. (2004). Cultural threat and
perceived realistic group conflict as dual predictors of prejudice. *Journal
of Experimental Social Psychology, 40*(1), 99–105.

Zárate, M. A., Reyna, C., & Alvarez, M. J. (2019). Cultural inertia, identity, and
intergroup dynamics in a changing context. *Advances in Experimental
Social Psychology, 59*, 175–233.

Zárate, M. A., & Shaw, M. P. (2010). The role of cultural inertia in reactions to
immigration on the U.S./Mexico border. *Journal of Social Issues, 66*, 45–57.
doi:10.1111/j.1540-4560.2009.01632.x

Zhang, Q. (2010). Asian Americans beyond the model minority stereotype: The
nerdy and the left out. *Journal of International and Intercultural Communication, 3*(1), 20–37.

Zimmerman, J. (2018). Commentary: One group definitely faces prejudice in
college admissions. It's not who you think it is. *Chicago Tribune.* Retrieved
from https://www.chicagotribune.com/news/opinion/commentary/ct-per
spec-shy-asian-americans-college-admissions-discrimination-0815
-story.html

Zou, L. X., & Cheryan, S. (2017). Two axes of subordination: A new model of
racial position. *Journal of Personality and Social Psychology, 112*(5), 696.

CHAPTER NINE

Model Minorities and Perpetual Foreigners: Stereotypes of Asian Americans

Stacey J. Lee and Joan J. Hong

If asked to close their eyes and imagine an Asian American person, chances are good that most non-Asians would imagine an academically focused student who plays the piano or violin and/or struggles to speak English. The image of the high achieving student and the non-English speaking person reflect the two most enduring and consequential stereotypes of Asians Americans: *model minority* and *perpetual foreigner*. The model minority stereotype characterizes Asian Americans as academically successful, hardworking, obedient, family-oriented, and entrepreneurial. According to the model minority stereotype, the economic and academic success of Asian Americans proves that equal opportunity exists for all races. The perpetual foreigner stereotype is based on the assumption that Asians are unwilling and/or unable to assimilate to the United States. Cast as perpetual foreigners, Asian Americans are denied acceptance as authentic and equal Americans. While seemingly oppositional stereotypes, the model minority stereotype and the perpetual foreigner stereotype are closely related and mutually reinforcing stereotypes that work to marginalize Asian Americans (Park, 2008; Wu,

2002). Historian Gary Okihiro (1994) argued that the model minority stereotype is simply a benign version of the yellow peril/perpetual foreigner
stereotype. In this chapter, we will explore the persistence of these stereotypes throughout U.S. history and in the daily lives of Asian Americans in
the twenty-first century, and we will review recent research on the impact of
the stereotypes on Asian American communities.

Historical Roots and Contemporary Expressions of Racial Stereotypes of Asian Americans

The perpetual foreigner stereotype and the model minority stereotype
have long histories in the United States, and both stereotypes emerge in current political debates and in popular culture. The perpetual foreigner stereotype is a contemporary expression of the yellow peril racial stereotype that
was prominent in the late nineteenth and early twentieth century. The idea
that Asian immigrants represented a "yellow peril" was based on the perceived threat of Asian immigrants to the identity of the nation. The yellow
peril discourse positioned Asian immigrants as cultural, economic, and
moral threats to the White nation (Chan, 1994; Okihiro, 1994). According to
this discourse, Asian immigrants were sneaky, inscrutable, and unable to
assimilate to the dominant European American norms. During wartime conflict and economic distress, the idea of foreignness can lead Asian Americans
to be seen as the enemy (Lowe, 1996; Saito, 2001; Wu, 2002). The perpetual
foreigner/yellow peril stereotypes led to fears about an Asian invasion that
contributed to various discriminatory immigration policies aimed at Asian
Americans, and the internment of Japanese Americans during World War II.
History demonstrates that the most virulent expressions of the perpetual
foreigner/yellow peril stereotype emerge when Asian nations are understood
to be a threat to the United States. The increasing nationalist sentiments and
xenophobic discourses in the present time have once again led to Asians and
Asian Americans being seen as threatening the nation.

Since the 1960s, Asian Americans have been intractably associated with
the model minority, which suggests that Asian Americans have "made it" and
no longer experience racial discrimination or other structural barriers.
Importantly, the "model minority" term was coined in the 1960s by the dominant press to silence Civil Rights protests (Feagin, 2000; Lee, 2009). The
model minority rhetoric was used to prove that anyone can make it in the U.S.
and to confirm that the U.S. is the land of equal opportunity (Lee, 2015).
Thus, the model minority stereotype played a central role in forming racial
hierarchies and inter-group relations, including being a racial wedge between
Asian Americans and African American communities. Park (2008) argues,

"the model minority myth functions as a political mechanism of control that alters one's sense of reality to justify the unequal social order" (p. 136).

The perpetual foreigner stereotype lives on in popular cultural representations of Asian American cultures and languages, which are depicted as being exotic and quintessentially un-American (Lee, 1999). Images of Asian and Asian American martial artists represent one example of how the perpetual foreigner stereotype operates in popular culture. Another common expression of the perpetual foreigner stereotype in popular culture centers around jokes about Asian languages and accents. In 2016 Jesse Watters of Fox News, for example, produced a "Chinatown" segment that called on overtly racist stereotypes and included culturally insensitive jokes made at the expense of Chinatown residents. Elderly Chinese residents who didn't speak English were made the brunt of jokes. In response to the infamous segment, Ronny Chieng, an Asian American comedian who is frequently mocked due to his thick accent, attempted in his own segment to upend the stereotypes of Asian Americans and present the community with counter-narratives that they too have nuanced political opinions and are able to hold intellectual conversations. In popular culture, the model minority stereotype lives on in Asian American characters who are portrayed as smart and nerdy. The ABC comedy *Dr. Ken*, staring Ken Jeong as a "brilliant physician with no bed side manner," draws on and perpetuates the model minority stereotype (https://abc.go.com/shows/dr-ken). The current debate surrounding affirmative action and the admissions policies at Harvard also calls upon stereotypes of Asian American students as high-achieving model minorities. Garces and Poon (2018) argue that in the current lawsuit, Asian Americans are used, once again, as a "racial cover" in efforts to abolish affirmative action, as opponents are "capitalizing on a unique and recent rise of Chinese American immigrant opposition to affirmative action" (Garces & Poon, 2018, p. 2). The characterization of Asian Americans as high achieving students "hurt" by affirmative action fails to recognize the diversity of Asian Americans, including many who do not experience model minority success.

Research illustrates that the model minority and perpetual foreigner stereotypes play out differently for girls/women and boys/men. The model minority stereotype, particularly the idea that Asian Americans are obedient, has contributed to the dominant image that Asian American men are asexual, effeminate, and lacking virility (Eng, 2001). These emasculating stereotypes require Asian men to demonstrate stereotypical heterosexual behaviors to reject their perceived "feminine" nature (Kumashiro, 1999). Asian American women, on the other hand, are framed as exotic and sexually submissive beings who draw on supposedly foreign ways to please their partners (Cho, 2003; Prasso, 2005). These examples illustrate the ways racialized stereotypes intersect with other identities in the lives of Asian Americans.

Racial Stereotype Threats and Collateral Damage

While the model minority stereotype suggests that Asian Americans have overcome racism, the scholarship on Asian Americans reveals that some Asian Americans may embrace model minority behavior as a strategy for dealing with racism. Several studies have revealed that Asian American families encourage their children to perform well in school as a way of coping with racism in the dominant society (Lee, 2009; Lee & Zhou, 2015; Louie, 2004). Asian immigrant parents adopt a narrow frame of achievement and success to better prepare and protect their children from the prejudice of being non-White and to assure their legitimate place in society (Park, 2008) and the pathway to success (Louie, 2004). Thus, Asian immigrants' focus on narrow pathways and a single narrative of success can be understood as a way of coping with potential discrimination in a highly hostile society (Conchas & Pérez, 2003; Lee, 2009; Lee & Zhou, 2015). Indeed, research suggests that the "Tiger Mom" parenting style associated with Asian Americans may be a response to concerns regarding racial discrimination (Lee & Zhou, 2015). Despite the motivations, however, their actions confirm the model minority stereotype in the dominant imagination.

A central danger of the model minority stereotype is that it simplifies the lived experiences of a diverse racial group thereby rendering invisible the experiences of Asian Americans who do not experience model minority success. Asian Americans are a heterogeneous group, consisting of various ethnic, cultural, linguistic, and religious groups with diverse economic and educational backgrounds. Indeed, an examination of the disaggregated data on Asian Americans reveals that not all Asian American groups are high achieving and successful. Students who fail to meet the standards set by the model minority often feel like failures (Lee, 1994; Lee & Zhou, 2015; Louie, 2004). The "loss of face" may even lead to distancing themselves from their ethnic community and their peers in school (Lew, 2004). Asian American youth are not immune from internalizing and believing in prescribed biases about their racial or ethnic background although they discern the negative effects that stereotypes might have on them (McGee, Thakore, & LaBlance, 2017). Lee and Zhou (2015) found that many Asian American students have internalized the belief that "real" Asians are high achieving, and those who fail to meet these standards of success struggle with self-doubt. Chou and Feagin (2014) argue that the internalization of the model minority stereotype reflects the "double consciousness" that many Asian Americans experience.

Gupta, Szymanski, and Leong (2011) have shown that greater affirmation and confirmation of the model minority stereotypes led to higher level of psychological distress and more negative attitudes toward mental health support. The same research found that internalized racism is a significant factor that resulted in psychological distress from not being able to meet the expectations of the model minority and viewing the need for mental health support as another sign of incompetence (Gupta et al., 2011). This research highlights the fact that the acceptance of "positive" stereotypes can lead to similar detrimental effects just like the endorsement of overtly "negative" stereotypes does, suggesting that the internalization of all stereotypes is problematic (Gupta et al., 2011).

Studies have shown that Asian American students report the highest level of emotional distress among ethnic minority groups (Lorenzo, Frost, & Reinherz, 2000). Numerous studies have found that the pressure to live up to the model minority stereotype leads to anxiety, depression, and other mental health issues. Stereotypes and experiences with racism are correlated with negative mental health outcomes among Asian American students (Lee & Ahn, 2011). Among four racial minority groups of adolescent youth, Asian Americans scored one of the highest levels of social stress and family conflicts (Choi, Meininger, & Roberts, 2006). Compared to White Americans, Asian Americans had lower levels of self-esteem (Choi et al., 2006). Furthermore, national statistics show that one out of every five Asian American adolescents experience suicidal ideation (Center for Disease Control and Prevention, 2017). Yet, research shows that Asian Americans access mental health services at lower rates than other minority groups (Lee et al., 2009). Shame and social stigma, along with lack of awareness of resources and parents' lack of knowledge, are believed to be strong determinants that hinder youth in Asian American communities from utilizing mental health services (Lee et al., 2009; Ling, Okazaki, Tu, & Kim, 2014).

Recent research reveals that Asian American youth and college-aged students experience microaggressions, marginalization, and overt racial harassment (Huynh, Devos, & Smalarz, 2011; Ong, Burrow, Fuller-Rowell, Ja, & Sue, 2013; Sue, Bucceri, Lin, Nadal, & Torino, 2007). Microaggressions ranged from being assumed to be good at math (i.e., model minority) to being assumed to be from another country (i.e., perpetual foreigner). For example, most Asian Americans, including third-, fourth-, and fifth-generation Americans, have had the frustrating experience of trying to convince a non-Asian that they are from the United States. While questions such as "Where are you *really* from?" may appear to be innocent, they reflect an assumption that Asian Americans can't be Americans. These racialized microaggressions serve to remind Asian Americans that they are not equal members of society.

Asian Americans report being unfairly treated because of their race or ethnicity, their native language, and/or Asian accent (Goto, Gee, & Takeuchi, 2002; Kim, Wang, Deng, Alvarez, & Li, 2011). Although Asian Americans might fully identify themselves as Americans, they consistently experience being perceived as foreigners and thus feel the need to validate their membership in the nation. Cheryan and Monin (2005), for example, found that Asian Americans do not report being any less American than other White

Americans and introduces the term "identity denial" to explain the practice of denying one's Asian identity and connection to Asian culture and eliminating any trace or indication that might make them seem less American when faced with acceptance threat. Hence, Asian Americans continuously attempted to prove their belongingness and reassert themselves to be portrayed as fully integrated members of the dominant society by demonstrating their knowledge in popular American culture (Cheryan & Monin, 2005). Chinese Americans with low levels of English language proficiency or those who speak English with an accent struggle to adjust in schools, which contributes to depressive symptoms (Kim et al., 2011). The perpetual foreigner stereotype was correlated with a lower sense of belonging to the dominant culture and was a strong predictor for identity conflict. The stereotype also had a significant impact for lower hope and life satisfaction for Asian Americans (Huynh et al., 2011).

Both the model minority and perpetual foreigner stereotypes are also implicated in anti-Asian harassment of Asian American youth. Ironically, both living up to the standards of the model minority stereotype and failure to do so contribute to the perpetual foreigner stereotype, which positions Asian Americans as inherently different from other "regular" Americans. Asian Americans report higher levels of racial discrimination than other diverse racial groups (Mouttapa, Valente, Gallaher, Rohrbach, & Unger, 2004). Chinese American youth suffered from harassment from their peers because they were perceived to receive favorable treatment from teachers who viewed Asian Americans as hardworking, well-behaved, and academically inclined (i.e., model minority) (Qin, Way, & Rana, 2008). Asian American youth were trapped between parents who pushed them to do well academically and peers who harassed them for focusing too much on academics.

Asian Americans youth experienced racial discrimination including physical (e.g., slapping and pushing) and verbal harassment (e.g., name-calling) by non-Asian peers despite exhibiting fewer behavioral issues (Lorenzo et al., 2000). Some male students responded to the constant physical harassment by attempting to grow their physique (Lorenzo et al., 2000). Asian American youth's experiences with discrimination and marginalization have led many to be reluctant to build relationships with peers outside of their racial or ethnic group (Rosenbloom & Way, 2004). This reluctance to build relationships with non-Asian peers contributed to their lower social status in the school. Moreover, they were positioned lower in the social hierarchy because they were less likely to fight back and were seen as weak and defenseless in the eyes of African American and Latino students (Rosenbloom & Way, 2004).

Finally, the research suggests that stereotypes impact both mental and physical health. Self-reported discrimination among Asian Americans was found to be associated with cardiovascular conditions and may be a potential factor for respiratory problems (Gee, Spencer, Chen, & Takeuchi, 2007).

Racial discrimination was also a correlate of pain (e.g., chronic back or neck problems), frequent or severe migraines, and ulcers (Gee et al., 2007). We have not found extensive studies that have investigated physical health-related problems associated with Asian Americans beyond this literature; however, prior studies that have found stressors to have an effect on health such as blood pressure (Ryan, Gee, & LaFlamme, 2006) and hypertension (Guyll, Matthews, & Bromberger, 2001) of other ethnic minority groups could be applied to predict similar effects on those who belong to Asian American communities. Further research is needed on the impact of stereotype threats on Asian American communities.

Conclusion

The persistence of both the model minority and perpetual foreigner stereotypes in popular culture, public discourse and in schools negatively impacts Asian American communities. Asian American youth and college students encounter the model minority and the perpetual foreigner stereotype in their daily lives. Both stereotypes are implicated in the social and emotional stress faced by Asian Americans. Despite the dire need for psychosocial and mental health support for Asian American youth, economic barriers (e.g., lack of insurance), cultural norms circulated in Asian American families and communities (e.g., stigmatization of mental health illness and misconceptions about mental health support), and the model minority stereotype are all barriers to receiving proper mental health services (Spencer, Chen, Gee, Fabian, & Takeuchi, 2010).

Educational institutions and mental health providers must work toward fostering counter-narratives that challenge the dominant narratives (Bamberg, 2004). We call for liberating educational practices and efforts that help empower Asian American youth to be the authors of their own counter-stories, to retell and share their experiential knowledge in order to truly challenge racial stereotypes. As the population of Asian Americans continues to grow, and as globalization brings various Asian cultural forms (e.g., anime and K-pop) to the United States, it will be important to examine whether and how stereotypes of Asian Americans are reproduced and/or challenged. Future research should also examine the ways the racialized stereotypes of Asian Americans as model minorities and perpetual foreigners intersect with other identities (e.g., age, social class, religion, disability, sexuality, etc.).

References

Bamberg, M. (2004). Considering counter narratives. In M. Bamberg & M. Andrews (Eds.), *Considering counter narratives: Narrating, resisting, making sense.* Amsterdam, The Netherlands: John Benjamins.

Center for Disease Control and Prevention. (2017). *High school youth risk behavior survey.* Retrieved from https://nccd.cdc.gov/Youthonline/App/Results.aspx

Chan, S. (1994). *Hmong means free: Life in Laos and America.* Philadelphia, PA: Temple University Press.

Cheryan, S., & Monin, B. (2005). Where are you really from?: Asian Americans and identity denial. *Journal of Personality and Social Psychology, 89*(5), 717–730.

Cho, S. K. (2003). Converging stereotypes in racialized sexual harassment: Where the model minority meets Suzie Wong. In A. K. Wing (Ed.), *Critical race feminism: A reader* (pp. 349–356). New York: New York University Press.

Choi, H., Meininger, J. C., & Roberts, R. E. (2006). Ethnic differences in adolescents' mental distress, social stress, and resources. *Adolescence, 41*(162), 263–283.

Chou, R. S., & Feagin, J. R. (2014). *The myth of the model minority: Asian Americans facing racism* (2nd ed.). London: Routledge.

Conchas, G. Q., & Pérez, C. C. (2003). Surfing the "model minority" wave of success: How the school context shapes distinct experiences among Vietnamese youth. *New Directions for Youth Development, 2003*(100), 41–56.

Eng, D. L. (2001). *Racial castration: Managing masculinity in Asian America.* Durham, NC: Duke University Press.

Feagin, J. R. (2000). *Racist America.* New York: Routledge.

Garces, L. M., & Poon, O. (2018). Asian Americans and race-conscious admissions: Understanding the conservative opposition's strategy of misinformation, intimidation & racial division. *Civil Rights Project.* Retrieved from https://civilrightsproject.ucla.edu/research/college-access/affirmative-action/asian-americans-and-race-conscious-admissions-understanding-the-conservative-opposition2019s-strategy-of-misinformation-intimidation-racial-division/RaceCon_GarcesPoon_AsianAmericansRaceConsciousAdmi.pdf

Gee, G. C., Spencer, M. S., Chen, J., & Takeuchi, D. (2007). A nationwide study of discrimination and chronic health conditions among Asian Americans. *American Journal of Public Health, 97*(7), 1275–1282.

Goto, S. G., Gee, G. C., & Takeuchi, D. T. (2002). Strangers still? The experience of discrimination among Chinese Americans. *Journal of Community Psychology, 30*(2), 211–224.

Gupta, A., Szymanski, D. M., & Leong, F. T. L. (2011). The "model minority myth": Internalized racialism of positive stereotypes as correlates of psychological distress, and attitudes toward help-seeking. *Asian American Journal of Psychology, 2*(2), 101–114.

Guyll, M. M., Matthews, K. A., & Bromberger, J. T. (2001). Discrimination and unfair treatment: Relationship to cardiovascular reactivity among African American and European American women. *Health Psychology, 20*(5), 315–325.

Huynh, Q.-L., Devos, T., & Smalarz, L. (2011). Perpetual foreigner in one's own land: Potential implications for identity and psychological adjustment. *Journal of Social and Clinical Psychology, 30*(2), 133–162.

Kim, S. Y., Wang, Y., Deng, S., Alvarez, R., & Li, J. (2011). Accent, perpetual foreigner stereotype, and perceived discrimination as indirect links between English proficiency and depressive symptoms in Chinese American adolescents. *Developmental Psychology, 47*(1), 289–301.

Kumashiro, K. K. (1999). Supplementing normalcy and otherness: Queer Asian American men reflect on stereotypes, identity, and oppression. *International Journal of Qualitative Studies in Education, 12*(5), 491–508.

Lee, D. L., & Ahn, S. (2011). Racial discrimination and Asian mental health: A meta-analysis. *The Counseling Psychologist, 39*(3), 463–489.

Lee, E. (2015). *The making of Asian America: A history.* New York: Simon & Schuster Paperbacks.

Lee, J., & Zhou, M. (2015). *The Asian American achievement paradox.* New York: Russell Sage Foundation.

Lee, R. G. (1999). *Orientals: Asian Americans in popular culture.* Philadelphia, PA: Temple University Press.

Lee, S., Juon, H.-S., Martinez, G., Hsu, C. E., Robinson, E. S., Bawa, J., & Ma, G. X. (2009). Model minority at risk: Expressed needs of mental health by Asian American young adults. *Journal of Community Health, 34*(2), 144–152.

Lee, S. J. (1994). Behind the model-minority stereotype: Voices of high- and low achieving Asian American students. *Anthropology & Education Quarterly, 25*(4), 413–429.

Lee, S. J. (2009). *Unraveling the "model minority" stereotype* (2nd ed.). New York: Teachers College Press.

Lew, J. (2004). The "other" story of model minorities: Korean American high school dropouts in an urban context. *Anthropology & Education Quarterly, 35*(3), 303–323.

Ling, A., Okazaki, S., Tu, M.-C., & Kim, J. J. (2014). Challenges in meeting the mental health needs of urban Asian American adolescents: Service providers' perspectives. *Race and Social Problems, 6*(1), 25–37.

Lorenzo, M., Frost, A., & Reinherz, H. (2000). Social and emotional functioning of older Asian American adolescents. *Child and Adolescent Social Work Journal, 17,* 289–304.

Louie, V. S. (2004). *Compelled to excel.* Stanford, CA: Stanford University Press.

Lowe, L. (1996). *Immigrant acts: On Asian American cultural politics.* Durham, NC: Duke University Press.

McGee, E. O., Thakore, B. K., & LaBlance, S. S. (2017). The burden of being "model": Racialized experiences of Asian STEM college students. *Journal of Diversity in Higher Education, 10*(3), 253–270.

Mouttapa, M., Valente, T., Gallaher, P., Rohrbach, L. A., & Unger, J. B. (2004). Social network predictors of bullying and victimization. *Adolescence, 39,* 315–334.

Okihiro, G. Y. (1994). *Margins and mainstreams: Asians in American history and culture*. Seattle, WA: University of Washington Press.

Ong, A. D., Burrow, A. L., Fuller-Rowell, T. E., Ja, N. M., & Sue, D. W. (2013). Racial microaggressions and daily well-being among Asian Americans. *Journal of Counseling Psychology, 60*(2), 188–199.

Park, L. S.-H. (2008). Continuing significance of the model minority myth: The second generation. *Social Justice, 35*(2), 134–144.

Prasso, S. (2005). *The Asian mystique: Dragon ladies, Geisha girls, & our fantasies of the exotic Orient*. New York: Public Affairs.

Qin, D. B., Way, N., & Rana, M. (2008). The "model minority" and their discontent: Examining peer discrimination and harassment of Chinese American immigrant youth. *New Directions for Child and Adolescent Development, 2008*(121), 27–42.

Rosenbloom, S. R., & Way, N. (2004). Experiences of discrimination among African American, Asian American, and Latino adolescents in an urban high school. *Youth & Society, 35*(4), 420–451.

Ryan, A. M., Gee, G. C., & LaFlamme, D. J. (2006). The association between self-reported discrimination, physical health and blood pressure: Findings from African Americans, black immigrants, and Latino immigrants in New Hampshire. *Journal of Health Care for the Poor and Underserved, 17*, 116–132.

Saito, N. T. (2001). Symbolism under siege: Japanese American redress and the "racing" of Arab Americans as "terrorists." *Asian Law Journal, 8*, 1–32.

Spencer, M. S., Chen, J., Gee G. C., Fabian, C. G., & Takeuchi, D. T. (2010). Discrimination and mental health–related service use in a national study of Asian Americans. *American Journal of Public Health, 100*(12), 2410–2417.

Sue, D. W., Bucceri, J., Lin, A. I., Nadal, K. L., & Torino, G. C. (2007). Racial microaggressions and the Asian American experience. *Cultural Diversity and Ethnic Minority Psychology, 13*(1), 72–81.

Wu, F. H. (2002). *Yellow: Race in America beyond black and white*. New York: Basic Books.

CHAPTER TEN

Gender Stereotypes

Maya Gann-Bociek and Richard D. Harvey

"Gender parity is not just good for women, it's good for *societies*."
—Angelica Fuentes, gender equality advocate and president of
the Angelica Fuentes Foundation, an organization that focuses on
gender equality and female empowerment

Gender issues have often been pushed to the side, deeming them as a "women's issue" rather than a "human issue." Above, Angela Fuentes gives this as a response to this dilemma, mirroring the thoughts and frustrations of gender experts, equalists, and activists across the globe. In the U.S. specifically, this is all too often the response when someone mentions the 21.4 percent pay gap between women and men (U.S. Department of Labor, 2014) or the underrepresentation of high-ranking female faculty in STEM (science, technology, engineering, mathematics) fields across the nation (Van Miegroet & Glass, 2017).

Similarly, gender stereotypes are also overlooked as an important human issue, despite gender stereotypes (and the gender norms associated with them) having damaging effects to individuals of all genders. A recent study by Blum, Mmari, and Moreau (2017) investigated adolescents around the world to better understand the gender-based beliefs they held. Some themes found in these gendered beliefs were that girls were perceived to be vulnerable, potential victims, and in need of protection, whereas boys were considered to be independent, strong, and even considered to be troublemakers and predators. Alarmingly, the study found that in addition to these themes being present, real-life consequences stemmed from these themes. For example, girls have higher rates of being victims of violence, pregnancy, sexually transmitted infections, and, in countries where it is legal, higher rates of child marriage. Boys have higher rates of engaging in violent behaviors, having a higher mortality rate (both in childhood and adulthood), and higher rates of substance abuse (Blum et al., 2017).

This chapter will be discussing gender stereotypes broadly to help the reader understand gender, gender stereotypes, and the areas of life that stereotypes affect. We will begin by defining the terms that will be important to clarify the discussion of gender stereotypes, including the gender-sex distinction. Following the clarification of terms, we will then discuss the mechanisms surrounding gender stereotypes, and how gender stereotypes infiltrate everyday life.

We will then talk about several life domains that gender stereotypes touch, discussing some of the origins of gender stereotypes, as well as how gender stereotypes have been found to affect these domains, as found by recently published empirical research. Following the overview of current research within the specific domains, we will discuss gender stereotypes from an intersectional perspective, primarily exploring the differences in gender stereotyping for those with different ethnic and cultural backgrounds, as well as discuss how gender stereotypes are affecting individuals who are transgender and gender nonconforming. Finally, we will discuss implications that counteract the negative effects of gender stereotyping. These will focus on interventions and practices that have decreased gender stereotyping, bias, and the outcomes that these beliefs affect.

Defining Terms

We begin by explaining the sex-gender distinction. Sex (or biological sex) generally refers to what sex is assigned to someone at birth or during an ultrasound based on the appearance of the external genitals and other biological traits (chromosomes, etc.). The sex of an individual usually falls under three categories: female, male, and intersex (Sex, n.d.), the latter being more rarely assigned than the first two, but still making up a substantial portion of the population (Intersex Society of North America, n.d.).

Gender refers to the attitudes, behaviors, and feelings that society associates with biological sex, as well as the cultural aspects of being female or male (i.e., femininity, masculinity). Further, it is society's interpretation of what characteristics (physical, behavioral, and attitudinal) each sex possesses (Gender, n.d.). While much of the population's assigned sex and gender are congruent with each other (cisgender), it is important to note that there is a significant portion of the population whose assigned sex and gender identification do not align with each other (i.e., transgender individuals, gender nonconforming individuals, etc.; Genderqueer, n.d.; Transgender, n.d.).

Gender stereotypes are primarily built on of perceptions of gender. The Office of the High Commissioner for Human Rights (United Nations) has defined a gender stereotype as a generalized view of what characteristics ought to be possessed by someone of a certain gender or about the roles and behaviors that should be performed by someone of a certain gender. The Gender Equality Commission of the Council of Europe (2015) provides an alternative definition: Gender stereotypes are "preconceived ideas whereby females and males are arbitrarily assigned characteristics and roles determined and limited by their gender." The act of gender stereotyping is the practice of applying these stereotypical beliefs to other individuals (Gender Stereotype, n.d.).

Gender stereotypes, like all stereotypes, are generalized beliefs about a group based on their attributes and do not necessarily reflect the frequency of certain behaviors, attitudes, and characteristics of these individuals in the real world. The gender stereotypes we recognize today are derived from a variety of different sources including (but not limited to) perceptions of sex, perceptions of gender, gender roles from the past, and perceptions of the frequency of behaviors performed by people of a certain gender. Gender stereotypes have been known to affect a variety of life domains, including work, politics, and education, to name a few. In the next few sections, we will discuss the models and mechanisms that lead to gender stereotyping, followed by looking at some specific domains that gender stereotypes affect.

Illusory Correlations

The concept of illusory correlations has been key to understanding the structure and content of stereotypes in general, and gender stereotypes particularly. Illusory correlations have largely been understood to be the building blocks of stereotypes, as they form stereotypes, help maintain stereotypes, and allow them to endure (Hamilton & Rose, 1980). While the definition has evolved since Chapman's (1967) initial coining of the term, illusory correlations are understood to be a phenomenon where individuals believe there is a relationship between two variables, even when a relationship doesn't actually exist. In stereotype literature specifically, the variables are typically a particular group of people's relationships with certain events, behaviors, or attitudes (Hamilton & Gifford, 1976).

Much of the illusory correlation research within the stereotyping literature looks at stereotyping broadly or in relation to racial stereotypes, but within the illusory correlation literature around gender, this phenomenon is known to affect individuals of all ages and academic backgrounds, from young children (Susskind, 2003) to seasoned academics (Brown & Smith, 1989). Illusory correlations are so infectious, that Risen, Gilovich, and Dunning (2007) found that illusory correlations can form from even a single, unusual event that happens with someone of a particular group (termed "one-shot illusory correlations"). For instance, if a woman who has a very visible and public emotional outburst, someone who is affected by the illusory correlation phenomenon might believe that this occurrence happened because she is a woman, rather than something that might be actually correlated to the outburst, such as high amounts of stress.

Contemporary Models

Within the past two decades, a number of models have been developed through empirical research that have direct implications for understanding gender stereotypes. Among these models are the Stereotype Content Model (Fiske, Cuddy, Glick, & Xu, 2002), Stereotype Threat (Steele & Aronson, 1995), and the Shifting Standards Model (Biernat, 1995; Manis, Biernat, & Nelson, 1991). Each of these models and their implications for understanding gender stereotypes will be discussed below.

Stereotype Content Model

Stereotype Content Model (SCM) proposes that group stereotypes are formed along the dimensions of warmth and competence (Fiske et al., 2002). The dimension of warmth refers to the extent that an individual believes that someone else or a group has the intent to harm or threaten the individual (i.e., high in warmth indicates low intent to harm and high intent to cooperate). The dimension of competence is essentially the individual's perception of whether or not a person or group is competent enough to carry out their intentions (i.e., high competence indicates beliefs that a person or group is generally capable, intelligent, skillful, etc.; Cuddy, Fiske, & Glick, 2008; Fiske et al., 2002).

Further, perceptions of warmth and competence about the person or group can be low or high, and the combinations of low and high warmth/ competence results in four different stereotypes and attitudes. For instance, groups that are seen as being high in warmth but low in competence may be groups that an individual pities and assigns "paternalistic" stereotypes (that they are low in status and not competitive; i.e., the traditional housewife or disabled people). This stereotyping results in passive facilitation, such as cooperating with the group when it's convenient for the individual or associating with them because they're obligated to (Cuddy, Fiske, & Glick, 2008).

Conversely, individuals who perceive a group as low in warmth and high in competence may be envious of that group, assigning "envious" stereotypes (such as the belief that they are high status, and competitive; i.e., those who are rich, Jewish individuals). This stereotype results in the passive harm of the group, such as neglect or ignoring them. In gender stereotype research, women are often targeted as the high warmth/low competence (paternalistic stereotype) group, whereas men are targeted as the low warmth/high competence (envious stereotype) groups (Eckes, 2002).

Stereotype Threat

Stereotype threat, or the threat of confirming negative stereotypes about an individual's gender, racial, or cultural group in a situation where the stereotype may apply (Spencer, Steele, & Quinn, 1999; Steele & Aronson, 1995), is another way that gender stereotypes can negatively influence real-life outcomes. Stereotype threat can push an individual to perform in a way that confirms the stereotype about their group.

Stereotype threat is particularly interesting because it is manipulatable. Hivley and El-Alayli (2014) found that female athletes performed worse when told that women perform worse than men on a particular, moderately difficult task that was relevant to their sport. However, there was no difference in performance when the women were told that there were no performance differences between female and male athletes (a strategy that was used to remove any preexisting stereotype). Indeed, stereotype threat can be induced or eliminated with only a minor comment. Pansu et al. (2016) found similar occurrences in young boys' reading performance scores when they were told that boys don't read as well as girls do (Pansu et al., 2016).

Shifting Standards Model

The Shifting Standards Model (Biernat, 1995) proposes that when we evaluate and judge individuals of other groups, we tend to use a different standard than when we judge people from our own group. This is what many might call a "double standard" (Gaunt, 2013). For instance, one might judge a woman's height of five feet and eight inches as "tall," which would be true only if one is comparing her to other women. However, if she were compared to males, she might be considered "short." In both cases, the woman is the same height, what differs is the standard (i.e., norm) that is being used. Of course, norms for males and females exist for more than height. They also differ along issues like intelligence, leadership ability, and assertiveness. In all these instances, the standards for men and women are "shifted."

To illustrate this phenomenon, Biernat and Kobrynowicz (1997) performed a study that shows how shifting standards can infiltrate organizational research and settings. In their study, they found that in an mock evaluation setting where the participant evaluated mock-job applicants, participants set competency standards for women and African American applicants much lower than male and Caucasian applicants, but also set higher ability standards for the same women and African American applicants (i.e., these same group members needed to perform at a higher level once in the position, despite having lower initial competency standards). Because of these shifting standards, while it may be easier for women and minority group members to hit minimum standards initially, they are also expected to work harder and to "prove" their performance and abilities once in the position (Biernat & Kobrynowicz, 1997).

The models discussed above have given us a way to understand how gender stereotypes are formed and how they are able to infiltrate and affect life. To better understand the outcomes of gender stereotypes specifically, we will now move into reviewing contemporary empirical research that identifies the consequences of gender stereotypes and stereotyping.

Consequences of Gender Stereotypes

In addition to the research that has focused on the structure and/or content of stereotypes, there has been a large amount of research that has focused on how gender stereotypes affect real-world outcomes. What appears to be crucial is that gender stereotypes impact real-world outcomes primarily through the process of bias. Thus, bias is a key mediational mechanism through which gender stereotypes impact real-world phenomena.

The Stereotype-Bias Relationship

The stereotype-bias relationship implies that stereotypes that are held by society inform bias, and these biases influence decision-making (Heilman, 2001, 2012, 2015). This most often occurs when individuals who are not male enter into life domains that have historically been held by men, such as politics or higher-level positions in organizations; however, stereotype-informed bias is known to result in a variety of consequences. We will talk about these in more depth later on in this chapter.

Heilman (2012) explains in a series of research that stereotypes affect bias because stereotypes are made up of descriptive gender stereotypes (what characteristics women and men *actually* have) and prescriptive gender stereotypes (what characteristics women and men *ought* to have). These types of stereotypes inform bias, which is known to influence decision-making, particularly in leadership domains (Heilman, 2012). These biased decisions ultimately create obstacles for individuals who are not male who desire upward movement within a work setting, especially those that are male-dominated work settings (Heilman, 2012, 2015). It is also important to note that gender stereotypes and bias can affect decision-making, regardless of whether the rater or decision maker is consciously aware of the stereotype and believes it (explicit bias), or if the rater is unconsciously influenced by the bias (implicit bias; Reuben, Sapienza, & Zingales, 2014).

Further, violating gender stereotypes could result in poorer evaluations from a rater because of a concept called gender-role congruity bias, which is a preference for people of a certain gender to perform in ways that are consistent with their known gender roles (Kock, D'Mello, & Sackett, 2015). This bias is formed from gender-role stereotypes that individuals learn throughout life, and is one of the biases that can manifest from the stereotype-bias relationship. This bias is known to affect people of all genders when they violate their traditional gender norms and will be underlying some of the contemporary consequences that we will talk about in the next several sections.

Gender Stereotypes and Education

To further explore the more specific issues that gender stereotypes affect, such as work and politics, it is important to discuss gender stereotypes broadly within the education domains, as most gender stereotypes are learned much earlier than when an individual first enters into a workplace or begins to participate in politics.

The concept of gender is something that is learned early on in childhood. Incidentally, gender stereotypes are learned around the same time that gender is learned, or at least when we begin to teach children about the differences between genders—this is something researchers have known for decades. Nearly three decades ago, Fagot, Leinbach, and O'Boyle (1992) found that children who are educated about labels related to gender tend to also know more stereotypes related to gender.

Children learn about gender and the stereotypes relating to gender, not only from their families (Eckert & McConnell-Ginet, 2013; Fagot et al., 1992) and at school, but also in their communities, from their friends (Eckert & McConnell-Ginet, 2013), and from different forms of medias (Grau & Zotos, 2016). More often than not, gender and gender stereotypes are not taught to children and adolescents with ill intentions. However, we know from the stereotype threat literature that even the most mundane comments and ideas regarding gender stereotypes have the ability to affect behavior and cognitive outcomes.

Earlier, we discussed how things that children around the world learn about gender can influence major life outcomes such as mortality rates, pregnancy, and violent behaviors (Blum et al., 2017). Likewise, stereotypes find their way into even more specific, significant areas of life. Cundiff, Vescio, and Lo (2013) found that the more that gender-science stereotypes were believed by women, the less they identified with science. The opposite effect was found in men. Even implicitly, gender-science stereotypes were associated with intent to persist in the science domain, meaning that gender stereotypes about STEM (science, technology, engineering, and mathematics) fields were enough to influence whether or not someone wanted to pursue STEM, directly impacting the gender disparities we see within the field (Cundiff et al., 2013; Nosek & Smyth, 2011).

A few years later, Bian, Leslie, and Cimpian (2017) found that gender stereotypes can influence children as young as six years old. In their study, they found that gender stereotypes about high-level intellect being associated with men more than women can influence young girls, as even the youngest girls in their sample were less likely to think that people of their gender were "really, really smart." This not only influenced their perceptions of gender but also the activities they were interested in.

Even when children and adolescents don't agree with gender stereotypes and norms, it is not easy for them to resist or challenge them. Mulvey and Killen (2015) found that children were willing to resist stereotypical gender norms, but they didn't expect their peers to resist them as much as they did. This expectation about their peers also declined with age. Further, because the children recognized that their peers may not resist gender norms to the same extent they did, they reported that going against their peer-group would likely result in exclusion. This shows that while Western culture encourages individuality, it is still very hard for children to go against their peers. Finally, while the children recognized that girls may be able to get away with challenging gender stereotypes despite their perception of their peers' ideas, boys would not have the same success (Mulvey & Killen, 2015).

While the explicit conversation about gender may not be as prevalent after the initial years a child is exposed to the world, Grau and Zotos (2016) explain that media and advertisements may perpetuate the continuous learning of stereotypical ideas with both explicit and implicit usage of gender stereotypes in media and advertising. They explain that generally, media used to play with gender stereotyping, putting men in more agentic, masculine, and "superior" roles and women into roles that were soft, egalitarian, and "inferior" roles. While media has not totally outgrown its use of putting people in gender-stereotypic roles, it is evolving to a place with more equity. Now, roles with women and men are becoming increasingly more positive and androgynous, showing that women and men are not constrained to performing stereotypical gender roles, many of which are outdated.

Gender Stereotypes and Work

Throughout this chapter, we've briefly discussed gender issues that we see in employment. These issues touch on the wage-gap putting an imaginary worth on the work and performance of people based on their gender (U.S. Department of Labor, 2014) and disparities between women and men in higher-level positions within STEM fields (Van Miegroet & Glass, 2017). We will add to this by discussing more studies that have found disparities in employment fueled by gender stereotypes.

In an extensive review and meta-analysis of gender stereotypes' effects on employment decisions, Kock et al. (2015) found several themes from an extensive number of experimental studies that examined nearly twelve-thousand participants. These themes surrounded the concept of gender-role congruity bias that was mentioned earlier. For jobs that were majority dominated by a specific gender, major disparities were found: there was a preference for men when the jobs were in male-dominated fields (Kock et al., 2015). This was especially true for decision makers who were male. However, there was no strong preference by decision makers for men or women when the jobs were in female-dominated fields or jobs in fields with no majority. Additionally, this bias was not as prevalent when the decision makers were encouraged to make careful decisions, or when the decision makers were experienced professionals (Kock et al., 2015).

In another review focused on emotionality and employment, the researcher found that gender stereotypes that are focused on emotion impede a woman's ability to rise up in the ranks within an organization and be successful leaders (Brescoll, 2016). Much of this review focuses on how women are responded to when they express particular emotions. For instance, women are generally penalized when they show emotion at all, but especially so when expressing emotions that imply dominance (i.e., pride). Interestingly, they also found that women are reprimanded for not showing any emotion at all, as they are not satisfying the stereotypes that insist that women should be communal and warm. This complicated relationship grows in complexity when race and ethnicity are introduced. This will be covered in depth later on in the chapter.

Hoyt and Murphy (2016) found in their review of leadership literature that women may face stereotype threat in leadership because of a perceived "lack of fit" issue, affecting women because they don't fit the White, male stereotype traditionally prescribed to leaders. Additionally, this stereotype threat can be cued to prospective female leaders in several different ways, from having a sexist (or potentially sexist) interviewer to just being in an environment that doesn't appear to support or have representation of women leaders (Hoyt & Murphy, 2016; Walton, Murphy, & Ryan, 2015).

With leadership specifically, the "glass ceiling" is a concept that is frequently used. The glass ceiling was first coined as early as the 1980s, when Morrison, White, and Van Velsor (1987) described it as an "impenetrable barrier" that women will face during their careers, often keeping them from advancing within an organization (Morrison, White, & Van Velsor, 1987). In Heilman (2001), they went on to say that the glass ceiling was a consequence of gender stereotypes and went on to research stereotypes in leadership even today, as the glass ceiling's effects are still present in many contemporary organizations (Heilman, 2012, 2015). Interestingly, we do see the glass ceiling being broken by women and minority CEOs, sometimes more often than White men—however, instances of this change in leadership preferences are found most often for organizations that are performing badly (Cook & Glass, 2014).

While much of the workplace research has shown disparities toward women, men are not free from the negative effects of workplace gender stereotyping. As mentioned earlier, adolescent children are aware that it is harder for boys to resist gender stereotypes than it is for girls (Mulvey & Killen, 2015). Unfortunately, this may not change into adulthood. Since the mid-nineties, women have been entering into male-dominated fields more often, where female-dominated fields have not seen an increase of men, despite the potential of male interest in these fields (Croft, Schmader, & Block, 2015).

In cases where a male does enter into an occupational role that is incongruent with gender stereotypes, they are often paid less, and their status is negatively affected. Brescoll, Uhlmann, Moss-Racusin, and Sarnell (2012) also found that working under a supervisor whose gender was incongruent with the domain they worked in (i.e., a female supervisor in a masculine field) was enough for male workers to be perceived of having lower status and were often paid less.

Once established in an organization, these issues persist even in the most necessary of situations. Rudman and Mescher (2013) found that men that requested family leave were perceived to have more stereotypically feminine traits, such as being weak and uncertain, and lacking stereotypically masculine traits, like being agentic, competitive, and ambitious. Further, more penalties and less rewards were present for men who were seen as weak (i.e., less recommendations for promotions, leadership positions, etc.; Rudman & Mescher, 2013). These instances show that stereotypically feminine characteristics can be problematic for the men that hold them. However, in an earlier paper, Rudman (1998) explained that anyone violating gender-stereotypical norms may receive backlash.

Gender Stereotypes in Politics

As one would expect, the leadership stereotypes mentioned earlier can also affect the political domain. Similar occurrences that Brescoll (2016) discussed can also be found for women leaders who work within politics. In a study performed by Ditonto, Allison, and Redlawsk (2014), competence was a frequently searched topic when seeking information about female candidates in elections, relating to the leadership "fit" theme that has previously discussed in this chapter (Heilman, 2015; Hoyt & Murphy, 2016). Additionally, the female candidate's stance on compassion issues was also searched for more than their male counterparts (Ditonto, Allison, & Redlawsk, 2014).

As for actual voter outcomes and decision-making, the role that stereo-types play is less clear. While older research showed that women who violated their stereotypical communal roles by being perceived as seeking power had worse voting outcomes (Okimoto & Brescoll, 2010), more recent research by Dolan (2014) found that women candidates were evaluated more on what political party they ascribed to than what stereotypes surround women leaders. Further, in an experimental study performed by Dolan and Lynch (2014), they confirmed this idea once again when they found that very little evidence of gender stereotypes playing an important part in vote choice.

Gender Stereotypes and Identity

Intersectionality

Gender stereotypes become more complicated when an individuals' other identities become involved. Intersectionality, or "the complex, cumulative way in which the effects of multiple forms of discrimination (such as racism, sexism, and classism) combine, overlap, or intersect" (Intersectionality, n.d.) is a unique way that a person's multiple identities may alter the ways that gender stereotypes affect individuals. Intersectionality is a unique concept, as it does not imply that individuals that occupy more than one role (i.e., Person of Color and woman) will experience the roles additively, but that the individual will have an experience unique to the combination of these roles (Ghavami & Peplau, 2013). These individuals will also experience unique stereotyping, such as women who are Black facing the stereotype of the "angry Black woman" (Ashley, 2014).

Empirical research has investigated the relationship between stereotyping and intersectionality. Rosenthal and Lobel (2016) investigated the stereotypes that Black women face regarding motherhood. They found that Black women (pregnant or not) were perceived more negatively for topics related to motherhood, sexual activity, and risk, and socioeconomic status than White women (pregnant or not). Pregnant Black women were also perceived as more likely to need public assistance and being single mothers more often than pregnant White women (Rosenthal & Lobel, 2016). Ashley (2014) also found that the "angry Black woman" stereotype has the potential to decrease the usefulness and affect the proper application of mental health treatments for women who are Black when they seek them out.

People of Color who are men are also affected by these intersectional stereotypes. At the beginning of this chapter, we discussed that Blum et al. (2017) found that boys were more likely to be seen as violent, but this perception becomes increasingly more complicated when race is involved. Black and Hispanic men receive harsher prison sentences than men of other races or women, showing that the stereotypes surrounding violent tendencies of certain racial groups, as well as the stereotypes of the men within those racial groups, have real-world consequences (Steffensmeier, Painter-Davis, & Ulmer, 2017).

In organizational domains, intersectionality presents a different effect. In a study performed by Livingston, Rosette, and Washington (2012), they found that Black women leaders and White male leaders did not receive the same backlash for behaving in agentic ways, where the opposite occurred for White women leaders and Black male leaders.

Transgender and Gender Nonconforming Identities

Research investigating gender stereotypes' effect on transgender and gender nonconforming individuals is severely lacking. While research has shown that violating gender-stereotypic norms has negative effects (Livingston et al., 2012; Rudman, 1998; Rudman & Mescher, 2013), there has not been much research to investigate how this affects or differs for transgender and gender nonconforming individuals specifically.

In the little research that has been done on gender stereotypes within this population, research has shown that trans* individuals have their own unique stereotypes and struggle with stereotype threat when these stereotypes are introduced. McKinnon (2014) reported that three primary stereotypes that transwomen endure are stereotypes that they are being deceiving ("passing" as a biological woman, often portraying her as strong, dominant, and often "dangerous" to unsuspecting straight men), that they are pathetically "playing" a woman ("unpassable" as a woman; sad, tragic, and "bad" at being a woman), or that they do not exist at all (implying that transwomen are not real; they will always be men "no matter what they do to their bodies"). Stereotype threat from these stereotypes has been found to affect transwomen's gender presentation and expression (often resulting in an inability to express her authentic self) and other behaviors. Additionally, the fear of stereotype threat results in situational avoidance behaviors (where she may avoid any situation where these stereotypes may be present) (McKinnon, 2014), which could result in a number of outcomes, including lack of career and social opportunities and experience.

The shortage of literature regarding gender stereotypes and their effects surrounding gender nonconforming and transgendered individuals does not insist that they (the effects, the stereotypes, or even the individuals) do not exist. Rather, they are likely very prevalent among the LGBTQIA+ populations and are likely just as complex and impactful as how traditional gender-stereotypes affect cisgender individuals. More research needs to be done to have a more in-depth, empirical understanding of how all transgender and gender nonconforming individuals are affected by gender stereotypes.

The Hope for an Optimistic Future: Decreasing Gender Stereotypes' Effects

While empirical research has identified the consequences of gender stereotypes, they also have looked into how to decrease the negative effects of gender stereotyping. This final section of the chapter will discuss several different ways that gender stereotypes damaging effects can be mitigated.

Education Is Key

Education about gender stereotypes, their origins, and their effects are a straightforward way to help decrease gender stereotyping and bias. This idea is effective and is often the approach that is taken in the early stages of many bias-reduction interventions. To tackle gender stereotypes at the root, the illusory correlation literature has suggested a variety of ideas on how to help decrease gender stereotyping—before they even have the chance to affect real-world outcomes. Eagly and Steffen (1984) have suggested in their early literature that changing the roles we stereotypically divide women and men into will need to cease, and there needs to be a push for nonsexist portrayals of women and men in textbooks. Contemporary efforts have taken this suggestion, particularly in media, as we now see in children's shows violating stereotypic gender norms (i.e., children's show character *Doc McStuffins*, a woman of color, as a medical doctor) and media putting people in androgynous or gender nonconforming roles (i.e., men taking care of babies in diaper commercials). Susskind (2003) suggested similar ideas but said that for this approach to work (particularly for children), exposure to people performing behaviors that are counterstereotypic needs to be done often, not only once or twice.

With one-shot illusory correlations, Risen et al. (2007) noted that in cases of unusual behaviors where these false relationships may arise, more elaborate stereotypes could be created from this single event. In these cases, simply being aware that illusory correlations exist and can occur from single events could potentially help individuals realize that these relationships are not real and encourage them to make a conscious effort to prevent themselves from adopting stereotypical ideas and beliefs.

Macro-Level Gender Stereotype and Bias Interventions

As alluded to earlier, gender bias interventions are one way to help tens of hundreds of people at once decrease the effects of bias and stereotypes surrounding gender. These are actively utilized by many different types of organizations to help them solve issues they may be having around gender stereotypes. Within STEM fields, these types of interventions have helped reduce gender bias in STEM faculty, shift cultural climates of departments to a climate that supports the career advancement of women in STEM, and encourage positive behavioral change from faculty (Carnes et al., 2015; Girod et al., 2016).

Perrault (2015) stresses the importance of institutional change to properly encourage gender diversity. In organizations, Perrault remarks that institutional change requires stakeholders questioning legitimacy in a current practice. Within organizations, change can be aimed at the double standards implied in the Shifting Standards Model discussed above (Biernat, 1995). Whether these standards be embedded within the criteria for promotions, delegation and assignments, or leadership emergence, they are likely targets for organizational-level interventions and thereby opportunities to reduce the impact of gender stereotypes in organizations.

Micro-Level Gender Stereotype and Bias Interventions

Mentoring has had success in helping individuals enter into and maintain upward momentum in a variety of fields. Tran (2014) noted that prior to the study they conducted, mentoring has led to the success of women of color in faculty positions. Lopez (2013) noted that mentoring style is also important to see success in a diverse range of mentees and encouraged the use of collaborative mentorships (Lopez, 2013).

To the degree to which gender stereotypes are likely to vary along the dimensions of competency and warmth as discussed in the Stereotype Content Model (Fiske et al., 2002), interventions aimed at dispelling the notion that women are "warm" but "incompetent" might make a substantial impact. Primarily, these interventions could untangle the illusory correlation that all women, simply by virtue of being women, are incompetent. However, they might also, in turn, untangle the notion that all women, simply by virtue of being women, are necessarily warm.

In addition to interventions that focus on change within the perpetrators of gender stereotypes, there might also be ways to effect change for those who are typically the targets of gender stereotypes. Women and other gendered minorities are likely to face struggles that result from the internalizing of gender stereotypes. Also, even when the stereotypes aren't necessarily internalized, their mere salience in a given situation might impede performance, as suggested by the Stereotype Threat (Steele & Aronson, 1995) Model discussed earlier. Thus, the effects of gender stereotypes on women can be reduced by reducing stereotype threat. In the Stereotype Threat section earlier in this chapter, the studies described indicated that stereotype threat was induced by a cue, and that these cues could be as mundane as a sexist comment, or as elaborate as an organization's appearance of supporting female employees. While it isn't always possible to manipulate these cues, as these studies were able to do, trying to reduce cues that foster negative stereotypes whenever possible should be encouraged.

Summary

This chapter explored and discussed gender stereotypes and bias, identifying what they are, how they work, and the variety of life domains and people that they affect. The majority of the information and empirical research mentioned in this chapter is from the last five years, with the hope that contemporary research can be built off existing knowledge over gender stereotypes and bias. It is important to note that while this chapter covered a variety of topics within the gender stereotype domain, it only scratched the surface of information available on the topic and is meant to be a general overview of gender stereotypes and bias. The authors hope that this chapter will help inform a better understanding of gender, gender stereotypes, and bias and that the reader will be encouraged to critically think about how gender stereotypes affect them and the world around them.

References

Ashley, W. (2014). The angry black woman: The impact of pejorative stereotypes on psychotherapy with black women. *Social Work in Public Health, 29(1),* 27–34.

Bian, L., Leslie, S., & Cimpian, A. (2017). Gender stereotypes about intellectual ability emerge early and influence children's interests. *Science, 355*(6323), 389–391.

Biernat, M. (1995). The shifting standards model: Implications of stereotype accuracy for social judgment. In Y.-T. Lee, L. J. Jussim, & C. R. McCauley (Eds.), *Stereotype accuracy: Toward appreciating group differences* (pp. 87–114). Washington, D.C.: American Psychological Association.

Biernat, M., & Kobrynowicz, D. (1997). Gender-and race-based standards of competence: Lower minimum standards but higher ability standards for devalued groups. *Journal of Personality and Social Psychology, 72*(3), 544.

Blum, R. W., Mmari, K., & Moreau, C. (2017). It begins at 10: How gender expectations shape early adolescence around the world. *Journal of Adolescent Health, 61*(4 Suppl), S3–S4.

Brescoll, V. L. (2016). Leading with their hearts? How gender stereotypes of emotion lead to biased evaluations of female leaders. *The Leadership Quarterly, 27,* 415–428.

Brescoll, V. L., Uhlmann, E. L., Moss-Racusin, C., & Sarnell, L. (2012). Masculinity, status, and subordination: Why working for a gender stereotype violator causes men to lose status. *Journal of Experimental Social Psychology, 48*(1), 354–357.

Brown, R., & Smith, A. (1989). Perceptions of and by minority groups: The case of women in academia. *European Journal of Social Psychology, 19*(1), 61–75.

Carnes, M., Devine, P. G., Manwell, L. B., Byars-Winston, A., Fine, E., Ford, C. E., . . . Palta, M. (2015). Effect of an intervention to break the gender bias habit for faculty at one institution: A cluster randomized, controlled trial. *Academic Medicine: Journal of the Association of American Medical Colleges, 90*(2), 221.

Chapman, L. (1967). Illusory correlation in observational report. *Journal of Verbal Learning and Verbal Behavior, 6*(1), 151–155. doi:10.1016/S0022-5371(67)80066-5

Cook, A., & Glass, C. (2014). Above the glass ceiling: When are women and racial/ethnic minorities promoted to CEO? *Strategic Management Journal, 35*(7), 1080–1089.

Croft, A., Schmader, T., & Block, K. (2015). An underexamined inequality: Cultural and psychological barriers to men's engagement with communal roles. *Personality and Social Psychology Review, 19*(4), 343–370.

Cuddy, A. J., Fiske, S. T., & Glick, P. (2008). Warmth and competence as universal dimensions of social perception: The stereotype content model and the BIAS map. *Advances in Experimental Social Psychology, 40*, 61–149.

Cundiff, J. L., Vescio, E. L., & Lo, L. (2013). Do gender–science stereotypes predict science identification and science career aspirations among undergraduate science majors? *Social Psychology Education, 16*, 541–554.

Ditonto, T. M., Allison, J. H., & Redlawsk, D. P. (2014). Gender stereotypes, information search, and voting behavior in political campaigns. *Political Behavior, 36*(2), 335–358.

Dolan, K. (2014). Gender stereotypes, candidate evaluations, and voting for women candidates: What really matters? *Political Research Quarterly, 67*(1), 96–107.

Dolan, K., & Lynch, T. (2014). It takes a survey: Understanding gender stereotypes, abstract attitudes, and voting for women candidates. *American Politics Research, 42*(4), 656–676.

Eagly, A. H., & Steffen, V. J. (1984). Gender stereotypes stem from the distribution of women and men into social roles. *Journal of Personality and Social Psychology, 46*(4), 735.

Eckert, P., & McConnell-Ginet, S. (2013). *Language and gender.* Cambridge: Cambridge University Press.

Eckes, T. (2002). Paternalistic and envious gender stereotypes: Testing predictions from the stereotype content model. *Sex Roles, 47*(3–4), 99–114.

Fagot, B. I., Leinbach, M. D., & O'Boyle, C. (1992). Gender labeling, gender stereotyping, and parenting behaviors. *Developmental Psychology, 28*(2), 225–230.

Fiske, S. T., Cuddy, A. J., Glick, P., & Xu, J. (2018). A model of (often mixed) stereotype content: Competence and warmth respectively follow from perceived status and competition (2002). In *Social cognition* (pp. 171–222). London: Routledge.

Gaunt, R. (2013). Breadwinning moms, caregiving dads: Double standard in social judgments of gender norm violators. *Journal of Family Issues, 34*(1), 3–24.

Gender. (n.d.). *APA dictionary of psychology* (2nd ed.). Retrieved from https://www.apa.org/pi/lgbt/resources/sexuality-definitions.pdf

Gender Equality Commission of the Council of Europe. (2015). *Gender equality glossary.* Retrieved from https://www.coe.int/en/web/genderequality

Gender Stereotype. (n.d.). *Women's rights and gender section, OHCHR Research and Right to Development Division, Rule of Law, Equality and Non-Discrimination Branch.* Retrieved from https://www.ohchr.org/Documents/Issues/Women/WRGS/OnePagers/Gender_stereotyping.pdf

Genderqueer. (n.d.). *APA dictionary of psychology* (2nd ed.). Retrieved from https://www.apa.org/pi/lgbt/resources/sexuality-definitions.pdf

Ghavami, N., & Peplau, L. A. (2013). An intersectional analysis of gender and ethnic stereotypes: Testing three hypotheses. *Psychology of Women Quarterly, 37*(1), 113–127.

Girod, S., Fassiotto, M., Grewal, D., Ku, M. C., Sriram, N., Nosek, B. A., & Valantine, H. (2016). Reducing implicit gender leadership bias in academic medicine with an educational intervention. *Academic Medicine, 91*(8), 1143–1150.

Grau, S. L., & Zotos, Y. C. (2016). Gender stereotypes in advertising: A review of current literature. *International Journal of Advertising, 35*(5), 761–770.

Hamilton, D. L., & Gifford, R. K. (1976). Illusory correlation in interpersonal perception: A cognitive basis of stereotypic judgements. *Journal of Experimental Social Psychology, 12*, 392–407.

Hamilton, D. L., & Rose, T. L. (1980). Illusory correlation and the maintenance of stereotypic beliefs. *Journal of Personality and Social Psychology, 39*(5), 832–845. doi:10.1037/0022-3514.39.5.832

Heilman, M. E. (2001). Description and prescription: How gender stereotypes prevent women's ascent up the organizational ladder. *Journal of Social Issues, 57*(4), 657–674.

Heilman, M. E. (2012). Gender stereotypes and workplace bias. *Research in Organizational Behavior, 32*, 113–135.

Heilman, M. E. (2015). Gender stereotypes: Impediments to women's career progress. In *Auswahl von Männern und Frauen als Führungskräfte* (pp. 73–84). Wiesbaden: Springer Gabler.

Hivley, K., & El-Alayli, A. (2014). "You throw like a girl": The effect of stereotype threat on women's athletic performance and gender stereotypes. *Psychology of Sport and Exercise, 15*(1), 48–55.

Hoyt, C. L., & Murphy, S. E. (2016). Managing to clear the air: Stereotype threat, women, and leadership. *The Leadership Quarterly, 27*(3), 387–399. doi:10.1016/j.leaqua.2015.11.002.

Intersectionality. (n.d.). *Merriam-Webster Dictionary* online. Retrieved from https://www.merriam-webster.com/dictionary/intersectionality

Intersex Society of North America. (n.d.). *ISNA.* Retrieved October 10, 2018, from www.isna.org

Kock, A. J., D'Mello, S. D., & Sackett, P. R. (2015). A meta-analysis of gender stereotypes and bias in experimental simulations of employment decision making. *Journal of Applied Psychology, 100*(1), 128–161.

Livingston, R. W., Rosette, A. S., & Washington, E. F. (2012). Can an agentic Black woman get ahead? The impact of race and interpersonal dominance on perceptions of female leaders. *Psychological Science, 23*(4), 354–358.

Lopez, A. E. (2013). Collaborative mentorship: A mentoring approach to support and sustain teachers for equity and diversity. *Mentoring & Tutoring: Partnership in Learning, 21*(3), 292–311.

Manis, M., Biernat, M., & Nelson, T. F. (1991). Comparison and expectancy processes in human judgment. *Journal of Personality and Social Psychology, 61*, 203–211.

McKinnon, R. (2014). Stereotype threat and attributional ambiguity for trans women. *Hypatia, 29*(4), 857–872.

Morrison, A. M., White, R. P., & Van Velsor, E. (1987). *Breaking the glass ceiling.* Reading, MA: Addison-Wesley.

Mulvey, K. L., & Killen, M. (2015). Challenging gender stereotypes: Resistance and exclusion. *Child Development, 86*(3), 681–694.

Nosek, B. A., & Smyth, F. L. (2011). Implicit social cognitions predict sex differences in math engagement and achievement. *American Educational Research Journal, 48*, 1124–1154. doi:10.3102/0002831211410683

Okimoto, T. G., & Brescoll, V. L. (2010). The price of power: Power seeking and backlash against female politicians. *Personality and Social Psychology Bulletin, 36*(7), 923–936.

Pansu, P., Régner, I., Max, S., Colé, P., Nezlek, J. B., & Huguet, P. (2016). A burden for the boys: Evidence of stereotype threat in boys' reading performance. *Journal of Experimental Social Psychology, 65*, 26–30.

Perrault, E. (2015). Why does board gender diversity matter and how do we get there? The role of shareholder activism in deinstitutionalizing old boys' networks. *Journal of Business Ethics, 128*(1), 149–165.

Reuben, E., Sapienza, P., & Zingales, L. (2014). How stereotypes impair women's careers in science. *Proceedings of the National Academy of Sciences USA, 111*(12), 4403–4408.

Risen, J. L., Gilovich, T., & Dunning, D. (2007). One-shot illusory correlations and stereotype formation. *Personality and Social Psychology Bulletin, 33*(11), 1492–1502.

Rosenthal, L., & Lobel, M. (2016). Stereotypes of Black American women related to sexuality and motherhood. *Psychology of Women Quarterly, 40*(3), 414–427.

Rudman, L. A. (1998). Self-promotion as a risk factor for women: The costs and benefits of counter stereotypical impression management. *Journal of Personality and Social Psychology, 74*, 629–645.

Rudman, L. A., & Mescher, K. (2013). Penalizing men who request a family leave: Is flexibility stigma a femininity stigma? *Journal of Social Issues, 69*(2), 322–340.

Sex. (n.d.). *APA dictionary of psychology* (2nd ed.). Retrieved from https://www.apa.org/pi/lgbt/resources/sexuality-definitions.pdf

Spencer, S. J., Steele, C. M., & Quinn, D. M. (1999). Stereotype threat and women's math performance. *Journal of Experimental Social Psychology, 35*(1), 4–28. doi:10.1006/jesp.1998.1373

Steele, C. M., & Aronson, J. (1995). Stereotype threat and the intellectual test performance of African Americans. *Journal of Personality and Social Psychology, 69*(5), 797.

Steffensmeier, D., Painter-Davis, N., & Ulmer, J. (2017). Intersectionality of race, ethnicity, gender, and age on criminal punishment. *Sociological Perspectives, 60*(4), 810–833.

Susskind, J. E. (2003). Children's perception of gender-based illusory correlations: Enhancing preexisting relationships between gender and behavior. *Sex Roles, 48*(11–12), 483–494.

Tran, N. A. (2014). The role of mentoring in the success of women leaders of color in higher education. *Mentoring & Tutoring: Partnership in Learning, 22*(4), 302–315.

Transgender. (n.d.). *APA dictionary of psychology* (2nd ed.). Retrieved from https://www.apa.org/pi/lgbt/resources/sexuality-definitions.pdf

U.S. Department of Labor, Bureau of Labor Statistics. (2014). *Women's Bureau.* Retrieved from https://www.dol.gov/wb/stats/stats_data.htm

Van Miegroet, H., & Glass, C. (2017). Status, recruitment, and retention of women in STEM between 2008 and 2014. *Technical Report.*

Walton, G. M., Murphy, M. C., & Ryan, A. M. (2015). Stereotype threat in organizations: Implications for equity and performance. *Annual Review of Organizational Psychology and Organizational Behavior, 2,* 523–550.

CHAPTER ELEVEN

Sexuality Stereotyping in Politics, the Media, Schools, and the Workplace

Kyle J. Page, Charnetta R. Brown,
and Zuzuky Robles

This chapter continues the discussion on stereotypes by focusing the lenses on sexuality and the pitfalls and progress related to sexual orientation. According to Blashill and Powlishta (2009), stereotypes based on sexual orientation originated in Freud's gender inversion theory. The gender inversion theory stated that gay men are more similar to heterosexual females than heterosexual males, whereas gay women are more similar to heterosexual males than heterosexual females. This notion has encouraged the use of stereotypic cues to make inferences about sexual orientation. In today's culture, this is known as "gaydar," which is a form of sixth sense or intuition that helps inform judgments about sexual orientation (Bronski, Pellegrini, & Amico, 2013). While some research has suggested that people are able to accurately identify someone's sexual orientation based on physical characteristics (e.g., Rule, Ambady, Adams, & Macrae, 2008), some researchers argue that "gaydar" comes with fallacies that may indirectly promote discrimination (e.g., Blashill & Powlishta, 2009).

Throughout this century, we have seen several events that have influenced beliefs and perceptions about sexual orientation. According to Blashill and Powlishta (2009), changes in beliefs about sexual orientation, as well as gender roles, have affected stereotypes relating to sexual orientation. Stereotypes of lesbian, gay, bisexual, and transgender (LGBT) individuals have historical rooting that has continued to take shape within politics, media, education, and the workplace and have led to prejudice and discrimination. This chapter will explore stereotypes by examining historical progression, different existing stereotypes, and contributions that are more recent.

History

From the time that the United States was established (1776), crimes such as sodomy and buggery were considered capital offenses in some states and cross dressing was considered a felony punishable by imprisonment (Painter, 2005). Although it has been speculated that some prominent historical figures, such as Abraham Lincoln (Herndon & Weik, 1889), were homosexual, little change in laws or opinions of society seemed to take place until the sexual revolution (the mid-1960s). In 1963, Illinois first decriminalized consensual sexual relations in same-sex couples. By 1973, four more states (Connecticut, Colorado, Oregon, and Delaware) had followed, and by the end of the 1970s, fifteen additional states (Ohio, Massachusetts, North Dakota, New Mexico, New Hampshire, California, West Virginia, Iowa, Maine, Indiana, South Dakota, Wyoming, Nebraska, Washington, and New York) did the same. Pennsylvania and Wisconsin followed suit in the 1980s with Kentucky, Nevada, Tennessee, Montana, and Rhode Island joining the cause in the 1990s. It was not until 2003 that the Supreme Court decriminalized homosexuality (*Lawrence v. Texas*) in the final fourteen states.

From a psychological perspective, the American Psychiatric Association removed the diagnosis of "homosexuality" from the second edition of the Diagnostic and Statistical Manual in 1968 (Drescher, 2015) but did not remove "Gender Identity Disorder" until December of 2012 (GLAAD, 2012). Further, the World Health Organization did not remove "Transsexualism" until June of 2018 (Fitzsimons, 2018). It is also important to note that, from a medical perspective, LGBT individuals still face pervasive health disparities and barriers to high-quality care (Keuroghlian, Ard, & Makadon, 2017). This possibly stems from the HIV/AIDS epidemic, which began in 1981 and perpetuated many negative sex stereotypes. Headlines such as "'Gay plague' may lead to blood ban on homosexuals" that appear in the *Daily Telegraph* (1983) provide a poignant example of the repercussions of this health crisis and movies such as *The Normal Heart* attempt to portray this time period. In many locations, LGBT individuals are "high risk" candidates for blood donations, which often deters LGBT participation. On a positive note, some progress is apparent as new drugs, such as the Pre-Exposure Prophylaxis (PrEP), begin to permeate the market.

In summation, although it may seem to some that LGBT individuals have had a voice throughout history, it has not been until recently that equal rights have made substantial progress. Additionally, although it is beyond the scope of this chapter, it would be foolish to not mention that, for those who display more than one characteristic that is not considered the norm (i.e., gender, race, religion, culture, etc. . . .), there are intersectional effects. In other words, the challenges faced by LGBT individuals can be exacerbated if that individual happens to also be a stigmatized religion or stereotyped race.

Politics

The monumental progress within the LGBT community around equality has increased more rapidly over the years with the passage of marriage and employment laws (Herek, 2015). The Human Rights Campaign (HRC) is at the forefront of the political movement for LGBT Americans with success in the Defense of Marriage Act and the repeal of the long-standing "Don't Ask, Don't Tell" act of the 1990s. For anyone who might not be familiar with these acts, the "Don't Ask, Don't Tell" act was a military policy that took effect under the Clinton Administration; it prohibited discrimination or harassment on closeted (those not disclosing their sexual orientation) gay and bisexual service members or applicants and barred openly gay and bisexual service members (Burks, 2011). Further, the Defense of Marriage Act was a federal law that defined marriage as the union between a man and a woman as a way to refuse recognition of same-sex marriage at the federal level (Adam, 2003). Though the HRC has made significant progress, it was not the first organization to fight for the equal rights of LGBT individuals.

Some of the first political engagements in the LGBT community developed around the Stonewall riots of 1969 (Clendinen & Nagourney, 2001). The Stonewall riots erupted after the police raided a late nightclub outing at a local gay bar. The patrons (and later identified activists) included revolutionaries, drag queens, and "butch" (masculine) lesbians, all of whom were involved in physical altercations with the police ("street fights") and resulted in the LGBT community participating in various political demonstrations. This event ultimately paved the way to the beginning of the gay liberation movement (Clendinen & Nagourney, 2001). In addition to political action, the LGBT community began to boycott local brands who did not accept their way of life. One example is the boycotting of Florida orange juice, who supported the "Save Our Children, Incorporated" campaign that sought to overturn legislation that banned housing, employment, and public discrimination based on sexual orientation (Niedwiecki, 2013). This political activity continues to this day. For example, in the 2012 elections, the LGBT community accounted for 66 percent of the six million votes for that election year, which lead to an "Equality Landslide" (Human Rights Campaign, 2012). Following this, the Obama administration named June as LGBT Pride Month (Semm & Sanchez-Watson, 2012), extended the Family Leave Act to cover same-sex couples (Landau, 2012), and improved the Uniting American Families Act to afford binational LGBT and heterosexual couples the same rights as American citizens (Semm & Sanchez-Watson, 2012). Furthermore, President Obama included sexual orientation and gender identity to anti-hate crimes legislation such as the Matthew Shepard and James Byrd Jr. Hate Crimes Prevention Act (Weiner, 2010). The Supreme Court has also contributed to significant advancements during the Obama administration by extending equal marriage rights for the LGBT community by recognizing that Americans have the right to marry regardless of gender (i.e., *Obergefell v. Hodges*, 2015).

Beyond political approval and marriage equality, the Pew Research Center reported that same-sex marriage support/acceptance has risen from 35 percent (2001) to 62 percent (2016). However, despite social and political trends, the Trump administration continues to threaten the substantial progress that the HRC and other political activists within the LGBT community have made to date. Within one year of the Trump administration, the president and his staff have greatly diminished information on LGBT individuals on the White House website (Robertson, 2018) and proposed a ban on transgender individuals serving in the military (Belkin, Barrett, Eitelberg, & Ventresca, 2017; Philipps, 2017). Shortly after, the administration discriminated against transgender students by reversing workplace protections and bathroom bills leading to the emphasis on gendered bathrooms and the reduction of gender-neutral restrooms (Restar & Reisner, 2017). This ban targeted sixteen states that have restricted bathroom use for transgender individuals and fourteen states that have bans specifically in public schools, thereby impacting the gender dysphoria faced by individuals who do not identify with their sex at birth (Restar & Reisner, 2017).

The focus on sexual orientation within the political space has spanned the course of several decades with more significant progress in support than in opposition. In the early 1990s, a Colorado for Family Values (CFV) board member tried several times to ban local gay rights laws by publicly expressing disgust and hate during state campaigns (Nussbaum, 2010). Moreover, CFV board members suggested that homosexuals are radically deviant, express militant gay aggression, and are responsible for a large proportion of child molestation (Nussbaum, 2010). Despite various conservative states efforts to ban homosexuals, these attempts shaped the expansion of Title VII to cover sexual orientation (Marcosson, 1992). Activism started with the notion that sexual orientation disorders were a mental illness (American Psychiatric Association, 1952) and that has since evolved into the idea that sexual orientation is not only fluid but also a normal sexual variant (American

Psychiatric Association, 1968). Further, a contributing factor to the socialization of sexual orientation is the value of diversity that has permeated social, political, and educational spheres.

Public Opinion and Media

There are a variety of books written about understanding the interaction of media representation and gay people (e.g., Wolf & Kielwasser, 2014). Throughout the world, few shifts in public opinion have been as durable or changing as attitudes involving those of the LGBT community. Although some more rural areas of America are openly less accepting, there has been a general trend toward acceptance. For example, when analyzing over 325 national public opinion surveys on LGBT rights from 1977 to 2014, trends indicate a rapid and significant increase of support in the United States (Flores, 2014). Further, public support for marriage equality (55%) and for adoption rights (63%) have more than doubled since the early 2000s, and about 72 percent of the public currently supports laws protecting lesbians and gay men from job discrimination. Additionally, approximately 92 percent of America's LGBT adults say that society has become more accepting in the past decade and an equal number expect it to grow even more accepting in the decade ahead (Taylor, 2013). It is important to note that even though more than half of Americans (55%) say they favor allowing gays and lesbians to marry legally, 37 percent remain opposed (Weigel & Tumulty, 2017). So what does this mean for LGBT individuals?

Despite acceptance, the depiction of LGBT individuals in the media has plenty of room for improvement. Typically, gay men are stereotyped as being hyper-feminine (Linneman, 2008) and lesbian women are stereotyped to be hyper-masculine (Blashill & Powlishta, 2009). When homosexual TV characters are caricaturized in this manner, negative stereotypes are reinforced (Bond, 2014) and permeate through society. For example, if men display feminine behavior, their sexuality is often questioned (Madon, 1997), and individuals are often surprised if someone that doesn't "seems gay" turns out to be homosexual (Rapp, 2013). Following gender-congruence theory, when individuals do not follow their societal role of either masculinity or femininity, they may become the recipient of bias (Tokar & Jome, 1998). Addressing these stereotypes is vitally important as the public, children and adults alike, learn about LGBT culture primarily through the media (Croteau & Hoynes, 1997).

Research has shown that media consumption and freedom of press predict positive attitudes toward homosexuality among younger cohorts (Ayoub & Garretson, 2017; Calzo & Ward, 2009). Luckily, there has been an unparalleled increase in the representation of gay people in news, television, and movies since the 1990s (Gross, 2002). There is a vast array of portrayals of LGBTQ individuals in shows targeting a wide variety of audiences such as general/family (i.e., *Modern Family, The Fosters*), younger audiences (i.e., *Teen Wolf, Glee, The Originals, Shadow Hunters*), and even superhero audiences (i.e., *The Umbrella Academy*). There are also movies ranging from online providers such as Netflix (i.e., *Alex Strangelove*), international films (i.e., *Call Me by Your Name*), political films (i.e., *Milk*), short films (i.e., *The Way He Looks*), musicals (i.e., *Rent*), and younger audience films (i.e., *GBF, Noah's Ark*). However, the frequency of representation does not allow us to understand the effects of stereotyping in the media. For example, although reality shows such a *Big Brother* and *Alabama Shore* include all types of cast members, they often do so in a way that fits pre-existing stereotypes (Chung, 2007). Further, shows often rely on stereotypical characters to tell stories more efficiently (Vargas & DePyssler, 1998). One example is *Queer as Folk*, which depicts LGBT individuals living in unrealistic, erotic lifestyles revolving and evolving around drugs, gay clubs, and casual sex. A second example is *Will & Grace*. Although this show has had a long-running career (1998–2006) and has been renewed, Will and Jack, the two homosexual main characters, are generally obsessed with fashion, beauty, the idolization of younger, handsome, masculine men, and bar scenes. Typically, these heterocentric forms of stereotyping have negative influences on public perception and lead individuals to believe that being gay is an act or performance (Newton & Williams, 2003).

Contrary to television and media growth and popularity, only 125 films (18%) released by major motion pictures include LGBT individuals, with 23 (43%) of those films giving less than one minute of screen time for LGBT characters and only 9 (7%) passing the Vito Russo test (GLAAD, 2017). To pass the Vito Russo test, which assesses the narrative of LGBT individuals, a film must (a) contain a LGBT individual, (b) the character is not be solely or predominantly defined by their sexual orientation/gender identity, and (c) the character must be tied into the plot in such a way that their removal would have a significant effect. In essence, LGBT portrayal in major motion pictures tends to have LGBT individuals depicted as the butt of juvenile jokes or being the unfortunate recipients of miserable and loveless existences (Blacklow, 2018). Further, when gay men are portrayed in stereotypical effeminate roles, they are perceived to be warmer (i.e., more helpful, kind, friendly, etc.) but less competent than gay characters that are portrayed as more masculine (Sink, Mastro, & Dragojevic, 2018). Despite this, in terms of Oscar representation (2016–2018), films like *Moonlight*, which stars Black, gay males, *Call Me By Your Name*, which stars White, European, gay males, and *A Fantastic Woman*, which stars a transgender woman, respectively are breaking ground in the representation of LGBT individuals. The trend continues (2019) with films such as *Bohemian Rhapsody* and *The Favourite*.

Beyond film, television, and general public opinion surveys, the area that seems to have the most tumultuous relationship with the LGBT community, as well as individuals of color, is social media and advertising. It is best to look at examples when discussing this topic. In 2015, Campbell's Soup Company released an advertisement with gay dads. There was a large cry of outrage and support on the Campbell's Facebook page (Nichols, 2015). In several cases, people often use their religious views and opinions as a reason behind why they are bigoted toward the LGBT community and as a reason why they believe certain populations deserve fewer rights. For example, the aforementioned "Save Our Children, Inc." was highly supported by Christian fundamentalists such as Anita Bryant, a celebrity singer, who claimed that removing sexuality discrimination was actually discriminating against her right to teach her children biblical morality. Often the religious stereotype of homosexual individuals is that their way of life is unnatural and in opposition to the will of their deity. Some individuals have even gone as far as to blame natural disasters, such as Hurricane Sandy and Joaquin, as well as a slew of earthquakes (Salandra, 2017), on gay equality. This is not to say that all religious entities are adverse to the LGBT community. In fact, a survey from the Pew Research Center (2011) reported that 79 percent of White Catholics and 65 percent of White "mainline" Protestants, compared to 29 percent of White evangelical Protestants, say that homosexuality should be accepted. In the same survey, Hispanics (64%) supported homosexuality at higher rates than White Americans (58%) or African Americans (49%). Additionally, there has been substantial, yet mixed, pro-gay support from Pope Francis since 2013. Ultimately, this leads to a conversation about cultural, as well as religious attitudes, toward the LGBT community that is beyond the ability of this chapter. Suffice it to say that although some cultural and religious attitudes are in contrast to the gay rights movement, other campaigns, such as It Gets Better and Where Love Is Illegal, support equal rights and acceptance for all individuals no matter where they lie in relation to gender or sexual identity.

This bigotry has not stopped companies like Coca-Cola, which, in 2014, released a Super Bowl (American football) advertisement called "It's Beautiful" where LGBT and non-LGBT individuals sang "America the Beautiful." Since then, Coca-Cola has released other commercials such as "Pool Boy," which features a young woman pining after the pool-cleaning man while her brother does the same thing from up in his room. They both rush to give him a Coke, only to find their mother has already done so. Coca-Cola has also created "The Wonder of Us," which targets and supports LGBT consumers using presumed genderqueer-identity individuals wearing a rainbow collar. It seems that, in our opinion, every time a company takes a stance on LGBT inclusion, there is an outcry from the public on both sides. This is particularly troublesome, as despite an increase in public support, there seems to be a vocal minority that opposes LGBT inclusion in advertisement. However, after initial stance, it seems that the outcry on subsequent advertisements decreases. It is imperative that companies continue to provide diverse media portrayal in advertisements as heterosexism has effects on the lives of homosexual individuals. For example, when individuals were exposed to heterosexist rap music, individuals gave gay job applicants lower evaluations than those who were exposed to no music (Binder & Ward, 2016).

In summation, although there has been vast growth and development in the portrayal of LGBT individuals in the media, there is still much progress that can be made. As media portrayal can affect individuals in a plethora of ways (e.g., Croteau & Hoynes, 1997), it is key to know how LGBT community is being represented. If it is in a manner that supports the negative reinforcement of stereotypes, there will be deleterious effects for those who are exposed.

Educational Systems

Outside of the home, schools are not only instrumental in providing education, but also in shaping societal norms. Historically, schools have helped encourage the differentiation of boys and girls based on stereotypes. Often, in high school, deviation from the norm is viewed as a punishable social act. For example, girls have often been encouraged to register for home economics or humanities courses, whereas boys have often been encouraged to take science and shop courses (Kemp-Jackson, 2016; Wirtenberg & Nakamura, 1976). These stereotypical gender roles not only affect the courses students are allowed to enroll in but have also affected their ability to express their sexuality at school.

While a positive step for LGBT rights occurred in *Fricke v. Lynch* (1980), where public high schools were prohibited from discriminating against students who wanted to bring same-sex dates to prom, there is clearly still pushback. According to the 2015 National School Climate Survey (NSCS), 26.5 percent of students reported that their schools prevented students from attending a school dance with same-sex dates (Kosciw, Greytak, Giga, Villenas, & Danischewski, 2016). To date, schools receive public and judiciary scrutiny when students are prohibited from attending school events for wearing clothing deemed unconventional for their gender or for bringing same-sex dates (e.g., *Byshop Elliot v. Buffalo School District*; Besecker, 2017).

Stereotypes regarding gender norms and sexuality lead to viewing LGBT individuals as violating cultural standards of masculinity and femininity, exacerbating negative attitudes toward the LGBT community (e.g., Herek, 1993; Whitley, 2001). The Gay, Lesbian, and Straight Education Network (GLSEN) surveyed 10,528 students between the ages of thirteen and twenty-one across the United States. Their findings revealed that 95.8 percent of LGBT students experienced homophobic remarks (e.g., name-calling) at school (Kosciw et al., 2016). In addition, 27 percent of students reported being physically harassed due to sexual orientation, while 20.3 percent reported being physically harassed for gender expression. Moreover, 29.8 percent of students reported disciplinary actions for public displays of affection that were tolerated among non-LGBT students. More concerning, transgender students reported being more victimized than their LGB peers, with higher rates of verbal and physical harassment, as well as physical assault due to sexual orientation preferences and gender expression (Kosciw et al., 2016).

Perceptions and stereotypes that transgender individuals are perverse is one contributing factor to the harassment and victimization they endure on a daily basis. Recent focus has increased the spotlight on the transgender community with the introduction of "bathroom bills." Proponents of the bathroom bills argue that allowing transgender individuals (especially transgender women) to use bathrooms that align with their gender identity increases sexual assault and voyeurism toward cisgender (a person whose gender and identity matches their assigned sex at birth) individuals (Steinmetz, 2015). In 2016, the Obama administration instructed public schools that they must allow transgender students to use bathrooms and locker rooms that align with their gender identity. However, to the chagrin of the LGBT community, the Trump administration formally rescinded that guidance in 2017 (Brammer, 2018). This was a particularly devastating decision for the transgender community, as a recent survey revealed that 70 percent of transgender individuals reported being harassed, abused, or denied access to public restrooms (Herman, 2013). Additionally, around 2015, NSCS found that two-thirds of transgender students avoid school bathrooms due to feeling uncomfortable or unsafe (Kosciw et al., 2016).

Indeed, stereotypes help engender negative false perceptions that can manifest in discrimination against the LGBT community and can have detrimental effects on children's education and self-esteem (Cvencek, Meltzoff, & Greenwald, 2011). The 2015 National School Climate Survey (NSCS) reported that 60.5 percent of LGBT students wanted to drop out of school due to hostile school climate (e.g., unsupportive peers and teachers, harassment). Furthermore, LGBT students with high victimization and discrimination reported lower self-esteem and school belonging as well as higher depression compared to LGBT students that had low-victimization and discrimination (Kosciw et al., 2016). More alarmingly, Kisch, Leino, and Silverman (2005) found that LGBT students were 2.6 times more likely to consider or attempt suicide compared with heterosexual students.

Movements toward creating safe, antibullying, spaces for LGBT students exist. In 1993, Massachusetts was the first to lead in promoting safe spaces for LGBT youth with its Safe School Program for LGBTQ Students. Washington State followed suit with its Safe School Coalition. While all states now have antibullying policies or laws, only thirteen states (California, Colorado, Connecticut, Illinois, Iowa, Maine, Massachusetts, Minnesota, New

Jersey, New York, Oregon, Vermont, and Washington) have antibullying laws designed to protect students based on sexual orientation and gender identity (GLSEN, 2018). Many schools have introduced "safe zones," which are often indicated by stickers on the classroom or office doors. These first started appearing in the 1990s and serve to indicate that educators are LGBT-friendly and will not tolerate harassments. In 2010, GLSEN sent "safe space kits" to every public middle and high school in the United States. These kits included safe space posters and guides for LGBT allies. However, schools still have a long way to go, as a recent survey revealed that only 26 percent of students reported that their school promoted safe spaces (Kosciw et al., 2016).

One way schools can promote safe spaces is by adding educational content that accurately portrays the LGBT community; however, stereotypes about the LGBT community have also affected educational content. Currently, eight states (Alabama, Arizona, Louisiana, Mississippi, Oklahoma, South Carolina, Texas, and Utah) have anti-LGBT laws prohibiting health education teachers and staff from discussing LGBT issues at school. Moreover, some states (Alabama, Arizona, Louisiana, Mississippi, Oklahoma, South Carolina, and Texas) have state education laws that prohibit the "promotion of homosexuality," which are often referred to as *"no promo homo"* laws. These laws apply explicitly to teachers to forbid them from discussing LGBT people or topics in a positive manner (GLSEN, 2018). Some laws go as far as requiring teachers to portray LGBT individuals in a negative light that is often false. Laws such as these only serve to increase the stigmatization of LGBT individuals by providing K–12 students inaccurate and misleading information which may be internalized and lead to a belief that being gay is shameful and wrong (Rodriguez, 2013).

Recent surveys provide some evidence toward the negative impact of the No Promo Homo rhetoric. For example, in a survey of middle and high school students, LGBT students in states with No Promo Homo policies reported much less support from teachers and administrators. Additionally, these students are less likely to report having LGBT-related resources in school (e.g., comprehensive school harassment/assault policies, school personnel supportive of LGBT students, and Gay-Straight Alliances) compared to students in states without No Promo Homo policies (GLSEN, 2009). This is detrimental because having these resources could potentially prevent LGBT bullying, as well as help students feel safer (Abreu, Black, Mosley, & Fedewa, 2016). Compared to students attending schools with an anti-LGBT curriculum, students attending schools with an LGBT-inclusive curriculum reported that they were less likely to feel unsafe because of their sexual orientation, less likely to miss school in the past month, and less likely to hear homophobic remarks (e.g., "fag" or "dyke"), as well as more likely to report peer acceptance of their sexual orientation (Hamed-Troyansky, 2016).

LGBT stereotypes also heavily affect teachers, as many teachers that identify as LGBT are not allowed to disclose their sexual preference. Common
misconceptions about homosexuality have led people to believe that teachers
will influence children to become gay if they disclose it or that teachers are
trying to push a homosexual agenda. Currently, there are no federal laws that
protect teachers from workplace discrimination based on sexual orientation,
as they are subject to state and local laws. As such, there are multiple cases of
discrimination. For example, in 2014, a Special Education teacher in Oregon
was fired for openly disclosing his sexual preference during a speech after
winning State Teacher of the Year Award (Lopez, 2015). In 2017, an Elementary School teacher in Texas was suspended for showing the class a picture of
her wife in an introductory slide on the first day of class (Hauser, 2018).

Yet, supporters and allies of the LGBT community have been working
hard to fight stereotypes and misconceptions. For example, Planned Parent-
hood has led efforts to promote learning about gender identity in preschool.
In addition, California passed Senate Bill 48 (SB48), the Fair Education Act,
which provides for the inclusion of LGBT perspectives in K–12 textbooks.
Illinois followed in the footsteps of California and also voted to require LGBT
history in school textbooks.

Overall, stereotypes based on sexual orientation have not only hindered
educational content but have also yielded unfriendly, sometimes hostile,
school environments for LGBT youth. Though progress has been made, there
is still a long way to go in the fight for equality in educational settings and
even more in the workplace.

Workplace

The scope of sexuality extends outside the home, community, and schools
into the workplace. A public policy research institute estimates that there are
around 7 million private sector, 1 million state and local, and 200,000 federal employees who identify as LGBT in the current workforce (Sears, Mallory, & Hunter, 2009). Additionally, there are areas of the country that
employ more LGBT individuals within their state and local governments—
while there are 30 percent employed within California and New York, there
are less than half of 1 percent in Montana, North Dakota, and Wyoming
combined (Sears et al., 2009). Though these numbers are impactful, there
may be far more employees who do not self-identify in the workplace due to
formal and informal discrimination and fears of retaliation despite some
employment protections.

Stereotypes of the LGBT community in the workplace are similar to those
assumptions outside of work: gay men are effeminate and weak (Herek,
1984), and lesbian women are "butch" (more masculine) in their body language and attire (Hoel, Lewis, & Einarsdottir, 2014). This stereotyping has

exposed employees to hostility, harassment, and homophobic remarks (Hoel et al., 2014; Pedulla, 2014). Moreover, studies have identified several stereotypes associated specifically with lesbian individuals. Some examples include, but are not limited to, a concern that their lesbian counterparts would "hit on them," "push their beliefs on them," or that lesbians are unnatural and immoral (Giddings & Smith, 2001). Though these are considered negative connotations, other researchers have found that lesbian women who have agentic characteristics are seen as more competent on task-related work compared to their heterosexual counterparts (Niedlich, Steffens, Krause, Settke, & Ebert, 2015). These stereotypes affect not only LGBT individuals in terms of employment progress, such as low salary and missed opportunities for promotion, but also in their affective identities. Employees who identify as LGBT feel as though they are living a double life, as if they have to remain closeted or isolated from their peers, and often feel shame and self-loathing because of treatment in the workplace (Giddings & Smiths, 2001; Pedulla, 2014). This stereotyping of LGBT individuals is not a new phenomenon; in fact, there have been laws throughout the past century that have attempted to address the plight of these individuals and overall refocus the treatment of all employees within the workplace.

Research exploring discrimination within the workplace reviewed the historical progression of laws dating from the 1970s, following the first Employment Nondiscrimination Act (ENDA) of the 1990s, and eventually the more recent Equality Act of 2015 (Dixon, Kane, & DiGrazia, 2017). More specifically, the ENDA was an employment legislation that prohibits discrimination in hiring employees based on their sexual orientation and gender identity if employers have at least fifteen employees (Gao & Zhang, 2016). The Equality Act of 2015 amends the Civil Rights Act of 1964 and provides consistent, explicit nondiscrimination protections to LGBTQ individuals for a variety of areas of life, including employment, education, and public spaces (H.R.3185—Equality Act). Of further interest, only twenty-two states within the United States have specific employment protections against sexual orientation and gender identity, and of the employees who identify as LGBT, 39 percent live in states without formal employment protections (Dixon et al., 2017).

LGBT employees have noted experiences of formal and informal discrimination in the workplace. Both formal discrimination, such as overt firing and barriers to promotion, and informal discrimination, such as verbal and nonverbal harassment, homophobic jokes, and loss of credibility, have been found (Ozeren, 2014). Retaliation against homosexuality includes, but is not limited to, pay discrimination, such that LGBT individuals are given less pay than their heterosexual counterparts (Klawitter, 2015), promotion opportunities being decreased (Zugelder & Champagne, 2018), or even denial of employment (Eliason, Dibble, & Robertson, 2011). In a review of studies conducted in the workplace for LGBT individuals facing discrimination, findings indicate that transgender employees are reporting higher rates of unemployment, low earnings, and denial of promotion based on gender identity (Badgett, Lau, Sears, & Ho, 2007; Holman, Fish, Oswald, & Goldberg, 2018). These fears and discriminations persist despite employment legislation and policies around nondiscrimination laws.

Given the laws within the United States on nondiscrimination workplaces, LGBT individuals would hope to feel safer at work than in their communities. However, as the aforementioned studies indicate, this is not always the case. To further perpetuate uncertainty within the workplace, LGBT individuals who outwardly possess and display effeminate or "butch" characteristics can be direct targets of formal and informal discrimination. Despite the stereotypes LGBT individuals face within the workplace, companies who value these individuals for their contributions may give LGBT employees more comfort in the places they choose to work. More importantly, if hiring and staffing methods are centered on valuing the different perspectives of LGBT individuals and the reduction of stereotyping in the workplace, companies can begin to show LGBT individuals that they are valued and that discrimination is not accepted in their workplace.

Conclusion

It is our belief that only through a holistic lens do we have the ability to understand the effect of stereotyping. With relevance to this chapter, by looking at the stereotypes that permeate multiple areas of life, such as the educational system, the workplace, the political sphere, and the media, we can better understand the experiences of the LGBT community. Although lasting and influential changes exist, there are still powerful stereotypes that affect the way LGBT individuals learn, work, and socialize. By supplementing findings from stereotyping literature, with public opinion surveys, political doctrines, discrimination literature, and the current media examples, we hope that you are better able to understand how stereotypes affect this community.

References

Abreu, R. L., Black, W. W., Mosley, D. V., & Fedewa, A. L. (2016). LGBTQ youth bullying experiences in schools: The role of school counselors within a system of oppression. *Journal of Creativity in Mental Health, 11*(3–4), 325–342.

Adam, B. D. (2003). The Defense of Marriage Act and American exceptionalism: The "gay marriage" panic in the United States. *Journal of the History of Sexuality, 12*(2), 259–276.

American Psychiatric Association. (1952). *Diagnostic and statistical manual of mental disorders* (1st ed.). Washington, D.C.: Author.

American Psychiatric Association. (1968). *Diagnostic and statistical manual of mental disorders* (2nd ed.). Washington, D.C.: Author.

Ayoub, P. M., & Garretson, J. (2017). Getting the message out: Media context and global changes in attitudes toward homosexuality. *Comparative Political Studies, 50*(8), 1055–1085.

Badgett, M. V., Lau, H., Sears, B., & Ho, D. (2007). *Bias in the workplace: Consistent evidence of sexual orientation and gender identity discrimination.* Retrieved from https://heinonline.org/HOL/LandingPage?handle=hein .journals/chknt84&div=25&id=&page=

Belkin, A., Barrett, F., Eitelberg, M., & Ventresca, M. (2017). Discharging transgender troops would cost $960 million. *Blueprints for Sound Public Policy.* Doctoral dissertation, School of Business and Public Policy, Naval Postgraduate School.

Besecker, A. (2017, September 6). *Lawsuit settled over LGBTQ rights at McKinley High.* Retrieved from https://buffalonews.com/2017/09/05/lawsuit-settled -lgbtq-rights-mckinley-high-school/

Binder, K., & Ward, L. M. (2016). Can heterosexist music cause hiring discrimination against sexual minority men? Testing the effects of prejudicial media messages. *The Journal of Sex Research, 53*(6), 666–677.

Blacklow, J. (2018, February 21). *Why 2018 is a banner year for LGBTQ representation at the Oscars (Guest Column).* Retrieved from https://variety.com/2018 /film/opinion/lgbtq-gay-oscars-2018-glaad-column-1202705989/

Blashill, A. J., & Powlishta, K. K. (2009). Gay stereotypes: The use of sexual orientation as a cue for gender-related attributes. *Sex Roles, 61*(11–12), 783–793.

Bond, B. J. (2014). Sex and sexuality in entertainment media popular with lesbian, gay, and bisexual adolescents. *Mass Communication and Society, 17*(1), 98–120.

Brammer, J. P. (2018). *Education Department says it won't investigate transgender bathroom complaints.* Retrieved from https://www.nbcnews.com/feature /nbc-out/education-department-says-it-won-t-investigate-transgender -bathroom-complaints-n847626

Bronski, M., Pellegrini, A., & Amico, M. (2013). *" You can tell just by looking": And 20 other myths about LGBT life and people* (Vol. 9). Boston: Beacon Press.

Burks, D. J. (2011) Lesbian, gay, and bisexual victimization in the military: An unintended consequence of "Don't Ask, Don't Tell"? *The American Psychologist, 66*(7), 604–613. doi:10.1037/a0024609

Calzo, J. P., & Ward, L. M. (2009). Media exposure and viewers' attitudes toward homosexuality: Evidence for mainstreaming or resonance? *Journal of Broadcasting & Electronic Media, 53*(2), 280–299.

Chung, S. K. (2007). Media literacy art education: Deconstructing lesbian and gay stereotypes in the media. *International Journal of Art and Design Education, 26*(1), 98–107.

Clendinen, D., & Nagourney, A. (2001). *Out for good: The struggle to build a gay rights movement in America*. New York: Simon and Schuster.

Croteau, D., & Hoynes, W. (1997). Social inequality and media representation. In D. Croteau, & W. Hoynes (Eds.), *Media/Society. Industries, images and audiences*. London: Pine Forge Press.

Cvencek, D., Meltzoff, A. N., & Greenwald, A. G. (2011). Math–gender stereotypes in elementary school children. *Child development*, 82(3), 766–779.

Daily Telegraph. (1983). "Gay plague" may lead to blood ban on homosexuals. *Daily Telegraph*, 2, 5.

Dixon, M., Kane, M., & DiGrazia, J. (2017). Organization, opportunity, and the shifting politics of employment discrimination. *Social Currents*, 4(2), 111–127.

Drescher, J. (2015). Out of DSM: Depathologizing homosexuality. *Behavioral Sciences*, 5(4), 565–575.

Eliason, M. J., Dibble, S. L., & Robertson, P. A. (2011). Lesbian, gay, bisexual, and transgender (LGBT) physicians' experiences in the workplace. *Journal of Homosexuality*, 58(10), 1355–1371.

Fitzsimons, T. (2018, June 20). *"Transsexualism" removed from World Health Organization's disease manual*. Retrieved from https://www.nbcnews.com /feature/nbc-out/transsexualism-removed-world-health-organization -s-disease-manual-n885141

Flores, A. (2014). National trends in public opinion on LGBT rights in the United States. *The Williams Institute*. Retrieved from https://williamsinstitute.law .ucla.edu/research/census-lgbt-demographics-studies/natl-trends-nov -2014

Fricke v. Lynch, 491 F. Supp. 381. (1980). U.S. District Court for the District of Rhode Island. Retrieved from https://law.justia.com/cases/federal /district-courts/FSupp/491/381/1799237

Gao, H., & Zhang, W. (2016). Employment nondiscrimination acts and corporate innovation. *Management Science*, 63(9), 2982–2999.

Giddings, L. S., & Smith, M. C. (2001). Stories of lesbian in/visibility in nursing. *Nursing Outlook*, 49, 14–19.

GLAAD. (2012, December 06). *The APA removes "gender identity disorder" from updated mental health guide*. Retrieved from https://www.glaad.org/blog /apa-removes-gender-identity-disorder-updated-mental-health-guide

GLAAD. (2017). *The GLAAD Studio Responsibility Index (SRI)*. Retrieved from http://www.glaad.org/files/2017_SRI.pdf

GLSEN. (2009). *National Climate Survey. Gay Lesbian and Straight Education Network*. Retrieved from http://www.glsen.org/cgi-bin/iowa/all/research /index.html

GLSEN. (2018). *Laws prohibiting "promotion of homosexuality" in schools: Impacts and implications (research brief)*. New York: GLSEN.

Gross, L. (2002). Minorities, majorities and the media. In *Media, ritual and identity* (pp. 97–112). London: Routledge.

Hamed-Troyansky, R. (2016). Erasing gay from the blackboard: The unconstitutionality of no promo homo education laws. *20 U.C. Davis Journal of Juvenile Law & Policy, 85,* 90.

Hauser, C. (2018, May 10). Texas teacher showed a photo of her wife, and was barred from the classroom. *The New York Times.* Retrieved from https://www.nytimes.com/2018/05/10/us/gay-teachers-wife-texas.html

Herek, G. M. (1984). Beyond "homophobia": A social psychological perspective on attitudes toward lesbians and gay men. *Journal of Homosexuality, 10*(1–2), 1–21.

Herek, G. M. (1993). Gender gaps in public opinion about lesbians and gay men. *Public Opinion Quarterly, 66,* 40–66.

Herek, G. M. (2015). Beyond "homophobia": Thinking more clearly about stigma, prejudice, and sexual orientation. *American Journal of Orthopsychiatry, 85*(5S), S29.

Herman, J. L. (2013). Gendered restrooms and minority stress: The public regulation of gender and its impact on transgender people's lives. *Journal of Public Management & Social Policy, 19*(1), 65.

Herndon, W. H., & Weik, J. W. (1889). *Herndon's Lincoln: The true story of a great life: Etiam in minimis major: The history and personal recollections of Abraham Lincoln* (Vol. 1). Chicago, IL, New York, and San Francisco, CA: Belford, Clarke & Co.

Hoel, H., Lewis, D., & Einarsdottir, A. (2014). *The ups and downs of LGBs workplace experiences: Discrimination, bullying and harassment of lesbian, gay and bisexual employees in Britain.* Manchester, England: Manchester Business School.

Holman, E. G., Fish, J. N., Oswald, R. F., & Goldberg, A. (2018). Reconsidering the LGBT climate inventory: Understanding support and hostility for LGBTQ employees in the workplace. *Journal of Career Assessment, 27*(3), 544–559.

Human Rights Campaign. (2012, November 13). *LGB and allied voters critical to 2012 electoral successes.* Retrieved from https://www.hrc.org/press/lgb-and-allied-voters-critical-to-2012-electoral-successes

Kemp-Jackson, S. (2016). *It's time to bring back shop and home economics classes.* Retrieved from https://www.huffingtonpost.ca/samantha-kempjackson/bring-back-home-ec-and-shop-class_b_11398220.html

Keuroghlian, A. S., Ard, K. L., & Makadon, H. J. (2017). Advancing health equity for lesbian, gay, bisexual and transgender (LGBT) people through sexual health education and LGBT-affirming health care environments. *Sexual Health, 14*(1), 119–122.

Kisch, J., Leino, E. V., & Silverman, M. M. (2005). Aspects of suicidal behavior, depression, and treatment in college students: Results from the spring 2000 National College Health Assessment Survey. *Suicide and Life Threatening Behavior, 35,* 3–13.

Klawitter, M. (2015). Meta-analysis of the effects of sexual orientation on earnings. *Industrial Relations: A Journal of Economy and Society, 54*(1), 4–32.

Kosciw, J. G., Greytak, E. A., Giga, N. M., Villenas, C., & Danischewski, D. J. (2016). *The 2015 National School Climate Survey: The experiences of lesbian, gay, bisexual, transgender, and queer youth in our nation's schools.* New York: GLSEN.

Landau, J. (2012). DOMA and presidential discretion: Interpreting and enforcing federal law. *Fordham Law Review, 81,* 619.

Linneman, T. J. (2008). How do you solve a problem like Will Truman? The feminization of gay masculinities on Will & Grace. *Men and Masculinities, 10*(5), 583–603.

Lopez, G. (2015). *Oregon's Teacher of the Year spoke openly about being gay—And then he was fired.* Retrieved from https://www.vox.com/2015/7/6/8900589 /gay-discrimination-oregon-teacher

Madon, S. (1997). What do people believe about gay males? A study of stereotype content and strength. *Sex Roles, 37*(9–10), 663–685.

Marcosson, S. A. (1992). Harassment on the basis of sexual orientation: A claim of sex discrimination under Title VII. *Georgetown Law Journal, 81,* 1–38.

Newton, J. H., & Williams, R. (2003). The avocado and the asparagus: Searching for masculine and feminine archetypes within the stereotyping theater of sexualized mediatypes. In P. M. Lester & S. D. Ross (Eds.), *Images that injure: Pictorial stereotypes in the media* (p. 214). Westport, CT: Praeger.

Nichols, J. M. (2015, October 15). *When bigots freaked out about Campbell's ad with gay dads, this man had a brilliant response.* Retrieved from https://www .huffingtonpost.com/entry/when-bigots-freaked-out-about-campbells -ad-with-gay-dads-this-man-had-a-brilliant-response_us_561fc302 e4b028dd7ea6d7f3

Niedlich, C., Steffens, M. C., Krause, J., Settke, E., & Ebert, I. D. (2015). Ironic effects of sexual minority group membership: Are lesbians less susceptible to invoking negative female stereotypes than heterosexual women? *Archives of Sexual Behavior, 44*(5), 1439–1447.

Niedwiecki, A. (2013). Save our children: Overcoming the narrative that gays and lesbians are harmful to children. *Duke Journal Gender Law & Policy, 21,* 125.

Nussbaum, M. C. (2010). *From disgust to humanity: Sexual orientation and constitutional law.* Oxford, England: Oxford University Press.

Obergefell v. Hodges, 576 U.S. (2015, June 26). Retrieved from https://www .supremecourt.gov/opinions/14pdf/14-556_3204.pdf

Ozeren, E. (2014). Sexual orientation discrimination in the workplace: A systematic review of literature. *Procedia—Social and Behavioral Sciences, 109,* 1203–1215.

Painter, G. (2005, February). *Sodomy laws.* Retrieved from https://www.glapn.org /sodomylaws/sensibilities/introduction.htm

Pedulla, D. S. (2014). The positive consequences of negative stereotypes: Race, sexual orientation, and the job application process. *Social Psychology Quarterly, 77*(1), 75–94.

Pew Research Center. (2011). *Most say homosexuality should be accepted by society.* Retrieved from https://www.people-press.org/2011/05/13/most-say-homo sexuality-should-be-accepted-by-society

Philipps, D. (2017, October 30). *Judge blocks Trump's ban on transgender troops in military.* Retrieved from https://www.nytimes.com/2017/10/30/us /military-transgender-ban.html

Rapp, T. (2013). Meet Jason Collins, the NBA's first openly gay active player. *Bleacher Report.* Retrieved from https://bleacherreport.com/articles /1622705-meet-jason-collins-nbas-first-active-openly-gay-player

Restar, A. J., & Reisner, S. L. (2017). Protect trans people: Gender equality and equity in action. *The Lancet, 390*(10106), 1933–1935.

Robertson, A. (2018, January 20). *Trump's White House website is one year old. It's still ignoring LGBT issues, climate change, and a lot more.* Retrieved from https://www.theverge.com/2018/1/20/16909218/trump-white-house -website-update-lgbt-climate-change-disabilities-one-year-anniversary

Rodriguez, M. (2013). See no evil, hear no evil, speak no evil: Stemming the tide of no promo homo laws in American schools. *The Modern American, 8*(1), 5.

Rule, N. O., Ambady, N., Adams, R. B., Jr., & Macrae, C. N. (2008). Accuracy and awareness in the perception and categorization of male sexual orien-tation. *Journal of Personality and Social Psychology, 95*(5), 1019.

Salandra, A. (2017). *7 natural disasters Evangelicals have blamed on gay people.* Retrieved from http://www.newnownext.com/natural-disasters-evan gelicals-blame-gay-people/09/2017/

Sears, B., Mallory, C., & Hunter, N. D. (2009). Estimates of LGBT public employ-ees. *UCLA: The Williams Institute.* Retrieved from https://escholarship.org /uc/item/6cz123ww

Semm, P. T., & Sanchez-Weston, C. (2012). Waiting for change: Obama and the LGBT community. *Grading the 44th President: A report card on Barack Obama's First Term as a Progressive Leader: A Report Card on Barack Obama's First Term as a Progressive Leader, 203.*

Sink, A., Mastro, D., & Dragojevic, M. (2017). Competent or warm? A stereotype content model approach to understanding perceptions of masculine and effeminate gay television characters. *Journalism & Mass Communication Quarterly, 95*(3), 588–606.

Steinmetz, K. (2015, March 6). States battle over bathroom access for transgen-der people. *Time.* Retrieved from http://time.com/3734714/transgender -bathroom-bills-lgbt-discrimination/

Taylor, P. (2013). *A survey of LGBT Americans: Attitudes, experiences and values in changing times.* Washington, D.C.: Pew Research Center.

Tokar, D. M., & Jome, L. M. (1998). Masculinity, vocational interests, and career choice traditionality: Evidence for a fully mediated model. *Journal of Counseling Psychology, 45*(4), 424.

Vargas, L., & DePyssler, B. (1998). Using media literacy to explore stereotypes of Mexican immigrants. *Social Education, 62*(7), 407–412.

Weigel, D., & Tumulty, K. (2017). A gift and a challenge for democrats: A restive, active and aggressive base. *The Washington Post*. Retrieved from https://www.washingtonpost.com/powerpost/a-gift-and-a-challenge-for-democrats-a-restive-active-and-aggressive-base/2017/02/11/e265dd44-efef-11e6-b4ff-ac2cf509efe5_story.html

Weiner, R. (2010). Hate crimes bill signed into law 11 years after Matthew Shepard's death. *Huffington Post*. Retrieved from https://www.huffpost.com/entry/hate-crimes-bill-to-be-si_n_336883

Whitley, B. E. (2001). Gender-role variables and attitudes towards homosexuality. *Sex Roles, 45*, 691–612.

Wirtenberg, T. J., & Nakamura, C. Y. (1976). Education: Barrier or boon to changing occupational roles of women? *Journal of Social Issues, 32*(3), 165–179.

Wolf, M., & Kielwasser, A. (2014). *Gay people, sex, and the media*. London: Routledge.

Zugelder, M. T., & Champagne, P. J. (2018). A management approach to LGBT employment: Diversity, inclusion and respect. *Journal of Business Diversity, 18*(1), 40–50.

CHAPTER TWELVE

Stereotypes of Veterans

Christopher Stone

Each year, roughly 200,000 service members transition from military service into the civilian sector (Executive Office of the President, 2013). Further, approximately 8 percent of the working-age population in the United States is considered a veteran. U.S. Code (U.S.C.): Title 38 § 101 defines a veteran as "a person who served in the active military, naval, or air service, and who was discharged or released there-from under conditions other than dishonorable." Veterans have been identified by employers as possessing a number of positive traits that are valued in the workplace, including leadership and teamwork skills, comfortability with structure and discipline, and demonstrated effectiveness in getting tasks done (Harrell & Berglass, 2012). Although military experience on a résumé should signal to employers the increased potential for some of these traits, potentially making it easier for veterans to find a job, a large percentage of veterans report having difficulty finding and retaining suitable employment. In a study conducted by Prudential (2012), "finding a job" was listed by veterans as the hardest part of the transition process. Additionally, 80 percent of the veterans surveyed in the Prudential (2012) study reported difficulty translating their skills for the civilian workforce. On the employer side, Harrell and Berglass (2012) reported that most companies in their study identified risks and challenges to hiring veterans, even those companies that actively seek out veteran applicants. This suggests that employers associate both positive and negative characteristics with veterans. Nearly 25 percent of veterans believe that employers avoid hiring veterans entirely (Prudential, 2012). A survey conducted by the Pew Research Center (2011) demonstrated the ever-increasing gap between the military and the civilian population. The results of the survey show a downward trend (by generation) in the likelihood that an individual will report having a relative in the military. For example, 33 percent of those surveyed between the ages of eighteen and twenty-nine reported having a family connection to the military compared to 57 percent of those aged thirty to forty-nine. Additionally, the report noted that less than one-half of 1 percent of the adult population in the United States has served on activity duty at any point in their lives. Based on the small percentage of the population that has served, and the widening gap between those that have some familial connection to the military and those that do not, it is not surprising that there continues to be a disconnect between the civilian world and the realities of military service.

The purpose of this chapter is to review what we know about stereotypes of veterans and provide some examples of research in the various areas surrounding the topic. The following sections will first describe the similarities between the military and civilian workplace and then discuss the role of stereotyping of veterans and where these stereotypes come from, how stereotypes are applied to veterans, and how stereotypes may be mitigated, as well as provide recommendations for practice and future research.

Similarities between the Military and Civilian Workplace

Acknowledging that few individuals are familiar with the military and the experiences that veterans have while serving in the military, it is important to take a moment to provide some context. Although there are a number of unique aspects of military service, there are a number of ways serving in the military is much like a regular job. First, most members of the armed forces do not serve in combat or train for combat roles (Bureau of Labor Statistics, 2019b). As is the case with any organization, a large component of the military is made up of support staff. These may include mechanics, medical and legal professions, human resources personnel, intelligence officers, civil engineers, and so on. These individuals lead relatively normal lives, work a schedule, wear a uniform, get promoted, take vacations, and have families. Although the hierarchy and control structure within the military is more rigid than that of most civilian organizations, much of the day-to-day work looks just like any civilian workplace. In fact, many military units employ civilians who are integrated with the active duty military members working side by side doing the same jobs.

Evidence of Actual Differences between Veterans and Civilians

Like any work experience, military service provides an individual with new knowledge, skills, abilities, and work preferences that they take with them into their future employment. As is true with all stereotypes, the assumption that *all* veterans leave military service with the same set of characteristics is preposterous. However, there are some traits that may be found more frequently in veterans than in civilians based on their unique experience. Very little empirical work has been done to discern actual differences between those who have or have not served in the armed forces but recent pressure to identify a return on investment (ROI) on veteran hiring has stimulated initial research in this area. The Institute for Veterans and Military Families (Haynie, 2016) published a report in which they lay out the case for why a veteran may be a good choice for an organization and provide ten empirically supported characteristics of veterans that may set them apart from their civilian peers. Those characteristics included being entrepreneurial, exhibiting high levels of organizational commitment, possessing advanced team-building skills, and demonstrating high levels of resiliency among others. A study conducted by the Korn Ferry Institute (2017) provides evidence that veterans possess higher levels of mental agility and people agility, which are two subcomponents of learning agility, when compared to a normed civilian group. With the increased emphasis on building diverse organizations, people agility, or the "degree to which one is open-minded toward others, enjoys interacting with a diversity of people, understands his or her strengths, interests, and limitations, and uses them effectively to accomplish organizational goals" (p. 4), should be a skill of particular interest to hiring managers. It is important to point out that the findings from these studies suggest that veterans are simply more likely to have these traits, based on their unique work experience, not that all veterans do.

Sources of Veteran Stereotypes

In the absence of firsthand experience with the military or with veterans (Pew Research Center, 2011), individuals "fill in the blanks" with information they gather from third-party sources. The majority of the information we consume today comes from news and other media, which have been criticized for their portrayal of veterans as well as other groups (Alderton, 2015; Parrott, Albright, Dyche, & Steele, 2018). Because the major goal of mass media (e.g., news, television, movies) is to capture the interest of the consumer, often only stories that are heartwarming or tragic are conveyed. This emphasis on attention-grabbing stories provides the general public with only a distorted and extreme view of who veterans really are.

Stereotypes from Social Media

Social media has become a popular means of exchanging ideas over the last decade. For many, social media may be their main source of news and primary means of communication with others. In fact, approximately

66 percent of Americans rely on social media for their news (Matsa & Shearer, 2018). In a *Psychology Today* (Mobbs, 2018) opinion piece, Mobbs, a clinical psychologist and veteran, describes her observations while searching social media for a series of veteran-related hashtags (e.g., #veterans, #military). Hashtags are user-created metadata, or keywords, that users include in their social media posts so others who are interested in similar topics can locate them. For example, an individual may post a photo, news story, or simple comment about veterans and include the hashtag "#veterans" so that others interested in veterans can easily locate it. In this article, the author posits that the portrayals of veterans that were observed while searching for veteran-related hashtags fell within three broad categories. These categories included portrayals of mental illness (e.g., PTSD, "ticking time bomb"), heroism, or masculine culture (e.g., guns, bravery). The author labels these categories as "Punisher," "Captain America," and "outraged vet." Mobbs' categories overlap with similar academic research in the area that will be discussed in the following sections. Given the increasing gap between the military and civilian cultures and the fact that approximately two-thirds of Americans choose to get their news through social media (Matsa & Shearer, 2018), these observations are especially troubling. Whether social media consumers are primarily exposed to positive (Captain America) or negative (Punisher, outraged vet) representations of veterans, extreme examples reinforce and potentially enhance skewed perceptions of veterans as a group.

Stereotypes in Movies and Television

Just as social media has been shown to provide a distorted view of veterans, movies and television also play a role in shaping public perception. Exposure to Vietnam War movies has previously been identified as a factor in shaping public perception of government assistance to Vietnam War veterans. In a field study conducted by Griffin and Sen (1995), participants' attributions were found to be related to exposure to Vietnam War movies. Participants who reported more exposure to films in which the character was attempting to cope with the circumstances of war reported higher levels of external (War) attributions, meaning that they perceived veterans of the Vietnam War as victims of circumstance rather than being in control of their own fate. The inverse result (i.e., lower levels of external attributions) was observed for those who reported watching films in which characters were in control of their own situation. This study highlights how powerful television and film can be in shaping perceptions of real-world events.

The fact that Mobbs (2018) used the names of superheroes to label two of three categories, namely the Punisher and Captain America, is telling of a trend in the entertainment industry. Veteran characters in movies and television shows are often portrayed based on the same aforementioned stereotypes, whether it be the war-torn, rage-filled fighting machine (e.g., the Punisher) or the unwavering do-no-wrong patriot who stands for honor and freedom (e.g., Captain America). One organization, Got Your 6, works to combat the use of veteran stereotypes in media and entertainment. According to Rob Gordon, president of Be the Change Inc., "we believe that the entertainment industry plays a vital role in America by shaping perceptions that can then shape and affect behavior" (Alderton, 2015). Got Your 6 works with studios, networks, and agencies to write realistic, nonstereotypical characters who have military experience but are not exclusively defined by it. Got Your 6 has worked with and certified a number of projects, including the movie *American Sniper.*

Stereotypes in the News

Like social media, movies, and television, news media contributes to and perpetuates veteran stereotypes. Even if the intent of a story is not to harm, headlines alone can be damaging. Consider the following headlines: "Are military veterans more likely for shooting sprees?" and "Experts: Vets' PTSD, violence a growing problem" (Hayes, 2012; Steele, 2017). These headlines may be all it takes to introduce and reinforce perceptions of veterans as violent and dangerous. Although both news articles go on to explain that not all veterans are prone to violence and even include quotes from academic and industry experts backing up this assertion, the damage may have already been done for readers who never get past the headline.

In a study conducted by Parrott et al. (2018) that analyzed news outlets across the United States, researchers identified three major themes that portrayals of veterans fell into: charity (representing 35% of stories), victim (30%), and hero (35%). Charity stories are those focused on providing some sort of assistance to veterans in need. These stories typically emphasize the sacrifices made by veterans, such as combat injuries, psychological trauma, or separation from their families while deployed and highlight the need of society to return the favor. Stories that fall in the victim category are those that refer to mistreatment of veterans by the federal government (e.g., Veterans Administration) or society. Hero stories are those that emphasize honor and pride. Although hero stories may invoke more positive perceptions of veterans and potentially lead to positive outcomes for veterans in turn, reliance on positive stereotypes by hiring managers can conceivably lead to negative consequences for the veteran group as a whole. For example, if a veteran is hired on the presumption that they fit the hero archetype and subsequently fail to live up to that standard, an employer may decide to avoid hiring veterans altogether in the future. This study provides empirical evidence for what those working with veterans already believed: that news outlets provide only a narrow depiction of veterans. The story that goes untold is that of the average veteran: Those that prepare for their eventual military separation by attending college while in the armed forces and those that successfully find meaningful civilian employment upon leaving the service. Because stories of the average veteran do not make interesting headlines, what the general public does not see is that the majority of veterans are employed, although typically at a lower rate than civilians, and veterans are more likely to be enrolled in college than are civilians (Kleykamp, 2013).

Application of Stereotypes

As military members transition into their new roles as veterans they face the daunting task of finding suitable employment. Employment is crucial to an individual's well-being. For most, jobs are not just how we earn an income but also how we establish an identity or where we find purpose. After leaving military service, where veterans once earned a respectable income with full benefits, suddenly finding themselves unemployed may lead to feelings of worthlessness as they potentially go from breadwinner to burden. Not only does their income and lifestyle change, but veterans also find themselves with a loss of identity that is strongly tied to their military service (Gonzalez, 2019; Mael, 2019). Unemployment has been identified as a potential risk factor for suicide by scholars from psychology, sociology, and economics. Although the specific role of unemployment and the causal pathways associated with this link are still unclear, multiple studies provide evidence that suggests unemployment is related to suicide (Classen & Dunn, 2012; Kposowa, 2001; Van Orden et al., 2010). Given that veterans are 22 percent more likely to commit suicide than nonveterans (Veterans Administration, 2017), identifying and eliminating barriers to employment is crucial.

Stereotypes in Employment

Although veterans cannot be identified based on their appearance alone, veteran status is not easily concealed when seeking employment. Unless the veteran chooses to have a multiyear gap in their employment history, which could potentially do even more harm, their military work experience is listed on their résumés and application forms. Therefore, any perceptions that hiring managers have of veterans will be activated early in the employment process, before the veteran is granted an interview. In one study conducted by Prudential (2012), nearly one-quarter of veterans surveyed believed that employers avoid hiring veterans. Another study by the Center for New American Society (Harrell & Berglass, 2012) noted that "some employers report concerns about the effects of combat stress, including post-traumatic stress issues, anger management and tendencies toward violence" (p. 6). Because the selection process is often a search for negative information (Cascio &

Aguinis, 2008) these negative perceptions can be especially damaging to the veteran while seeking employment. As hiring managers use heuristics such as group membership (i.e., veteran) to make assumptions about a collection of knowledge, skills, abilities, and other qualifications (KSAOs) they may unintentionally dismiss an otherwise qualified applicant simply because of their military experience.

Although very little empirical work has been conducted in this area to date, some researchers have successfully demonstrated the application of stereotypes in employment situations. Bordieri and Drehmer (1984) were interested in the impact that military service had on Vietnam veterans in employment decisions. In the study, hiring managers reviewed a job applicant's résumé and a job description. Some managers were given a Vietnam veteran's résumé, and others were given a non-Vietnam veteran's résumé. Despite the fact that the résumés were identical except for the applicant's veteran status, Vietnam veterans received significantly lower recommendations for hire and were perceived to be more predisposed to psychological problems. This study demonstrated that the presence of military experience on a résumé may activate harmful stereotypes that ultimately influence hiring decisions.

Stone, Lengnick-Hall, and Muldoon (2018) conducted an experiment similar to that of Bordieri and Drehmer (1984) in which participants were given a series of résumés and asked to make judgments about them. The researchers found that veterans (i.e., résumés with military experience listed in the work history) were perceived to have higher levels of leadership and teamwork skills but lower levels of social skills. This is interesting, given that one would assume social skills are a necessary component of leadership or teamwork skills. However, the social skills stereotype has been identified in previous work (e.g., Harrell & Berglass, 2012). It is believed that veterans are perceived as lacking social skills due to the false assumption that all veterans are simply trained to follow orders without question.

Studying stereotypes in general is difficult due to the potential for social desirability bias (Nederhof, 1985). Participants may respond to prompts in a way that they believe will be viewed favorably by others. One solution researchers have used to overcome the difficulties in studying stereotypes is through implicit association tests, or IAT (Greenwald, McGhee, & Schwartz, 1998). In an IAT, participants are presented with target concepts (e.g., military and civilian) and attributes (e.g., aggressive or brave) and asked to sort them over a series of timed stages. These tests attempt to measure implicit biases, or the strength of association between concepts and attributes, by comparing response times of participants across the different stages of the test. Klinefelter, Irving, and Huffman (2018) used an IAT to understand participants' perceptions of military members and civilians. They also used explicit measures to collect data on perceptions of veterans. On average, participants reported no significant difference in explicit attitudes toward veterans or civilians, and in fact, explicit measures demonstrated a positive evaluation of veterans overall. However, the results of the implicit associations test revealed a moderate mental health stigma associated with veterans. This suggests that, despite having no outwardly expressed or acknowledged biases against veterans, individuals may hide their biases or are unaware of their existence. However, these results should be interpreted with caution due to the fact that the IAT has received a great deal of criticism from researchers, including challenges to both the validity and reliability of the test, over the last two decades since its introduction (Arkes & Tetlock, 2004; Fiedler, Messner, & Bluemke, 2006).

Using semi-structured interviews Kato, Jinkerson, Holland, and Soper (2016) identified several themes related to the adjustment process of veterans after deployments to combat zones. Their sample included student veterans who were currently enrolled in college. One theme, labeled "battling the stereotypes," emerged from participant experiences such as encountering civilians, including in some cases their own family members, who believed that all veterans return from deployment with PTSD. It is essential to note the importance of this particular finding: The mere fact that in some cases family members can hold such inaccurate stereotypes of veterans (and, relatedly, seem unaware of the realities of the military experience) demonstrates just how pervasive these stereotypes are. Even those closest to the veteran can in some cases hold potentially damaging stereotypes. Another interesting finding detailed in the study is that despite the fact that 10 percent of the veteran population (Bureau of Labor Statistics, 2019a) and 16 percent of the total enlisted military forces are women (Reynolds & Shendruk, 2018), female veterans reported surprise and even pushback from others after making their veteran status known. Although it is true that the majority of the members of the U.S. armed forces are men, women have served in the military for decades with some restrictions (mostly on combat roles) and since 2016 without such restrictions.

Across a series of three qualitative studies (i.e., focus groups and interviews) exploring the military to civilian transition experience conducted by the Center for Innovation and Research on Veterans & Military Families, the researcher (Keeling, 2018) identified three consistent themes: (1) planning, preparation, and personal agency; (2) civilian culture and shifting identity; and (3) veteran stereotypes and discrimination. Although these findings are based on self-report data from veterans, the repeated appearance of the stereotype and discrimination theme across multiple studies cannot be dismissed. In another qualitative study, using responses to open-ended questions about the transition experience, Furst-Holloway and Stone (2018) found that among other stated barriers there was a perception that it's possible that all veterans have PTSD and that many do. For example, many participants reported employers expressing concern about their military experience. If the characteristics associated with the position are incongruent with those attributed to veteran status, many employers may arbitrarily disqualify a job applicant (Stone & Stone, 2015).

Stereotype Mitigation

Of major concern to practitioners and researchers alike is how to combat stereotypes of veterans. Fortunately, some progress has been made in this area. Stone and Stone (2015) describe several strategies that can be employed by both organizations and veterans to improve veteran employment outcomes. One proposed strategy involves the use of educational programs within organizations to dispel stereotypes. Hammer et al. (2018) developed and tested such a training program. Their supervisor training intervention, Veteran-Supportive Supervisor Training (VSST), increased supervisor knowledge of the military- and veteran-related topics by nearly 80 percent. The researchers also found increases in positive perceptions of veteran employees and family-supportive supervisor behaviors. The findings from this study demonstrate that educational programs can increase awareness, change perceptions of veterans, and ultimately benefit veterans and organizations.

As proposed by Stone and Stone (2015), veterans can also engage in strategies to effectively mitigate negative perceptions while emphasizing positive ones. One mechanism that has been suggested is the use of impression management. For example, when veterans respond to interview questions with direct, short responses, as they might be expected to in the military, a civilian hiring manager may perceive this as indicative of a lack of social skills. In some cases, this misunderstanding can be explained by a lack of interview skills on the part of the hiring manager (e.g., asking simple yes/no questions). Regardless, a veteran can be taught to elaborate when answering interview questions in order to demonstrate their communication skills as well as their creativity. Aside from actively working to override potentially negative stereotypes in an interview, veterans can increase their chances of making it to the interview by seeking out help in translating their military experience and preparing a civilian résumé.

Recommendations for the Future

As stated by Mobbs (2018), "it's important to clarify this is not an 'us' (veterans) vs. 'them' (civilian) problem. This is an everyone problem" (p. 1). Organizations, veterans, and nonveterans all have the ability to effect change when it comes to closing the gap between perceptions of military veterans and the realities of the impact of military experience and what lasting changes it creates in veterans. Additionally, unemployment affects everyone in some form; therefore, it is in the best interest of all citizens to participate in helping to reduce it.

Recommendations for Practice

Rather than view a veteran as a standard set of characteristics that either fit or do not fit with any given job, hiring managers should take the time to look deeper into what specific military jobs entail. O*Net Online (www .onetonline.org) is a website sponsored by the Department of Labor that contains several tools a hiring manager or job seeker may find useful. The Military Crosswalks tool can be used to identify general KSAOs needed for any given military job code. Both hiring managers and veterans can use this tool to help translate military work experience into civilian language.

Recommendations for Research

There is still much we do not know about veteran stereotypes. Of primary concern to researchers should be teasing out the distinction between real differences and unfounded stereotypes of veterans. It is difficult to suggest that veterans should not be stereotyped based on their group membership while simultaneously suggesting that hiring veterans can be good for organizations. Research in this area should focus on specific characteristics of interest to organizations, such as motivation, commitment, resiliency, and soft skills, among others. Second, researchers need to identify where these stereotypes are being applied. Are we seeing the same outcomes across industries, or are they focused within specific types of jobs? What other factors determine when and how stereotypes are applied? Previous research on other disadvantaged populations have explored interaction effects of demographic factors such as race and gender. More research should be conducted to identify other variables that may be at play in making attributions about veterans. Finally, although there is some evidence that stereotypes can be mitigated through educational programs, more work needs to be done to identify factors related to training success. Demographic factors of employees and supervisors should be explored to determine, for example, if a one-size-fits-all approach to training interventions is sufficient.

Conclusion

Stereotypes of veterans are particularly interesting considering that, unlike other groups recognized in this book, veterans are one of the few groups that individuals self-select into. This makes such stereotypes inherently different in that the assumption is not that veterans were born with any particular set of characteristics but rather that they acquired them through experience. Theoretically and practically, therefore, they must be viewed differently than group membership based on factors such as age, gender, race, or nationality. Through a greater understanding of how veteran stereotypes are created, applied, and mitigated, multiple stakeholders will benefit. Not only will the lives of veterans and their families be improved, but workplaces and society as a whole will also benefit from the diversity of ideas and experiences that veterans bring with them into civilian life.

References

Alderton, M. (2015, November 11). Veterans group Got Your 6 uses Hollywood to shatter stereotypes. *USA Today.* Retrieved from https://www.usatoday.com/story/life/2015/11/11/veterans-group-got-your-6-shatters-hollywood-stereotypes/75512556/

Arkes, H. R., & Tetlock, P. E. (2004). Attributions of implicit prejudice, or "would Jesse Jackson 'fail' the Implicit Association Test?" *Psychological Inquiry, 15*(4), 257–278.

Bordieri, J. E., & Drehmer, D. E. (1984). Vietnam veterans: Fighting the employment war. *Journal of Applied Social Psychology, 14*(4), 341–347.

Bureau of Labor Statistics. (2019a). *Employment situation of veterans summary.* Retrieved from https://www.bls.gov/news.release/vet.nr0.htm

Bureau of Labor Statistics. (2019b). *Occupational outlook handbook: Military careers.* Retrieved from https://www.bls.gov/ooh/military/military-careers.htm

Cascio, W. F., & Aguinis, H. (2008). *Applied psychology in human resource management* (6th ed.). Upper Saddle River, NJ: Prentice Hall.

Classen, T. J., & Dunn, R. A. (2012). The effect of job loss and unemployment duration on suicide risk in the United States: A new look using mass layoffs and unemployment duration. *Health Economics, 21*(3), 338–350.

Executive Office of the President. (2013). The fast track to civilian employment: Streamlining credentialing and licensing for service members, veterans, and their spouses. *The White House.* Retrieved from https://www.whitehouse.gov/sites/default/files/docs/military_credentialing_and_licensing_report_2-24-2013_final.pdf

Fiedler, K., Messner, C., & Bluemke, M. (2006). Unresolved problems with the "I," the "A," and the "T": A logical and psychometric critique of the Implicit Association Test (IAT). *European Review of Social Psychology, 17*(1), 74–147.

Furst-Holloway, S., & Stone, C. (2018, April). The veteran mindset during transitions to the civilian sector: A qualitative study. In P. Reilly (Chair), *Beyond the unemployment headlines: Examining veteran transition issues and solutions.* Symposium presented at the Society for Industrial and Organizational Psychology, Chicago, IL.

Gonzalez, J. (2019, April). Veteran transition into civilian employment and identity challenges. In P. Reilly (Chair), *From warrior to civilian: Military veteran identity and the transition process.* Symposium presented at the Society for Industrial and Organizational Psychology, National Harbor, MD.

Greenwald, A. G., McGhee, D. E., & Schwartz, J. L. (1998). Measuring individual differences in implicit cognition: The implicit association test. *Journal of Personality and Social Psychology, 74*(6), 1464–1480.

Griffin, R. J., & Sen, S. (1995). Causal communication: Movie portrayals and audience attributions for Vietnam veterans' problems. *Journalism & Mass Communication Quarterly, 72*(3), 511–524.

Hammer, L., Anger, W. K., Wipfli, B., Olson, R., Mahoney, L., Brockwood, K., & Bird, P. (2018). Online training improves supervisor knowledge and attitudes toward veteran employees. In P. Reilly (Chair), *Beyond the unemployment headlines: Examining veteran transition issues and solutions.* Symposium presented at the Society for Industrial and Organizational Psychology, Chicago, IL.

Harrell, M. C., & Berglass, N. (2012). *Employing America's veterans: Perspectives from businesses.* Washington, D.C.: Center for a New American Security.

Hayes, A. (2012, January 17). Experts: Vets' PTSD, violence a growing problem. *CNN.* Retrieved from https://www.cnn.com/2012/01/17/us/veterans-violence/index.html

Haynie, J. M. (2016, April). *Revisiting the business case for hiring a veteran: A strategy for cultivating competitive advantage* (Workforce Readiness Briefs, Paper No. 2). Syracuse, NY: Institute for Veterans and Military Families, Syracuse University.

Kato, L., Jinkerson, J. D., Holland, S. C., & Soper, H. V. (2016). From combat zones to the classroom: Transitional adjustment in OEF/OIF student veterans. *The Qualitative Report, 21*(11), 2131–2147.

Keeling, M. (2018, April). A qualitative psychology approach to understanding military to civilian transition. In P. Reilly (Chair), *Calling for reinforcements: IGNITING military veteran transition research and practice.* Symposium presented at the Society for Industrial and Organizational Psychology, Chicago, IL.

Kleykamp, M. (2013). Unemployment, earnings and enrollment among post 9/11 veterans. *Social Science Research, 42*(3), 836–851.

Klinefelter, Z., Irving, L., & Huffman, A. (2018, April). Employees' perceptions of veterans: The role of explicit and implicit attitudes. In P. Reilly (Chair), *Beyond the unemployment headlines: Examining veteran transition issues and solutions.* Symposium presented at the Society for Industrial and Organizational Psychology, Chicago, IL.

Korn Ferry Institute. (2017). *Debunking myths in veteran hiring.* Retrieved from https://www.kornferry.com/institute/download/download/id/18111/aid/2200

Kposowa, A. J. (2001). Unemployment and suicide: A cohort analysis of social factors predicting suicide in the US National Longitudinal Mortality Study. *Psychological Medicine, 31*(1), 127–138.

Mael, F. (2019, April). An enduring military identity complicates transition. In P. Reilly (Chair), *From warrior to civilian: Military veteran identity and the transition process.* Symposium presented at the Society for Industrial and Organizational Psychology, National Harbor, MD.

Matsa, K., & Shearer, E. (2018, September 10). News use across social media platforms 2018. *Pew Research Center.* Retrieved from http://www.journalism.org/2018/09/10/news-use-across-social-media-platforms-2018/

Mobbs, M. (2018, January 24). What you think about veterans is likely wrong. *Psychology Today.* Retrieved from https://www.psychologytoday.com/us/blog/the-debrief/201801/what-you-think-about-veterans-is-likely-wrong

Nederhof, A. J. (1985). Methods of coping with social desirability bias: A review. *European Journal of Social Psychology, 15,* 263–280.

Parrott, S., Albright, D., Dyche, C., & Steele, H. (2018). Hero, charity case, and victim: How U.S. news media frame military veterans on Twitter. *Armed Forces & Society,* 1–21. doi:10.1177/0095327X18784238

Pew Research Center. (2011). *The military-civilian gap: Fewer family connections.* Retrieved from www.pewsocialtrends.org/2011/11/23/the-military-civilian-gap-fewer-family-connections/

Prudential. (2012). *Veterans employment challenges: Perceptions and experiences of transitioning from military to civilian life.* Retrieved from https://www.voced.edu.au/content/ngv%3A60692

Reynolds, G., & Shendruk, A. (2018). *Demographics of the U.S. military.* Retrieved from https://www.cfr.org/article/demographics-us-military

Steele, J. (2017, January 11). Are military veterans more likely for shooting sprees? *The San Diego Union-Tribune.* Retrieved from https://www.sandiegouniontribune.com/military/veterans/sd-me-veterans-violence-20170109-story.html

Stone, C., & Stone, D. L. (2015). Factors affecting hiring decisions about veterans. *Human Resource Management Review, 25*(1), 68–79.

Stone, C. B., Lengnick-Hall, M., & Muldoon, J. (2018). Do stereotypes of veterans affect chances of employment? *The Psychologist-Manager Journal, 21*(1), 1–33.

Van Orden, K. A., Witte, T. K., Cukrowicz, K. C., Braithwaite, S. R., Selby, E. A., & Joiner, T. E., Jr. (2010). The interpersonal theory of suicide. *Psychological Review, 117*(2), 575.

Veterans Administration. (2017, September 15). VA releases veteran suicide statistics by state. *Veterans Administration.* Retrieved from https://www.va.gov/opa/pressrel/pressrelease.cfm?id=2951

CHAPTER THIRTEEN

Weight Stereotypes

Lynn Bartels

I went to a job interview . . . where the guy right in front of me (the interviewer), right at the beginning of the interview, he wrote "Too Fat!" on the form that he had in front of him.

—Female focus group participant from Cossrow, Jeffery, and McGuire (2001, p. 212)

Overweight individuals are often perceived through the lens of damaging weight stereotypes, which lead to devastating forms of discrimination in many aspects of their lives, including health care, interpersonal relationships, education, and employment. Unlike other stereotypes, for which there is pressure to conceal discriminatory attitudes, weight stereotypes are often openly acknowledged. This may be a function of the perceived controllability of weight (Crandall & Martinez, 1996). As obesity rates in the United States increase, more than 70 percent of American adults are considered overweight (Body Mass Index, BMI[1] = 25 – 29.9) or obese (BMI = 30+) (National Health and Nutrition Examination Survey, 2013–2014). Given U.S. weight statistics, weight discrimination is a pervasive concern, affecting most people in the United States. The purpose of this chapter is to review the current research on weight stereotypes and their consequences, noting where additional research is needed. Given the large number of people affected and the serious

---

[1]Body mass index is calculated by multiplying weight in pounds by 703 and then dividing that number by height in inches squared. Note that BMI is criticized as a flawed measure of obesity. For example, BMI does not take muscle into account.

consequences, it's important to also consider ways of reducing the effects of weight stereotypes.

Weight Stereotyping

The stereotypical traits associated with being overweight are harsh. For example, as overweight individuals are perceived to have failed to control their weight, they may be viewed as having low self-control and discipline (Puhl & Brownell, 2003). Individuals who are overweight may also be perceived as lazy (Ryckman, Robbins, Kaczor, & Gold, 1989), careless (Ruggs, Hebl, & Williams, 2015), sloppy (Vartanian & Silverstein, 2013), and so on. Additionally, being overweight may be linked to broader, negative attributes such as incompetence and unattractiveness (Teachman, Gapinski, Brownell, Rawlings, & Jeyaram, 2003). When undergraduates were asked to match body silhouettes with various characteristics, large body shapes were associated with traits such as slow, lazy, unfriendly, and boring (Greenleaf, Stark, Gomez, Chambiss, & Martin, 2004).

In an effort to examine whether there is evidence to support the undesirable weight stereotypes, Roehling, Roehling, and Odland (2008) examined the relationship between body weight and four of the Big Five personality factors (i.e., neuroticism, extraversion, agreeableness, and conscientiousness). They did not find meaningful differences in personality based on weight. Thus, the widely held negative stereotypes of individuals who are overweight were not evidenced by personality differences, suggesting the stereotypes may be invalid.

There are important differences between how weight stereotypes and other types of stereotypes operate. Unlike other stereotypes (e.g., race), it is often considered socially acceptable to express negative attitudes toward individuals who are overweight (Crandall, 1994; Crandall & Biernat, 1990; Morrison & O'Connor, 1999). Obese people have been labeled "the last acceptable targets of discrimination" (Puhl & Brownell, 2001, p. 788). There is less social desirability pressure to suppress negative weight attitudes, which may be a function of perceptions of weight controllability (Crandall & Martinez, 1996). To understand the strength of the negative attitudes toward obesity, 46 percent of survey participants said they would be willing to give up one year of their lives rather than be obese, while 15 percent reported that they would rather give up ten years of their lives than be obese (Schwartz, Vartanian, Nosek, & Brownell, 2006). In comparison with other forms of bias (i.e., Muslim and gay), weight bias was significantly stronger (Latner, O'Brien, Durso, Brinkman, & MacDonald, 2008) but not as commonly reported as perceived gender, age, and race discrimination (Puhl, Andreyeva, & Brownell, 2008).

Development of Weight Stereotypes

It's unclear exactly how weight stereotypes develop, but it is clear they exist from a young age. Using several different tasks, Cramer and Steinwert (1998) found that preschool children as young as three years old associated negative characteristics with body weight. For example, preschool children identified the overweight target in a story as "mean" and possessing other undesirable characteristics. The stereotype that fat is bad starts at an early age.

Mass media is often blamed for perpetuating weight bias. Based on cultivation theory, the onslaught of media images shapes our perceptions of idealized reality (Gerbner, Gross, & Morgan, 2002). Models who appear underweight, often through the use of photo manipulation techniques such as Photoshop, are often portrayed desirably in the mass media, creating unrealistic representations of female bodies (Silverstein, Perdue, Peterson, & Kelly, 1986). In contrast, overweight individuals are rarely seen on television shows or in movies. When they are included, they are presented negatively (Greenberg, Eastin, Hofschire, Lachlan, & Brownell, 2003). As Chrissy Metz (2018, front book cover) put it, "Hollywood gave women two options: size zero or sight gag." Overweight actors are often the target of jokes and unlikely to be in romantic roles (Puhl & Brownell, 2003). Stigmatizing media images include seminaked, headless bodies engaging in unhealthy behaviors (Pearl, Puhl, & Brownell, 2012). Popular media presents people who are obese as "grotesque, uncontained, destined for ill-health, and an early death, and a burden on the public purse" (Lupton, 2017, p. 120). The result of exposure to media images can be high rates of body dissatisfaction and increased rates of disordered eating behaviors in women (Grabe, Ward, & Hyde, 2008).

Recently, there have been some signs of increased acceptance of larger bodies. There are now media platforms to counter the fat-shaming narrative (e.g., the Adipositivity project, #body positivity, #fatbabe) (Lupton, 2017). Plus-size models have been included in the *Sports Illustrated* swimsuit edition. Dove soap's Real Beauty campaign presents more realistic female body images. Even Barbie doll bodies have been transformed to present a wider range of body sizes. In social media, fat shamers are often called out. Body acceptance may reduce weight stigmatization (Murakami & Latner, 2015). Murakami and Latner (2015) found that overweight targets who were described as accepting of their weight (e.g., Ahsyley believes her body shape and body weight are attractive, and her body is satisfactory at her current weight) were less stigmatized by others and were perceived by others to have better self-esteem and mental health.

Characteristics of Those Who Hold Negative Weight Stereotypes

Although negative attitudes are widely held, there are differences between groups in how they stigmatize others based on weight. Weight stigma means that weight as a social identity is devalued and associated with negative consequences such as bias and discrimination (Crocker, Major, & Steele, 1998). For example, men tend to report higher antifat attitudes than women (Brochu & Morrison, 2007; Harris, Walters, & Waschull, 1991; Morrison & O'Connor, 1999) and to stigmatize obesity in men and women (Hebl & Turchin, 2005). Compared to White men, African American men have a wider range of acceptable weights for women (Hebl & Turchin, 2005). That is, African American men find thin and medium women desirable, while White men only view thin female body types favorably. White women rated heavy women lower than they rated other women, and they gave the lowest ratings to heavy, White women. African American women were less likely to stigmatize women based on weight (Hebl & Heatherton, 1998).

There are cultural differences as well. For example, Crandall and Martinez (1996) found that Mexicans were more accepting of being overweight. Also, there are likely differences among Whites based on culture (e.g., Eastern European), but little research has examined within-group differences. Thus, certain groups are more likely to hold negative attitudes toward individuals who are overweight.

In addition to demographic differences in weight attitudes, there are also relationships with other attitudes. There were positive correlations between antifat attitudes and authoritarianism, homonegativity, and political conservatism (Crandall & Biernat, 1990; Morrison & O'Connor, 1999), such that people who are authoritarian, antigay, and politically conservative were more likely to report higher antifat attitudes. Even though antifat attitudes are widely held, people with certain characteristics have stronger antifat attitudes.

Implicit versus Explicit Attitudes

In addition to the widespread expression of negative, explicit self-reported antifat attitudes, individuals may also possess implicit, negative, weight biases that are outside of their conscious awareness and control. An obesity implicit association test measures the extent to which participants are more likely to associate negative terms (e.g., lazy) than positive ones (e.g., determined) with fat people. Even when antifat attitudes aren't explicitly endorsed, implicit biases can exist. For example, weight management health care providers who did not report negative, explicit attitudes toward the obese had strong negative, implicit attitudes (Teachman & Brownell, 2001). Individuals with low BMIs tended to have both negative explicit and implicit attitudes (Schwartz et al., 2006). Implicit bias was higher when thin people and obese people were presented doing stereotype-congruent activities (e.g., obese person watching television, thin person preparing vegetables) (Hinman, Burmeister, Kiefner, Borushok, & Carels, 2015).

Although there is some inconsistent research, another way weight stereotypes may differ from other types of stereotypes (e.g., race, ethnicity) is that there is limited ingroup, protective bias. Ingroup protective bias occurs when individuals from the social identity group hold positive attitudes about the group. With protective ingroup bias, ingroup members may protect their self-esteem by blaming outgroup members for being prejudiced. In contrast, some previous research has shown that overweight individuals also express weight bias (Crandall, 1994; Crandall & Biernat, 1990; Harris et al., 1991; Latner et al., 2008) which is demonstrated when antifat attitudes are not related to one's own weight. Other research has provided some evidence of ingroup protective bias (Morrison & O'Connor, 1999). For example, Schwartz et al. (2006) found a negative correlation between BMI and antifat attitudes such that weight bias decreased, but was still present, among heavier individuals. Their findings may be a result of having a larger participant weight range than previous research. Nonetheless, overweight individuals may not experience a strong, protective, ingroup bias.

One explanation for the widespread acceptance of weight stereotypes is the belief that people can control their weight through diet and exercise. If weight is controllable, and overweight people choose not to control it, then they may be viewed as responsible for their weight. Those who have strong beliefs in a just world, which is the idea that people get what they deserve, may be more likely to support the idea that weight is personally controllable (Crandall & Martinez, 1996). The idea that weight is controllable has been challenged by those who believe that weight is a complex interaction between individuals and their environments (Puhl & Brownell, 2003). Beliefs in the causes of weight gain are associated with different levels of blame on overweight individuals. This has implications for weight stigma interventions, which will be discussed later. Next, we'll explore the different effects of weight for various target groups.

Weight and Its Stigma across Target Groups

Weight means different things for different groups. Weight intersects with other personal characteristics (e.g., gender, age, socioeconomic status and race) in interesting and unique ways. There are differences across demographic groups in weight, weight stigma and weight bias internalization. Weight bias internalization is self-stereotyping that involves accepting blame for negative weight-related experiences and is associated with increased psychological distress (O'Brien et al., 2016).

Taking a look at gender differences, more men (74%) than women (67%) are considered overweight or obese (National Health and Nutrition Examination Survey, 2013–2014). Research has shown that stereotypes of overweight women were more negative than stereotypes of overweight men (Harris et al., 1991). In the National Survey of Midlife Development in the United States (MIDUS) of adults between the ages of twenty-five and seventy-four, women reported higher levels of daily and lifetime weight/height discrimination than men (Puhl et al., 2008). Yet newer research (Himmelstein, Puhl, & Quinn, 2017) shows similar rates of weight stigma for men and women, with women showing higher rates of weight bias internalization. The patterns of weight stigma appear to differ between men and women. Women tend to show a linear trend, with weight discrimination increasing with BMI, and men show a U-shaped relationship between BMI and weight stigma, with discrimination occurring at both low and high BMI extremes (Himmelstein, Puhl, & Quinn, 2018). It is important to note the different relationships between weight and stigma that emerge for men compared to women. Researchers should not assume that weight stereotypes operate similarly for males and females who are overweight.

Looking at race/ethnicity and obesity, Asian Americans (11.7%) were least likely to be obese and African Americans (48.1%) were most likely to be obese, with White (34.5%) and Hispanic (42.5%) obesity rates between the other two groups. Some research has examined weight stigma for African Americans compared with Whites and identified important race and gender differences. There was less stigmatization of overweight, African American men than overweight, White men (Hebl & Turchin, 2005). White women reported less satisfaction with their weight than African American women (Harris et al., 1991; Stevens, Kumanyika, & Keil, 1994). Similarly, researchers (Himmelstein et al., 2017; Puhl, Himmelstein, & Quinn, 2018) found weight bias internalization was lower among Hispanics and Blacks and higher among Whites and Asians, suggesting that Whites and Asians experience more weight-related guilt and psychological distress. Recent research suggests that the thin ideal is increasingly being accepted by ethnic minorities, especially those who are exposed to and identify with mainstream, White culture (Keel & Forney, 2013), which may perpetuate the effects of weight bias internalization. Within racial/ethnic groups, there may be cultural differences, too.

Obesity is more prevalent among people from low socioeconomic status (SES) backgrounds, especially low SES women (Ogden, Lamb, Carroll, & Flegal, 2010). Educated women are less likely to be obese than women who aren't educated (Ogden et al., 2010). Based on MIDUS survey data, women with little education reported higher levels of height/weight discrimination. On the other hand, uneducated men reported few occurrences of height/weight discrimination (Puhl et al., 2008). Again, gender moderates the effects of weight on discriminatory outcomes. In terms of weight bias internalization, Puhl et al. (2018) found negative relationships with income and education.

Obesity is more common among middle-aged (40.2%) and older adults (37%) compared to young adults (32.3%) (Ogden, Carroll, Fryar, & Flegal, 2015). Younger MIDUS participants reported the highest rates of height/weight discrimination (Puhl et al., 2008) and weight stigma (Himmelstein et al., 2017). Future research should examine the impact of age on weight discrimination. Higher weight may be more expected and accepted for older individuals, tempering weight stigmatization. Thus, weight stereotypes may be differentially applied across groups. Next, we'll briefly explore the consequences of weight stereotypes.

Consequences of Weight Stereotypes

Weight stereotypes can result in devastating effects in many areas of life such as health, interpersonal relationships, education, and employment. Weight discrimination in each of these contexts is examined next.

Health

Being overweight has negative effects on physical and mental health. Its effects on health are both direct and indirect. Weight can directly affect health by contributing to conditions such as heart disease, Type II diabetes, high blood pressure, and so on (Haslam & James, 2005). Weight can also have less direct effects on health. Weight-based teasing during adolescence has been shown to prompt maladaptive eating patterns and obesity later in life (Puhl & Heuer, 2009; Puhl et al., 2017).

Obese patients frequently reported feeling stigmatized by health care providers (Puhl & Brownell, 2006) and may be less likely to seek care (Puhl & Heuer, 2009). Puhl and Heuer (2009) reviewed research that showed that health care professionals (doctors, nurses, medical students, fitness professionals, and dietitians) stigmatize people who are obese. They characterized obese individuals as lazy and noncompliant. They also felt unprepared and ineffective in treating obesity, which may lead to spending insufficient time with obese patients (Puhl & Heuer, 2009).

In terms of mental health, weight discrimination may lead to higher rates of depression, anxiety, body dissatisfaction, and suicidality (Carpenter, Hasin, Allison, & Faith, 2000; Puhl & Heuer, 2009). Some research points to gender differences in weight stigma's effects on mental health. In their meta-analysis, Miller and Downey (1999) found a small negative correlation between weight and self-esteem, with a stronger relationship for women than men. Ciciurkaite and Perry (2018) used data from the National Health Measurement study to look at the mental health consequences of weight and perceived weight discrimination for American women from different racial/ethnic and SES groups. Obese Hispanic and obese low SES women showed lower levels of mental health than obese White women and obese high SES women. Obese African American women who experienced weight discrimination did not show significant decreases in mental health, which may be due to a rejection of the thinness ideal (Keel & Forney, 2013). Ciciurkaite and Perry (2018) concluded that socioeconomic status can buffer the effects of weight stigma on psychological health. Overall, there are significant health effects of weight that may vary across groups.

Interpersonal Relationships

Overweight individuals may also be penalized socially (Gortmaker, Must, Perrin, Sobol, & Dietz, 1993). They can face weight stigmatization in relationships with others. Overweight individuals said that family and friends were the source of the most negative weight-related experiences (Puhl, Moss-Rascusin, Schwartz, & Brownell, 2008). Participants reported weight-based teasing and name-calling from family members. Lydecker, O'Brien, and Grilo (2018) found pervasive weight bias among parents. Nearly all parents (93%) reported moderate or strong explicit weight bias. Fathers did report more explicit weight bias than mothers. Obese and overweight parents reported less explicit bias. Parents also exhibited implicit biases (Lydecker et al., 2018).

Brochu and Morrison (2007) found that participants had lower intentions to engage socially with or befriend overweight individuals. Participants reported more discriminatory, behavioral intentions toward individuals who are overweight. Not surprisingly, overweight women reported having fewer close friends (Sarlio-Lähteenkorva, 2001).

Weight also affects dating prospects. In one study, more men responded to a personal advertisement from a woman with a history of drug problems than an obese woman (Smith, Schmoll, Konik, & Oberlander, 2007). In another study, overweight men and women were ranked lower as potential sexual partners in comparison to people with various disabilities, mental illness, or a history of sexually transmitted diseases (Chen & Brown, 2005). Weight, especially for women, can make it difficult to develop strong interpersonal relationships.

Education

A 1994 National Education Association Report on Discrimination due to Physical Size concluded: "For fat students, the school experience is one of ongoing prejudice, unnoticed discrimination, and almost constant harassment. From nursery school through college, fat students experience ostracism, discouragement, and sometimes violence. Often ridiculed by their peers and discouraged by even well-meaning education employees." Very overweight adolescent girls (63%) and boys (58%) reported weight-based teasing (Neumark-Sztainer et al., 2002). Weight-based teasing is associated with lower self-esteem and body satisfaction and increased risk of depression and suicidal thoughts (Eisenberg, Neumark-Sztainer, & Story, 2003).

Despite their commitment to student well-being, teachers reported negative stereotypes toward overweight students (Neumark-Sztainer, Story, & Harris, 1999), and students reported being aware of teachers' attitudes (Bauer, Yang, & Austin, 2004). These negative attitudes may be more prevalent among male teachers and those with less professional training (Hague & White, 2005).

Crandall (1991) sought to extend earlier research showing that obese (particularly obese female) students were less likely to be accepted into college compared with students with equivalent backgrounds (Canning & Mayer, 1966). Crandall (1991) found that overweight students (particularly daughters) received less financial support from their parents than normal-weight students. In a review of university outcomes for overweight men and women (Hill, Lopez, & Caterson, 2018), the U.S. studies revealed lower GPAs for overweight students and mixed findings for graduation rates. Some studies revealed lower likelihood of enrollment for overweight women than men. There are many challenges in pursuing an education for obese individuals, particularly obese females.

Employment

Employers may also hold stereotypical views of employees, which can lead to work-related discrimination. Unlike many other stigmatized groups, weight is not a federally protected group, although some states and municipalities do have laws that prohibit weight-based employment discrimination, and limited forms of protection may be available through the Americans with Disabilities Act. Without legal protection, weight discrimination is legal in many work contexts (Roehling, 1999).

There is evidence of weight discrimination in every part of the employment process, from hiring through termination, in both lab and field studies (Roehling, 1999). In their meta-analysis of experimental studies, Roehling, Pichler, and Bruce (2013) found that overweight individuals were more negatively evaluated across workplace outcomes, including hiring, suitability, and salary. Weight had the strongest effect on perceptions of the target as a desirable coworker. Another meta-analysis (Vanhove & Gordon, 2014) looked at correlational studies and the outcomes faced by job applicants and incumbents and found evidence of weight discrimination, especially for women.

There are wage penalties as well, with obese individuals consistently earning less compared to nonobese individuals, and the salary differences are greater for females than men (Baum & Ford, 2004; Mason, 2012). The relationship between weight and pay are very different for females and males and reflect gender weight ideals (Judge & Cable, 2011). Judge and Cable (2011) examined data from 12,686 participants in the National Longitudinal Survey of Youth over a twenty-five-year time span with numerous control variables, including gender, marital status, children, and so on. For women, there was a linear trend whereby very thin women experienced the largest salary penalty for initial weight gains. Additional weight gains were not punished as harshly. For men, a different U-shaped trajectory was identified. Very thin males were rewarded for weight gain until they reached the point of obesity. Thus, very thin and obese males were stigmatized while all women except the very thin were stigmatized (Judge & Cable, 2011). The relationship between weight and salary matches the patterns of weight stigmatization identified by Himmelstein et al. (2018).

Interventions to Reduce Weight Stigma

Methods that have worked to decrease other forms of stigma have met with limited success in reducing weight stigma. For example, stories or videos of weight discrimination designed to elicit empathy were not successful in decreasing stigma (Teachman et al., 2003). In some cases, interpersonal contact with the stigmatized individuals can decrease stigma. However, Puhl and Brownell (2003) pointed out that given the prevalence of obesity, it's unlikely that people lack contact with obese people.

Other efforts have focused on attributions of controllability (Crandall, 1994; Teachman et al., 2003). Teachman et al. (2003) provided participants with information about the causes of obesity. Some participants were provided information that said the primary cause of weight is genetic. Others were told that weight is controllable through diet and exercise. Presenting weight as controllable led to more negative attitudes. Yet, providing information about weight as less controllable and mainly due to genetics did not decrease negative attitudes. Implicit weight bias did decrease for overweight participants exposed to the genetic manipulation.

Another approach involves social consensus, which involves shared beliefs or norms. When stigmatizing beliefs are perceived to be shared by others, those stigmatizing beliefs are strengthened (Zitek & Hebl, 2007). In one study (Puhl, Schwartz, & Brownell, 2005) participants were given with false information about others' views of obesity. When participants were told that others held more positive attitudes toward individuals who are obese than they did, participants' attitudes became more positive. This approach appears promising.

Based on the justification/suppression model, efforts to suppress prejudice can reduce interpersonal discrimination. In a study examining how overweight customers are treated in a retail context, King, Shapiro, Hebl, Singletary, and Turner (2006), found that when the overweight customer did things like carrying a Diet Coke, talking about dieting, and participating in a half marathon, interpersonal discrimination was reduced. The customer's comments were intended to evoke the notion that weight is controllable, which led to the suppression of prejudice.

Another promising intervention targets media portrayals of individuals who are overweight. In their studies, Pearl et al. (2012) portrayed individuals who were overweight in positive images (e.g., shopping for produce at the grocery store) or stigmatizing images (e.g., eating junk food on the couch). Participants who viewed the positive images expressed more positive attitudes and lower preference for social distance than participants who viewed the stigmatizing images. These results suggest that more positive media portrayals of individuals who are overweight may lead to more accepting attitudes and behaviors. Despite the prevalence and strength of weight bias (Latner et al., 2008), some interventions may show promise in reducing it.

Future Research

There are many areas where future research can help improve our understanding of weight-based discrimination. More research is needed on the effects of formal (connected to job decisions like hiring, promotion, or salary) versus interpersonal discrimination (negative verbal and nonverbal social interactions). A recent meta-analysis (Dhanani, Beus, & Joseph, 2018) compared the effects of formal discrimination and interpersonal discrimination. Contrary to their hypothesis, they found had that both types of discrimination had similarly harmful relationships with work outcomes. They expected that formal discrimination, because of its significant relationships with employment decision-making, would lead to more negative workplace outcomes. However, they found that interpersonal discrimination had equally or more harmful effects. Additional research should examine the effects of formal versus interpersonal discrimination, looking specifically at weight discrimination in other contexts (e.g., education, health care).

More research is needed on the effects of experienced versus observed bystander or ambient discrimination. In their meta-analysis, Dhanani et al. (2018) unexpectedly found that observed discrimination had stronger relationships with negative workplace outcomes (e.g., affective commitment, turnover intentions, mental health) than experienced discrimination. This research conclusion implies that negative impacts of discrimination expand beyond the target to witnesses. Although this conclusion was reached based on a study of discrimination in general, it may have similar effects in the area of weight discrimination. Even observers who aren't currently overweight can likely imagine being overweight in the future, as weight is more modifiable than other stigmatized characteristics (e.g., race, gender). On the other hand, perhaps observed weight discrimination isn't as impactful as other forms of discrimination because of the strength of negative attitudes toward overweight individuals and the weaker protective ingroup bias (Latner et al., 2008).

We need more precise manipulations of weight, particularly when trying to understand gender differences in weight discrimination. Often, studies contrast "normal weight" targets with overweight targets and don't consider the entire weight range or carefully equate weight perceptions of male and female targets (Roehling et al., 2013). Different patterns of weight discrimination are emerging for men and women. Being underweight may be beneficial to women but not men, and being average weight may be beneficial to men but not women (Himmelstein et al., 2018; Judge & Cable, 2011). Current weight stereotyping and discrimination research does not effectively take these gender/weight differences into account.

Conclusion

Weight stereotypes are widely held and associated with negative characteristics such as being lazy and unmotivated. There are differences across groups in how much they stigmatized and are stigmatized by weight stereotypes, with women experiencing more negative consequences. The effects of weight stereotypes appear across significant life experiences such as health, interpersonal relationships, education and employment. We need to find ways to decrease the negative stereotypes and the toll they take on their targets. These efforts may exist on formal levels through legislation and organizational policies and diversity efforts, but they also need to occur at the interpersonal level where much of the damage takes place (Puhl et al., 2008).

References

Bauer, K. W., Yang, Y. W., & Austin, S. B. (2004). "How can we stay healthy when you're throwing all of this in front of us?" Findings from focus groups and interviews in middle schools on environmental influences on nutrition and physical activity. *Health Education & Behavior, 31*(1), 34–46.

Baum, C. L., & Ford, W. F. (2004). The wage effects of obesity: A longitudinal study. *Health Economics, 13*(9), 885–899.

Brochu, P. M., & Morrison, M.A. (2007). Implicit and explicit prejudice toward overweight and average-weight men and women: Testing their correspondence and relation to behavioral intention. *The Journal of Social Psychology, 147*(6), 681–706.

Canning, H., & Meyer, J. (1966). Obesity—Its possible effect on college acceptance. *New England Journal of Medicine, 275,* 1172–1174.

Carpenter, K. M., Hasin, D. S., Allison, D. B., & Faith, M. S. (2000). Relationships between obesity and DSM-IV major depressive disorder, suicide ideation, and suicide attempts: Results from a general population study. *American Journal of Public Health, 90*(2), 251–257.

Chen, E. Y., & Brown, M. (2005). Obesity stigma in sexual relations. *Obesity Research, 13,* 1393–1397.

Ciciurkaite, G., & Perry, B. L. (2018). Body weight, perceived weight stigma and mental health among women at the intersection of race/ethnicity and socioeconomic status: Insights from the modified labelling approach. *Sociology of Health & Illness, 40*(1), 18–37.

Cossrow, N. H. F., Jeffery, R. W., & McGuire, M. T. (2001). Understanding weight stigmatization: A focus group study. *Journal for Nutritional Education, 33*(4), 208–214.

Cramer, P., & Steinwert, T. (1998). Thin is good, fat is bad: How early does it begin? *Journal of Applied Developmental Psychology, 19*(3), 429–451.

Crandall, C. S. (1991). Do heavy-weight students have more difficulty paying for college? *Personality and Social Psychology Bulletin, 17*(6), 606–611.

Crandall, C. S. (1994). Prejudice against fat people: Ideology and self-interest. *Journal of Personality and Social Psychology, 66*(5), 882–894.

Crandall, C. S., & Biernat, M. (1990). The ideology of anti-fat attitudes. *Journal of Applied Social Psychology, 20*(3), 227–243.

Crandall, C. S., & Martinez, R. (1996). Culture, ideology, and antifat attitudes. *Personality and Social Psychology Bulletin, 22*(11), 1165–1176.

Crocker, J., Major, B., & Steele, C. (1998). Social stigma: The psychology of marked relationships. *The Handbook of Social Psychology, 2,* 504–553.

Dhanani, L. Y., Beus, J. M., & Joseph, D. L. (2018). Workplace discrimination: A meta-analytic extension, critique, and future research agenda. *Personnel Psychology, 71,* 147–179.

Eisenberg, M. E., Neumark-Sztainer, D., & Story, M. (2003). Associations of weight-based teasing and emotional well-being among adolescents. *Archives of Pediatric and Adolescent Medicine, 157,* 733–738.

Gerbner, G., Gross, L., & Morgan, M. (2002). Growing up with television: Cultivation processes. In J. Bryant & D. Zillman (Eds.), *Media effects: Advances in theory and research* (2nd ed., pp. 43–67). Mahwah, NJ: Erlbaum.

Gortmaker, S. L., Must, A., Perrin, J. M., Sobol, A. M., & Dietz, W. H. (1993). Social and economic consequences of overweight in adolescence and young adulthood. *New England Journal of Medicine, 329,* 1008–1012.

Grabe, S., Ward, L. M., & Hyde, J. S. (2008). The role of the media in body image concerns among women: A meta-analysis of experimental and correlational studies. *Psychological Bulletin, 134,* 460–476.

Greenberg, B. S., Eastin, M., Hofschire, L., Lachlan, K., & Brownell, K. D. (2003). Portrayals of overweight and obese individuals on commercial television. *American Journal of Public Health, 93*, 1342–1348.

Greenleaf, C., Starks, M., Gomez, L., Chambliss, H., & Martin, S. (2004). Weight-related words associated with figure silhouettes. *Body Image, 1*, 373–384.

Hague, A. L., & White, A. A. (2005). Web-based intervention for changing attitudes of obesity among current and future teachers. *Journal of Nutrition Education and Behavior, 37*(2), 58–66.

Harris, M. B., Walters, L. C., & Waschull, S. (1991). Gender and ethnic differences in obesity-related behaviors and attitudes in a college sample. *Journal of Applied Social Psychology, 21*(19), 1545–1566.

Haslam, D. W., & James, W. P. (2005). Obesity. *Lancet, 366*, 1197–1209.

Hebl, M. R., & Heatherton, T. F. (1998). The stigma of obesity in women: The difference is black and white. *Personality and Social Psychology Bulletin, 24*(4), 417–426.

Hebl, M. R., & Turchin, J. M. (2005). The stigma of obesity: What about men? *Basic and Applied Social Psychology, 27*, 267–275.

Hill, A. J., Lopez, R. R., & Caterson, I. D. (2018). The relationship between obesity and tertiary education outcomes: A systematic review. *International Journal of Obesity, 42*, 1–9.

Himmelstein, M. S., Puhl, R. M., & Quinn, D. M. (2017). Intersectionality: An understudied framework for addressing weight stigma. *American Journal of Preventive Medicine, 53*(4), 421–431.

Himmelstein, M. S., Puhl, R. M., & Quinn, D. M. (2018). Weight stigma in men: What, when, and by whom? *Obesity, 26*(6), 968–976.

Hinman, N. G., Burmeister, J. M., Kiefner, A. E., Borushok, J., & Carels, R. A. (2015). Stereotypical portrayals of obesity and the expression of implicit weight bias. *Body Image, 12*, 32–35.

Judge, T. A., & Cable, D. M. (2011). When it comes to pay, do the thin win? The effect of weight on pay for men and women. *Journal of Applied Psychology, 96*(1), 95–112.

Keel, P. K., & Forney, K. J. (2013). Psychosocial risk factors for eating disorders. *International Journal of Eating Disorders, 46*(5), 433–439.

King, E. B., Shapiro, J. R., Hebl, M. R., Singletary, S. L., & Turner, S. (2006). The stigma of obesity in customer service: A mechanism for remediation and bottom-line consequences of interpersonal discrimination. *Journal of Applied Psychology, 91*(3), 579–593.

Latner, J. D., O'Brien, K. S., Durso, L. E., Brinkman, L. A., & MacDonald, T. (2008). Weighing obesity stigma: The relative strength of different forms of bias. *International Journal of Obesity, 32*(7), 1145–1152.

Lupton, D. (2017). Digital media and body weight, shape, and size: An introduction and review. *Fat Studies, 6*(2), 119–134.

Lydecker, J. A., O'Brien, E., & Grilo, C. M. (2018). Parents have both implicit and explicit biases against children with obesity. *Journal of Behavioral Medicine, 41*, 1–8.

Mason, K. (2012). The unequal weight of discrimination: Gender, body size, and income inequality. *Social Problems, 59*(3), 411–435.

Metz, C. (2018). *This is me: Loving the person you are today.* New York: Dey St. Books.

Miller, C. T., & Downey, K. T. (1999). A meta-analysis of heavyweight and self-esteem. *Personality and Social Psychology Review, 3*(1), 68–84.

Morrison, T. G., & O'Connor, W. E. (1999). Psychometric properties of a scale measuring negative attitudes toward overweight individuals. *The Journal of Social Psychology, 139*(4), 436–445.

Murakami, J. M., & Latner, J. D. (2015). Weight acceptance versus body dissatisfaction: Effects on stigma, perceived self-esteem, and perceived psychopathology. *Eating Behaviors, 19,* 163–167.

National Education Association. (1994). *National Education Association report on discrimination due to physical size.* Retrieved from https://www.lectlaw .com/files/con28.htm

National Health and Nutrition Examination Survey (2013–2014). Retrieved from https://www.niddk.nih.gov/health-information/health-statistics/over weight-obesity

Neumark-Sztainer, D., Falkner, N., Story, M., Perry, C., Hannan, P. J., & Mulert, S. (2002). Weight-based teasing among adolescents: Correlations with weight status and disordered eating behaviors. *International Journal of Obesity Related Metabolic Disorders, 26*(2), 123–131.

Neumark-Sztainer, D., Story, M., & Harris, T. (1999). Beliefs and attitudes about obesity among teachers and school health care providers working with adolescents. *Journal of Nutrition Education, 31*(1), 3–9.

O'Brien, K. S., Latner, J. D., Puhl, R. M., Vartanian, L. R., Giles, C., Griva, K., & Carter, A. (2016). The relationship between weight stigma and eating behavior is explained by weight bias internalization and psychological distress. *Appetite, 102,* 70–76.

Ogden, C. L., Carroll, M. D., Fryar, C. D., & Flegal, K. M. (2015). *Prevalence of obesity among adults and youth: United States, 2011–2014* (pp. 1–8). Washington, D.C.: U.S. Department of Health and Human Services, Centers for Disease Control and Prevention, National Center for Health Statistics.

Ogden, C. L., Lamb, M. M., Carroll, M. D., & Flegal, K. M. (2010). *Obesity and socioeconomic status in adults: United States 1988–1994 and 2005–2008.* NCHS data brief no 50. Hyattsville, MD: National Center for Health Statistics.

Pearl, R. L., Puhl, R. M., & Brownell, K. D. (2012). Positive media portrayals of obese persons: Impact on attitudes and image preferences. *Health Psychology, 31*(6), 821–829.

Puhl, R. M., Andreyeva, T., & Brownell, K. D. (2008). Perceptions of weight discrimination: Prevalence and comparison to race and gender discrimination in America. *International Journal of Obesity, 32,* 992–1000.

Puhl, R. M., & Brownell, K. D. (2001). Bias, discrimination and obesity. *Obesity Research, 9*(12), 788–805.

Puhl, R. M., & Brownell, K. D. (2003). Psychosocial origins of obesity stigma: Toward changing a powerful and pervasive bias. *Obesity Reviews, 4,* 213–227.

Puhl, R. M., & Brownell, K. D. (2006). Confronting and coping with weight stigma: An investigation of overweight and obese adults. *Obesity, 14*(10), 1802–1815.

Puhl, R. M., & Heuer, C. A. (2009). The stigma of obesity: A review and update. *Obesity, 17,* 941–964.

Puhl, R. M., Himmelstein, M. S., & Quinn, D. M. (2018). Internalizing weight stigma: Prevalence and sociodemographic considerations in U.S. adults. *Obesity, 26*(1), 167–175.

Puhl, R. M., Moss-Rascusin, C. A., Schwartz, M. B., & Brownell, K. D. (2008). Weight stigmatization and bias reduction: Perspectives of overweight and obese adults. *Health Education Research, 23*(2), 347–358.

Puhl, R. M., Schwartz, M. B., Brownell, K. D. (2005). Impact of perceived consensus on stereotypes about obese people: A new approach for reducing bias. *Health Psychology, 24*(5), 517–525.

Puhl, R. M., Wall, M. M., Chen, C., Austin, S. B., Eisenberg, M. E., & Neumark-Sztainer, D. (2017). Experiences of weight teasing in adolescence and weight-related outcomes in adulthood: A 15-year longitudinal study. *Preventive Medicine, 100,* 173–179.

Roehling, M. V. (1999). Weight-based discrimination in employment: Psychological and legal aspects. *Personnel Psychology, 52*(4), 969–1016.

Roehling, M. V., Pichler, S., & Bruce, T. A. (2013). Moderators of the effect of weight on job-related outcomes: A meta-analysis of experimental studies. *Journal of Applied Social Psychology, 43*(2), 237–252.

Roehling, M. V., Roehling, P. V., & Odland, L. M. (2008). Investigating the validity of stereotypes about overweight employees: The relationship between body weight and normal personality traits. *Group & Organization Management, 33*(4), 392–424.

Ruggs, E. N., Hebl, M. R., & Williams, A. (2015). Weight isn't selling: The insidious effects of weight stigmatization in retail settings. *Journal of Applied Psychology, 100*(5), 1483–1496.

Ryckman, R. M., Robbins, M. A., Kaczor, L. M., & Gold, J. A. (1989). Male and female raters' stereotyping of male and female physiques. *Personality and Social Psychology Bulletin, 15*(2), 244–251.

Sarlio-Lähteenkorva, S. (2001). Weight loss and quality of life among obese people. *Social Indicators Research, 54*(3), 329–354.

Schwartz, M. B., Vartanian, L. R., Nosek, B.A., & Brownell, K. D. (2006). The influence of one's own body weight on explicit anti-fat bias. *Obesity, 14,* 440–447.

Silverstein, B., Perdue, L., Peterson, B., & Kelly, E. (1986). The role of the mass media in promoting a thin standard of bodily attractiveness for women. *Sex Roles, 14,* 519–532.

Smith, C. A., Schmoll, K., Konik, J., & Oberlander, S. (2007). Carrying weight for the world: Influence of weight descriptors on judgments of large-sized women. *Journal of Applied Social Psychology, 37*(5), 989–1006.

Stevens, J., Kumanyika, S. K., & Keil, J. E. (1994). Attitudes toward body size and dieting: Differences between elderly black and white women. *American Journal of Public Health, 84*(8), 1322–1325.

Teachman, B. A., & Brownell, K. D. (2001). Implicit anti-fat bias among health professionals: Is anyone immune? *International Journal of Obesity, 25*(10), 1525–1531.

Teachman, B. A., Gapinski, K. D., Brownell, K. D., Rawlins, M., & Jeyaram, S. (2003). Demonstrations of implicit anti-fat bias: The impact of providing causal information and evoking empathy. *Health Psychology, 22*(1), 68–78.

Vanhove, A., & Gordon, R. A. (2014). Weight discrimination in the workplace: A meta-analytic examination of the relationship between weight and work-related outcomes. *Journal of Applied Social Psychology, 44*(1), 12–22.

Vartanian, L. R., & Silverstein, K. M. (2013). Obesity as a status cue: Perceived social status and the stereotypes of obese individuals. *Journal of Applied Social Psychology, 43*, 319–328.

Zitek, E. M., & Hebl, M. R. (2007). The role of social norm clarity in the influenced expression of prejudice over time. *Journal of Experimental Social Psychology, 43*(6), 867–876.

CHAPTER FOURTEEN

Stereotypes about People with Disabilities

Alecia M. Santuzzi and LaWanda Cook

Disability is often a forgotten category in definitions of diversity and initiatives intended to increase inclusion. Most of nearly 70 percent of U.S. companies that report use of some type of diversity training attend to differences in gender, race/ethnicity, and sexual orientation in the workplace (Kalinoski et al., 2013); much less attention has been paid to disability as a type of diversity (Bezrukova, Jehn, & Spell, 2012; McLaughlin, Bell, & Stringer, 2004). A recent systematic review of literature on disability-focused workplace diversity training indicated that of 1,322 articles, only three articles featured empirical investigation of work-based, disability-focused diversity training (Phillips, Deiches, Morrison, Chan, & Bezyak, 2016). Stensrud's (2007) research suggested that disability might be viewed as different from other types of diversity, more as "a problem to be accommodated rather than a difference to be celebrated" (p. 234).

Under the most comprehensive disability civil rights law, the Americans with Disabilities Act of 1990 (ADA) and the ADA Amendments Act of 2008 (ADAAA), a person is considered to have a disability if they: (1) have a physical or mental impairment that substantially limits one or more major life activities (e.g., working, relating to others, learning, breathing, walking), (2) have a history or record of such an impairment, or (3) are perceived by others as having such an impairment (U.S. Department of Justice, 2009). The primary intent of the ADA is to ensure the inclusion of people with disabilities in work and all aspects of community life. The ADA's definition is intended to offer people with a wide range of conditions equal access and protections against disability related discrimination.

Like other protected social categories typically considered in discussions about diversity,[1] observers frequently do not acknowledge the important differences among individuals with disabilities. This lack of recognition of diversity within the disability community is evidenced by the increased call for disability justice. Beyond the pursuit of disability rights, disability justice acknowledges the ways in which society and social movements (i.e., disability rights, women's rights, etc.), have failed to consider the needs of people with a range of physical and mental impairments and have addressed disability as a singular issue, without regard for class, race, gender, and other intersecting identities (Berne, 2015).

Disabilities vary in a variety of important features, including visibility, origin, timing of onset, and controllability of the impairment. Importantly, these features may influence how observers react to a person's disability (e.g., how stigmatizing the disability is; Jones et al., 1984). As noted above, disability also exists with other important demographic identities (e.g., gender identity, racial/ethnic identity), as well as family roles and occupational identity. Yet, the disability identity often takes center stage for observers. When observers view disability as the focus (or "master status"; Goffman, 1963), they filter information about the person through what they know about people with disabilities. In many cases, this "knowledge" is informed by stereotypes about disability. Consequently, stereotypic beliefs might inform how observers evaluate an individual's qualifications for and performance in other important identities (e.g., family and occupational roles).

This chapter describes the nature of disability stereotypes and their implications for individuals with disabilities. We further highlight recent literature discussing how stereotypes are expressed by others and affect day-to-day life for people with disabilities, particularly in performance-related domains (i.e., employment). We then provide some insight into evolving areas of research to inspire continued investigation of this topic.

Traits Connected to Disability Stereotypes

Stereotypes encourage observers to infer certain traits of individuals based on social category membership. The stereotypic traits associated with disability most directly are associated with generalized low ability, as the

---

[1]According to the U.S. Equal Employment Opportunity Commission, U.S. federal civil rights legislation prohibits discrimination on the basis of age (age forty and up), disability, pregnancy, national origin, race/color, religion, and sex (including transgender status and sexual orientation). Source: US EEOC website, "Discrimination by Type," n.d.

presence of a disability via the "spread effect" (Dembo, Leviton, & Wright, 1975), is often assumed to affect all aspects and attributes of a person, including perceptions of their intelligence, attractiveness, and employability (Olkin, 1999; Wright, 1983). Thus, while the term "disability" itself implies an impaired ability, the stereotypic traits extend beyond ability into social and motivational traits. Defining people by their disabilities and, consequently, as less capable and less valuable to society than people without disabilities, is referred to as "ableism" (Campbell, 2008; Goodley, 2014; Linton, 1998). Stereotypes grounded in ableism reflect the socially constructed belief that individuals with disabilities are not "normal" or complete human beings. The pervasiveness of ableism in everyday encounters, as well as realities such as transportation barriers, may limit opportunities to engage with other members of the disability community, contribute to internalized ableism, and discourage development of a positive disability identity (Campbell, 2008; Gill, 1997).

Individuals with all types of disabilities face the challenges presented by stigma and ableism. Much of the existing research has focused on people with physical impairments and infers that people with physical disabilities are perceived as "quiet, honest, gentlehearted, nonegotistical, benevolent, helpless, hypersensitive, inferior, depressed, distant, shy, unappealing, unsociable, bitter, nervous, unaggressive, insecure, dependent, unhappy, aloof, and submissive" (Stone & Colella, 1996, p. 358, citing Fichten & Amsel, 1986). Additional research notes inferences that people with physical disabilities are more "saintlike, courageous, deserving of a break, and less capable of competing with others" (Makas, 1988).

More recently, the literature has expanded to highlight people with psychological disabilities. For instance, Lapsle, Nikora, and Black (2002) argue that the association of mental health disabilities with "unreason, excess, incapacity and unreliability are historically entrenched attitudes in Western societies" (p. 4). Further, Corrigan and Watson (2002) note that individuals with these types of disabling conditions tend to experience greater stigma than persons with physical disabilities, and in cases such as substance abuse, may be viewed as in control of and responsible for their disabilities. People with obvious physical impairments may be subjected to immediate stigma due to the visibility of difference. However, when the disability is not readily apparent, people with disabilities may experience difficulty being recognized as "truly" disabled by self and others, making access to accommodations and decisions about disability disclosure even more problematic (Caldwell, 2010; Pilling, 2012; Samuels, 2003). Although the content of the stereotypes and attitudes might differ depending on features of the disability (e.g., physical or psychological), acquiring a disability label generally can adversely affect social experiences and one's physical and mental wellbeing.

The content of disability stereotypes has been classified into dimensions to better understand how they relate to stereotypes of other social categories. Accordingly, the content of disability stereotypes has mostly been classified as low competence and high warmth (Fiske, Cuddy, Glick, & Xu, 2002; Fiske, Xu, & Cuddy, 1999). This suggests that, in general, people with disabilities may be expected to be nice but not smart. This classification indicates that individuals with disabilities of various types might need to work hard to overcome expectations of poor competence and related performances. In addition, the expectation of warmth might create more emotion work (Hochschild, 1983) in order to sustain positive relationships in the workplace and other social settings, which can be particularly difficult for individuals with disabilities in situations where they might need to decline a request or provide negative feedback.

Some recent research suggests that the higher warmth ratings of people with disabilities might be a function of explicitly reported ratings rather than internally held beliefs. Mik-Meyer (2016) found that employers often discussed employees with visible disabilities as "different" despite their explicit claims that individuals with disabilities should be treated equally in the workplace. This suggests that observers might outwardly endorse what they believe to be right or just (e.g., all people should be treated equally) but then behave in subtle ways that contradict those beliefs. Relying on an implicit association measurement strategy, Rohmer and Louvet (2018) found implicit judgments of both competence and warmth to be lower when evaluating visible disability cues as compared to a person showing no signs of disability. This might suggest that observers rely on explicitly stated warmth judgments as a strategy to compensate for their beliefs about low competence. Importantly, such implicitly held beliefs may be better predictors of how individuals with disabilities are treated by observers, compared to explicitly stated beliefs.

Situation-specific Stereotype Activation

Stereotypes might be especially active in situations in which the content of the stereotype is most relevant (Bodenhausen, 2010). Inferences of low competence that typically accompany disability stereotypes might be especially salient to observers in work and other performance-related contexts (Rohmer & Louvet, 2018). Unfortunately, it is in those domains in which such inferences are likely to yield the most damage to the individual's image. In a work environment, for example, individuals might have to overcome expectations of helplessness and slow performance. Such expectations might prevent workers with disabilities from being considered for additional tasks and other opportunities to demonstrate competence and potential for advancement. Corroborating this notion, recent research found that workers with physical, intellectual, and mental health disabilities might be disproportionately selected for low-complexity jobs and viewed as not fit for high-complexity jobs (Nota, Soresi, & Perry, 2006). Further, Louvet (2007) found that people with highly visible physical disabilities were more likely to be overlooked for jobs involving significant levels of customer interaction. Research by Gouvier, Sytsma-Jordan, and Mayville (2003) demonstrates that people with chronic mental health conditions are less likely to be hired even for low-complexity tasks. These patterns might also be evident into educational contexts; students with disabilities might be excluded from full participation in classroom activities when instructors and others assume they will not want to engage in difficult tasks or have the ability to engage in advanced opportunities. Disability stereotype activation in a performance-related domain might be especially threatening to individuals who value roles and identities in that domain more than their disability identities (Galer, 2012).

Stereotypical reactions to disability might be driven more by the need for accommodation than a disability identity per se. The need for accommodations might provide an observable cue for attributions of being dependent and a "burden." Negative reactions toward the disability might thus be in effort to avoid the burden expected from fulfilling accommodation requests rather than the individual who may need accommodations. For example, research on accommodation use in employment settings suggests that reluctance to use visible accommodations may be due to individuals' concerns about possible adverse treatment from colleagues and supervisors who may feel burdened by the expense and effort of providing those accommodations (von Schrader, Cook, & Gower, in press; von Schrader, Xu, & Bruyère, 2014). By reducing visible cues of disability and associated costs of accommodations, individuals may be able to control the activation of disability stereotypes.

Much of the research and discussion about disability stereotypes and their consequences for individuals with disabilities focuses on situations in which the disability stereotype is most relevant, namely when competence and ability are of primary importance. Thus, subsequent discussion about the impact of disability stereotypes largely targets employment and related performance domains. However, similar concerns might arise in nonwork roles with performance expectations, such as parenting as a family role. Indeed, "people with disabilities face significant barriers to creating and maintaining families" due to obstacles "created by the child welfare system, family law system, adoption agencies, assistive reproductive technology providers and society as a whole" (National Council on Disability, 2012). These barriers are suspected to be due to stereotypical beliefs about the child-rearing abilities of people with disabilities.

Consequences of Disability Stereotypes for Individuals with Disabilities

Most recent research related to disability stereotypes highlights how stereotypes translate into others' attitudes and behaviors in reaction to disability as well as individuals' decisions about how to manage their own disability-related information in social situations. We summarize developments on these themes in the following sections.

Attitudes

The complexity of traits in the disability stereotype is reflected in complexity in reported attitudes toward people with disabilities. Past research suggests that traits associated with disability stereotypes are generally undesirable (Fichten & Amsel, 1986). However, the nature of the traits can sometimes mask negative evaluation behind what on the surface appears to be positive regard. For example, the expectation that people with disabilities are courageous may seem like a positive attribution. Even those seemingly positive attributions may be connected to discrimination and other potentially harmful outcomes, such as reluctance to ask for assistance that would enable better self-care, when paired with other stereotypic attributions (e.g., dependent; Miles, 2018).

Why would positive attributions lead to negative outcomes for individuals with disabilities? Research suggests that the *source* of explicitly endorsed positive traits for individuals with disabilities should be carefully considered (Biernat & Manis, 1994). Explicit positive reactions might be driven by observations that the individual with a disability is performing better than expected (i.e., better than the stereotype suggests). Given low performance expectations, individuals with disabilities also face unsolicited "praise" if they exhibit unexpected good performance. Such behavior may be met with feedback that the individual is admired for overcoming challenges or a source of inspiration. On the surface, this might be interpreted as positive regard and healthy experiences for individuals with disabilities. However, research suggests that these reactions may be due to low expectations driven by stereotypes held by observers (Biernat, Vescio, & Manis, 2013). When an individual with a disability performs in a way that is better than the low expectation, it might be met with extreme praise, even if the performance was average in an absolute sense. In this way, observers might hold a "shifting standard" (Biernat & Manis, 1994) that is lower for individuals with disabilities than for those without disabilities. Demonstrating this phenomenon, Lynch and Finkelstein (2015) found that employees with disabilities received lower objective performance ratings and were ranked lower in deservingness of resources compared to employees without disabilities. Despite those differences, employees with disabilities and without disabilities received similar subjective ratings of performance. The findings suggest that subjective evalu-ations might be high for individuals with disabilities despite receiving low absolute performance scores, and ultimately resources (e.g., bonuses) are allocated in line with that objective decision rather than the inflated subjec-tive evaluation.

It is also possible that observers genuinely hold positive and negative atti-tudes toward individuals with disabilities, creating ambivalence (Katz, 1981). However, most recent research suggests that the negative attitude is domi-nant in the way observers with reported ambivalence actually behave toward individuals with disabilities in the form of displayed discomfort (Fichten, Robillard, Judd, & Amsel, 1989; Hebl & Kleck, 2000; Kleck, Ono, & Has-torf, 1966) and social avoidance (Snyder, Kleck, Strenta, & Mentzer, 1979). Research on intergroup emotions corroborates the complex "positive but really negative" attitudes encountered by people with disabilities (Chan, Livneh, Pruett, Wang, & Zheng, 2009; Findler, Vilchinsky, & Werner, 2007; Pruett, Lee, Chan, Wang, & Lane, 2008). For example, when coupled with traits of low competence, the positive regard translates into pity. Rather than experiencing the typically promoting effects of positive regard, pity rein-forces negative stereotypes about competence and related behavioral expec-tations among individuals with disabilities. This creates a paternalistic regard, such that observers assume individuals with disabilities need sup-port to perform well. Pity reactions to disability could explain why men with disabilities may be more stigmatized than women with disabilities (Stone & Colella, 1996), as the disability stereotype contradicts stereotypes of men as being independent and capable.

Explicit positive attitudes toward disability also might be context-specific, diminishing in situations in which observers are personally threatened or otherwise directly affected by an individual's disability. For example, a co-worker may report positive regard for a colleague with a disability until that co-worker has to work directly with the person with a disability. A per-ceived burden due to working with someone who has a disability may over-ride explicit positive attitudes or values of equality (Colella & Stone, 2005; Stone & Colella, 1996). Moreover, if accommodations are required, they might be perceived as providing an unfair advantage to individuals with dis-abilities in competitive work environments (Colella, 2001).

Legal protections under the ADA (1990) and other policies are in place to protect people from the negative consequences of stereotypes and stigma. However, recent research suggests that such top-down approaches to chang-ing attitudes are ineffective and sometimes backfire. For example, hundreds of studies have reported that diversity training does not reduce bias toward stereotyped group (Paluck & Green, 2009). At a general level, observers may have a negative reaction to the legislation or policies that exacerbate negative attitudes toward disability (Stone & Colella, 1996). The next section describes patterns of discrimination that might be faced by individuals with disabilities despite these known legal protections.

Discrimination

The generally negative stereotypes about individuals with disabilities have been shown to translate into discrimination against those individuals despite existing legislation designed to protect against such events. Ren, Paetzold, and Colella (2008) conducted a meta-analysis and found that adults with physical disabilities received generally positive evaluations but significantly lower performance expectations. Importantly, hiring decisions seemed to be aligned with performance expectations, such that individuals with disabilities had a lower probability of being selected for hiring. Based on those findings, it is not surprising that research shows lower employment rates for individuals with disabilities compared to those who do not have disabilities. For instance, in 2008 the employment rate for adults aged twenty-one to sixty-four with a disability was 39.5 percent as compared to 79.9 percent among their nondisabled peers; and in 2017, the rate for people with disabilities versus those without was 37.3 percent versus 79.4 percent, respectively (Erickson, Lee, & von Schrader, 2017). Curiously, employment rates have decreased rather than increased since implementation of the ADA (Kruse & Schur, 2003; Weathers & Wittenburg, 2009). These rates suggest that the intended purpose of the ADA and related legislation might not be meeting the objective of preventing disability-related employment discrimination.

One major feature of the ADA aimed at fully including individuals with disabilities is the mandate for reasonable accommodations in employment and access to goods and services offered by both public and private entities. Individualized accommodations, such as sign language interpreter services, and changes in policies or practices that do not fundamentally alter the nature of an activity or service, as well as broader accessibility adjustments (e.g., structural changes to buildings) may be required for the full participation of people with disabilities in all aspects of community life. Although notable improvement is evident in decreased education gaps between students with and without disabilities (Kessler Foundation, 2015) and improving physical access (e.g., ramps for people who require stairless entry, blinking lights to signal alarms for people who cannot hear), individual accommodations are often denied in the workplace. Disability stereotypes might influence decisions about whether supervisors fulfill an accommodation request. If the disability is inferred to be controllable by the individual, and/or the accommodation request is perceived to be burdensome or unreasonable, supervisors might be less likely to comply (Florey & Harrison, 2000).

Discrimination also might emerge through more subtle behaviors among observers. For instance, perceptions of low competence implied by disability stereotypes might be conveyed through unsolicited helping behavior. Although helping is typically viewed as a prosocial activity with positive intentions for the receiver of such help, these behaviors also might convey to a receiver that he or she is assumed to need such help. Receiving unsolicited help can negatively affect the receiver's perceptions of self-worth (Schneider, Major, Luhtanen, & Crocker, 1996). In the context of a performance domain, such as in employment or education, providing unsolicited assistance may communicate and reinforce the stereotype that a person with a disability is weak, dependent, and cannot perform as well as others. If internalized, this conveyed message can be threatening to the individual's educational or occupational identity. Individuals with disabilities could get "tracked" into less challenging and advanced opportunities that require training (Stone & Colella, 1996).

Identity Management Strategies

Disability stereotypes might also affect the behavior of individuals with disabilities themselves. With the expectation of stereotyping and stigma, individuals with disabilities might adjust the ways they present themselves in social situations. One major behavior exhibited by individuals with disabilities is avoidance of situations in which they expect to be targets of stereotyping and stigma (Silverman & Cohen, 2014). This might lead individuals with disabilities to form fewer social relationships, with the consequence of having fewer opportunities for social support. This also might lead adults to avoid certain career directions that would make them more susceptible to stereotypes and negative evaluation, instead selecting careers that value their disability identity (Santuzzi & Waltz, 2016).

Some performance-related situations such as education and employment cannot be avoided completely, at least not without severe consequences to one's financial stability and quality of life. Identity management strategies might be especially important for individuals with disabilities to successfully navigate the social environment in such performance-focused domains. Individuals with disabilities might engage in a variety of identity management strategies that range from explicitly acknowledging the disability to completely concealing or "passing" as a person without the disability (Hebl & Kleck, 2000; Lyons et al., 2018). Some research suggests that openly acknowledging the disability in an interview context might yield positive outcomes (Hebl & Kleck, 2000; Lyons et al., 2018); however, the positive outcomes might only emerge for individuals with disabilities that are perceived to be uncontrollable (i.e., no attributions of blame for the condition).

Elements of avoidance might be indicated by behaviors that downplay the presence or severity of a disability. For example, Baldridge and Veiga (2006) found that anticipated negative social consequences discourage accommodation requests by workers with hearing impairments. By not requesting accommodations, an individual may keep their disability at a low level of awareness in the workplace or completely out of observers' awareness (if the disability is concealable). A recent study showed that downplaying a disability may yield fewer negative consequences for individuals with uncontrollable impairments (hearing loss) as compared to those who are believed to be responsible for the disability (Lyons, Volpone, Wessel, & Alonso, 2017). Downplaying the disability in a hiring context might yield more reactions of pity and lower hiring intentions by observers for individuals with controllable hearing loss.

In addition to potentially being ineffective, recent research also suggests that effortful identity management to downplay or conceal a disability might have negative health and well-being consequences for individuals with disabilities, even though such strategies might avoid an immediate reaction of social stigma from observers (DeJordy, 2008; Santuzzi, Waltz, Rupp, & Finkelstein, 2014). Thus, efforts to avoid social consequences of stereotyping might instigate negative consequences to health and well-being for individuals with disabilities. Concealing is generally associated with more social isolation (Beatty & Kirby, 2004, 2006), feelings of inauthenticity (Newheiser, Barreto, & Tiemersma, 2017), psychological distress (Chaudoir & Quinn, 2010; Quinn & Earnshaw, 2011), and cognitive interference during tasks (Smart & Wegner, 1999). Thus, in an effort to avoid negative social reactions, individuals with disabilities might put themselves at risk of poor functioning and well-being as a consequence of effortfully concealing or downplaying disability.

Recent Trends in Disability Research

Over the past five years, research on the impact of disability stereotypes has evolved along several themes. Below, we summarize the current research trends in this topic.

Invisible Disabilities

Guided by clarifications in the ADAAA of 2008, it is becoming more apparent that the majority of qualifying conditions under the ADA are nonvisible or concealable. Thus, for the majority of qualifying conditions, the person with the impairment must disclose the disability to others in order for others to know about it. Such disclosures are often met with skepticism from observers (Davis, 2005; Emens, 2013; Mills, 2017), especially if the discloser will have access to accommodations or otherwise gains from qualifying as a person with a disability (Colella, 2001; Colella, Paetzold, & Belliveau,

2004). Recent work has demonstrated that adults with service dogs experience significantly more discrimination in public places if the disability is invisible as compared to visible (Mills, 2017). Adults with invisible disabilities but visible accommodations frequently face skepticism and doubts about the legitimacy of the disability and thus worthiness of accommodations (Cook, von Schrader, Malzer, & Mimno, in press; Mills, 2017; von Schrader et al., in press).

Recent research on nonvisible disabilities also highlights the difficulty for people with qualifying conditions to detect and label their own challenges as disabilities (Santuzzi & Keating, 2019; Santuzzi, Waltz, Finkelstein, & Rupp, 2014). Without visible cues of disability presence, both outside observers and individuals with ADA-covered impairments may feel uncertain about whether or not a qualifying disability is present. Individuals with concealable conditions may not detect the disability until they engage in social comparison processes to identify whether what they are experiencing is an impairment or just normal variation (Santuzzi, Keating, Martinez, Finkelstein, Rupp, & Schulz, forthcoming). The extent and frequency with which an invisible disability is salient to the individual may determine whether the person adopts a disability identity and discloses the disability in social contexts.

Psychological Disabilities

Mental health disabilities and other psychological impairments are among the most stigmatized disabilities (Colella & Stone, 2005; Stone & Colella, 1996), and have received increased attention in recent research on disability reactions and experiences. Recent research suggests that although mental health conditions (Corrigan & Watson, 2002; Huskin, Reiser-Robbins, & Kwon, 2018; Livingston & Boyd, 2010; Sharac, Mccrone, Clement, & Thornicroft, 2010), ADHD (Patton, 2009), traumatic brain injury (TBI) and other cognitive impairments (Blanck, 2015; Hagger & Riley, 2017; Riley & Hagger, 2015), and autism spectrum disorder (ASD; Kinnear, Link, Ballan, & Fischbach, 2016; Werner & Shulman, 2015) qualify for legal protections under the ADA, they are also subject to high levels of social stigma. Note that these specific disabilities tend to be concealable rather than immediately apparent to observers.

Part of the stigmatization associated with mental health and other psychological disabilities might be connected to the fact that most are invisible or concealable. Observers might question whether an individual's condition is "real" or how it might differ from anyone else who occasionally feels "down" or stressed. Additionally, the ways in which people with such disabilities may need to be accommodated in the workplace and other community settings are often perceived as even more inconvenient than accommodations for persons with physical disabilities. Further, the impairments from mental illness and psychological disabilities are not limited to psychological states; they also can contribute to poor physical well-being (Chesney, Goodwin, & Fazel, 2014; Ladwig et al., 2017). As a nonvisible, highly stigmatized disability type, the recent literature has discussed mental health as its own unique category of disability and whether or not it should be considered a disability at all (Anderson, Sapey, & Spandler, 2011; Lester & Tritter, 2005).

Positive Disability Identity

Past literature on experiences of individuals with disabilities largely focuses on negative consequences and misfortunes. Recent work has adjusted the conversation by introducing positive and healthy aspects of disability experiences. For example, work by Jammaers, Zanoni, and Hardonk (2016) and Sundar et al. (2018) describes how individuals with disabilities can form and maintain positive identities despite ableist work environments. More generally, Bogart (2014, 2015) provides evidence for positive health and well-being experiences associated with adopting a valued disability identity. The benefits may include higher levels of self-esteem, lower levels of anxiety, and lower levels of depressive symptoms. Such work brings disability into the same arena as other social identities as it is not discussed as something that needs "fixed," but rather an individual difference to be embraced and serving a self-protective function.

Intersectionality

To date, the bulk of disability research has tended to consider disability as the primary or most salient identity of an individual (Bell, 2006; Miles, Nishida, & Forber-Pratt, 2017). As noted throughout this chapter, the diversity within the disability community (e.g., psychological versus physical, visible versus concealable) has made the focus on disability challenging enough on its own. However, in order to more fully understand how disability stereotypes and stigma influence the lives of people with disabilities, researchers and practitioners must consider how other social identities and roles intersect with disability to yield unique, complex experiences. Currently, approximately 5.3 percent of employed adults aged twenty-one to sixty-four have a disability (Erickson et al., 2017). According to U.S. Census Bureau (2014) population projections, the population will continue to age and become more ethnically diverse over the next several decades. Both older people and racial/ethnic minorities have higher rates of disability (Erickson et al., 2017). Thus, the possibility for more social challenges exists as historically dominant groups are required to adjust to and work collaboratively with individuals toward whom they may hold conscious or unconscious negative bias.

Most notable in the research literature over the past several years are the examinations of gender and age as intersecting with disability (Baldridge & Swift, 2013; Bend & Priola, 2018; Schur, 2003; Schur, Kruse, & Blanck, 2005; Shakespeare, 2006). Older individuals and women seem more likely to embrace disability identities and act on them (e.g., request accommodations). However, research also has examined intersections with race (Williams, Yu, Jackson, & Anderson, 1997) and ethnicity (Araújo & Borrell, 2006), providing avenues for continued research on disability stereotypes in the context of other social identities. Additional research highlights intersections with social roles. For example, Dwertmann and Boehm (2016) found interpersonal disconnections in supervisor-subordinate relationships when the supervisor had a disability but the subordinate did not. As the negative impact of stereotypes are most evident in performance-related roles, an obvious direction for continued research is to examine how disability stereotypes intersect with specific roles that may involve performance expectations that conflict with stereotypic expectations.

Conclusion

Like other legally protected groups, people with disabilities are often targets of negative stereotypes and social stigma. Perceptions of low competence that are central to the typical disability stereotype, may leave individuals with disabilities be particularly susceptible to disability stereotypes and their consequences in performance-related domains, such as employment. Current research highlights the negative consequences of disability stereotypes in the form of negative attitudes, persistent discrimination, and costs to the individuals with disabilities as they expend resources to manage their disabilities in social contexts. Recent research also shows signs of emerging areas of study not previously emphasized in the literature on disability stereotypes and social experiences. Emerging literature on invisible disabilities, psychological disabilities, positive disability identities, and intersectionality may enhance understanding of disability as one of many social identities that contributes to human diversity in the workplace and other social environments.

References

Americans with Disabilities Act (ADA). (1990). *The Americans with Disabilities Act of 1990*. Retrieved from https://www.eeoc.gov/eeoc/history/35th/1990s/ada.html

Anderson, J., Sapey, B., & Spandler, H. (2011). Distress or disability. In *Proceedings of a Symposium Held at Lancaster University, November 15–16, 2011.*

Araújo, B. Y., & Borrell, L. N. (2006). Understanding the link between discrimination, mental health outcomes, and life chances among Latinos. *Hispanic Journal of Behavioral Sciences, 28*(2), 245–266. doi:10.1177/073 9986305285825

Baldridge, D. C., & Swift, M. L. (2013). Withholding requests for disability accommodation: The role of individual differences and disability attributes. *Journal of Management, 39*(3), 743–762. doi:10.1177/014920631 0396375

Baldridge, D. C., & Veiga, J. F. (2006). The impact of anticipated social consequences on recurring disability accommodation requests. *Journal of Management, 32*(1), 158–179. doi:10.1177/0149206305277800

Beatty, J. E., & Kirby, S. L. (2004). *Feeling misunderstood: The emotional experiences of people with invisible identities.* Paper presented at the Academy of Management Annual Conference, New Orleans, LA.

Beatty, J. E., & Kirby, S. L. (2006). Beyond the legal environment: How stigma influences invisible identity groups in the workplace. *Employee Responsibilities and Rights Journal, 18*(1), 29–44. doi:10.1007/s10672-005 -9003-6

Bell, C. (2006). Introducing white disability studies: A modest proposal. In L. J. Davis (Ed.), *The disability studies reader* (2nd ed., pp. 275–282). New York: Routledge.

Bend, G. L., & Priola, V. (2018). What about a career? The intersection of gender and disability. In A. M. Broadbridge & S. L. Fielden (Eds.), *Research handbook of diversity and careers* (pp. 193–208). Cheltenham, England: Edward Elgar Publishing.

Berne, P. (2015). Disability justice: A working draft. *Sins Invalid, 10.* Retrieved from https://www.sinsinvalid.org/blog/disability-justice-a-working-draft -by-patty-berne

Bezrukova, K., Jehn, K. A., & Spell, C. S. (2012). Reviewing diversity training: Where we have been and where we should go. *Academy of Management Learning & Education, 11*(2), 207–227. doi:10.5465/amle.2008.0090

Biernat, M., & Manis, M. (1994). Shifting standards and stereotype-based judgments. *Journal of Personality and Social Psychology, 66*(1), 5–20.

Biernat, M., Vescio, T. K., & Manis, M. (2013). Judging and behaving toward members of stereotyped groups: A shifting standards perspective. C. Sedikides, J. Schopler, & C. A. Insko (Eds.), *Intergroup cognition and intergroup behavior* (151–175). Mahwah, NJ: Psychology Press.

Blanck, P. (2015). eQuality: Web accessibility by people with cognitive disabilities. *Inclusion, 3*(2), 75–91. doi:10.1352/2326-6988-3.2.75

Bodenhausen, G. V. (2010). Diversity in the person, diversity in the group: Challenges of identity complexity for social perception and social interaction. *European Journal of Social Psychology, 40*(1), 1–16. doi:10.1002/ejsp.647

Bogart, K. R. (2014). The role of disability self-concept in adaptation to congenital or acquired disability. *Rehabilitation Psychology, 59*(1), 107–115. doi:10.1037/a0035800

Bogart, K. R. (2015). Disability identity predicts lower anxiety and depression in multiple sclerosis. *Rehabilitation Psychology, 60*(1), 105–109. doi:10.1037/rep0000029

Caldwell, K. (2010). We exist: Intersectional in/visibility in bisexuality & disability. *Disability Studies Quarterly, 30*(3/4). doi:10.18061/dsq.v30i3/4.1273

Campbell, F. A. K. (2008). Exploring internalized ableism using critical race theory. *Disability & Society, 23*(2), 151–162. doi:10.1080/09687590701841190

Chan, F., Livneh, H., Pruett, S. R., Wang, C.-C., & Zheng, L. X. (2009). Societal attitudes toward disability: Concepts, measurements, and interventions. In F. Chan, E. Da Silva Cardoso, & J. A. Chronister (Eds.), *Understanding psychosocial adjustment to chronic illness and disability: A handbook for evidence-based practitioners in rehabilitation* (pp. 333–367). New York: Springer Publishing Company.

Chaudoir, S. R., & Quinn, D. M. (2010). Revealing concealable stigmatized identities: The impact of disclosure motivations and positive first disclosure experiences on fear of disclosure and well-being. *Journal of Social Issues, 66*(3), 570–584. doi:10.1111/j.1540-4560.2010.01663.x

Chesney, E., Goodwin, G. M., & Fazel, S. (2014). Risks of all-cause and suicide mortality in mental disorders: A meta-review. *World Psychiatry, 13*(2), 153–160. doi:10.1002/wps.20128

Colella, A. (2001). Coworker distributive fairness judgments of the workplace accommodation of employees with disabilities. *Academy of Management Review, 26*, 100–116. doi:10.5465/amr.2001.4011984

Colella, A., Paetzold, R., & Belliveau, M. A. (2004). Factors affecting coworkers' procedural justice inferences of workplace accommodations of employees with disabilities. *Personnel Psychology, 57*(1), 1–23. doi:10.1111/j.1744-6570.2004.tb02482.x

Colella, A., & Stone, D. L. (2005). Workplace discrimination toward persons with disabilities: A call for some new research directions. In R. Dipboye & A. Colella (Eds.), *Discrimination at work: The psychological and organizational bases* (pp. 227–253). Mahwah, NJ: Lawrence Erlbaum.

Cook, L., von Schrader, S., Malzer, V., & Mimno, J. (in press). Unwelcoming workplaces: Bullying and harassment of employees with disabilities. *Labor and Employment Relations Association (LERA) Annual Research Volume.*

Corrigan, P. W., & Watson, A. C. (2002). Understanding the impact of stigma on people with mental illness. *World Psychiatry: Official Journal of the World Psychiatric Association, 1*(1), 16–20. Retrieved from https://www.ncbi.nlm.nih.gov/pmc/articles/PMC1489832/

Davis, N. A. (2005). Invisible disability. *Ethics, 116*(1), 153–213.

DeJordy, R. (2008). Just passing through: Stigma, passing, and identity decoupling in the work place. *Group & Organization Management, 33*(5), 504–531. doi:10.1177/1059601108324879

Dembo, T., Leviton, G. L., & Wright, B.A. (1975). Adjustment to misfortune: A problem of social-psychological rehabilitation. *Rehabilitation Psychology, 22*(1), 1–100. doi:10.1037/h0090832

Dwertmann, D. J., & Boehmn, S. A. (2016). Status matters: The asymmetric effects of supervisor-subordinate disability incongruence and climate for inclusion. *Academy of Management Journal, 59*(1), 44–64.

Emens, E. (2013). Disabling attitudes: U.S. disability law and the ADA amendments act. In L. Davis (Ed.), *The disability studies reader* (pp. 42–60). New York: Routledge.

Erickson, W., Lee, C., & von Schrader, S. (2017). *Disability statistics from the American Community Survey (ACS)*. Ithaca, NY: Cornell University Yang-Tan Institute (YTI). Retrieved from the Cornell University Disability Statistics website: http://www.disabilitystatistics.org/

Fichten, C. S., & Amsel, R. (1986). Trait attributions about college students with a physical disability: Circumplex analyses and methodological issues. *Journal of Applied Social Psychology, 16*(6), 410–427.

Fichten, C. S., Robillard, K., Judd, D., & Amsel, R. (1989). College students with physical disabilities: Myths and realities. *Rehabilitation Psychology, 34*(4), 243–257. doi:10.1037/h0079074

Findler, L., Vilchinsky, N., & Werner, S. (2007). The multidimensional attitudes scale toward persons with disabilities (MAS): Construction and validation. *Rehabilitation Counseling Bulletin, 50*(3), 166–176. doi:10.1177/00343 552070500030401

Fiske, S. T., Cuddy, A. J. C., Glick, P., & Xu, J. (2002). A model of (often mixed) stereotype content: Competence and warmth respectively follow from perceived status and competition. *Journal of Personality and Social Psychology, 42*(6), 878–902. doi:10.1037//0022-3514.82.6.878

Fiske, S. T., Xu, J., & Cuddy, A. C. (1999). (Dis)respecting versus (dis)liking: Status and interdependence predict ambivalent stereotypes of competence and warmth. *Journal of Social Issues, 55*(3), 473–489.

Florey, A. T., & Harrison, D. A. (2000). Responses to informal accommodation requests from employees with disabilities: Multistudy evidence on willingness to comply. *The Academy of Management Journal, 43*(2), 224–233.

Galer, D. (2012). Disabled capitalists: Exploring the intersections of disability and identity formation in the world of work. *Disability Studies Quarterly, 32*(3). Retrieved from http://dsq-sds.org/article/view/3277/3122

Gill, C. J. (1997). Four types of integration in disability identity development. *Journal of Vocational Rehabilitation, 9*(1), 39–46. doi:10.1016/S1052-2263(97)00020-2

Goffman, E. (1963) *Stigma: Notes on the management of spoiled identity.* New York: Prentice-Hall.

Goodley, D. (2014). *Dis/ability studies: Theorising disablism and ableism*. London: Routledge.

Gouvier, W. D., Systma-Jordon, S., & Mayville, S. (2003). Patterns of discrimination in hiring job applications with disabilities: The role of disability type, job complexity, and public contact. *Rehabilitation Psychology, 48*(3), 175–181. doi:10.1037/0090-5550.48.3.175

Hagger, B. F., & Riley, G. A. (2017). The social consequences of stigma-related self-concealment after acquired brain injury. *Neuropsychological Rehabilitation, 29*(7), 1129–1148. doi:10.1080/09602011.2017.1375416

Hebl, M. R., & Kleck, R. E. (2000). The social consequences of physical disability. In T. F. Heatherton, R. E. Kleck, M. R. Hebl, & J. G. Hull (Eds.), *The social psychology of stigma* (pp. 273–306). New York: Guilford Publications, Inc.

Hochschild, A. R. (1983). *The managed heart: Commercialization of human feeling*. Berkeley: University of California Press.

Huskin, P. R., Reiser-Robbins, C., & Kwon, S. (2018). Attitudes of undergraduate students toward persons with disabilities: Exploring effects of contact experience on social distance across ten disability types. *Rehabilitation Counseling Bulletin, 62*(1), 53–63. doi:10.1177/0034355217727600

Jammaers, E., Zanoni, P., & Hardonk, S. (2016). Constructing positive identities in ableist workplaces: Disabled employees' discursive practices engaging with the discourse of lower productivity. *Human Relations, 69*, 1365–1386. doi:10.1177/0018726715612901

Jones, E. E., Farina, A., Hastorf, A. H., Markus, H. M., Miller, D. T., & Scott, R. A. (1984). *Social stigma: The psychology of marked relationships*. New York: Freeman.

Kalinoski, Z. T., Steele-Johnson, D., Peyton, E. J., Leas, K. A., Steinke, J., & Bowling, N. A. (2013). A meta-analytic evaluation of diversity training outcomes. *Journal of Organizational Behavior, 34*(8), 1076–1104. doi:10.1002/job.1839

Katz, I. (1981). *Stigma: A social-psychological perspective*. Hillsdale, NJ: Erlbaum.

Kessler Foundation. (2015). *National employment and disability survey: Report of main findings*. West Orange, NJ: Author.

Kinnear, S. H., Link, B. G., Ballan, M. S., & Fischbach, R. L. (2016). Understanding the experience of stigma for parents of children with autism spectrum disorder and the role stigma plays in families' lives. *Journal of Autism and Developmental Disorders, 46*(3), 942–953. doi:10.1007/s10803-015-2637-9

Kleck, R., Ono, H., & Hastorf, A. H. (1966). The effects of physical deviance upon face-to-face interactions. *Human Relations, 19*, 425–436. doi:10.1177/001872676601900406

Kruse, D., & Schur, L. (2003). Employment of people with disabilities following the ADA. *Industrial Relations, 42*(1), 31–66.

Ladwig, K. H., Baumert, J., Marten-Mittag, B., Lukaschek, K., Johar, H., Fang, X., . . . KORA Investigators. (2017). Room for depressed and exhausted mood as a risk predictor for all-cause and cardiovascular mortality beyond the contribution of the classical somatic risk factors in men. *Atherosclerosis, 257*, 224–231. doi:10.1016/j.atherosclerosis.2016.12.003

Lapsley, H., Nikora, L. W., & Black, R. M. (2002). *"Kia mauri tau!" Narratives of recovery from disabling mental health problems*. Wellington, New Zealand: Mental Health Commission.

Lester, H., & Tritter, J. Q. (2005). "Listen to my madness": Understanding the experiences of people with serious mental illness. *Sociology of Health & Illness, 27*(5), 649–669.

Linton, S. (1998). *Claiming disability: Knowledge and identity*. New York: New York University Press.

Livingston, J. D., & Boyd, J. E. (2010). Correlates and consequences of internalized stigma for people living with mental illness: A systematic review and meta-analysis. *Social Science & Medicine, 71*(12), 2150–2161. doi:10.1016/j.socscimed.2010.09.030

Louvet, E. (2007). Social judgment toward job applicants with disabilities: Perception of personal qualities and competences. *Rehabilitation Psychology, 52*(3), 297–303.

Lynch, J. E., & Finkelstein, L. M. (2015). An experimental investigation into judgment and behavioral implications of disability-based stereotypes in simulated work decisions: Evidence of shifting standards. *Journal of Applied Social Psychology, 45*(11), 613–628. doi:10.1111/jasp.12324

Lyons, B. J., Martinez, L. R., Ruggs, E. N., Hebl, M. R., Ryan, A. M., O'Brien, K. R., & Roebuck, A. (2018). To say or not to say: Different strategies of acknowledging a visible disability. *Journal of Management, 44*(5), 1980–2007. doi:10.1177/0149206316638160

Lyons, B. J., Volpone, S. D., Wessel, J. L., & Alonso, N. M. (2017). Disclosing a disability: Do strategy type and onset controllability make a difference? *Journal of Applied Psychology, 102*(9), 1375–1383. doi:10.1037/apl0000230

Makas, E. (1988). Positive attitudes toward disabled people: Disabled and nondisabled persons' perspectives. *Journal of Social Issues, 44*(1), 49–61. doi:10.1111/j.1540-4560.1988.tb02048.x

McLaughlin, M. E., Bell, M. P., & Stringer, D. Y. (2004). Stigma and acceptance of persons with disabilities: Understudied aspects of workforce diversity. *Group & Organization Management, 29*(3), 302–333. doi:10.1177/1059601103257410

Mik-Meyer, N. (2016). Othering, ableism and disability: A discursive analysis of co-workers' construction of colleagues with visible impairments. *Human Relations, 69*(6), 1341–1363. doi:10.1177/0018726715618454

Miles, A. L., Nishida, A., & Forber-Pratt, A. J. (2017). An open letter: Dear white disability studies and ableist institutions of higher education. *Disability Studies Quarterly, 37*(3). doi:10.18061/dsq.v37i3.5997

Mills, M. L. (2017). Invisible disabilities, visible Service Dogs: The discrimination of Service Dog handlers. *Disability & Society, 32*(5), 635–656. doi:10.1080/09687599.2017.1307718

National Council on Disability. (2012). *Rocking the cradle: Ensuring the rights of parents with disabilities and their children* (pp. 185–192). Washington, D.C.: National Council on Disability. Retrieved from https://www.ncd.gov/sites /default/files/Documents/NCD_Parenting_508_0.pdf

Newheiser, A. K., Barreto, M., & Tiemersma, J. (2017). People like me don't belong here: Identity concealment is associated with negative workplace experiences. *Journal of Social Issues, 73*(2), 341–358. doi:10.1111 /josi.12220

Nota, L, Soresi, S., & Perry, J. (2006). Quality of life in adults with intellectual disability: The evaluation of Quality of Life Instrument. *Journal of Intellectual Disability Research, 50*(5), 371–385.

Olkin, R. (1999). *What psychotherapists should know about disability.* New York: Guilford Press.

Paluck, E. L., & Green, D. P. (2009). Prejudice reduction: What works? A critical look at evidence from the field and the laboratory. *Annual Review of Psychology, 60*, 339–367. doi:10.1146/annurev.psych.60.110707.163607

Patton, E. (2009). When diagnosis does not always mean disability: The challenge of employees with attention deficit hyperactivity disorder (ADHD). *Journal of Workplace Behavioral Health, 24*(3), 326–343.

Phillips, B. N., Deiches, J., Morrison, B., Chan, F., & Bezyak, J. L. (2016). Disability diversity training in the workplace: Systematic review and future directions. *Journal of Occupational Rehabilitation, 26*(3), 264–275. doi:10.1007/s10926-015-9612-3

Pilling, M. D. (2013). Invisible identity in the workplace: Intersectional madness and processes of disclosure at work. *Disability Studies Quarterly, 33*(1). Retrieved from http://dsq-sds.org/article/view/3424/3204

Pruett, S. R., Lee, E. J., Chan, F., Wang, M. H., & Lane, F. J. (2008). Dimensionality of the contact with disabled persons scale. *Rehabilitation Counseling Bulletin, 51*, 210–220. doi:10.1177/0034355207311310

Quinn, D. M., & Earnshaw, V. A. (2011). Understanding concealable stigmatized identities: The role of identity in psychological, physical, and behavioral outcomes. *Social Issues and Policy Review, 5*(1), 160–190. doi:10.1111 /j.1751-2409.2011.01029.x

Ren, L. R., Paetzold, R. L., & Colella, A. (2008). A meta-analysis of experimental studies on the effects of disability on human resource judgments. *Human Resource Management Review, 18*(3), 191–203. doi:10.1016/j.hrmr .2008.07.001

Riley, G. A., & Hagger, B. F. (2015). Disclosure of a stigmatized identity: A qualitative study of the reasons why people choose to tell or not tell others about their traumatic brain injury. *Brain injury, 29*(12), 1480–1489. doi:1 0.3109/02699052.2015.1071427

Rohmer, O., & Louvet, E. (2018). Implicit stereotyping against people with disability. *Group Processes & Intergroup Relations, 21*(1), 127–140. doi: 10.1177/1368430216638536

Samuels, E. J. (2003). My body, my closet: Invisible disability and the limits of coming-out discourse. *GLQ: A Journal of Lesbian and Gay Studies, 9*(1–2), 233–255. doi:10.1215/10642684-9-1-2-233

Santuzzi, A. M., & Keating, R. T. (2019). Managing invisible disabilities in the workplace: Identification and disclosure dilemmas for workers with hidden impairments. In S. Fieldsen, M. Moore, & G. Wright (Eds.), *The Palgrave handbook for disability at work*. London: Palgrave.

Santuzzi, A. M., Keating, R., Martinez, J., Finkelstein, L., Rupp, D., & Schulz, N. (forthcoming). Uncovering antecedents and consequences of identity management strategies for workers with concealable disabilities. *Journal of Social Issues, 28.*

Santuzzi, A. M., & Waltz, P. R. (2016). Disability in the workplace: A unique and variable identity. *Journal of Management, 42*(5), 1111–1135. doi:10.1177/0149206315626269

Santuzzi, A. M., Waltz, P. R., Rupp, D., & Finkelstein, L. M. (2014). Invisible disabilities: Unique challenges for employees and organizations. [Focal Article]. *Journal of Industrial and Organizational Psychology: Perspectives on Science and Practice, 7*(2), 204–219.

Schneider, M. E., Major, B., Luhtanen, R., & Crocker, J. (1996). Social stigma and the potential costs of assumptive help. *Personality and Social Psychology Bulletin, 22*(2), 201–209. doi:10.1177/0146167296222009

Schur, L. A. (2003). Barriers or opportunities? The causes of contingent and part-time work among people with disabilities. *A Journal of Economy and Society, 42*(4), 589–622. doi:10.1111/1468-232X.00308

Schur, L., Kruse, D., & Blanck, P. (2005). Corporate culture and the employment of persons with disabilities. *Behavioral Science and the Law, 23,* 3–20. doi:10.1002/bsl.624

Shakespeare, T. (2006). The social model of disability. *The Disability Studies Reader, 2,* 197–204.

Sharac, J., Mccrone, P., Clement, S., & Thornicroft, G. (2010). The economic impact of mental health stigma and discrimination: A systematic review. *Epidemiology and Psychiatric Sciences, 19*(3), 223–232. doi:10.1017/S11211 89X00001159

Silverman, A. M., & Cohen, G. L. (2014). Stereotypes as stumbling-blocks: How coping with stereotype threat affects life outcomes for people with physical disabilities. *Personality and Social Psychology Bulletin, 40*(10), 1330–1340. doi:10.1177/0146167214542800

Smart, L., & Wegner, D. M. (1999). Covering up what can't be seen: Concealable stigma and mental control. *Journal of Personality and Social Psychology, 77*(3), 474–486.

Snyder, M. L., Kleck, R. E., Strenta, A., & Mentzer, S. J. (1979). Avoidance of the handicapped: An attributional ambiguity analysis. *Journal of Personality and Social Psychology, 37*(12), 2297–2306.

Stensrud, R. (2007). Developing relationships with employers means considering the competitive business environment and the risks it produces.

Rehabilitation Counseling Bulletin, 50(4), 226–237. doi:10.1177/003435520 70500040401

Stone, D. L., & Colella, A. (1996). A model of factors affecting the treatment of disabled individuals in organizations. *Academy of Management Review, 21*(2), 352–401.

Sundar, V., O'Neill, J., Houtenville, A. J., Phillips, K. G., Keirns, T., Smith, A., & Katz, E. E. (2018). Striving to work and overcoming barriers: Employment strategies and successes of people with disabilities. *Journal of Vocational Rehabilitation, 48*(1), 93–109.

United States Census Bureau. (2014). *2014 national population projections tables.* Retrieved from https://www.census.gov/data/tables/2014/demo/popproj /2014-summary-tables.html

U.S. Department of Justice. (2009). Retrieved from https://www.ada.gov/cguide .htm

von Schrader, S., Cook, L., & Gower, W. S. (in press). Supporting workplace performance: Encouraging disability disclosure and managing reasonable accommodations requests. *Labor and Employment Relations Association (LERA) Annual Research Volume.*

von Schrader, S., Malzer, V., & Bruyère, S. (2014). Perspectives on disability disclosure: The importance of employer practices and workplace climate. *Employee Responsibilities and Rights Journal, 26*(4), 237–255. doi:10.1007 /s10672-013-9227-9

von Schrader, S., Xu, X., & Bruyère, S. M. (2014). Accommodation requests: Who is asking for what? *Rehabilitation Research, Policy, and Education, 28*(4), 329–344.

Weathers, R., & Wittenburg, D. (2009). Measuring trends in the employment rate of people with disabilities. In A. J. Houtenville (Ed.), *Counting working-age people with disabilities: What current data tell us and options for improvement.* Kalamazoo, MI: W. E. Upjohn Institute.

Werner, S., & Shulman, C. (2015). Does type of disability make a difference in affiliate stigma among family caregivers of individuals with autism, intellectual disability or physical disability? *Journal of Intellectual Disability Research, 59*(3), 272–283. doi:10.1111/jir.12136

Williams, D. R., Yu, Y., Jackson, J. S., & Anderson, N. B. (1997). Racial differences in physical and mental health: Socio-economic status, stress and discrimination. *Journal of Health Psychology, 2*(3), 335–351. doi:10.1177 /135910539700200305

Wright, B. A. (1983). *Physical disability: A psychosocial approach* (2nd ed.). New York: Harper & Row.

CHAPTER FIFTEEN

Stereotyping Religion

Ain Simpson

Religion is among the oldest and most foundational institutions in the history of civilization (Norenzayan, 2013). It is thus unsurprising to observe a rich tapestry of religious diversity throughout the world ("theodiversity"; Norenzayan, 2016). Even in relatively modern nations such as the United States (founded largely by puritan Christians), we see much variety in religious belief, practice, identity, and belonging. Accompanying such religious diversity, of course, is a plethora of stereotypes. The present chapter focuses on the contributions of *psychological science* to our understanding of religious stereotypes in the United States.

So, how to proceed? To understand stereotypes of a particular category (e.g., religion), we must consider not only exemplars of category membership (e.g., Abrahamic religions) but also exemplars of category *non-membership* (e.g., astrology). Accordingly, religious stereotypes can be understood first by comparing religion to categories that are defined in contradistinction to religion. The first comparison naturally arises by considering the fundamental attribute of religion—belief in supernatural agents—thus pitting religion against atheism. A second comparison emerges by recognizing that religion has endured, for millennia, as an ultimate explanation of worldly phenomena, and this has come into conflict with another major source of ultimate explanation: science. Finally, beyond comparisons between religious and nonreligious phenomena, a third area in which we see categorical distinctions is *among* religions (e.g., Catholicism, Protestantism, Islam, Jainism). Hence, we have three primary contexts in which to discuss religious stereotypes:

i.   Religion versus Atheism
ii. Religion versus Science
iii. Religion A versus Religion B, C, D. . . .

The present chapter is organized according to these three sets of distinctions. I will focus on (i) and (ii), because this allows the broadest possible considerations of *religion* (although (iii) is interesting, we could get fixated on specific "trees" and lose sight of the overall "forest," especially given the *thousands* of religions that still exist in the world; Norenzayan, 2016). In addition, because morality and trustworthiness are central features in the social psychology of religion (e.g., Gervais, 2013; Norenzayan & Shariff, 2008), *emphasis is placed on the moral attributes of religious stereotypes.*

Definitions

Both *Religion* and the *psychology of religion* can be defined primarily with reference to their most salient and unique features—supernatural beliefs, deference to supernatural superiors, collective belonging and ritual/worship, and social organization built around belief in objective moral truths. A similar definition has been offered by Saroglou (2011), who distinguished beliefs, rituals/emotions, moral rules, and shared identity as the four pillars of religion. Each facet is important in an analysis of religious stereotypes; however, the *belief* component may be central, as beliefs undergird: (i) the other facets, to some degree (e.g., basic religious beliefs shape identity formation and the structure of rituals); (ii) differences between religions (e.g., the divergent beliefs that led to Martin Luther's reformation and the protestant departure from Catholicism); and (iii) the chief distinction between religion and atheism (indeed, *lack of* belief is likely the most reasonable and empirically valuable definition of atheism; Bullivant, 2013).

Stereotypes of Religion versus Atheism

Moral Trustworthiness

Perhaps the most predominant characteristic that is psychologically (indeed, unconsciously) associated with religion is *morality*, and with it the associated phenomena of selflessness, trustworthiness, and prosociality. As many as 57 percent of U.S. citizens may believe that one cannot be moral without belief in God (Pew Research Center, 2014). Why might this be? Anthropological evidence suggests that, throughout the history of civilization, "world religions may have evolved to create a potent linkage between the supernatural and the prosocial" (Atran & Henrich, 2010, p. 19), and that this has been a crucial factor in explaining societal expansion from small tribes of kith and kin to large networks of unrelated individuals (Norenzayan et al., 2016). For example, Roes and Raymond (2003) analyzed the Standard Cross-Cultural Sample, featuring data from 186 societies chosen to represent the various cultures of the entire world. The authors found that watchful and punishing deities were far more common in relatively large and complex societies, suggesting that socio-moral regulation via shared belief in a supernatural moral order was a necessary precondition to civilization.

Psychological evidence reveals the same pattern. Moral trustworthiness is reflexively associated with religiosity among most participants (even among some atheists), as demonstrated via the inverse association between atheism and *immorality* (Gervais, Shariff, & Norenzayan, 2011). North American participants were presented with a target individual who behaved in a morally distrustful manner (e.g., removing cash from a lost wallet), and were given a standard conjunction task that asked whether the immoral target is more likely to be a member of one category (e.g., "teacher") or two categories (e.g., "teacher" and ____). The latter is objectively less frequent and thus incorrect (it is a subclass of the former), but is more likely to be chosen if participants draw on stereotypes that override statistical logic. Gervais et al. (2011) experimentally manipulated the second social category (e.g., Muslim; Jew; atheist; rapist), and found that only atheists and rapists elicited the conjunction fallacy at high rates (with no differences between these conditions). Importantly, atheists were described with the description "does not believe in God," meaning that effects weren't driven by reactions to a hypothetically tainted social label (but see Simpson, Rios, and Cowgill [2017] for evidence that the label "atheist" amplifies some negative attitudes toward nonbelievers). In other words, absent religious belief and its accompanying stereotype of moral virtue, nonbelievers trigger a stereotype of untrustworthiness as readily as do rapists!

Crucially, this effect has been replicated in at least four ways (and with literally thousands of participants). First, several North American samples revealed the same effect in response to various types of moral violation (e.g., callous harm, disrespecting authority, disgusting acts; Gervais, 2014). Second, beyond North America, harm-based immorality was more readily associated with atheists than with believers in Australia, the UK, the Netherlands, Czech Republic, Singapore, China, Hong Kong, India, the UAE, and Mauritius (only in Finland and New Zealand was this effect nonsignificant, albeit trending in the same direction; Gervais et al., 2017). Third, returning to U.S. participants, Gervais et al. (2017; supplemental studies) also found that this category-conjunction effect did not emerge when other forms of nonbelief were tested (e.g., disbelief in evolution or global warming), suggesting that *religious* nonbelief is psychologically categorized as a unique type of disbelief. Finally, the same authors even found that a moral violation explicitly associated with a particular religion (child abuse among Catholic priests) was more readily attributed to a priest who lacked belief in God than one who believes in God. In short: extensive and diverse evidence, obtained from across the globe, reveals unconscious and potent stereotypes that associate theistic belief with morality and atheism with immorality.

Such stereotypes also manifest in mental imagery. Brown-Iannuzzi, McKee, and Gervais (2018) formed 800 pictorial variants of a human face (originally a blend of Black, White, male, and female faces), randomly sorted these into 400 pairs, and gave participants a binary-choice activity consisting of 400 trials, each trial displaying one face-pair. The only activity in the study, half the sample selected which one of the two faces looks most like a person who does believe in God, and the other half of the sample selected which one of the two faces looks most like a person who does *not* believe in God. Across the entire sample, the authors then averaged all atheist and theist images, forming one composite image for each. A subsequent sample of 332 U.S. online participants (unaware of the prior image selection task) then rated each of the two images on a variety of attributes (half rated morality- and religion-relevant traits, while half rated traits such as attractiveness and competence). The theist image was rated as significantly more trustworthy and moral, and less hostile and inhuman, compared to the atheist image (very large effect sizes; $Fs = 86–130$). (Supplemental analyses revealed that atheist participants generated slightly more positive images of atheists and slightly less positive images of theists compared to theist participants, but still, a separate sample judged these atheist-generated images with the same pattern of "atheist bad, theist good"). Another sample of 273 U.S. participants online was presented with the same two images in ten critical trials (intermixed with twenty distractor trials featuring randomly generated faces). In each trial, participants read either a moral or immoral scenario (e.g., "left food out for a stray cat" vs. "kicked a dog for no reason") and were asked to connect the scenario with one of the two faces on display. Participants (theists *and* atheists alike) were much more likely to choose the atheist image than the theist image when the scenario was immoral than when it was moral. Overall, therefore, stereotypes of religious believers and nonbelievers likely include not only moral/behavioral attributes but also a suite of physical/visual attributes that are commonly associated with (im)morality. As Brown-Iannuzzi et al. (2018) describe, these findings suggest that atheist and theist labels carry a stigma that is "written in the face" (p. 296).

The same study revealed additional stereotypes. Theist images were judged more competent, warm, likeable, happy, and attractive, and less lazy. Hence, beyond moral attributes, religious believers benefit from a general "halo effect" in which they are stereotyped with a plethora of positive, appealing characteristics. Theist images were also judged more "feminine" and "White" (i.e., Caucasian). The latter result is difficult to interpret (the images were generated from only four base images—Black/White male/female, thus excluding consideration of other races), but the femininity stereotype perhaps suggests that, when juxtaposed against atheism, religion is stereotyped as gentle, caring, and nurturing. Might this mean that an intuitive response to the "threat" of atheism is a fondness for religious notions of kindness and mercy (archetypal "feminine" qualities) but not for religious notions of justice and order (archetypal "masculine" qualities)? Future research could address this question.

Types of Morality

Several categorically discrete types of moral concerns exist, as is plainly evident in moral trade-offs (consider, for example, the rally cry "No justice? No peace."). Increasingly, such moral diversity seems rooted in basic psychology and foundational moral intuitions. Moral Foundations Theory (MFT; Graham et al., 2013; Haidt, 2007) posits at least five such moral foundations that evolved to address basic needs of human survival and social living. We have intuitions for: providing care and minimizing harm (*Care*); discouraging cheating, freeloading, and general notions of unfairness (*Fairness*); group loyalty to strengthen solidarity/identity and for intergroup competition (*Loyalty*); deference to traditions and hierarchical social structures for social order and stability (*Authority*); and rendering certain things sacred or taboo to avoid breaching the purity and integrity of social structures (e.g., avoiding foul language in church, or carnal pleasures that could introduce selfish indecency into the socio-moral order; *Sanctity*).

Simpson and Rios (2016) used MFT to investigate intra- and intergroup moral stereotypes of U.S. Christians and atheists. Participants[1] completed the standard Moral Foundations Questionnaire from three perspectives: themselves, a "typical atheist," and a "typical Christian." This way, Christians' and atheists' actual, self-reported moral values could be compared against both intra- and intergroup stereotypes of said values. (Christian participants' responses are displayed in Figure 15.1.) Christians believed their ingroup endorsed *all* moral foundations much more strongly than atheists (except Fairness; the stereotyped difference was very small, but still favored Christians). In contrast, atheists typically perceived near-identical endorsement of Care, but stereotyped atheists as endorsing Fairness values moderately more than Christians and perceived much greater endorsement of Loyalty, Authority, and Sanctity values among Christians than atheists. With

---

[1]Despite relatively small samples (204 and 192, Studies 1 and 2, respectively), supplemental analyses found strong evidence that these samples were representative of U.S. Christians and atheists in general.

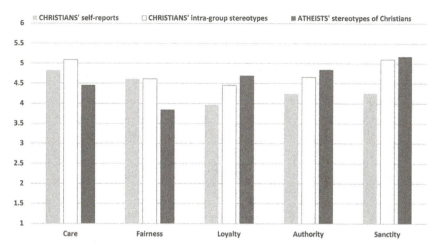

Figure 15.1 Christian participants' actual and stereotyped moral foundation endorsements (1–6 scale). (Adapted from Simpson and Rios [2016].)

the exception of atheists' stereotypes of Christians' fairness values (near the scale midpoint), all stereotypes put Christians well above the scale midpoints, suggesting a general perception of Christian moral virtuousness.

Atheists greatly exaggerated Christians' endorsements of Loyalty, Authority, and Sanctity; however, moderate-to-large exaggeration was also evident among Christian participants. Hence, the Christian stereotype seems rich with notions of ingroup loyalty and bounded group membership, deference to traditional authority and custom (e.g., gender roles), and puritanical concerns for decency and sacredness. Indeed, these types of morality are salient in most major religions (Graham & Haidt, 2010; Norenzayan, 2013), suggesting both a kernel of truth behind the stereotypes and the likelihood that stereotypes of *religion in general* bear the same moral features. Christians' concerns for caring/compassion were only mildly exaggerated among Christian participants' stereotypes and only mildly underestimated among atheist participants' stereotypes, but the raw-score estimate itself was high among Christians, suggesting that Christians' self-stereotypes are rich with notions of mercy and kindness (see below, "Intragroup Stereotypes," for further evidence). For both Christian and atheist participants, however, estimates of Christians' endorsement of Sanctity were the highest; hence, notions of purity, decency, sanctity, sacredness, and aversion to disgust and the profane perhaps dominate in collectively held stereotypes of Christian morality. All the above results remained the same when controlling for participants' self-reported left-right political identity.

In a second study, Simpson and Rios (2016) requested open-ended descriptions about outgroup morality from Christian and atheist participants.

Christians' responses were difficult to interpret, but atheists generally described Christian morality quite negatively regarding *all* moral foundations (except Care—atheists described Christians in both appealing and unappealing ways regarding caring/compassion). How might we explain this apparent inconsistency between Studies 1 and 2? It is possible that when responding from a Christian perspective in Study 1, atheist participants completed the morality items by considering how Christians would *respond*, but not how Christians *actually* think, feel, and act. This suggests that atheists perceive moral hypocrisy among Christians; a topic worthy of future research.

Essentialist Beliefs

If, as is presently argued, the *belief* component of religiosity is central to understanding religious stereotypes, then we must ask: What are people's *beliefs about belief itself*? To address this topic of meta-beliefs, Simpson et al. (2017) adapted measures of essentialist beliefs (i.e., beliefs about fixed "essences" that define and demarcate social groups). Factor analysis revealed three main dimensions of essentialist belief regarding theist-atheist differences. First, *discreteness*: Atheism and theism are perceived either as discrete and unbridgeable (rendering atheists a homogenous "categorical social other," detached from the spectrum of religious belief), or they are perceived simply as two ends of a common spectrum (rendering atheists as heterogeneous and just as much a part of human diversity as theists). This construct also reveals attitudes toward agnosticism: It is either seen as a valid position on a theism-atheism continuum, or it is seen as a nonsensical cultural artifact, incongruent with the supposed reality of atheist category discreteness. Second, *naturalness*: Put simply—is atheism perceived to be natural (e.g., part of God's plan), or is it a cultural artifact, specific to certain times and regions? Finally, *immutability*: Does one believe that atheists and theists can *truly* change their (ir)religious beliefs, or are these actually fixed, deep down? An online sample of 249 U.S. Christian theists, on average, (i) judged atheist-theist discreteness on a normal distribution around the scale midpoint (4.1/7), (ii) considered atheism a natural phenomenon (5.6/7), and (iii) were unlikely to believe that atheism and theism are fundamentally fixed and immutable ("inability to change"—2.7/7; "deeply fixed during childhood"—3.7/7). (Another item revealed middling scores on "heritability"—4.2/7.) However, in another online sample of 152 U.S. Christian theists, essentialist beliefs differed, between-subjects, depending on the social labels used. "Nonbelievers," compared to "atheists," were judged more likely to be "deeply fixed during childhood" (4.2 vs. 3.4/7. Hence, "atheist" may entail some degree of malleable social labeling, whereas "nonbeliever" may entail a deeper essence or "true self." Future research should investigate such beliefs among atheists themselves, as well as non-Christian religious believers.

Intragroup Stereotypes

As mentioned, Simpson and Rios (2016) found that Christians stereo-typed their own ingroup as strongly valuing caring and compassion. Schumann, McGregor, Nash, and Ross (2014) found similar results using a vastly different research design and a diverse sample of religious believers (including Christians, Muslims, Jews, and Hindus; all U.S. undergraduates). Under conditions of threat (e.g., reminders of death or induced fear and uncertainty about academic goals), priming religious identification reduced participants' hostile behavior and increased forgiveness, even when the reli-gious prime itself represented the hostile, vengeful aspects of religion (e.g., "an eye for an eye" versus "turn the other cheek"). In other words, indirectly reminding participants of their religious affiliation led them to respond to threat with kindness, selflessness, and generosity, regardless of the specific contents of the religious reminder. Evidence for such magnanimity included poorer recall of revenge-type words, less endorsement of violent revenge in response to a corruption scandal, and more intergroup generosity when dividing funds between ingroup and outgroup. The authors argued that these results suggest that religious believers generally perceive their religion as magnanimous; an interpretation bolstered by the fact that even reminders of hostile elements of one's religion led to increased magnanimity.

Imagining No Religion

How religious believers view their religious ingroup/s can be studied indi-rectly by asking them to imagine that atheism is correct. McAdams and Albaugh (2008) recruited 128 U.S. adults through Protestant and Catholic churches in and around Chicago, Illinois, in 2005–2007, for a two-hour life-story interview. Participants were asked to imagine and describe what their lives might have been like if they had never believed in God and/or been involved with a religious faith. Common themes included an empty life lack-ing richness and emotion (more common among politically left-leaning par-ticipants), and poor impulse control, selfishness, and base urges that would harm the broader social fabric (more common among politically right-lean-ing participants). In other words, *participants viewed religion as both a source of meaning/purpose and a buffer against the allure of desire, greed, and sin.* Although not explicitly tested, these results imply that the participants held stereo-types of believers and nonbelievers that differed sharply along these charac-teristics. (For additional evidence that religion is viewed by its adherents as a buffer against sin, much work by Ryan Ritter and Jesse Preston reveals an automatic disgust response among religious believers when thinking about atheism—e.g., Ritter & Preston, 2011; Ritter, Preston, Salomon, & Relihan-Johnson, 2016. In addition, Preston and Ritter [2012] found that values pertaining to religion and cleanliness, and the psychological activation thereof, exhibited a bidirectional causal relationship.)

Stereotypes of Religion versus Science

Perceptions of conflict between religion and science may be more prevalent than actual conflict itself. Between 2005 and 2008, Elaine Ecklund (2010) obtained quantitative data and qualitative interviews from almost 2000 scientists (spanning several disciplines) from the top twenty-one public and private U.S. universities, finding little evidence of hostility toward religion among scientists (but see Cragun [2010] for a critique). Nevertheless, religion and science are often *stereotyped* as being in conflict. Indeed, a Google search (December 11, 2018) of "science vs. religion" revealed 718 million results in less than one second! This included hundreds of articles and debates that explicitly pit science against religion.

Research in the cognitive science of religion suggests that such stereotypes may emerge not only from cultural forces (e.g., the separation of church and state) but also from basic psychological processes (note that typically both cultural and psychological forces are necessary for stereotypes to persist and spread through social networks). Regarding culture, both religion and science share a common goal of explaining complex, natural phenomena, meaning they are by default likely to conflict. More fundamental, however, are the pertinent psychological phenomena. Religious cognition (e.g., perceiving gods and spirits; teleological thinking) is essentially natural and may very well have evolved to facilitate survival (e.g., Atran & Norenzayan, 2004), whereas scientific reasoning relies on neural structures and cognitive processes that are far more recent in human evolution.

A particularly telling study is that of Preston and Epley (2009), who found that scientific and religious explanations of macro phenomena (e.g., the origins of the universe) compete, psychologically, in an all-or-nothing manner. When participants (undergraduates from the University of Western Ontario, University of Chicago, and Harvard) read text that discredited scientific explanations, they automatically expressed more negative evaluations of science *and* more positive evaluations of religion. The reverse effect was found when participants were exposed to information that discredited religion. (Note: Participants' religious identities were not reported.) In similar research, Preston, Ritter, and Hepler (2013) found that belief in souls typically decreased when participants were provided with convincing neuroscientific research that offered sophisticated mechanistic explanations for the human mind. However, when the researchers emphasized the presence of explanatory gaps in neuroscience research that suggested a limited capacity for science to address phenomena such as subjective experience, belief in souls increased. For example, in one study participants were asked to imagine they had contracted an incurable illness and had the option to freeze their body and "let their soul die." Prior to this, participants were presented with either mechanistic, neuroscientific explanations for the basis of love and morality or nonmechanistic, psychological explanations. Compared to a control, the neuroscientific condition revealed greater willingness to sacrifice the soul to save the body, whereas the psychological condition revealed less willingness to do so. In another experiment by Preston et al. (2013), participants were given an official-looking "soul card" that included their own initials and date of birth. Compared to a control (52%), participants who were exposed to strong neuroscience explanations of free will, love, and moral judgment were more likely to sell their soul card (72%), whereas participants exposed to weak neuroscience explanations were less likely to sell the card (40%). In short, scientific and religious explanations for the deep mysteries of life (e.g., love; the origins of the universe) "compete for explanatory space" and appear to compete, in zero-sum fashion, even in the human subconscious. In terms of stereotypes, therefore, science and religion seem to be categorized and processed as opposites, perhaps even as enemies.

Returning again to the cultural front, recent research suggests that U.S. Christians are stereotyped, *and* stereotype themselves, as lacking scientific ability. Across five studies, Rios, Cheng, Totton, and Shariff (2015) found such stereotypes expressed by participants of various (ir)religious backgrounds. Moreover, they found that Christians were prone to stereotype threat, as being reminded of their religious identity led them to actually perform worse on scientific tasks (e.g., logical reasoning) and to express less interest in science.

It thus follows that science and atheism may be psychologically and stereotypically associated, at least in contemporary U.S. society (obviously, the likes of Aristotle and Aquinas would beg to differ). Indeed, Scheitle and Ecklund (2017) found in a nationally representative sample of ~10,000 participants that reading about a religious scientist (Francis Collins, director of the National Institutes of Health and devout evangelist Christian) increased beliefs about the compatibility of religion and science, whereas reading about an atheist scientist (Richard Dawkins, a world-renowned biologist and self-avowed "militant atheist") exerted no effect on compatibility beliefs. This suggests that atheism-science associations are less surprising and more psychologically reflexive than theism-science associations. Similarly, in Simpson and Rios (2019), online samples of U.S. Christians estimated more atheists in the American sciences compared to Christians, even though Christians vastly outnumber *all* other (ir)religious groups in America. For example, one sample of 171 Christians estimated 52 percent of atheists and 43 percent of Christians among scientific faculty in U.S. higher education. (In contrast, most data suggest a clear religious majority across all levels of higher education and science. Gross and Simmons [2009] found that, of 1,417 U.S. professors at undergraduate and/or doctoral-program institutions, 10% identified as atheist and 13% as agnostic, and this 23% total rose to 37% at elite institutions. In addition, Pew Research Center [2015] found that among elite scientists affiliated with the American Association for the Advancement of Science, ~41% don't believe in a god, universal spirit, or higher power).

In short: Science and religion appear to be psychologically classified as distinct and competitive by many Americans. Atheism is more readily associated with science than religion, and U.S. Christians may be so aware of this that they actually underperform in and show less interest in science when merely reminded of their religious identity. Future research should investigate whether this latter effect is specific to Christians or whether it applies to religion in general. Whether or not atheism is experimentally made salient may be an important moderator of such an effect—for example, Jews may benefit from a stereotype of intelligence and scientific ability, but this stereotype may weaken if Jews are juxtaposed with atheists.[2]

Stereotypes of Specific Religions

How are specific religions stereotyped in the United States? This question is difficult to address adequately in such limited space. First, stereotypes of specific religions vary substantially across time and place. For example, Gordon Allport's (1954) seminal work on stereotypes and prejudice featured much discussion of how Americans stereotype Jews and Catholics, two groups that have since experienced large gains in public acceptance and social standing (for example, Gallup found in 1937 that 46% and 60% of respondents expressed willingness to vote for Jewish and Catholic presidential candidates, respectively, but in 2012, these had risen to 91% and 94%; see Gallup, 2012). Second, most psychological research relies on small samples (usually undergraduates) recruited in specific (and typically liberal, politically left-leaning) regions.

Nevertheless, we can gain valuable insight from public opinion polls regarding willingness to vote for political candidates from certain religious backgrounds. This serves the purpose of the present chapter not only because such polls typically recruit large, representative samples but also because their research questions align with the present focus on *moral trustworthiness* as a central feature of religious stereotypes (as moral trustworthiness is likely central in cognitive representations of religion; Gervais, 2013; Norenzayan & Shariff, 2008). Gallup (2012) asked a representative sample of 1004 participants from all fifty states (and D.C.), "If your party nominated a generally well-qualified person for president [in the upcoming 2012 presidential election] who happened to be __, would you vote for that person?" This question is an effective measure of trust because it removes confounding factors such as party affiliation and because answering "no" favors a rival party's

---

[2]For a comprehensive review of attitudes toward science, see Rutjens, Heine, Sutton, and van Harreveld (2018).

candidate—an action that voters would typically be very reluctant to do unless especially motivated. The following percentages of respondents expressed willingness to vote for a hypothetical candidate from the following religious groups: Catholic (94%), Jewish (91%), Mormon (80%), Muslim (58%), and atheist (54%). In similar research conducted in 2003, Edgell, Gerteis, and Hartmann (2006) polled a nationally representative sample of 2,081 Americans using the random-digit dial telephone technique. In follow-up research conducted in 2014, Edgell, Hartmann, Stewart, and Gerteis (2016) recruited 2,521 participants through an online platform that purportedly represents 97 percent of U.S. households. In response to the question "How much [do] you think people in this group agree with your vision of American society?" they found the following proportion of participants responding "not at all" per target group (2003 data in parentheses) [2014 data in brackets]: Atheists (39.6%) [41.9%], Muslims (26.3%) [45.5%], conservative Christians (13.5%) [26.6%], and Jews (7.4%) [17.6%]. In response to another question, the following proportions of participants indicated they would "disapprove if [their] child wanted to marry a member of this group" (2003 data in parentheses) [2014 data in brackets]: Atheist (47.6%) [43.7%], Muslim (26.3%) [48.9%], conservative Christian (6.9%) [17.2%], and Jew (11.8%) [17.8%]. These results suggest that, relatively speaking, Jews and (conservative) Christians are widely accepted in the social-moral fabric of American society, in both public and private spheres. Atheists, however, are rejected by almost half the country (assuming the samples are representative), while rejection of Muslims has surged to almost half the country over the past decade. For example, in the 2014 survey, 27 percent and 30 percent of participants believed that atheists and Muslims (respectively) don't share the participant's morals or values; 16 percent and 29 percent believed the respective group is socially intolerant; 9 percent and 18 percent believed that the group doesn't contribute to local communities; and 8 percent and 22 percent believed that the group is a threat to public order and safety. In terms of stereotypes, this suggests that the Judeo-Christian roots of America's founding still live on in the minds of many Americans—those who embrace such roots are mostly welcomed and are considered "one of us," whereas those who do not (in this case, atheists and Muslims) are considered "outsiders" who don't fit in with American cultural-moral values and beliefs. As the above statistics reveal, this leaves such "outsider" groups vulnerable to extreme prejudice and discrimination.

Recap: Future Directions

To review, in this chapter I have suggested the following as potentially fruitful topics for future research. First, given the findings regarding perceptions of facial features associated with atheism (Brown-Iannuzzi et al., 2018), might atheism be stereotyped with more archetypally masculine qualities and theism with more archetypally feminine qualities? Second, as some findings by Simpson and Rios (2016) could be interpreted in at least two different ways (participants either estimated outgroup moral values or estimated the outgroup's style of responding to surveys on morality), future research could further tease these interpretations apart and, in the process, investigate perceptions of outgroup moral hypocrisy. Third, no data reveal atheists' essentialist beliefs about the theism-atheism distinction or such beliefs among non-Christian theists. These beliefs appear to be deeply connected to attitudes toward atheists among U.S. Christians (Simpson et al., 2017), so further investigation among different religious or nonreligious groups could be informative. Finally, samples of atheists and other religious groups should be recruited to study beliefs about atheism-science associations.

Summary

A discussion of religious stereotypes could easily succumb to overly nuanced, time- and location-specific descriptions of particular religions and how they are viewed. Instead, I have found it more informative to focus on broader concerns that address fundamental definitions of religion and its counterparts. Religion, first and foremost, is a system of *belief*, and it can therefore be defined and discussed most comprehensively when juxtaposed against atheism and science. In this context of analysis, we find two major themes in human psychology that appear generalizable across the U.S. and perhaps even the world (and even human cultural history). First, religion is believed (stereotyped) to embody both moral virtue and an orientation toward moral behavior and socio-moral order. When judging the absence of religious belief (atheism), the human mind seems naturally inclined to perceive selfish abandon of moral virtue. Second, religion and science are mentally depicted (stereotyped) as opposites in competition for explanatory power. The world is full of mystery, and the human mind appears uninclined to embrace mechanistic/scientific explanations and religious, metaphysical explanations simultaneously—as the explanatory value of one goes up, that of the other seems to go down.

These observations appear to be generalizable and deeply rooted not just in culture but also human psychology. It thus follows that such observations should form a starting point in attempts to address stereotypes of religion, atheism, science, specific religions, and conflicts therein. I will illustrate this with two examples. First, consider President Obama's nomination for the head of the National Institutes of Health: Francis Collins, a major figure in American science, also happens to be a devout, evangelical Christian. This decision was received poorly by some scientists (consider, for example, Lawrence Krauss's [2015] contention that "all scientists should be militant atheists"). However, it may in fact have been the wisest decision to make in a Christian-majority country where religion is stereotyped as a wellspring of moral integrity *and* where fluctuations in public trust in science can yield serious consequences (consider the widespread decline in U.S. vaccination rates between 2015 and 2016,[3] accompanied by rising distrust in and fear of immunization science [e.g., Black & Rappuoli, 2010]). As a second illustration, prejudice and discrimination against religious nonbelievers (harmful in the United States and literally fatal in much of the world; e.g., CNN, 2015; Edgell et al., 2016; IHEU, 2012) are better understood *and* challenged upon recognition that human minds seem to automatically stereotype religion with morality and atheism with immorality. Recognizing this automaticity may help challenge the veracity of the stereotypes and thus facilitate intergroup tolerance and respect.

In short, understanding automatic stereotypes of religion can be put to the service of the public good. It is thus imperative that research on this topic continues.

References

Allport, G. W. (1954). *The nature of prejudice.* New York: Basic Books.

Atran, S., & Henrich, J. (2010). The evolution of religion: How cognitive by-products, adaptive learning heuristics, ritual displays, and group competition generate deep commitments to prosocial religions. *Biological Theory, 5*(1), 18–30.

Atran, S., & Norenzayan, A. (2004). Religion's evolutionary landscape: Counterintuition, commitment, compassion, communion. *Behavioral and Brain Sciences, 27*(6), 713–730.

Black, S., & Rappuoli, R. (2010). A crisis of public confidence in vaccines. *Science Translational Medicine, 2*(61), 61mr1.

Brown-Iannuzzi, J. L., McKee, S., & Gervais, W. M. (2018). Atheist horns and religious halos: Mental representations of atheists and theists. *Journal of Experimental Psychology: General, 147*(2), 292–297.

Bullivant, S. (2013). Defining "atheism." In S. Bullivant & M. Ruse (Eds.), *The Oxford handbook of atheism* (pp. 11–21). Oxford, England: Oxford University Press.

CNN. (2015, March). *Atheists: Inside the world of non-believers.* Retrieved from http://www.youtube.com/watch?v=83PeHIstSPM

Cragun, R. T. (2010). Review of *Science vs. Religion: What Scientists Really Think* by Elaine Howard Ecklund. *Journal for the Scientific Study of Religion, 49*(4), 776–768.

Ecklund, E. H. (2010). *Science vs. religion: What scientists really think.* New York: Oxford University Press.

---

[3]https://www.cdc.gov/nchs/hus/contents2017.htm?search=Vaccination.

Edgell, P., Gerteis, J., & Hartmann, D. (2006). Atheists as "other": Moral bound-aries and cultural membership in American society. *American Sociological Review, 71*(2), 211–234.

Edgell, P., Hartmann, D., Stewart, E., & Gerteis, J. (2016). Atheists and other cultural outsiders: Moral boundaries and the non-religious in the United States. *Social Forces, 95*(2), 607–638.

Gallup. (2012, June 21). *Atheists, Muslims see most bias as presidential candidates.* Retrieved from https://news.gallup.com/poll/155285/atheists-muslims-bias-presidential-candidates.aspx

Gervais, W. M. (2013). In godlessness we distrust: Using social psychology to solve the puzzle of anti-atheist prejudice. *Social and Personality Psychology Compass, 7*(6), 366–377.

Gervais, W. M. (2014). Everything is permitted? People intuitively judge immo-rality as representative of atheists. *PLoS One, 9*(4), e92302.

Gervais, W. M., Shariff, A. F., & Norenzayan, A. (2011). Do you believe in athe-ists? Distrust is central to anti-atheist prejudice. *Journal of Personality and Social Psychology, 101,* 1189–1206.

Gervais, W. M., Xygalatas, D., McKay, R. T., van Elk, M., Buchtel, E. E., Aveyard, M., . . . Klocová, E. K. (2017). Global evidence of extreme intuitive moral prejudice against atheists. *Nature Human Behaviour, 1*(8), s41562-017.

Graham, J., & Haidt, J. (2010). Beyond beliefs: Religions bind individuals into moral communities. *Personality and Social Psychology Review, 14*(1), 140–150.

Graham, J., Haidt, J., Koleva, S., Motyl, M., Iyer, R., Wojcik, S. P., & Ditto, P. H. (2013). Moral foundations theory: The pragmatic validity of moral plural-ism. In *Advances in experimental social psychology* (Vol. 47, pp. 55–130). New York: Academic Press.

Gross, N., & Simmons, S. (2009). The religiosity of American college and univer-sity professors. *Sociology of Religion, 70*(2), 101–129.

Haidt, J. (2007). The new synthesis in moral psychology. *Science, 316*(5827), 998–1002.

International Humanist and Ethical Union. (2012). *Freedom of thought report.* IHEU.org. Retrieved March 19, 2015, from http://iheu.org

Krauss, L. (2015, September 08). All scientists should be militant atheists. *The New Yorker.* Retrieved from http://www.newyorker.com/news/news-desk/all-scientists-should-be-militant-atheists

McAdams, D. P., & Albaugh, M. (2008). What if there were no God? Politically conservative and liberal Christians imagine their lives without faith. *Journal of Research in Personality, 42*(6), 1668–1672.

Norenzayan, A. (2013). *Big gods: How religion transformed cooperation and conflict.* Princeton, NJ: Princeton University Press.

Norenzayan, A. (2016). Theodiversity. *Annual Review of Psychology, 67,* 465–488.

Norenzayan, A., & Shariff, A. F. (2008). The origin and evolution of religious prosociality. *Science, 322*(5898), 58–62.

Norenzayan, A., Shariff, A. F., Gervais, W. M., Willard, A., McNamara, R., Sling-erland, E., & Henrich, J. (2016). The cultural evolution of prosocial reli-gions. *Behavioral and Brain Sciences, 39,* e1.

Pew Research Center. (2014). *Worldwide, Many see belief in God as essential to morality.* Retrieved from www.pewglobal.org/files/2014/03/Pew-Research-Center-Global-Attitudes-Project-Belief-in-God-Report-FINAL- March-13-2014.pdf.

Pew Research Center. (2015). *Religion and science.* Retrieved from http://www.pewinternet.org/2015/10/22/science-and-religion/

Preston, J., & Epley, N. (2009). Science and God: An automatic opposition between ultimate explanations. *Journal of Experimental Social Psychology, 45*(1), 238–241.

Preston, J. L., & Ritter, R. S. (2012). Cleanliness and godliness: Mutual association between two kinds of personal purity. *Journal of Experimental Social Psychology, 48*(6), 1365–1368.

Preston, J. L., Ritter, R. S., & Hepler, J. (2013). Neuroscience and the soul: Competing explanations for the human experience. *Cognition, 127*(1), 31–37.

Rios, K., Cheng, Z. H., Totton, R. R., & Shariff, A. F. (2015). Negative stereotypes cause Christians to underperform in and disidentify with science. *Social Psychological and Personality Science, 6*(8), 959–967.

Ritter, R. S., & Preston, J. L. (2011). Gross gods and icky atheism: Disgust responses to rejected religious beliefs. *Journal of Experimental Social Psychology, 47*(6), 1225–1230.

Ritter, R. S., Preston, J. L., Salomon, E., & Relihan-Johnson, D. (2016). Imagine no religion: Heretical disgust, anger and the symbolic purity of mind. *Cognition and Emotion, 30*(4), 778–796.

Roes, F. L., & Raymond, M. (2003). Belief in moralizing gods. *Evolution and Human Behavior, 24*(2), 126–135.

Rutjens, B. T., Heine, S. J., Sutton, R. M., & van Harreveld, F. (2018). Attitudes towards science. In *Advances in Experimental Social Psychology* (Vol. 57, pp. 125–165). San Diego, CA: Elsevier Academic Press.

Saroglou, V. (2011). Believing, bonding, behaving, and belonging: The big four religious dimensions and cultural variation. *Journal of Cross-Cultural Psychology, 42*(8), 1320–1340.

Scheitle, C. P., & Ecklund, E. H. (2017). The influence of science popularizers on the public's view of religion and science: An experimental assessment. *Public Understanding of Science, 26*(1), 25–39.

Schumann, K., McGregor, I., Nash, K. A., & Ross, M. (2014). Religious magnanimity: Reminding people of their religious belief system reduces hostility after threat. *Journal of Personality and Social Psychology, 107*(3), 432–453.

Simpson, A., & Rios, K. (2016). How do US Christians and atheists stereotype one another's moral values? *The International Journal for the Psychology of Religion, 26*(4), 320–336.

Simpson, A., Rios, K., & Cowgill, C. M. (2017). Godless in essence? Psychological essentialism, theistic meta-beliefs, and anti-atheist prejudice. *Personality and Individual Differences, 119*, 35–45.

Simpson, A., & Rios, K. (2019). Is science for atheists? Perceived threat to religious cultural authority explains US Christians' distrust in secularized science. *Public Understanding of Science, 28*(7), 740–758.

CHAPTER SIXTEEN

Stereotypes of Native Americans

Angela C. Bell, Edward Burkley, and Melissa Burkley

On November 27, 2017, President Trump met with a group of Navajo Code Talkers to honor their service to their country. Native Americans serve in the U.S. military at a higher rate than any other racial group (Brofer, 2003), yet their contributions often go unnoticed. For instance, code talkers from thirty-three tribal nations played an integral role in World War II, but their contributions remained classified and hidden for decades. Thus, this meeting with the president represented a rare moment in which Native Americans were being honored and recognized for their contributions to contemporary society. But it took an ugly turn when President Trump used the event to criticize political rival Senator Elizabeth Warren by invoking his nickname for her: Pocahontas. This nickname is a reference to her statement that she has Native American ancestry, a claim that President Trump disputed. The Pocahontas comment wasn't just offensive to Senator Warren. Native Americans protested its use, along with many other groups, because Pocahontas is considered to be a racial slur.

Why would invoking the name of a historical character and beloved Disney princess be considered a racial slur? As one NBC reporter put it, President Trump's comment was disrespectful because it "reduced the over 500 tribes in the United States to a caricature" (Martin, 2017).

Stereotypic depictions of Native Americans in our culture include images from popular movies (e.g., Disney's *Pocahontas*, *Dances with Wolves*), sports mascots (e.g., Cleveland Indians, Washington Redskins, Atlanta Braves), and product marketing (e.g., Land-O-Lakes Butter, Eskimo Pie). At first blush, these representations may seem harmless, but in truth they perpetuate stereotypes of Native people. In this chapter, we explore the nature of Native American stereotypes, how they are perpetuated by biased media representations, and how they affect Native people.

What Makes Native American Stereotypes Unique?

Although all racial groups suffer from inaccurate depictions, the stereotypes of Native Americans are unique in several ways. First, because Native Americans make up less than 2 percent of the U.S. population (U.S. Census Bureau, 2013), they are largely underrepresented in the media. In fact, the most common depiction of Native Americans is no depiction at all. Research indicates that less than 0.2 percent of TV and movie characters are Native American (Fryberg & Stephens, 2010). When depictions do exist, they largely represent historical images of Native Americans from the eighteenth and nineteenth century (e.g., Geronimo, Pocahontas). Contemporary depictions of Native Americans as doctors, lawyers, or business leaders are rare, if not nonexistent. When these two patterns are combined, it gives the impression that Native Americans do not exist as a *contemporary* racial group (Fryberg & Stephens, 2010).

Second, because the Native American population is small, most people have never had real-world interactions with Native American people. For example, a nationally representative survey conducted by the First Nations Development Institute (2018) found that two-thirds of Americans do not know a single person who, as far as they are aware, is a Native American. This means that most of what non-Native people know about Native Americans is based on just a handful of highly inaccurate media images. As a result, the few stereotypic portrayals that do exist have an even stronger impact on how the general public perceives Native people.

Third, portrayals of Native Americans within the context of product marketing is far more frequent than with other racial groups. Sports mascots is the most common example (and we will explore this topic in more detail later), but the commodification of Native culture is present in a wide range of domains. These include the marketing of food products (e.g., Eskimo Pie, Land-O-Lakes butter), alcohol (e.g., Crazy Horse Malt Liquor), tobacco (e.g., Natural American Spirit), clothing (e.g., Cherokee jeans) and various other businesses (e.g., Mutual of Omaha, Mohawk Carpet, Jeep Cherokee). In fact, according to the United States Patent and Trademark Office there are over 600 active trademarks for logos that feature Native American people (Wilson, 2014). This proliferation leads to the impression that Native Americans are more akin to a caricature than a contemporary social group (Fryberg & Stephens, 2010).

Finally, the lack of representation of Native Americans not only exists within the media, it also exists within the empirical literature. Research in which Native Americans are either the subject of the study (cf. Burkley, Durante, Fiske, Burkley, & Andrade, 2017; Chaney, Burke, & Burkley, 2011) or involved as participants (cf. Covarrubias & Fryberg, 2015; Fryberg, Markus, Oyserman, & Stone, 2008) is scarce. This empirical dearth means that the current body of psychological research fails to capture the complexity, variability, and nuance of the Native American experience.

Despite the fact that there are fewer empirical studies on Native American stereotypes compared to other racial stereotypes, a small collection of studies has tried to address this gap in the literature. And from these, we can extract invaluable information on the nature of such stereotypes.

Modern Examinations of Native American Stereotypes

A Dual-Sided Nature

One of the major insights to come out of research on Native American bias is the dual-sided nature of these stereotypes. For example, positive perceptions of Native Americans (e.g., peaceful, one with nature) often coexist with negative perceptions (e.g., aggressive, lazy, alcoholic; Burkley et al., 2017). A key to understanding how people can hold such contradictory perceptions lies in the concept of *subgroups*. Subgroups represent more narrowly defined categories than the broad social group (Richards & Hewstone, 2001). For example, the broader group "Blacks" consists of a wide range of subgroups, including poor Blacks, Black professionals, and Black athletes (Cuddy, Fiske, & Glick, 2007; Devine & Baker, 1991; Fiske, Bergsieker, Russell, & Williams, 2009), and each of these subgroups is associated with a different pattern of racial stereotypes. As a result, researchers who study stereotypes associated with subgroups, rather than the single broader social group, are able to capture stereotypes in a more richly defined, multi-level manner (Eckes, 1994).

To examine how subgroups impact Native American stereotypes, Burkley, Durante, Fiske, Burkley, and Andrade (2017) relied on the Stereotype Content Model (SCM; Fiske, Cuddy, Glick, & Xu, 2002). According to the SCM, most group stereotypes fall along two major dimensions: Groups are stereotyped to be high or low in *warmth* (e.g., friendly vs. cold; trustworthy vs. untrustworthy) and high or low in *competence* (i.e., hardworking vs. lazy; respected vs. disrespected). SCM is unique in that it allows researchers to identify a wide range of subgroups and then identify how these subgroups are uniquely stereotyped along the warmth and competence dimensions.

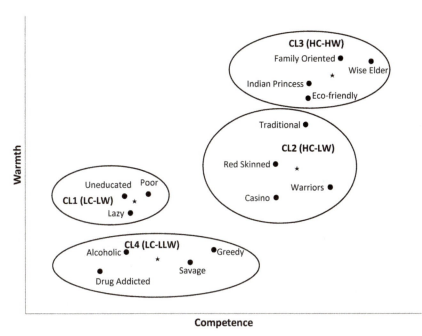

Figure 16.1 Results based on hierarchical cluster analysis of stereotypic ratings of various Native American subgroups. Stars indicate cluster centers. H = high, L = low, W = warmth, C = competence (Burkley, Durante, et al., 2017).

Using the SCM approach, Burkley et al. (2017) identified nine commonly held Native American subgroups: *alcoholic, casino, greedy, lazy, poor, red-skinned, warrior, traditional,* and *uneducated*. Furthermore, these various subgroups were found to cluster around four dominant stereotype patterns (Figure 16.1). The most dominant of these consisted of stereotypes depicting Native people as low in both warmth and competence. In fact, half of the subgroups conformed to this especially negative pattern (e.g., alcoholic, lazy, poor, uneducated) and were shown to elicit the emotion of contempt toward Native people. However, there was also evidence of a more ambivalent pattern. The casino, red-skinned, and warrior subgroups included stereotypes that depicted Native people as low in warmth but high in competence. This suggests that some Native American stereotypes have an ambivalent nature in that they contain both positive and negative qualities.

This research illustrates how people can have competing, coexisting attitudes toward Native American people as a whole. Some subgroups of Native Americans are perceived as warm and friendly, others as cold and hostile. Some subgroups are perceived as hardworking and competent, others as lazy and inferior. Thus, it is important that future work on Native American stereotypes (as well as that of other social groups) take into account the variability affording by subgroups.

The Noble/Ignoble Warrior

A second major insight to come from the work on Native American stereotypes is the proliferation of the warrior stereotype (Burkley et al., 2017). The depiction of Native people as aggressive and war-like has deep historical roots. In the Declaration of Independence, Thomas Jefferson refers to the "merciless Indian savages, whose known rule of warfare, is undistinguished destruction of all ages, sexes, and conditions." And Jefferson was not alone in this perception of Native Americans as savage brutes. Throughout history, this biased perception of Native savagery was used to justify the removal of Native and indigenous people from their land and to justify the systemic dissolution of their language and culture in the name of assimilation. As a result, the image of the ignoble, contemptible savage has remained largely unchanged since Jefferson's time.

But existing side-by-side with the hostile stereotype is the image of the noble warrior or chief. These images depict Native American warriors as brave and honorable (Burkley et al., 2017), and they can be seen in popular movies like *Dances with Wolves* and *The Last of the Mohicans*.

One realm where this tug-of-war between noble and ignoble warrior depictions is most evident is in the use of sports mascots. Native American sports mascots have had a long, tumultuous history. Opponents of these mascots claim they perpetuate disparaging, stereotypic images of Native people (Farnell, 2004; Fryberg & Watts, 2010; King, 2010). Instead, mascot supporters claim they honor the traditions and bravery of Native people (Price, 2002), or they argue that such mascots are merely harmless symbols that have little impact on how Native people are treated or perceived. Thus, the sports mascot issue represents a particularly unique aspect of the Native American experience.

Although public opinion on the nature of sports mascots has been split, the scientific literature largely supports the claims that Native American mascots are harmful. In particular, several studies have demonstrated how exposure to Native Americans mascot imagery results in negative outcomes for Native American people.

For example, Freng and Willis-Esqueda (2011) found that White participants primed with the Chief Wahoo mascot responded faster to negative Indian stereotypes and slower to positive Indian stereotypes than those primed with a Yankees or Pirates mascot image. This indicates that merely viewing the Chief Wahoo image activated harmful stereotypes toward Native Americans in the minds of the perceivers. Similarly, Angle, Dagogo-Jack, Forehand, and Perkins (2016) found in their first study that exposure to a Native American mascot led to a stronger automatic association between

Native Americans and warlike adjectives (e.g., savage, vicious, barbaric) than exposure to a kangaroo mascot; however, this was only among participants with more malleable (i.e., liberal) political views. Thus, results from these studies collectively suggest that everyday encounters with Native American sports mascots can activate negative stereotypes about Native people.

But does this mean that exposure to these mascots causes people to judge Native people in stereotypic ways? Not necessarily. Stereotype activation, as measured in these studies, is not the same as stereotype *application*. Activation means the stereotype is more readily available in the person's mind. Application means the person relies on the stereotype when forming an impression of a target person (Kunda & Spencer, 2003). The distinction is important because stereotype application is far more likely to lead to real-world consequences in the form of discrimination than stereotype application.

The Freng and Willis-Esqueda (2011) study only found evidence that Indian mascot exposure causes stereotype activation. What it didn't test was whether those activated stereotypes are more likely to be applied toward a Native American target and produce biased judgments. If this were the case, it would suggest that despite what some may think, Native sports mascots are harmful to Native people because they facilitate biased perceptions (and perhaps eventually biased behaviors).

To determine the impact of mascots on stereotype application, Burkley et al. (2017) asked participants to memorize a series of images. Some viewed a collection of Native American mascots (e.g., Washington Redskins, Florida Seminoles), some a collection of White mascots (e.g., Boston Celtics, Minnesota Vikings), and some viewed nonmascot images (e.g., cupcake, carrots). Next, all the participants read a diary entry describing a person engaging in ambiguously aggressive behavior. Everyone read the same entry, but some were told it was written by a Native American author, others were told it was a White author, and others were told it was a Black author (the Black author condition was included so that there was another racial minority group to compare to, but one unassociated with the sports mascot controversy). Participants then rated the author's level of aggression and indicated their own prejudice toward Native Americans. The variable of prejudice was included because prior research indicates stereotype activation is most likely to result in stereotype application among people who endorse prejudiced attitudes (e.g., Brown, Croizet, Bohner, Fournet, & Payne, 2003; Lepore & Brown, 1997). Thus, the prediction was that when people are exposed to Native mascots, those with a prejudicial attitude toward Native people would be more likely to stereotypically judge the Native target.

As expected, the impact of the mascot depended on the respondent's level of prejudice. High-prejudiced people who were exposed to the Native American mascots judged the Native American author more negatively than low-prejudiced people (Figure 16.2). Importantly, this pattern did not occur for

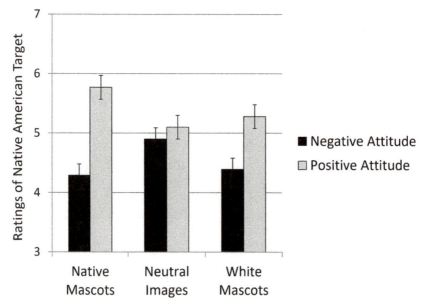

Figure 16.2   Trait ratings of Native American target as a function of image condition and attitude toward Native Americans. The lower the trait rating, the more negative (i.e., more stereotypic) the evaluation. A negative attitude is defined as 1 SD below the mean on the feeling thermometer and a positive attitude is defined as 1 SD above the mean. Error bars represent 95% confidence intervals. (Burkley, Burkley, et al., 2017).

judgments of the White or Black authors, suggesting that exposure to Native mascots only produces negative judgments of Native people, not all people in general. Furthermore, the pattern did not occur with exposure to the White mascot or nonmascot images, suggesting there is something unique about the Native mascot images. This pattern is consistent with research on other racial groups that shows racist depictions activate stereotypic thoughts among high-prejudice people and nonstereotypic thoughts among low-prejudice people (Kawakami, Dion, & Dovidio, 1998; Lepore & Brown, 1997). Thus, despite what mascot proponents say, it is clear that Native American sports mascots negatively alter the way Native American people are perceived.

The Vanishing Indian

A third major insight to come from the work on Native American stereotypes points to the social invisibility of Native Americans in modern society. When people think of bias and discrimination, they tend to think of prejudice by acts of commission (Fryberg & Eason, 2017). They focus on tangible acts of prejudice, such as bias in police shootings, discrimination in employee hiring, or the presence of degrading images (like sports mascots). However, prejudice can also occur through acts of *omission*. According to Fryberg and Eason (2017), prejudice through omission occurs whenever there is an absence or scarcity of cultural representations and a social group is (intentionally or unintentionally) left out of the public conscious.

Such omission occurs at a much higher rate for Native Americans than other major racial groups in the United States (Fryberg & Eason, 2017). As mentioned earlier, representations of Native Americans on TV, in commercials, and in film are rare. Even though Native Americans make up 2 percent of the American population (U.S. Census Bureau, 2013), they make up only 0.4 percent of prime-time TV and film characters (Mastro & Stern, 2003) and 0.09 percent of video game characters (Williams, Martins, Consalvo, & Ivory, 2009). Similarly, stories involving Native Americans rarely get coverage in the news. For example, the protests that occurred at Standing Rock Indian Reservation regarding the Dakota Access Pipeline threatened critical tribal resources and ecological resources, but it was not covered by mainstream media (Clark, 2016). Further, the largest radioactive accident in American history occurred at a New Mexico uranium mill in 1979. The incident left the Navajo nation without clean water for thirty-seven years, but the story received little public coverage. In comparison, the nuclear meltdown at Three Mile Island the same year received wide news coverage.

But media is just one example of Native American omission. Native Americans make up only 0.5 percent of primary/secondary teachers and 0.5 percent of college professors (Coopersmith, 2009; Keigher, 2009; Leavitt, Covarrubias, Perez, & Fryberg, 2015; Snyder, Dillow, & Hoffman, 2009). This means there is a low probability that Native American students will encounter a Native American teacher and role model during their academic career. As a result, they may come to question if they even belong in a school setting. Furthermore, an examination of state curricula revealed that most educational textbooks and course materials rarely mention Native Americans after the year 1900, and none contains content on current Indian issues or challenges (Shear, Knowles, Soden, & Castro, 2015). Such omission is made even worse given the new trend to remove precolonial history from AP History curriculum and therefore decrease any likelihood of exposure to indigenous history (Wong, 2018).

Such omissions can also be seen in criminal reporting. An examination of crime statistics found police brutality against Native Americans is frequently overlooked and underreported, despite the fact that Indians are, statistically speaking, the group most likely to be killed by police (Silva, 2017). A similar pattern occurs for the reporting and prosecuting of sexual assault. Two-thirds of sexual assault cases with Native American victims are not prosecuted, or if they are, they are tried in reservation courts, where many women report sexual bias in favor of male defendants (Edwards, 2017).

When taken together, this data suggests repeated omission and invisibility of Native Americans within society. Worse yet, it fuels a common perception that Native Americans no longer exist or are vanishing to extinction (Clark, Spanierman, Reed, Soble, & Cabana, 2011; Wolfe, 2006).

Unfortunately, this omission of Native Americans even extends to the scientific literature. Native Americans are rarely studied and rarely serve as participants in psychology research (Fryberg & Eason, 2017). This is even the case among prejudice researchers who, given their interests, should be especially sensitive to this insidious form of bias. For example, one analysis found that less than 0.5 percent of all prejudice research refers to Native Americans in any context (Fryberg & Eason, 2017). Theories focusing exclusively on prejudice and decimation toward Native Americans are hard to come by. Research on prejudice (or on any topic, for that matter) rarely includes predominately Native participants. Without such studies, it is impossible to fully assess how anti-Native American prejudices negatively affect Native people.

What are the Consequences of Native American Stereotypes?

Although small in number, there are a handful of studies that have examined how Native American stereotypes result in negative consequences for Native people. One such consequence is how such stereotypes affect the way Native Americans view themselves. For example, Leavitt et al. (2015) examined how the omission of Native people in the media shapes their identity and sense of self-worth. According to these researchers, the lack of contemporary Native American representations in the media severely limits how Native people see their place in society. Growing up without any examples or role models of Native doctors, professors, athletes, politicians, or entrepreneurs leads Native people to assume such opportunities are not available to them. As the Native American character in Sherman Alexie's (2007) novel *The Absolutely True Diary of a Part-Time Indian* puts it, "We reservation Indians don't get to realize our dreams. We don't get those chances. Or choices. We're just poor. That's all we are" (p. 13).

Because the few media representations that do exist are often antiquated and stereotypic, Native people may be more likely to internalize negative stereotypes about their group and use them to define their place in society. In support of this assertion, Fryberg et al. (2008) found that exposure to common media portrayals of Native Americans (like Chief Wahoo or Disney's Pocahontas) decreased Native American students' self-esteem, community worth, and sense of future academic success, compared to those who were not exposed to such images. In contrast, White students' self-esteem *increased* after exposure to these portrayals, suggesting that these images imply Whites' superiority over Native Americans. In another study, the decrease in self-worth after Native mascot exposure was even more pronounced among Native Americans who held a positive view of such mascots (Fryberg, 2003). Thus, it appears that when your only media role models are cartoonish, stereotypic caricatures, your sense of what you are and what you can accomplish becomes highly constrained.

Covarrubias and Fryberg (2015) examined how exposure to positive role models can help alleviate this effect. Native American students were presented with a biography and photograph of a successful academic role model. For one group, the role model was self-relevant (i.e., was also Native American). For a second group, the role was self-irrelevant (i.e., was European American). A third group received no role model information. The results indicated that the Native American students who read about a Native role model showed significantly higher feelings of school belonging than those in the other two groups. When combined, these studies show just how impactful good and bad role models can be on the Native American psyche.

Another consequence that results from Native American stereotypes is *stereotype threat*, which occurs when people feel they are at risk of confirming a negative stereotype about their group (Spencer, Logel, & Davies, 2016). When people perform a task where they might confirm a negative stereotype (e.g., a woman taking a math test), they are likely to suffer from stereotype threat and their test performance may become impaired.

Such stereotype threat is especially likely for minority students high in *ethnic identity*, which refers to how important being part of that racial group is to their identity (Tajfel, 1981). The stronger a racial minority's ethnic identity, the more they are motivated to not confirm the stereotype. For example, a common stereotype is that Native Americans are unintelligent and do not perform well academically. A Native American student with a strong sense of ethnic identity may be prone to worrying about confirming these stereotypes while taking a math test, and as a result, the student may be at risk of performing poorly on the test. For this reason, some researchers argue that stereotype threat helps explain why Native Americans have a high school dropout rate that is double that of their White counterparts (DeVoe & Darling-Churchill, 2008) and why only 1 percent of college students are Native American (Leavitt et al., 2015).

To examine the impact of stereotype threat empirically, Jaramillo, Mello, and Worrell (2015) studied a group of Native American high school students. They found that for Native American students high in ethnic identity, those who reported experiencing stereotype threat had worse GPAs than those who did not experience stereotype threat. However, for students low in ethnic identity, reported stereotype threat had no impact on their GPA. Thus, it was a combination of high ethnic identity and high stereotype threat that resulted in a low GPA. So the more Native American students care about disproving their group's negative stereotypes, the more they will likely suffer when under the shadow of stereotype threat.

How to Fix the Problem

The biggest issue in regard to Native American stereotypes has to do with the lack of social representations of Native people, but Native Americans are not the only group to have suffered from this problem. Not long ago, the same was true of African Americans. For example, in the early 1900s, the dominant media portrayal of Blacks centered around a single stereotypic representation: Sambo. Sambo refers to the image of Blacks as dim-witted, comical, bug-eyed, big-lipped buffoons, and the character was often depicted in Blackface. This image appeared in popular theater, TV shows, books, movies, and even children's cartoons. During the civil rights era, this stereotypical depiction of Sambo faded from view. Thanks to movies like *Black Panther*, *Get Out*, and *Moonlight*, and TV shows like *Black-ish*, *Empire*, *Atlanta*, and *Insecure*, today there is a much wider range of representations of Blacks and African Americans. This is not to say that stereotypic representations of Blacks no longer exist, but they exist side-by-side with more positive and accurate depictions. Nowadays, Black and African American characters are depicted as doctors, lawyers, politicians, presidents, professors, business leaders, and so on. Such a shift has surely resulted in more positive outcomes for African American people. For example, some have suggested that having an African American president in the hit TV show *24* paved the way for America's first Black president (Israel, 2008).

A similar trend is needed for Native Americans. The removal of sports mascots in one area where we have seen some progress in recent years, but it has been a slow and heavily resisted process. Similar attention should be paid to the 600+ company logos that appropriate Native American imagery and tribal names. The media should push for more contemporary depictions of Native people, such as those depicted in the recent bestselling book *There, There* by Tommy Orange. Furthermore, more Native American teachers and professors are needed to encourage Native Americans to expand their aspirations, reduce their school dropout rates, and increase their enrollment in college. Finally, Native Americans themselves should consider running for political offices so they have a more visible social voice. Currently, there are just two Native American members of Congress, but 2018 saw a record number of Native individuals (especially women) running for public office in the midterm elections (Fadel & Wiener, 2018).

A second solution is to target the omission of Native Americans within the scientific community (note that we provide specific suggestions for future research in the next section; here we discuss this issue more globally). When it comes to the study of stereotypes and prejudice, the approach that has dominated psychology (especially social psychology) over the past few decades has been a cognitive one. Spurred by the cognitive revolution of the 1970s, theories and research on racial bias have largely focused on how shared cognitive structures, like stereotypes and implicit attitudes, contribute to racial inequality. However, we seem to be on the precipice of a new revolution, one that emphasizes how inequality also results from a wide range of cultural factors and structural factors. According to this sociocultural approach, "each minority group has a unique history of racialized experience in American society" which shapes that group's experiences (Plaut, 2010, p. 92). The experiences of African Americans are inextricably tied to a history of slavery, Asian Americans to a history of being perceived as "perpetual foreigners," Latinos to a history of being perceived as invaders and illegal border crossers, and Middle Eastern Americans to a history of being perceived as religious extremists (Plaut, 2010). Although these racial groups share some experiences of discrimination, there are also noteworthy differences that researchers must consider when studying racial bias. The same is true of Native Americans.

In recognition of such unique experiences, there has been a recent call to arms in the literature for a need for "diversity science" (Fryberg & Stevens, 2010; Plaut, 2010). Diversity science moves beyond the White/Non-White division or the Black/White division typically seen in the current literature. Instead, diversity science honors the unique experiences of every social group and recognizes that in order to fully understand bias, one group cannot be substituted for another. This means that if researchers want to accurately capture the causes and consequences of racial bias, they must study the phenomenon within the full range of stigmatized groups. Never has there been a clearer call for more research on Native American stereotypes and Native people.

Saying more research is needed on Native Americans is easy; however, the issue is complex. Several factors are likely to blame for the current lack of research on Native American samples. First and foremost, Native Americans constitute the smallest racial group in America. A typical sample collected at a university, or even in an urban city, is not likely to include enough Native Americans for an accurate comparison. Add to this a recent push in psychological science for studies with large sample sizes, high power, and replicability, all of which pose as institutional barriers that hinder innovation in Native stereotype research. Thus, if researchers want to study Native populations, they will need to go the extra effort to seek out participants.

But the issue extends beyond sample recruitment. Native Americans have a long history of being lied to and exploited by White-led institutions. As a result, many hold a strong distrust of predominantly White institutions, including those associated with the fields of medicine, politics, and science.

For this reason, researchers must be sensitive to these issues and would benefit from seeking out collaborations with Native American scholars. Researchers who make connections with tribal nations and their representatives, rather than seeking out individuals, are likely to achieve more success and gain a greater understanding of the people they are trying to study.

Scientists must stop contributing to the invisibility of Native American people and start embracing a diversity science approach. They must work with Native people, who are stakeholders and are deeply affected by research, to examine the many causes and consequences of Native American stereotypes. And they must examine ways to provide Native Americans with protective factors to counteract the harmful effects of these stereotypes and subsequent biases.

But this gaping hole in the literature is also a sign of opportunity; consider the research on Native American sports mascots. For decades, people claimed that these stereotypic images were harmful, yet little scientific work had been done to test this assertion. However, in the last few years, several researchers have tackled this topic (e.g., Burkley et al., 2017; Chaney et al., 2011; Freng & Willis-Esqueda, 2011; Fryberg et al., 2008). Coinciding with this research was an increase in public criticism of mascots and legal proceedings against mascot-branded companies. Often, these criticisms and lawsuits cited the newly emerging mascot research as evidence of their assertion that such images produce negative consequences. In response, many sports teams and universities have said good-bye to their American Indian mascots, including the University of Illinois's Chief Illiniwek, the University of North Dakota's Fighting Sioux, and the Cleveland Indians' Chief Wahoo (although many have chosen to still keep words like "Indians" in their team name). This example shows that research on Native American issues can powerful and translational effects that fuel real-world improvements for Native people.

Specific Suggestions for Future Research

Clearly there is a lack of research on Native American stereotypes. But the issue is not just of quantity, there is also a lack in *quality*. This is because researchers often treat Alaskan Natives, Native Americans, and other indigenous people as a monolithic group. The problem is when researchers define Native people as a single, homogenous group, they "render invisible hundreds of diverse tribal cultures" (Leavitt et al., 2015, p. 43). There is an immense amount of diversity among Native people, perhaps more so than other racial groups. Native Americans (and First Peoples more broadly) vary greatly across tribes, regions, and geographic locations in terms of their culture, language, religion, and values. It remains to be seen if stereotypes also vary in regards to different tribes and regions, or if some tribes suffer from these stereotypes more than others. But here is the good news: the topic of Native American stereotypes is ripe for future research. In this final section we suggest a few topics that deserve further inquiry, but in no way is our list exhaustive.

First, more work is needed to examine how Native American stereotypes negatively impact Native people, not just psychologically but behaviorally and physiologically. For example, hundreds of studies have examined how stereotype threat impacts African Americans and women, yet only one study has examined this issue within the context of Native Americans (Jaramillo et al., 2015). Similarly, research on age stereotypes shows how internalizing such beliefs cause decrements in physical health among older adults (Dionigi, 2015). Future work could examine if Native people who internalize Native American stereotypes are more likely to suffer from psychological issues, behavioral issues or physiological issues as a result.

Second, future work should examine the harmful effects of Native American imagery beyond just sports mascots. As mentioned earlier, hundreds of brands and companies use Native American imagery in their logos (e.g., Land-O-Lakes butter, Eskimo Pie). Yet we know little about whether such imagery impacts how non-Natives view Native people or how Native people view themselves. Given the proliferation of such brand imagery, especially compared to other races, such research is greatly needed. Such work should also explore the *behavioral* consequences of imagery exposure. Most of the work on mascots has focused on the cognitive or emotional consequences for Native people, but to our knowledge there are no studies to date showing that mascots (or other imagery) result in discriminatory behaviors. Such work would greatly add to the literature.

Third, future work should examine how Native American stereotypes harm other groups in addition to Native people. For example, Kim-Prieto, Goldstein, Okazaki, & Kirschner (2010) found that exposure to American Indian sports mascots increased stereotyping of a different racial group (i.e., Asians). This suggests that exposure to stereotypic imagery of one group has a "contagion effect" that leads to heightened stereotyping of other stigmatized groups. Future work could explore whether this effect generalizes to other racial groups (e.g., Latinos, African Americans) as well as other stigmatized groups (e.g., women, homosexuals, the disabled). Future research should also examine if this contagion effect generalizes beyond sports mascot imagery. Such studies would add to the growing body of work on "stigma by prejudice transfer," which suggests that stigmatized groups are threatened by prejudice that is directed to all stigmatized groups, not just their own (Sanchez, Chaney, Manuel, Wilton, & Remedios, 2017).

Finally, future research should take a more nuanced approach by examining the interaction of both individual factors and environmental factors relevant to the impact of Native American stereotypes. For example, the effects of Native American stereotypes have been shown to be moderated by the respondent's level of prejudice (e.g., Burkley et al., 2017), their political affiliation (Angle et al., 2016), and the Native target's ethnic identity (Jaramillo et al., 2015). Future research should continue with this pattern and seek out other individual difference factors that interact with stereotype application.

References

Alexie, S. (2007). *The absolutely true diary of a part-time Indian.* New York: Little, Brown, and Co.

Angle, J. W., Dagogo-Jack, S. W., Forehand, M. R., & Perkins, A. W. (2016). Activating stereotypes with brand imagery: The role of viewer political identity. *Journal of Consumer Psychology, 27,* 84–90. doi:10.1016/j .jcps.2016.03.004

Brofer, J. (2003, November 14). *DoD honors culture, contributions of Native Americans.* Retrieved from https://www.tecom.marines.mil/News/News-Article -Display/Article/527780/dod-honors-culture-contributions-of-native-ameri cans/

Brown, R., Croizet, J., Bohner, G., Fournet, M., & Payne, A. (2003). Automatic category activation and social behaviour: The moderating role of prejudiced beliefs. *Social Cognition, 21,* 167–193. doi:10.1521/soco.21.3 .167.25339

Burkley, E., Durante, F., Fiske, S. T., Burkley, M., & Andrade, A. (2017). Structure and content of Native American stereotypic subgroups: Not just (ig) noble. *Cultural Diversity and Ethnic Minority Psychology, 23,* 209–219. doi:10.1037/cdp0000100

Burkley, M., Burkley, E., Andrade, A., & Bell, A. C. (2017). Symbols of pride or prejudice? Examining the impact of Native American sports mascots on stereotype activation. *The Journal of Social Psychology, 157,* 223–235. doi: 10.1080/00224545.2016.1208142

Chaney, J., Burke, A., & Burkley, E. (2011). Do American Indian mascots = American Indian people? Examining implicit bias towards American Indian people and American Indian mascots. *American Indian Alaska Native Mental Health Research, 18,* 42–62. doi:10.5820/aian.1801 .2011.42

Clark, D. A., Spanierman, L. B., Reed, T. D., Soble, J. R., & Cabana, S. (2011). Documenting weblog expressions of racial microaggressions that target American Indians. *Journal of Diversity in Higher Education, 4,* 39–50. doi:10.1037/a0021762

Clark, M. D. (2016). *Shallow coverage of Standing Rock is part of a bigger problem.* Retrieved from https://www.poynter.org/news/shallow-coverage-standing -rock-part-bigger-problem

Coopersmith, J. (2009). *Characteristics of Public, Private, and Bureau of Indian Education Elementary and Secondary School Teachers in the United States: Results*

From the 2007–08 Schools and Staffing Survey (NCES 2009–324). Washington, D.C.: National Center for Education Statistics, Institute of Education Sciences, U.S. Department of Education.

Covarrubias, R., & Fryberg, S. A. (2015). The impact of self-relevant representations on school belonging for Native American students. *Cultural Diversity and Ethnic Minority Psychology, 21,* 10–18. doi:10.1037/a0037819

Cuddy, A. J. C., Fiske, S. T., & Glick, P. (2007). The BIAS map: Behaviors from intergroup affect and stereotypes. *Journal of Personality and Social Psychology, 92,* 631–648. doi:10.1037/0022-3514.92.4.631

Devine, P. G., & Baker, S. M. (1991). Measurement of racial stereotype subtyping. *Personality and Social Psychology Bulletin, 17,* 44–50. doi:10.1177/0146167291171007

DeVoe, J. F., & Darling-Churchill, K. E. (2008). *Status and trends in the education of American Indians and Alaska Natives: 2008* (NCES 2008–084). Washington, D.C.: National Center for Education Statistics, Institute of Education Sciences, U.S. Department of Education. Retrieved November 24, 2013, from http://nces.ed.gov/pubs2008/2008084.pdf

Dionigi, R. A. (2015). Stereotypes of aging: Their effects on the health of older adults. *Journal of Geriatrics, 954027,* 1–9. doi.org/10.1155/2015/954027

Eckes, T. (1994). Explorations in gender cognition: Content and structure of female and male subtypes. *Social Cognition, 12,* 37–60. doi:10.1521/soco.1994.12.1.37

Edwards, M. (2017, November 14). *For Native Americans facing sexual assault, justice feels out of reach.* Retrieved from https://www.npr.org/2017/11/14/563059526/for-native-americans-facing-sexual-assault-justice-feels-out-of-reach

Fadel, L., & Wiener, T. (2018, July 4). *Record number of Native Americans running for office in midterms.* Retrieved from https://www.npr.org/2018/07/04/625425037/record-number-of-native-americans-running-for-office-in-midterms

Farnell, B. (2004). The fancy dance of racializing discourse. *Journal of Sport & Social Issues, 28,* 30–55. doi:10.1177/0193732503261887

First Nations Development Institute. (2018). *Reclaiming Native truth.* Retrieved from https://www.reclaimingnativetruth.com

Fiske, S. T., Bergsieker, H. B., Russell, A. M., & Williams, L. (2009). Images of Black Americans. *DuBois Review: Social Science Research on Race, 6,* 83–101. doi:10.1017/S1742058X0909002X

Fiske, S. T., Cuddy, A. J. C., Glick, P., & Xu, J. (2002). A model of (often mixed) stereotype content: Competence and warmth respectively follow from perceived status and competition. *Journal of Personality and Social Psychology, 82,* 878–902. doi:10.1037//0022-3514.82.6.87

Freng, S., & Willis-Esqueda, C. (2011). A question of honor: Chief Wahoo and American Indian stereotype activation among a university based sample. *The Journal of Social Psychology, 151,* 577–591. doi:10.1080/00224545.2010.507265

Fryberg, S. A. (2003). Really? You don't look like an American Indian: Social representations and social group identities. *Dissertation Abstracts International: Section B: The Sciences and Engineering, 64*, 3B.

Fryberg, S. A., & Eason, A. E. (2017). Making the invisible visible: Acts of commission and omission. *Current Directions in Psychological Science, 26*, 554–559. doi:10.1177/0963721417720959

Fryberg, S. A., Markus, H., Oyserman, D., & Stone, J. M. (2008). Of warrior chiefs and Indian Princesses: The psychological consequences of American Indian mascots. *Basic and Applied Social Psychology, 30*, 208–218. doi:10.1080/01973530802375003

Fryberg, S. A., & Stephens, N. M. (2010). When the world is colorblind, American Indians are invisible: A diversity science approach. *Psychological Inquiry, 21*, 115–119. doi:10.1080/1047840X.2010.483847

Fryberg, S. A., & Watts, A. (2010). We're honoring you dude: Myths, mascots, and American Indians. In H. R. Markus & P. M. Moya (Eds.), *Doing race: 21 essays for the 21st century.* New York: W. W. Norton & Company.

Israel, S. (2008, June 4). *Precedent for Black men in US film and TV.* Retrieved from https://www.jpost.com/International/Precedent-for-black-president -in-US-film-and-TV

Jaramillo, J., Mello, Z. R., & Worrell, F. C. (2015). Ethnic identity, stereotype threat, and perceived discrimination among Native American adolescents. *Journal of Research on Adolescence, 26*, 769–775. doi:10.1111 /jora.12228

Kawakami, K., Dion, K. L., & Dovidio, J. (1998). Racial prejudice and stereotype activation. *Personality and Social Psychology Bulletin, 24*, 407–416. doi:10 .1177/0146167298244007

Keigher, A. (2009). *Characteristics of public, private, and Bureau of Indian Education elementary and secondary schools in the United States: Results from the 2007– 08 schools and staffing survey* (NCES 2009–321). Washington, D.C.: National Center for Education Statistics, Institute of Education Sciences, U.S. Department of Education.

Kim-Prieto, C., Goldstein, L. A., Okazaki, S., & Kirschner, B. (2010). Effect of exposure to an American Indian mascot on the tendency to stereotype a different minority group. *Journal of Applied Social Psychology, 40*, 534–553. doi:10.1111/j.1559-1816.2010.00586.x

King, C. R. (2010). *The Native American mascot controversy: A handbook.* Lanham, MD: Scarecrow Press.

Kunda, Z., & Spencer, S. J. (2003). When do stereotypes come to mind and when do they color judgment? A goal-based theoretical framework for stereotype activation and application. *Psychological Bulletin, 129*, 522–544. doi:10.1037/0033-2909.129.4.522

Leavitt, P. A., Covarrubias, R., Perez, Y. A., & Fryberg, S. A. (2015). "Frozen in time": The impact of Native American media representations on identity and self-understanding. *Journal of Social Issues, 71*, 39–53. doi:10.1111 /josi.12095

Lepore, L., & Brown, R. (1997). Category and stereotype activation: Is prejudice inevitable? *Journal of Personality and Social Psychology, 72*, 275–287. doi:10.1037/0022-3514.72.2.275

Martin, A. (2017, November 28). *Trump's "Pocahontas" insult makes a mockery of Native Americans' diverse history.* Retrieved from https://www.nbcnews.com/think/opinion/trump-s-pocahontas-insult-makes-mockery-native-americans-diverse-history-ncna824471

Mastro, D. E., & Stern, S. R. (2003). Representations of race in television commercials: A content analysis of prime-time advertising. *Journal of Broadcasting & Electronic Media, 47*, 638–647. doi.org/10.1207/s15506878jobem4704_9

Plaut, V. C. (2010). Diversity science: Why and how difference makes a difference. *Psychological Inquiry, 21*, 77–99. doi:10.1080/10478401003676501

Price, S. L. (2002). The Indian wars. *Sports Illustrated.* Retrieved from http://vault.sportsillustrated.cnn.com/vault/article/magazine/MAG1025046/index.htm

Richards, Z., & Hewstone, M. (2001). Subtyping and subgrouping: Processes for the prevention and promotion of stereotype change. *Personality and Social Psychology Review, 5*, 52–73. doi:10.1207/S15327957PSPR0501_4

Sanchez, D. T., Chaney, K. E., Manuel, S. K., Wilton, L. S., & Remedios, J. D. (2017). Stigma by prejudice transfer: Racism threatens white women and sexism threatens men of color. *Psychological Science, 28*, 445–461. doi:10.1177/0956797616686218

Shear, S. B., Knowles, R. T., Soden, G. J., & Castro, A. J. (2015). Manifesting destiny: Re/presentations of Indigenous Peoples in K–12 U.S. *History Standards, Theory & Research in Social Education, 43*, 68–101. doi:10.1080/00933104.2014.999849

Silva, C. (2017, November 11). *Why are so many Native Americans killed by police?* Retrieved from https://www.newsweek.com/more-native-americans-are-being-killed-police-including-14-year-old-who-might-708728

Snyder, T. D., Dillow, S. A., & Hoffman, H. M. (2009). *Digest of education statistics 2008* (NCES 2009020). Washington, D.C.: National Center for Education Statistics, Institute of Education Sciences, U.S. Department of Education.

Spencer, S. J., Logel, C., & Davies, P. G. (2016). Stereotype threat. *Annual Review of Psychology, 67*, 415–437. doi:073115-103235

Tajfel, H. (1981). *Human groups and social categories: Studies in social psychology.* New York: Cambridge University Press. doi:10.1016/j.adolescence.2011.11.003

U.S. Census Bureau. (2013). *Facts for features: American Indian and Alaska Native heritage month.* Retrieved from https://www.census.gov/newsroom/facts-for-features/2013/cb13-ff26.html

Williams, D., Martins, N., Consalvo, M., & Ivory, J. D. (2009). The virtual census: Representations of gender, race and age in video games. *New Media & Society, 11*, 815–834. doi:10.1177/1461444809105354

Wilson, C. (2014, June 18). The 450 Companies that still have Indian mascots. *Time*. Retrieved from http://time.com/2894357/redskins-trademark-ind ian-interactive/

Wolfe, P. (2006). Settler colonialism and the elimination of the native. *Journal of Genocide Research, 8*, 387–409. doi:10.1080/14623520601056240

Wong, A. (2018, June 13). The controversy over just how much history AP World History should cover. *The Atlantic*. Retrieved from https://www.theatlantic .com/education/archive/2018/06/ap-world-history-controversy/562778

CHAPTER SEVENTEEN

Intersectionality and Future Research Directions

Elora C. Voyles and Joel T. Nadler

> *I was sitting there being black, and I was like "You know what? Give me another thing."*
>
> —*SOLOMON GEORGIO (Comedian)*

The aim of this book was look at stereotypes in modern society and, more specifically, provide short reviews of current research on major stereotyped groups existing in the United States. We began by providing an overview of the stereotyping process, including the impact of stereotypes and the measurement of stereotypes. In addition, we provided information on the qualities of stereotypes including explicit versus implicit and positive versus negative stereotypes. In addition, stereotype processes such as stereotype threat were discussed. After providing a foundation for understanding stereotypes, this book dedicated twelve chapters to stereotypes relating to specific group memberships. Dedicating an entire chapter to the discussion of specific stereotypes enabled a greater level of depth in the discussion of the formation and content of stereotypic beliefs as well as the consequences of these beliefs on members of stereotyped groups.

This final chapter serves as a brief summary of emerging trends in stereotype research and the intersectional nature of those falling into multiple stereotyped groups. Lastly, this chapter will conclude with suggestions for future research that will provide insight into current events influenced by stereotypes.

Intersectionality and Stereotypes

Researchers and social justice movements have become more aware of the intersectional nature of identities and the stereotypes that accompany combinations of marginalized identities (Arrington-Sanders et al., 2015; Babbitt, Gaither, Toosi, & Sommers, 2018; Ghavami & Peplau, 2013; Hancock, 2007; Parent, DeBlaere, & Moradi, 2013; Rosette, Koval, Ma, & Livingston, 2016; Sparks, 2017). Intersectionality acknowledges that people's identities are more complex than a single group membership. In addition, our perceptions of others also are also sensitive to multiple group identities within the others that we are perceiving. Simply adding an additional group membership can completely change our perceptions and accompanying stereotypes of another person. For example, when asked to picture a veteran, one image along with an associated stereotype may come to mind (likely a White man), but when instructed to picture a Black veteran, a different image and different stereotypes may come to mind.

Singularity and Stereotypes

Despite the intuitive understanding that stereotypes can change based on the intersection of multiple group memberships, much of the existing research on stereotypes and the chapters in this book have focused on the implications and impacts of a single stereotyped group. However, this does not reflect the reality that most members of stigmatized groups face. People possess multiple identities that intersect; these identities include race, gender, religions, and age. This research is valuable, but it is equally important to examine how different stereotyped identities interact. Some researchers have investigated combinations of marginalized statuses and found that the intersection of multiple identities elicits unique stereotypes and subsequently, unique outcomes for stereotyped individuals.

In most cases, when participants picture a member of a stereotyped group, they tend to have a default "schema" of how that person will look like. A schema is the cognitive lens that is used for recognizing and organizing patterns of information and characteristics (Leung & Morris, 2015). In the context of stereotypes, these schemas structure and organize information about different groups. Within schemas, there are prototypes that represent those typical characteristics of a category member (Jarymowicz, Kamińska-Feldman, & Szuster, 2016). Depending on the prototype that is primed, people will imagine the stereotyped group to fit with their working schema while imagining "default" categories for other areas of the stereotyped target's identity. Often, for stereotypes that are targeted toward categories besides race, people will often assume that a stereotyped target is White (Flagg, 1992). For example, when asked to picture a person with a disability, more likely than not, the person will picture a White person with a disability. Similarly, when asked to picture a member of a race, able-bodied is imagined as the default (Kattari, 2015). For example when asked to picture an Asian American, more than likely, people picture a physically able Asian American. In many cases, the prototype of different categories includes prototypical identities with more social power and status paired with representations of group members (e.g., picturing a person with a disability as being White). This tendency is referred to as the intersectional invisibility that can result in misrepresentations of group membership and systematic invisibility of group members who need representation within their identity (Purdie-Vaughns & Eibach, 2008).

Despite this tendency to rely on prototypes that focus on one social identity, every person belongs to a larger number of social categories. Stereotypes are intersectional in nature because membership to multiple social categories can influence perceptions and stereotypes of a person. Individuals with a particular configuration of marginalized statuses may be stereotypically viewed in ways that differ from others in their superordinate categories. As such, people with multiple marginalized identities often come to be recognized as a distinctive group, particularly when they do not conform to established stereotypes of those superordinate categories (Macrae, Bodenhausen, & Milne, 1995; Richards & Hewstone, 2001).

Summative or Multiplicative Effects

There are two ways to think about the effects of intersectional identities on stereotypes: the effects may be summative or multiplicative. The summative explanation suggests that people experience each social identity separately and independently of other social identities (Aranda et al., 2015). However, many researchers suggest that the perception and experience of multiple group identities results in multiplicity rather than summation (Bowleg, 2008; Purdie-Vaughns & Eibach, 2008; Warner & Shields, 2013). Multiplicity the interaction between multiple social identities is more than the sum of its parts. Intersectionality refers to the concept that there is a unique impact of having multiple marginalized social identities (Aranda et al., 2015; Hancock, 2007; Parent et al., 2013; Sparks, 2017). Past research suggests that stereotypes and discrimination do not independently influence based on social identities, instead stereotypes and discrimination are influenced by intersecting identities. Several researchers have examined the intersection of race and gender on stereotypes.

Ghavami and Peplau (2013) provided a broad, thorough study of qualitative stereotype content for different ethnic and gender group intersections. Participants' responses supported the intersectionality hypothesis by reporting unique characterizations or combinations of ethnicities and genders that create unique qualities not mentioned when the ethnicity and gender are examined separately. Another research study found that both White people and Black people viewed White men as having more prejudice compared to White women (Babbitt et al., 2018). In addition, most descriptions of ethnicities without consideration of gender fit more closely to men of that ethnicity rather than women of that ethnicity.

Within the social media domain, middle school students' perceptions intelligence, aggression, and gender typicality of targets on fictional Facebook profiles depended on gender, sexual orientation and race. Within the work domain, female leaders are perceived and evaluated very differently depending on their race (Ghavami & Peplau, 2018). Female Black leaders were perceived as dominant but lacking in competence. Female Asian leaders were perceived as being highly competent but not dominant. White female leaders were perceived to have moderate levels of competence and dominance (Rosette et al., 2016). Based on the current research, there is much support for the multiplicative impacts of belonging to multiple social identities. Sometimes intersectional identities can lead to privilege in certain circumstances and oppression in other circumstances (Warner, 2008). For example, being a Latino man brings privilege within the Latinx culture; however, being a person of color is still associated with discrimination in multiple contexts (Hurtado & Sinha, 2008). In the case for stigmatized group memberships, belonging to multiple stigmatized group identities can be especially deleterious.

The minority stress model suggests that members of stigmatized groups experience increased stress as a result of experiencing stereotypes, stigma, discrimination, and ostracism based on their group membership (Meyer, 2003). The effects of the minority stress model increases with each stigmatized social identity that one possesses. The multiplicative effects of minority stress has been tied to negative outcomes for minority group members including mental health problems, substance abuse, and internalized stigma (Lehavot & Simoni, 2011). In addition, with increasing numbers of stigmatized identities, reported discrimination and invisibility increased (Remedios & Snyder, 2018).

When considering multiple social identities, multiplicative effects may not always occur, in some cases other nonstigmatized identities may be disregarded. According to Sparks (2017) the intersectional trap occurs when generalizations are applied to groups such as races with little concern for the experiences and identities beyond the selected identity within the population. When the intersectional trap occurs, perceivers rely on stereotypes and make assumption based on one group membership while failing to recognize intersecting identities. This focus on one group membership while discounting others was illustrated in research examining perceptions of Black women. In the research study, Black women were viewed as less feminine compared to other women and they were rated as overall less attractive. The researchers' explanation for this finding suggested that Blackness is associated with maleness and Black women's Black identity overpowered perceptions of femininity in the eyes of outside perceivers (Goff, Thomas, & Jackson, 2008).

Researchers and society are quickly recognizing the importance of studying the intersection between identities and stereotypes. With this recognition, there has been a sharp increase in discussions and research examining intersectional identities and stereotypes (Warner, 2008). Research on intersectionality brings a host of challenges including which identities to examine and in what combinations. Warner (2008) recommends making a priori decision rules for the inclusion of identities and ensuring that the selected identities for research will answer the research questions. Warner and Shields (2013) advise against examining research for interactions between race and gender without theoretical support. In addition, Warner and Shields suggested that awareness of intersectional identities means that generalizations about men and women are less relevant and should be followed with the questions: Which men? Which women?

Immerging Trends

Trends in technology and societal views have influenced the immerging stereotype research trends in two ways: methodology and topics of research. Methodology in stereotypes research has evolved with advancing technology and increased use of data harvesting from social media. Meanwhile, topics of stereotype research have been influenced by changes within society that have driven a need for greater knowledge of the functions of prevalent stereotypes the subsequent outcomes.

Methodology

Society and academia have long maintained a relationship of influencing one another. Thus current research follows topics of interest within society and research findings inform professional practices and sometimes causal interactions through the occasional pop psychology news articles. For example, a recent research study by Ablett (2018) collected 5,364 tweets from Twitter users on comments related to a winter storm that occurred on February 23, 2017. These tweets were notable because the storm was named "Doris," a woman's name, as it is the convention to alternate between traditionally male names and traditionally female names when storm names are selected. Given that Doris is a female name and a traditionally older name, the researchers analyzed tweets for stereotyping responses and found trends of tweets with gendered insults and sexist language due to the female name. For example, "Doris out here giving everyone blows, what a slut #stormdoris." Such societal use of technology and social media has been harnessed by many social psychology researchers to better understand the influence of stereotypes in modern culture. Technological developments also include increased use of fMRI machines to determine areas of the brain are involved in stereotypical knowledge of groups (Delplanque, Heleven, & Van Overwalle, 2019).

Topics of Research

In addition to new trends in methods, stereotypes researchers have followed and investigated trends and topics within society. Some of the topics within the research are based on recent tragedy and controversy such as research on "shoot vs. don't shoot" and the #metoo movement. Other stereotypes topics such as gender stereotypes reflect an enduring interest that has persisted for over half a century (Eagly, Eaton, Rose, Riger, & McHugh, 2012). Another area of focus examines metastereotype, which refers to the phenomenon of being aware of stereotypes that others may hold about one's own group (Vorauer, Main, & O'Connell, 1998). The following paragraphs provide an overview of these growing areas of research; however, it is important to note that the body of research on stereotypes is constantly growing and that this is just a small sample of new knowledge.

Shoot vs. don't shoot began as an area of research after an unarmed Black man, Amadou Daillo, was shot nineteen times at close range by police (Correll, Hudson, Guillermo, & Ma, 2014). Consistently in research, untrained participants are more likely to shoot unarmed Black targets compared to unarmed White targets. Researchers who have investigated this troubling pattern suggest that the tendency to shoot unarmed Black men is based on stereotypes associating Black men with danger and weapons (Correll et al., 2014). The research focus on race and shootings of unarmed Black men has occurred simultaneously with the rise of the #BlackLivesMatter movement. It is likely that there are stereotypes regarding members and supporters of #BlackLivesMatter; however, no research has currently been published regarding this topic. Researchers should investigate the stereotypes of #BlackLivesMatter supporters in conjunction with race of the target and the perceiver. This would likely be an informative area of research given that others' perceptions of a speakers' knowledge and understanding of racial issues is influenced by the speakers' race (Chung, Bemak, Talleyrand, & Williams, 2018).

The #Metoo movement is focused on victims of harassment speaking out against sexual harassment and sexual assault. The #Metoo movement gained momentum after being tweeted to encourage women to share their stories of sexual harassment (Onwuachi-Willig, 2018). This movement recognizes workplace dynamics that are underpinned in stereotyping. In a research study by Berdahl (2007), competing explanatory theories for sexual harassment were tested to determine if sexual harassment was motivated by a sexual desire or to punish women who do not conform to traditional gender roles. Similar enforcement of stereotypes occurs when men are the targets of stereotypes, men who do not conform to prescribed masculinity stereotypes are often taunted with comments that are demeaning and commonly associated with women and femininity (Kitzinger, 2001; Schultz, 2018).

Research and media coverage of the #metoo movement can also have the power to influence images and stereotypes from consumers' perceptions and opinions (Matthes, 2009). Much of the media focus tends to be on cisgender women coming forward as victims and supporters (Evans, 2018; Onwuachi-Willig, 2018). Cisgender refers to a person whose gender matches the gender assigned at birth. This overrepresentation of White women in media covering the #metoo movement can contribute to a stereotype that the #metoo movement comprises of mostly White women, or a more deleterious stereotype that only White women are victims of sexual harassment and assault. In addition to the media's limited focus on race in the #metoo movement, there has also been little focus on how sexual harassment affects members of the LGBTQ community (Schultz, 2018). The limited coverage of the #metoo movement likely impacts stereotypes of supports and victims of the movement. Researchers should examine the impact of the #Metoo movement on stereotypes of sexual harassment victims, supporters of the #Metoo movement, and perpetrators of sexual harassment. The focus of the #Metoo movement media coverage on White female victims may counteract the very message that it seeks to promote. For White women, the #Metoo movement has provided role models of victims coming forward and receiving mostly supportive messages in response to their disclosure. However, for men, people of color, and LGBT people, the coverage featuring straight, cisgender women may promote a subtle but persistent stereotype that #Metoo is not for them (Rodino-Colocino, 2018).

The majority of the latest stereotypes research focuses on gender stereotypes. Research has focused on expanding upon areas such as the influence of subliminal gender stereotypes (Spears & Kuppens, 2018) and gender stereotypes on career opportunities (Balachandra, Briggs, Eddleston, & Brush, 2019). For example, a new study found that women who were highly identified with feminists but not with the broader group of women were especially likely to persist at a counterstereotypical task when subliminally exposed to a stereotype. Stereotype research has maintained a consistent focus on gender stereotypes; however, the tone of the research may be changing with shifting understanding and norms related to perceptions of gender identity and expression. One of the drivers of the shifts in gender perceptions is the recognition of people who have a gender identity that is different than their sex assigned at birth. Research on transgender stereotypes is just beginning to increase. To illustrate, studies of transgender stereotypes are first focusing on the valence and content of stereotypes about transgender people. Research has found that stereotype content about transgender people involved stereotypes of mental illness, sex reassignment, sexual orientation, and being an outcast from society (Gazzola & Morrison, 2014). There were also unique themes specifically targeting transmen (transmen identify as masculine) and specific themes targeting transwomen (transwomen identify as feminine).

Beyond stereotypes, research is beginning to add another layer by examining metastereotypes, which are what one person believes other groups think about their group (Vorauer et al., 1998). Much of the latest research on metastereotypes has focused on age metastereotypes in the workplace (Oliveira & Cabral-Cardoso, 2018; Peters, Van Der Heijden, Spurk, De Vos, & Klaassen, 2019; Voyles, Finkelstein, & King, 2014). For example, Peters et al. (2019) found the older adults' perceptions of their employability were negatively influenced by negative age metastereotypes. Oliveira and Cabral-Cardoso (2018) suggested human resource practices that focus on recognition and respect to buffer older workers from negative metastereotypes and a reduction in human resources management practices that focus on training for older adults, which can exacerbate negative metastereotypes. In addition to research on age in the workplace, metastereotypes are also being examined intersectionally with race and gender (Babbitt et al., 2018). Metastereotypes are a promising area of study that shows the impact of stereotype awareness on the cognitions and behaviors of individuals in stereotyped groups.

Future Research

Stereotypes researchers should continue to embrace trends in society to provide information on the process and impact of stereotypes on different groups. Stereotypes within society shift over time and as a result of cultural events, political environment, and media coverage. Researchers can inform society on the latest stereotypes. Stereotypes researchers are beginning to understand the complex and intersectional nature of stereotypes. As reflected in this chapter, the intersection between multiple identities has shown to have a powerful influence on the nuances of elicited stereotypes. It is especially important for researchers to keep up with intersectional stereotypes because there are particular stereotypes whose nature is constantly evolving. For example, analysis of word embedding in text and newspaper has captured the influence of historical events such as the women's movement corresponding to perceptions of women in particular occupations (Garg, Schiebinger, Jurafsky, & Zou, 2018).

In addition, stereotypes researchers now have more methods for data collection at their disposal. As such, researchers should embrace new methodology and technology to examine mental processes when stereotyping (e.g., fMRI and other physiological measures) as well as new platforms for the expression of stereotypes (e.g., social media and technology).

Final Words

Our culture shapes our stereotypes (Caprariello, Cuddy, & Fiske, 2009), and our stereotypes shape our culture (Godsil et al., 2016). As discussed throughout the course of this book, stereotypes, and their incidence and impacts are significant within our society. Many of the impacts of stereotypes can be negative, but it's important to recognize that stereotyping is a natural and automatic process that people engage in as a mental shortcut. There will probably never be a complex society that is without stereotypes in some form, they are unavoidable. Despite the fact that positive stereotypes do exist and can improve performance and outcomes for positively stereotypes group members (Shih, Pittinsky, & Ho, 2012), no stereotype is without negative implications. When a stereotype is positive for one group, it comes with a subtle implication that it is negative for another group. For example, men are positively stereotyped for abilities in spatial awareness and rotation (Doyle & Voyer, 2016), but this comes with a subtle implication that women are less skilled in this area. Another problem with stereotypes is that they are depersonalizing to group members, regardless of whether the stereotypes are positive or negative (Siy & Cheryan, 2013). In addition, for members of a group that is positively stereotyped in one domain, such as African Americans and athletic abilities, reminders of these positive stereotypes can subtly imply a stereotypic lack of competence in other areas such as academics (Stone, Harrison, & Mottley, 2012). However, when targets of positive stereotypes confront others who make comments on the stereotypes, they are evaluated more negatively than targets who confront negative stereotypes, making it more challenging to speak out against positive stereotypes (Alt, Chaney, & Shih, 2018). Overall, just as negative stereotypes can have negative consequences, so can positive stereotypes (Czopp, Kay, & Cheryan, 2015).

The final word in this book will be used to encourage readers to be aware of the stereotypes and biases that they possess toward other groups (and potentially themselves). Stereotypes are pervasive and they can have serious consequences, but they can be controlled.

While it would be ideal for all people to practice awareness and control of their stereotypic beliefs, not everyone will make this effort. For those who are targeted by stereotypes, there are two primary methods that can be used for reducing the negative impact: escaping and challenging (Wang, Whitson, Anicich, Kray, & Galinsky, 2017). Escaping can involve concealing a stereotyped identity (if possible) or denying that one possesses the negatively stereotyped traits. The escape methods can protect an individual from the deleterious effects of stereotypes, but it ultimately leaves the negative stereotypes intact. The other method is to challenge the stereotype. Challenging a stereotype can involve reframing the stereotype such that a stereotype that is purported to be a weakness is spun into a strength. For example, when leadership traits are characterized, they tend to better fit stereotypes of men rather than women (Powell, 2011). However, stereotypically feminine traits such as listening, communal behavior, and participative leadership strategies could be reframed as assets in leadership. Self-labeling is another strategy that challenges stereotypes by using a negative stereotype label and taking power away from the word. Wang et al. (2017) use the example of women invoking the term "slut walk" to raise awareness about rape culture, and to take power away from the word "slut." Escaping or challenging negative stereotypes offers options to people who are targeted because of their group membership, though some of these strategies may be more effective than others.

The onus should of managing the impacts of stereotypes should not be on the targets of stereotypes, but instead, should be the responsibility of all people. Devine and Sherman (1992) recommended education on the ways that stereotypes can influence our perceptions and behaviors toward stereotyped groups. However, education about stereotypes may be a catch-22 because awareness can sometimes lead people to engage in the behavior more by making people think that "everyone else is doing it" and so it must be normative (Duguid & Thomas-Hunt, 2015).

References

Ablett, R. (2018). 'Doris, You Bitch': The Sexist and Gendered Ageist Discourses of Twitter Users Concerning a Female-Named UK Storm. *Trent Notes on Linguistics, 1*, 75–88.

Alt, N. P., Chaney, K. E., & Shih, M. J. (2018). "But that was meant to be a compliment!": Evaluative costs of confronting positive racial stereotypes. *Group Processes & Intergroup Relations.* doi:10.1177/1368430218756493

Aranda, F., Matthews, A. K., Hughes, T. L., Muramatsu, N., Wilsnack, S. C., Johnson, T. P., & Riley, B. B. (2015). Coming out in color: Racial/ethnic differences in the relationship between level of sexual identity disclosure and depression among lesbians. *Cultural Diversity and Ethnic Minority Psychology, 21*(2), 247.

Arrington-Sanders, R., Oidtman, J., Morgan, A., Harper, G., Trent, M., & Fortenberry, J. D. (2015). 13. Intersecting identities in black gay and bisexual young men: A potential framework for HIV risk. *Journal of Adolescent Health, 56*(2), S7–S8.

Babbitt, L. G., Gaither, S. E., Toosi, N. R., & Sommers, S. R. (2018). The role of gender in racial meta-stereotypes and stereotypes. *Social Cognition, 36*(5), 589–601.

Balachandra, L., Briggs, T., Eddleston, K., & Brush, C. (2019). Don't pitch like a girl!: How gender stereotypes influence investor decisions. *Entrepreneurship Theory and Practice, 43*(1), 116–137.

Berdahl, J. L. (2007). The sexual harassment of uppity women. *Journal of Applied Psychology, 92*(2), 425–437.

Bowleg, L. (2008). When Black+ lesbian+ woman≠ Black lesbian woman: The methodological challenges of qualitative and quantitative intersectionality research. *Sex Roles, 59*(5–6), 312–325.

Caprariello, P. A., Cuddy, A. J., & Fiske, S. T. (2009). Social structure shapes cultural stereotypes and emotions: A causal test of the stereotype content model. *Group Processes & Intergroup Relations, 12*(2), 147–155.

Chung, R. C. Y., Bemak, F., Talleyrand, R. M., & Williams, J. M. (2018). Challenges in promoting race dialogues in psychology training: Race and gender perspectives. *The Counseling Psychologist, 46*(2), 213–240.

Correll, J., Hudson, S. M., Guillermo, S., & Ma, D. S. (2014). The police officer's dilemma: A decade of research on racial bias in the decision to shoot. *Social and Personality Psychology Compass, 8*(5), 201–213.

Czopp, A. M., Kay, A. C., & Cheryan, S. (2015). Positive stereotypes are pervasive and powerful. *Perspectives on Psychological Science, 10*(4), 451–463.

Delplanque, J., Heleven, E., & Van Overwalle, F. (2019). Neural representations of Groups and Stereotypes using fMRI repetition suppression. *Scientific Reports, 9*(1), 3190.

Devine, P. G., & Sherman, S. J. (1992). Intuitive versus rational judgment and the role of stereotyping in the human condition: Kirk or Spock? *Psychological Inquiry, 3*(2), 153–159.

Dionisi, A. M., & Barling, J. (2018). It hurts me too: Examining the relationship between male gender harassment and observers' well-being, attitudes, and behaviors. *Journal of Occupational Health Psychology, 23*(3), 303.

Doyle, R. A., & Voyer, D. (2016). Stereotype manipulation effects on math and spatial test performance: A meta-analysis. *Learning and Individual Differences, 47*, 103–116.

Duguid, M., & Thomas-Hunt, M. (2015). Condoning stereotyping? How awareness of stereotyping prevalence impacts expression of stereotypes. *Journal of Applied Psychology, 100*(2), 343–359.

Eagly, A. H., Eaton, A., Rose, S. M., Riger, S., & McHugh, M. C. (2012). Feminism and psychology: Analysis of a half-century of research on women and gender. *American Psychologist, 67*(3), 211.

Evans, A. (2018). # MeToo: A study on sexual assault as reported in the *New York Times. Occam's Razor, 8*(1), 3.

Flagg, B. J. (1992). Was blind, but now I see: White race consciousness and the requirement of discriminatory intent. *Michigan Law Review, 91*, 953.

Garg, N., Schiebinger, L., Jurafsky, D., & Zou, J. (2018). Word embeddings quantify 100 years of gender and ethnic stereotypes. *Proceedings of the National Academy of Sciences, 115*(16), E3635–E3644.

Gazzola, S. B., & Morrison, M. A. (2014). Cultural and personally endorsed stereotypes of transgender men and transgender women: Notable correspondence or disjunction? *International Journal of Transgenderism, 15*(2), 76–99.

Ghavami, N., & Peplau, L. A. (2013). An intersectional analysis of gender and ethnic stereotypes: Testing three hypotheses. *Psychology of Women Quarterly, 37*(1), 113–127.

Ghavami, N., & Peplau, L. A. (2018). Urban middle school students' stereotypes at the intersection of sexual orientation, ethnicity, and gender. *Child Development, 89*(3), 881–896.

Godsil, R. D., MacFarlane, J., Sheppard, B., LaFrance, S., Johnson, A. M., & Wong, T. (2016). Popculture, perceptions, and social change. Editorial Director: Liz Manne. *#Popjustice, 3*, 1–34.

Goff, P. A., Thomas, M. A., & Jackson, M. C. (2008). "Ain't I a woman?": Towards an intersectional approach to person perception and group-based harms. *Sex Roles, 59*(5–6), 392–403.

Hancock, A. M. (2007). When multiplication doesn't equal quick addition: Examining intersectionality as a research paradigm. *Perspectives on Politics, 5*(1), 63–79.

Hurtado, A., & Sinha, M. (2008). More than men: Latino feminist masculinities and intersectionality. *Sex Roles, 59*(5–6), 337–349.

Jarymowicz, M., Kamińska-Feldman, M., & Szuster, A. (2016). The asymmetry bias in me, we–others distance ratings. The role of social stereotypes. *Frontiers in Psychology, 7*, 50.

Kattari, S. K. (2015). Examining ableism in higher education through social dominance theory and social learning theory. *Innovative Higher Education, 40*(5), 375–386.

Kitzinger, C. (2001). Sexualities. In R. K. Unger (Ed.), *Handbook of the psychology of women and gender* (pp. 272–285). New York: John Wiley & Sons.

Lehavot, K., & Simoni, J. M. (2011). The impact of minority stress on mental health and substance use among sexual minority women. *Journal of Consulting and Clinical Psychology, 79*(2), 159.

Leung, K., & Morris, M. W. (2015). Values, schemas, and norms in the culture–behavior nexus: A situated dynamics framework. *Journal of International Business Studies, 46*(9), 1028–1050.

Macrae, C. N., Bodenhausen, G. V., & Milne, A. B. (1995). The dissection of selection in person perception: Inhibitory processes in social stereotyping. *Journal of Personality and Social Psychology, 69*(3), 397.

Matthes, J. (2009). What's in a frame? A content analysis of media framing studies in the world's leading communication journals, 1990–2005. *Journalism & Mass Communication Quarterly, 86*(2), 349–367.

Meyer, I. H. (2003). Prejudice, social stress, and mental health in lesbian, gay, and bisexual populations: Conceptual issues and research evidence. *Psychological Bulletin, 129*, 674–697.

Oliveira, E. A. D. S., & Cabral-Cardoso, C. J. (2018). Buffers or boosters? The role of HRM practices in older workers' experience of stereotype threat. *The Journal of Psychology, 152*(1), 36–59.

Onwuachi-Willig, A. (2018). What about# UsToo: The invisibility of race in the# MeToo movement. *Yale LJF, 128*, 105–120.

Parent, M. C., DeBlaere, C., & Moradi, B. (2013). Approaches to research on intersectionality: Perspectives on gender, LGBT, and racial/ethnic identities. *Sex Roles, 68*(11–12), 639–645.

Peters, P., Van Der Heijden, B., Spurk, D., De Vos, A., & Klaassen, R. (2019). Please don't look at me that way. An empirical study into the effects of age-based (meta-) stereotyping on employability enhancement among supermarket workers. *Frontiers in Psychology, 10*, 249.

Powell, G. N. (2011). The gender and leadership wars. *Organizational Dynamics, 40*, 1–9.

Purdie-Vaughns, V., & Eibach, R. P. (2008). Intersectional invisibility: The distinctive advantages and disadvantages of multiple subordinate-group identities. *Sex Roles, 59*(5–6), 377–391.

Remedios, J. D., & Snyder, S. H. (2018). Intersectional oppression: Multiple stigmatized identities and perceptions of invisibility, discrimination, and stereotyping. *Journal of Social Issues, 74*(2), 265–281.

Richards, Z., & Hewstone, M. (2001). Subtyping and subgrouping: Processes for the prevention and promotion of stereotype change. *Personality and Social Psychology Review, 5*(1), 52–73.

Rodino-Colocino, M. (2018). Me too, #MeToo: Countering cruelty with empathy. *Communication and Critical/Cultural Studies, 15*(1), 96–100.

Rosette, A. S., Koval, C. Z., Ma, A., & Livingston, R. (2016). Race matters for women leaders: Intersectional effects on agentic deficiencies and penalties. *The Leadership Quarterly, 27*(3), 429–445.

Schultz, V. (2018). Reconceptualizing sexual harassment, again. *Yale LJF, 128*, 22–66.

Shih, M. J., Pittinsky, T. L., & Ho, G. C. (2012). Stereotype boost: Positive outcomes from the activation of positive stereotypes. In M. Inzlicht & T. Schmader (Eds.), *Stereotype threat: Theory, process, and application* (pp. 141–156). New York: Oxford University Press.

Siy, J. O., & Cheryan, S. (2013). When compliments fail to flatter: American individualism and responses to positive stereotypes. *Journal of Personality and Social Psychology, 104*(1), 87–102.

Sparks, D. M. (2017). Navigating STEM-worlds: Applying a lens of intersectionality to the career identity development of underrepresented female students of color. *Journal for Multicultural Education, 11*(3), 162–175.

Spears, R., & Kuppens, T. (2018). Subliminal gender stereotypes: Who can resist? *Personality & Social Psychology Bulletin, 44*(12), 1648–1663.

Stone, J., Harrison, C. K., & Mottley, J. (2012). "Don't call me a student-athlete": The effect of identity priming on stereotype threat for academically engaged African American college athletes. *Basic and Applied Social Psychology, 34*(2), 99–106.

Vorauer, J. D., Main, K. J., & O'Connell, G. B. (1998). How do individuals expect to be viewed by members of lower status groups? Content and implications of meta-stereotypes. *Journal of Personality and Social Psychology, 75*(4), 917.

Voyles, E., Finkelstein, L., & King, E. (2014). A tale of two theories: Stereotype threat and metastereotypes. *Industrial and Organizational Psychology, 7*(3), 419–422.

Wang, C. S., Whitson, J. A., Anicich, E. M., Kray, L. J., & Galinsky, A. D. (2017). Challenge your stigma: How to reframe and revalue negative stereotypes and slurs. *Current Directions in Psychological Science, 26*(1), 75–80.

Warner, L. R. (2008). A best practices guide to intersectional approaches in psychological research. *Sex Roles, 59*, 454–463.

Warner, L. R., & Shields, S. A. (2013). The intersections of sexuality, gender, and race: Identity research at the crossroads. *Sex Roles, 68*(11–12), 803–810.

About the Editors and Contributors

Editors

Joel T. Nadler has a PhD in Applied Psychology, and he is a tenured professor and director of Southern Illinois University Edwardsville's Industrial/Organizational Psychology Master's program. He is also the cofounder of Alpha Omega Associates and has consulted with organizations ranging from small Charter Schools to Fortune 100 companies. As an academic, he has twenty-nine peer-reviewed published journal articles, six book chapters, and over one hundred conference presentations and workshops. Additionally, he has two books in print. His research interests include stereotypes, stereotype threat, gender bias in selection and performance appraisal, sexual harassment, organizational attractiveness, and adverse impact (EEO law). His work on stereotypes and stereotype threat has been published in journals such as *Journal of Applied Social Psychology*, *Sex Roles*, *American Journal of Evaluation*, and *Journal of Leadership and Organizational Studies*. He has consulted with organizations on areas such as organizational climate and culture, program evaluation, organizational development, and study design and methodology.

Elora C. Voyles has a PhD in Industrial Organizational Psychology and Social Psychology. She is assistant professor of psychology at Southern Illinois University Edwardsville. Her research focuses on age metastereotypes and stereotype threat. Her work has been published in academic journals such as *Career Development International*, *Industrial and Organizational Psychology: Perspectives on Science and Practice*, and *Work, Aging and Retirement*. In addition to research, she has also applied experience with job analysis, recruiting and interviewing, and employee performance appraisal.

Contributors

Phylicia C. Allen is a third-year doctoral student in the George Warren Brown School of Social Work at Washington University in St. Louis. She earned her BSW from Saginaw Valley State University and her MSW from the University of Michigan. Her current research examines strengths-based assessments on the structure of neighborhoods, the utilization of resources within neighborhoods, mechanisms for understanding academic outcomes, and risky behavior among African American adolescents.

Angel D. Armenta is currently a PhD student at the University of Texas at El Paso (UTEP). At UTEP, Angel studies prejudice and discrimination from two different perspectives. His first line of research involves the process by which social information of group members is consolidated into long-term memory and how this information changes over time. His work on memory consolidation suggests that time has a direct impact on prejudice formation. His second line of research involves studying reactions to cultural change. His research on cultural inertia suggests that change, in and of itself, is a good predictor of prejudice toward minority groups.

Lynn Bartels is professor of Industrial/Organizational Psychology at Southern Illinois University Edwardsville (SIUE). At SIUE, she also works as the director of Faculty Development. She earned her doctorate from the University of Akron. Her research interests include employee selection and development and all forms of employment discrimination, particularly weight discrimination.

Angela C. Bell is a social psychologist and assistant professor of Psychology at Lafayette College in Easton, PA. She earned her PhD in Psychology from Oklahoma State University and then spent a year as a Visiting Assistant Professor at Colby College. Dr. Bell's research has investigated cognitive biases that result when evaluating prejudice in the self and others, the positive and negative effects of endorsing ingroup stereotypes, and the underlying motivations for endorsing such stereotypes. Her work can be found in *Social Cognition*, *Psychology of Men & Masculinity*, *Social and Personality Psychology Compass*, and the *Journal of Social Psychology*.

Andrea Bellovary completed her undergraduate degree at Marquette University in Psychology and Criminal Justice. She is currently a PhD student at DePaul University and is a member of the Social and Intergroups Perception Lab at DePaul. Andrea researches the influence of stereotypes on attributional judgments, system-legitimizing ideologies, system perceptions, and political decision-making. Her research seeks to inform fellow researchers, the public, and policy makers.

Charnetta R. Brown has her MA in Industrial Organizational Psychology and is completing a PhD in Business Psychology with a concentration in Consulting. Her dissertation focuses on sexual orientation hiring discrimination, and it will highlight her work in diversity and inclusion. Her applied experience is in management consulting with multidisciplinary expertise in human capital, organizational design, change management, strategy, process improvement, and program management. She has consulted with public organizations, private organizations, and the federal government. She has her own career coaching company, Char Brown Solutions, and also serves as the Virtual Services Peer Group Coordinator for the Career Transition Center of Chicago, a nonprofit missioned to empower professionals to find meaningful employment.

Edward Burkley earned his doctoral degree in social psychology from the University of North Carolina at Chapel Hill and is associate professor of Psychology at Oklahoma State University. His research, which focuses on self-control, motivation, and goals, has been published in the *Journal of Personality and Social Psychology*, *Personality and Social Psychology Bulletin*, and *Self and Identity*. In his free time, he writes speculative fiction short stories (www .edwardburkley.com).

Melissa Burkley earned her doctoral degree from the University of North Carolina at Chapel Hill and worked as a professor at Oklahoma State University for over a decade. Her work, which focuses on stereotypes, prejudice, gender, and implicit racism, has been featured in the *New York Times*, *Cosmopolitan*, *Esquire*, and Oprah Radio. She has written articles for *Psychology Today*, *Poets & Writers*, and *Hinnom Magazine* and has served as a consultant for *TIME*, *O Magazine*, and, most recently, puresomni.com. Lastly, she runs two psychology-themed blogs: "The Social Thinker" for *Psychology Today* and "The Writer's Laboratory" (www.melissaburkley.com).

Sheretta T. Butler-Barnes is associate professor in the George Warren Brown School of Social Work at the Washington University in St. Louis. She earned her PhD in Developmental Psychology from Wayne State University. Her expertise and scholarly work are focused on the impact of racism and the use of culturally strength-based assets on the educational and health outcomes of Black American families.

LaWanda Cook is an extension faculty associate with the Yang-Tan Institute on Employment and Disability at Cornell University. Her research focuses on disability identity, well-being, and inclusion of individuals with disabilities in employment and leisure settings. Her work explores an array of issues, including the intersection of disability with other characteristics such as race, gender, and age, as well as concerns such as workplace bullying and harassment.

Cody Cox earned his PhD from Rice University in 2010 and has taught undergraduate and graduate students in business schools and psychology programs. Dr. Cox teaches in both the Greehey Business School where he currently serves as Chair of Marketing and Management and the graduate Industrial/Organizational Psychology program at St. Mary's University in San Antonio, Texas. He teaches graduate and undergraduate courses on topics such as organizational psychology, data analysis, human resource management, and leadership. His current research focuses on talent development and workplace diversity, with an emphasis on issues related to generational differences and the aging workforce.

Jessica L. Cundiff is assistant professor of Psychological Science at Missouri University of Science and Technology. She earned a dual PhD in Social Psychology and Women's Studies from Penn State University. Prior to joining the faculty of Missouri S&T, Dr. Cundiff was an applied researcher in Washington, D.C., where she evaluated programs aimed at increasing diversity in computer science. Her current research focuses on the psychological processes that contribute to social inequality, with an emphasis on subtle forms of sexism that are often unintentional and seemingly minor, yet consequential. Her work aims to educate about subtle bias and develop strategies for increasing diversity and inclusion, particularly in STEM fields. Her research has been published in outlets such as *Sex Roles, Journal of Social Issues, Group Processes and Intergroup Relations, Journal of Higher Education*, and *Journal of Experimental Social Psychology*. She also serves as a consulting editor for *Psychology of Women Quarterly*.

Maya Gann-Bociek is a graduate student in Saint Louis University's Industrial/Organizational Psychology doctoral program and is currently working under her mentor and coauthor, Dr. Richard Harvey. She currently works as a research assistant within the Collective Identity Laboratory and as a teaching assistant for two undergraduate psychology courses. Her primary research and applied interests focus within the areas of workplace diversity and inclusion; prejudice and discrimination surrounding marginalized populations within the workplace (with a focus on gender, race, and LGBTQIA+); and recently, program evaluation, not-for-profit organizations, and organizational development. Prior to her enrollment at Saint Louis University, she completed her bachelor's degree in Psychology at Southern Illinois University Edwardsville in May 2017.

Kara Harris graduated from the University of North Carolina at Greensboro in 2017 with a BA in Psychology. Currently, she is pursuing her PhD in Psychological Science with a specialization in Social Psychology at DePaul University in Chicago. She is a member of the Social and Intergroups Perception Lab at DePaul. Her research concentrates on intergroup relations, the influence of stereotypes, and identity. Specifically, she examines how such issues contribute to social perceptions and social injustice, by looking at both minority groups and the majority group.

Richard D. Harvey earned his PhD in Psychology from the University of Kansas. He currently holds a double appointment as associate professor in both the Social Psychology and Industrial/Organizational Psychology programs in the Department of Psychology at Saint Louis University. Dr. Harvey currently conducts and has published research on a variety of topics, including prejudice/racism, colorism, organizational identity, racial identity, and performance management/evaluation. He teaches graduate and/or undergraduate courses in Statistics, Research Methodology, Organizational Behavior/Development, Leadership, Prejudice, and Social Psychology. He is a recipient of a variety of research, teaching, and mentoring awards. Finally, Dr. Harvey is a fellow of the Center for the Application of Behavioral Sciences (CABS) and has over twenty years of organizational consulting experience in both for-profit and nonprofit organizations.

Amy L. Hillard is associate professor of Psychology at Adrian College, a small liberal arts college in southeast Michigan. Dr. Hillard is a social psychologist who studies prejudice and stereotyping. She earned her PhD in Psychology from the University of Nebraska-Lincoln and completed a postdoctoral fellowship through an NSF ADVANCE grant that examined workplace issues for women in areas in which they are underrepresented. Her research examines methods to reduce prejudice in everyday interactions (e.g., confronting prejudice) and in organizations (e.g., implicit bias training and educational interventions). Her research has been published in outlets such as *Sex Roles*, *Analyses of Social Issues and Public Policy*, *Advances in Gender Research*, and *Social Psychology of Education*.

Joan J. Hong is a PhD candidate in the Department of Educational Policy Studies at the University of Wisconsin–Madison. Her research interests include issues of race/ethnicity and social design research inspired by cultural historical activity theory to address disparities in student learning and emotional and behavioral outcomes.

Ashley N. Jackson is a doctoral student in the George Warren Brown School of Social Work. She earned her BS in Administration of Justice from

George Mason University and her MA from the University of Chicago, School of Social Service Administration (SSA). Her research interests include community-police relations, police violence, racial violence, and legal and racial socialization in connection to police contact among African American youth and families.

Jade S. Jenkins earned her PhD in Social and Industrial-Organizational Psychology from Northern Illinois University in 2014, in addition to an advanced graduate certificate in Women's and Gender Studies. She is currently the Institutional Effectiveness (IE) coordinator at Texas A&M University-Texarkana. She conducts research on the topics of stereotyping and discrimination (with a primary emphasis on gender and a secondary emphasis on age), work-life balance, technology, stress and well-being, and self-regulation. Her research has been presented at regional and national academic conferences and has been published in peer-reviewed outlets in both social psychology and organizational psychology. Some of these outlets include *Social Psychology* and *Stress & Health*.

Stacey J. Lee is professor of Educational Policy Studies and a faculty affiliate in Asian American Studies at the University of Wisconsin–Madison. She is the author of *Unraveling the Model Minority Stereotype: Listening to Asian American Youth* (2009) and *Up against Whiteness: Race, School & Immigrant Youth* (2005).

Kyle J. Page currently holds an MA in Industrial Organizational Psychology and is completing a PhD. His research focuses on Occupational Health Psychology, with a focus on work-family conflict, dispositions and worker/organizational health, and engagement and productivity. His publications are featured in *Occupational Health Science*. Currently he serves on the Communications Committee for the Society for Occupational Health Psychology to help disseminate occupational health findings through social media.

Christine Reyna earned her PhD in Social Psychology from the University of California, Los Angeles. She is currently a tenured professor at DePaul University in Chicago and the founder of the Social and Intergroup Perceptions Lab. Her research focuses on stereotypes, prejudice, and intergroup relations, with an emphasis on how people legitimize prejudice using attributions, values, and moral framing. She has examined these issues and their consequences on political and social policies and intergroup and intrapersonal outcomes. She has published in various outlets such as *Journal of Personality and Social Psychology*, *Advances in Experimental Social Psychology*, *Personality and Social Psychological Bulletin*, *Political Psychology*, *Behavior and Brain Science*, and *Cultural Diversity and Ethnic Minority Psychology*.

Zuzuky Robles is currently completing a PhD in Industrial Organizational Psychology. Her research focus is on Occupational Health Psychology, specifically on factors that contribute to employees' physical and psychological health. Her work in this area can be found in *Occupational Health Science*. Her applied experience is in employee relations consulting, where she has worked with both public and private organizations. She also has a background in clinical psychology research and has contributed to publications examining negative health behaviors and health disparities among minorities. Some of her research in this area are featured in *Addictive Behaviors*, *Journal of Anxiety Disorders*, and *Cognitive Behavior Therapy*.

Alecia M. Santuzzi is an associate professor of industrial-organizational psychology at Northern Illinois University. She has been conducting research and publishing on the experiences of social stigma and identity management for over fifteen years. Her most recent work focuses on experiences among working adults with concealable disabilities and the occupational health and well-being consequences of identity management decisions.

Ain Simpson graduated from the University of Melbourne (Australia) in 2009 with degrees in Liberal Arts and Music and was then trained in moral psychology under Dr. Simon Laham (also at the University of Melbourne). He graduated with a PhD in psychology in 2014. Subsequently, he completed three years of postdoctoral training under the guidance of Dr. Kimberly Rios at Ohio University and then taught as visiting assistant professor at Centre College. His research focuses on moral judgment and the social/evolutionary psychology of religion and how these topics intersect. Professionally, he currently divides his time between teaching undergraduate psychology at Miami University and piano performance.

Dr. John J. Skowronski is currently associated with the Northern Illinois University Center for the Study of Family Violence and Sexual Assault. There he is part of a team that explores when and why some parents aggress against their children. One research focus explores how parent violence follows from overly negative interpretations of child behavior. This research links to some of Dr. Skowronski's prior work, which explored how people think about others. His best-known research examined (a) our understanding of the causes of negativity biases and positivity biases in trait judgments made about others and (b) the pervasiveness and causes of spontaneous trait inferences that are made about others. Dr. Skowronski has also explored autobiographical memory and is probably best known for his studies on the fading affect bias in the feelings that people experience when remembering events from their personal past.

Dr. Christopher Stone serves as a Clinical Assistant Professor of Human Resource Management at Wichita State University, where he teaches selection and general human resources. He holds a PhD in business administration with an emphasis in organizational behavior and human resource management from the University of Texas at San Antonio. His research is primarily focused on barriers to employment for veterans and has been published in academic journals as well as presented at national conferences. Dr. Stone is actively engaged in the community by working with veterans' organizations and providing training for managers and service providers at organizations that seek to help veterans.

Courtney Thomas is currently a doctoral candidate in Social-Industrial/Organizational Psychology at Northern Illinois University. The training she receives at NIU allows her to focus on applying social psychological principles to the workplace. Her research focuses around person perception—how people perceive others and how that subsequently influences behaviors and emotions. Primarily, Courtney focuses on the effects of social category information on the discrimination and metastereotyping processes, especially within the aging population. In this work, Courtney has utilized implicit social cognition theories to inform the workplace literature on stereotype and metastereotype activation. Additionally, Courtney's research has investigated some forms of negative workplace interactions, like abusive supervision and self-control related to aggression. Research in this arena has focused on how to mitigate effects of abusive supervision, such as by using humor.

Maya A. Williams is a second-year doctoral student in the George Warren Brown School of Social Work. She earned her BA in Spanish with a minor in International Studies from the University of Michigan. Later, she attended the University of Texas at Austin, where she earned her MSW. Her research interests include school-based social work, interventions to the school-to-prison-pipeline, community engagement, and policy reform.

Friederike Young earned her MS in Industrial Organizational Psychology and her MBA in Leadership from St. Mary's University in 2018. Throughout her graduate studies, Friederike engaged in multiple research projects about the perception of generational differences in the workplace and their effects on various workplace scenarios. After graduation, Friederike's main focus is to help her organization understand the importance of data-driven decision-making and supports as a change agent throughout this continuous culture shift.

Michael A. Zárate earned his PhD in Social/Personality Psychology from Purdue University. He is a tenured professor of Psychology at UTEP. His research encompasses social and social cognitive processes involved in person and group perception. His research on cultural inertia has been published in multiple outlets, most recently in *Advances in Experimental Social Psychology*. His research on memory consolidation was published recently in *Psychological Science*. He has published in *Journal of Personality and Social Psychology*, *Psychological Review*, and *American Psychologist*, among other outlets. He also served as editor of *Cultural Diversity and Ethnic Minority Psychology*. His research often addresses social psychological issues from an ethnic minority perspective.

Index